Yamada-kun AND THE Seven Witches

13

MIKI YOSHIKAWA

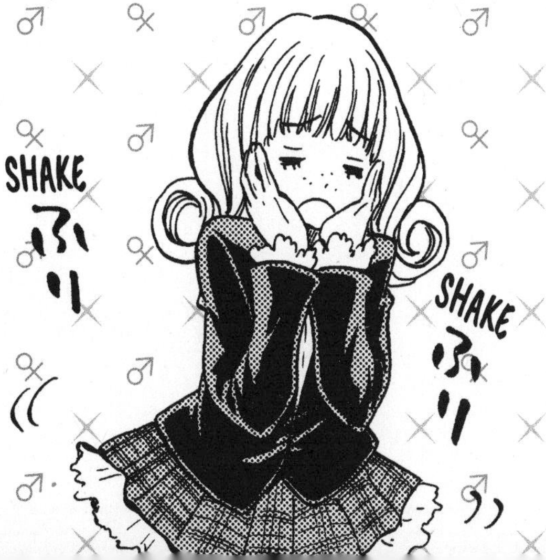
SHAKE
SHAKE

Urara Shiraishi

A second-year at Suzaku High School and president of the Supernatural Studies Club. An honor student with top marks in school who was formerly known as the "Switch Witch." She doesn't really express her true feelings very often, so she makes her boyfriend, Yamada, worry a lot!

Ryu Yamada

A second-year at Suzaku High School and part of the Supernatural Studies Club. Miyamura appointed him to the position of Student Council secretary. He's known as the "Copy Guy" and possesses the ability to copy the power of whichever witch he kisses. He loves Shiraishi.

Shinichi Tamaki

A second-year at Suzaku High School and treasurer for the Student Council. He's known as the "Capture Guy" and steals the power of the witch whom he kisses. He pretends to be an elite, but he's really just lonely.

Nene Odagiri

A second-year at Suzaku High School and clerk for the Student Council. She can be arrogant, but she's surprisingly caring, and she might actually be a nice girl.

Toranosuke Miyamura

A second-year at Suzaku High School and president of the Student Council. He's sharp-witted and is the most popular kid in school. He seems to get along with Yamada despite being pretty much his exact opposite.

Miyabi Itou

A second-year at Suzaku High School and part of the Supernatural Studies Club. She's totally into the occult, but it seems that she has yet to notice the appearance of new witches.

Jin Kurosaki

A first-year at Suzaku High School and one of the vice-presidents of the Student Council. He's always expressionless to everyone, but is totally obedient to Miyamura, whom he idolizes.

Midori Arisugawa

A first-year at Suzaku High School and one of the vice-presidents of the Student Council. She's a girl with an easy-going attitude who has a pretty nice chest. And the boys have already started a fan club for her?!

Rika Saionji

A third-year at Suzaku High School and the former seventh witch. She used to have the ability to erase memories. She has a bit of an abnormal personality.

Haruma Yamazaki

A third-year at Suzaku High School and the crafty, former president of the Student Council. He was once a member of the Supernatural Studies Club, but he had his memories erased by Rika. He now has his memories back.

Kentaro Tsubaki

A second-year at Suzaku High School and part of the Supernatural Studies Club. He used to live abroad and has a habit of frying up some tempura to keep himself from feeling sad and lonely.

Sid

A second-year at Suzaku High School and bad-boy punk. While observing the witches, he took notice of Yamada's power and looked into him, but…? His real name remains a mystery.

Nancy

A second-year at Suzaku High School and a mysterious girl filled with punk spirit. Along with her partner Sid, she planned an encounter with Yamada. What are her intentions?! Her real name remains a mystery.

Tsubasa Konno

A second-year at Suzaku High School and captain of the basketball time. She's one of the new witches. She's known as the "Submission Witch" and can give orders that render the recipient unable to defy her.

CONTENTS

CHAPTER 103: Google it later! — 005

CHAPTER 104: Going commando as a hobby. — 025

CHAPTER 105: Sorry-sshi! — 045

CHAPTER 106: She's got a dirty mind. — 065

CHAPTER 107: He looks bored. — 085

CHAPTER 108: A sorta bittersweet alliance. — 109

CHAPTER 109: The Masked JK. — 129

CHAPTER 110: So lame... — 155

EXTRA: Sobasshi's Cooking Time — 180

CHAPTER 103: Google it later!

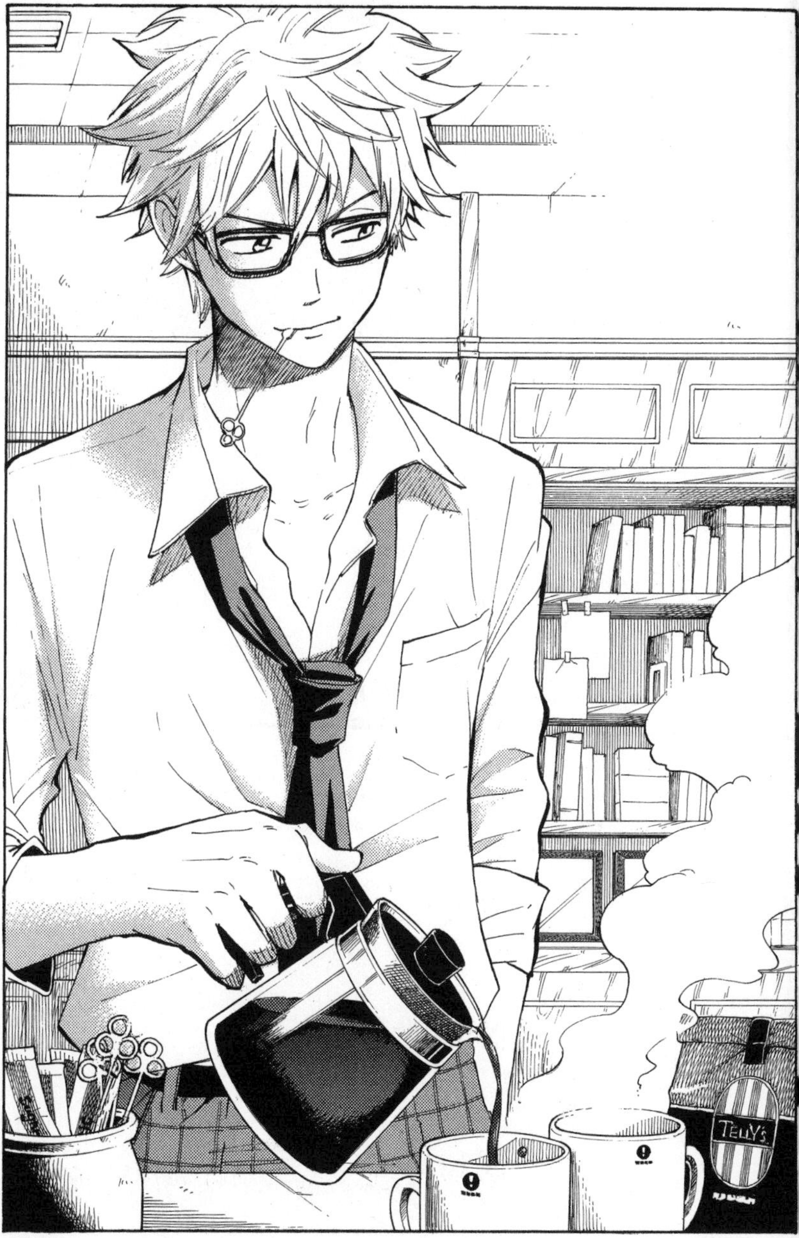
TELLY'S

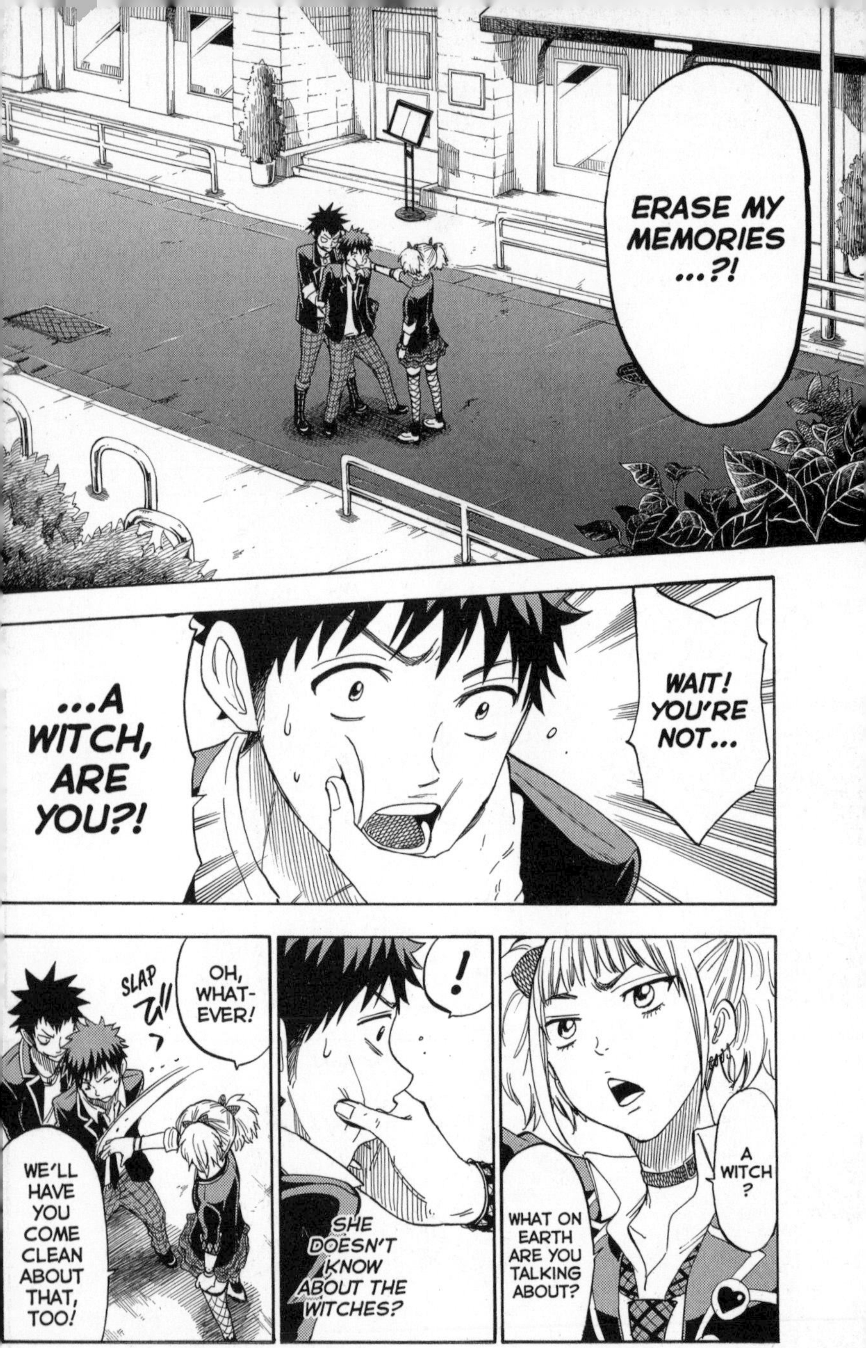

ERASE MY MEMORIES ...?!
WAIT! YOU'RE NOT...
...A WITCH, ARE YOU?!
A WITCH?
WHAT ON EARTH ARE YOU TALKING ABOUT?
!
SHE DOESN'T KNOW ABOUT THE WITCHES?
OH, WHAT-EVER!
SLAP
WE'LL HAVE YOU COME CLEAN ABOUT THAT, TOO!

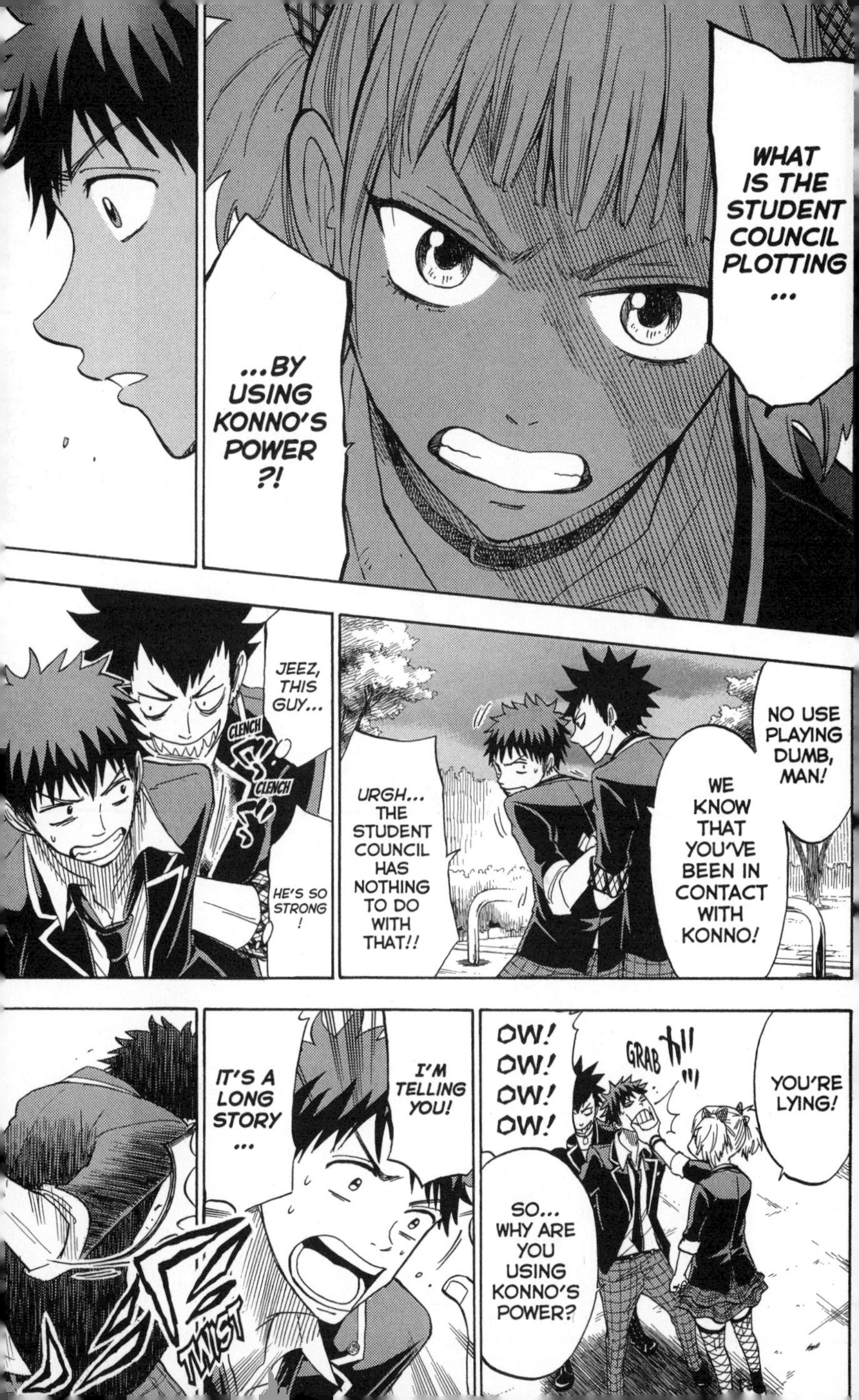
WHAT IS THE STUDENT COUNCIL PLOTTING...
...BY USING KONNO'S POWER?!
NO USE PLAYING DUMB, MAN!
WE KNOW THAT YOU'VE BEEN IN CONTACT WITH KONNO!
URGH... THE STUDENT COUNCIL HAS NOTHING TO DO WITH THAT!!
JEEZ, THIS GUY...
CLENCH
CLENCH
HE'S SO STRONG!
YOU'RE LYING!
GRAB
OW! OW! OW! OW!
SO... WHY ARE YOU USING KONNO'S POWER?
I'M TELLING YOU!
IT'S A LONG STORY...
TWIST

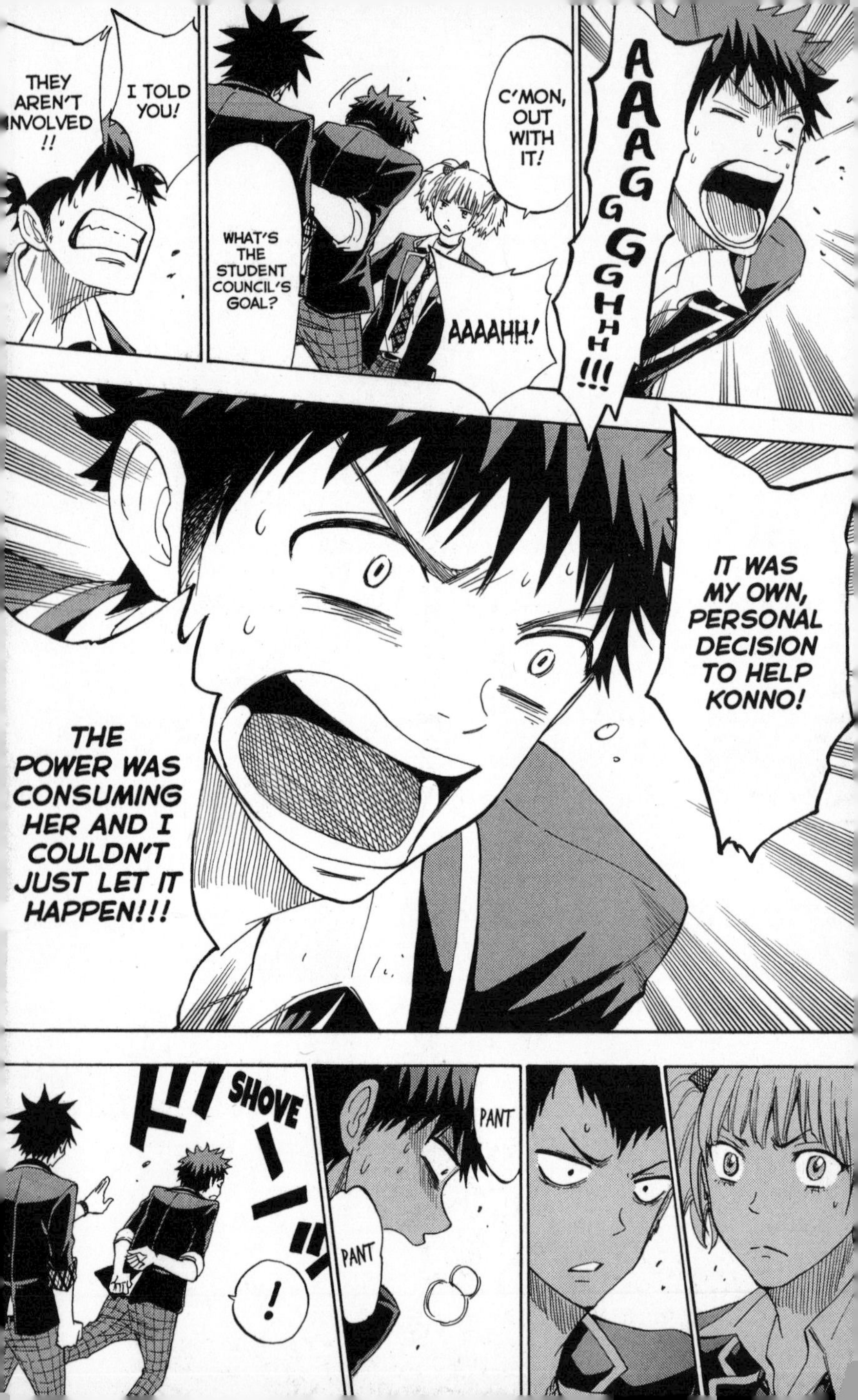
AAAAGGGGHHHH!!!
C'MON, OUT WITH IT!
WHAT'S THE STUDENT COUNCIL'S GOAL?
AAAAHH!
I TOLD YOU!
THEY AREN'T INVOLVED!!
IT WAS MY OWN, PERSONAL DECISION TO HELP KONNO!
THE POWER WAS CONSUMING HER AND I COULDN'T JUST LET IT HAPPEN!!!
PANT
PANT
SHOVE
!

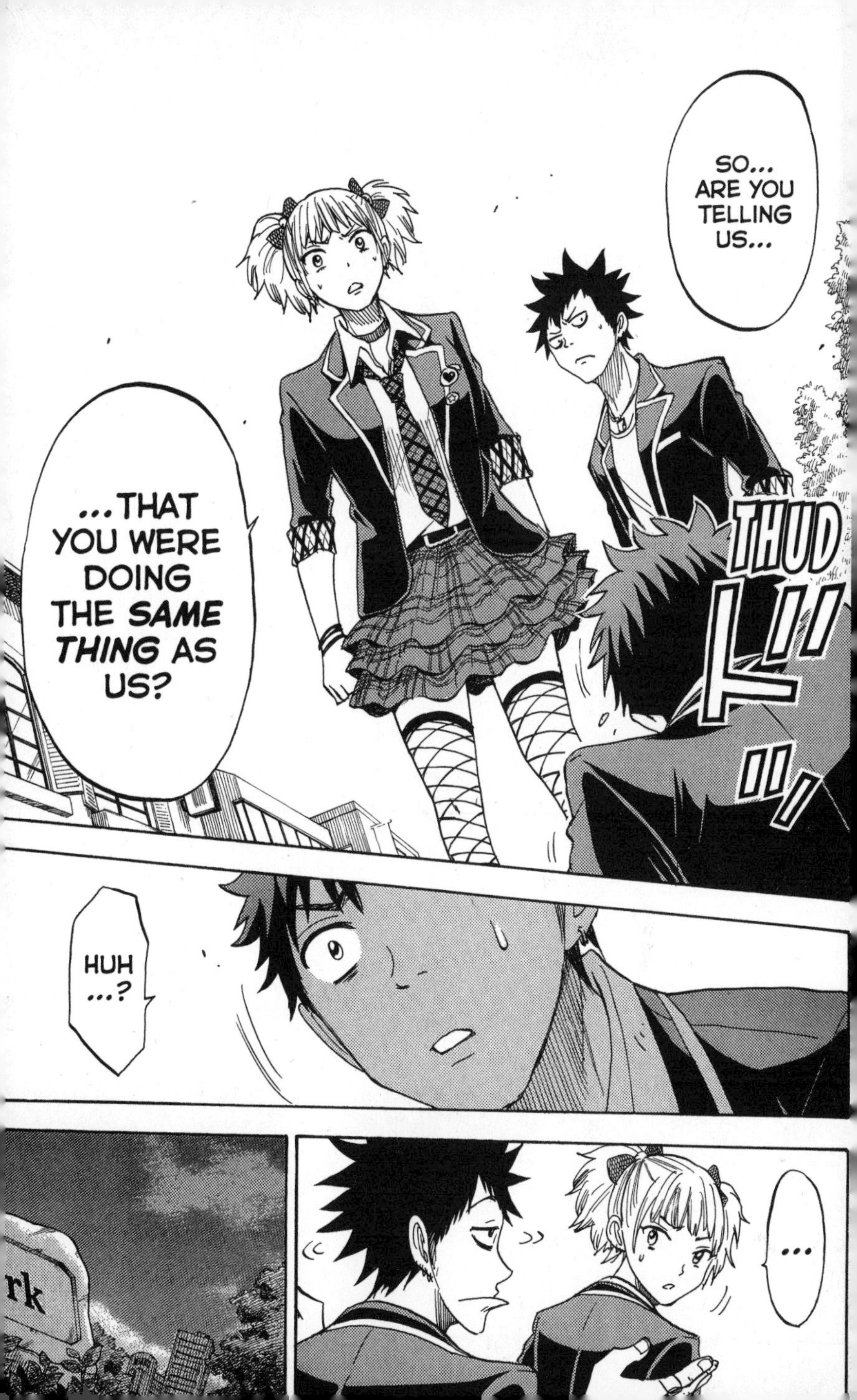
SO... ARE YOU TELLING US...
...THAT YOU WERE DOING THE *SAME THING* AS US?
THUD
HUH ...?
...

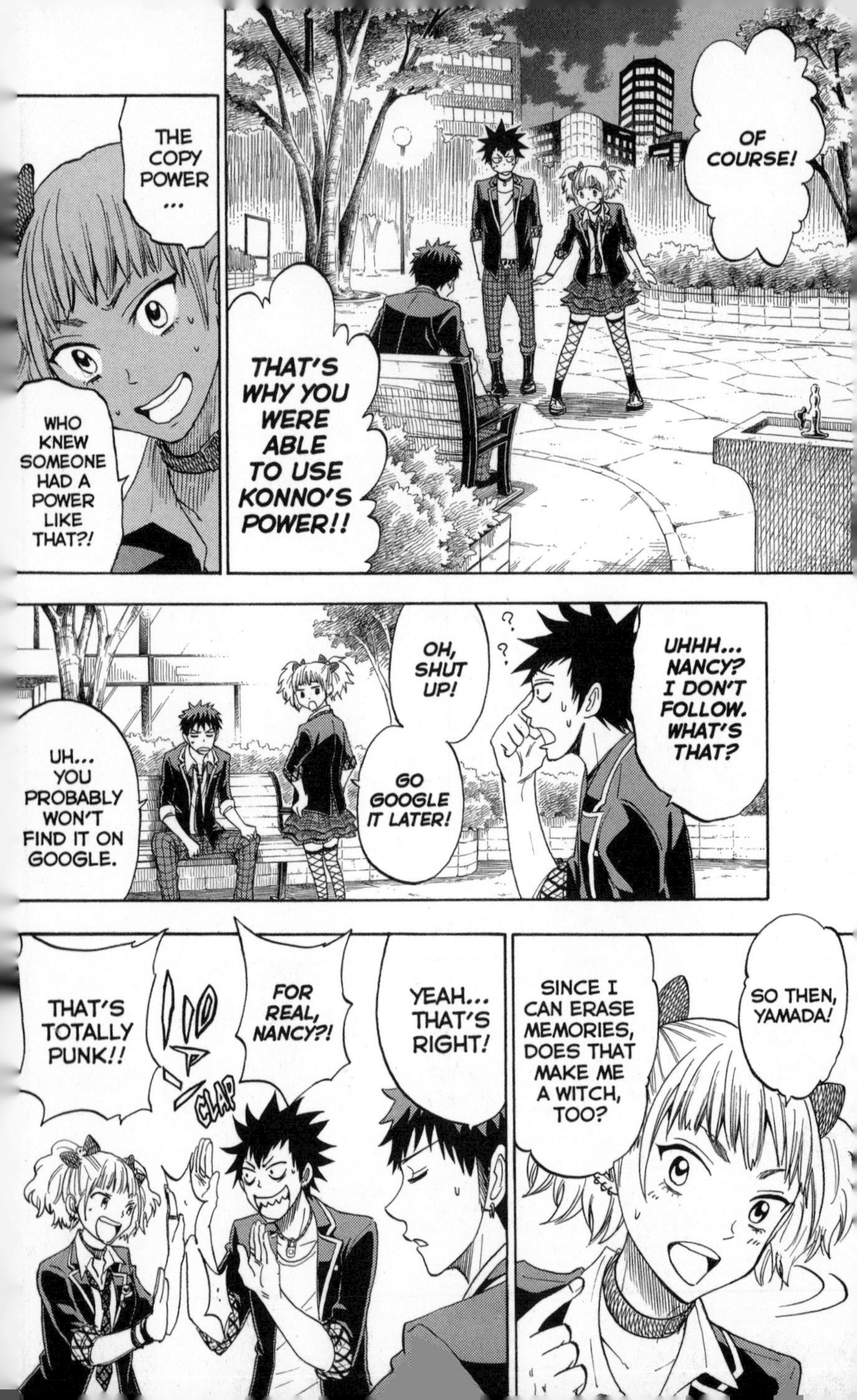
OF COURSE!
THAT'S WHY YOU WERE ABLE TO USE KONNO'S POWER!!
THE COPY POWER...
WHO KNEW SOMEONE HAD A POWER LIKE THAT?!
UHHH... NANCY? I DON'T FOLLOW. WHAT'S THAT?
OH, SHUT UP!
GO GOOGLE IT LATER!
UH... YOU PROBABLY WON'T FIND IT ON GOOGLE.
SO THEN, YAMADA!
SINCE I CAN ERASE MEMORIES, DOES THAT MAKE ME A WITCH, TOO?
YEAH... THAT'S RIGHT!
FOR REAL, NANCY?!
CLAP
THAT'S TOTALLY PUNK!!

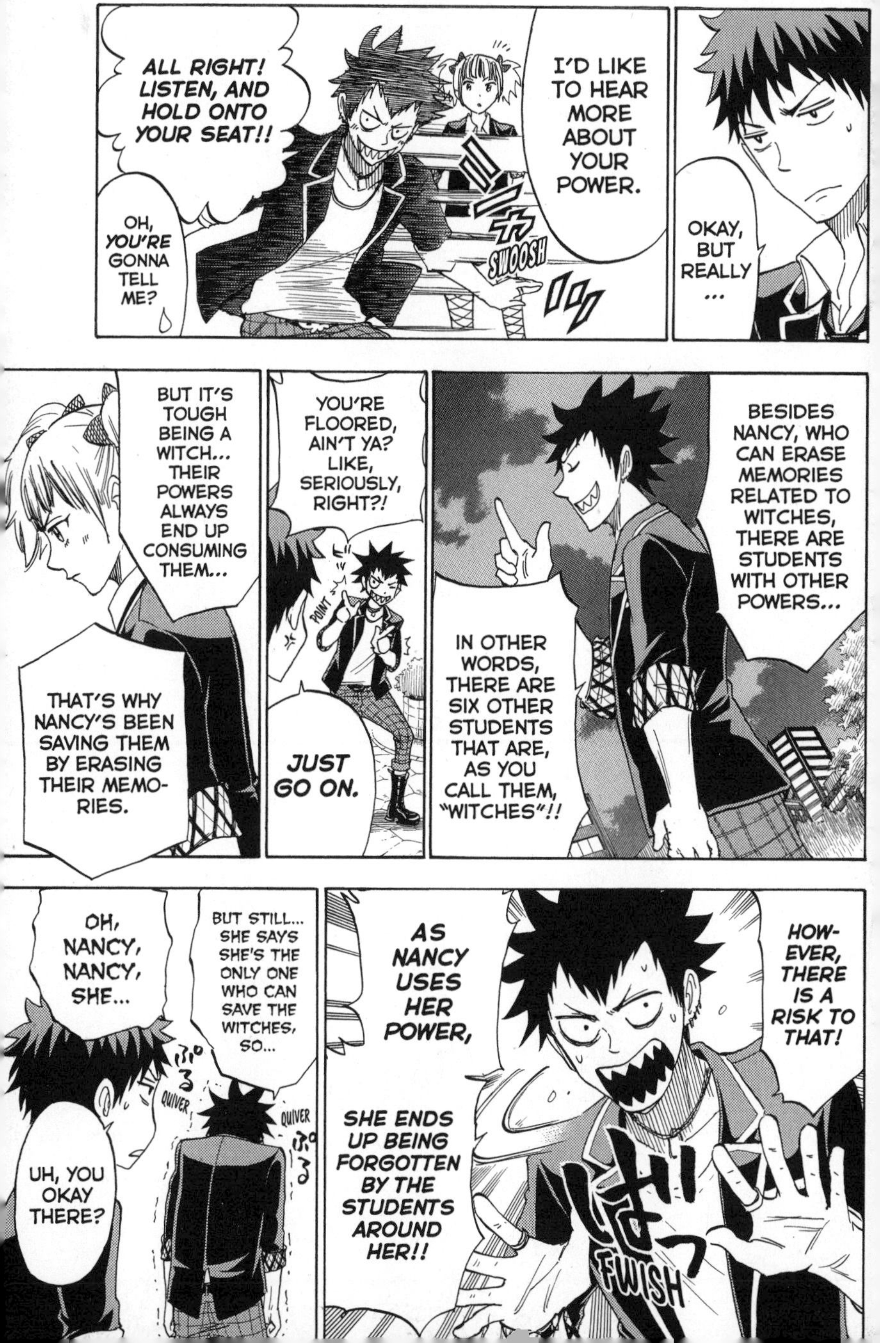
OKAY, BUT REALLY...
I'D LIKE TO HEAR MORE ABOUT YOUR POWER.
SWOOSH
ALL RIGHT! LISTEN, AND HOLD ONTO YOUR SEAT!!
OH, YOU'RE GONNA TELL ME?
BESIDES NANCY, WHO CAN ERASE MEMORIES RELATED TO WITCHES, THERE ARE STUDENTS WITH OTHER POWERS...
IN OTHER WORDS, THERE ARE SIX OTHER STUDENTS THAT ARE, AS YOU CALL THEM, "WITCHES"!!
YOU'RE FLOORED, AIN'T YA? LIKE, SERIOUSLY, RIGHT?!
POINT
JUST GO ON.
BUT IT'S TOUGH BEING A WITCH... THEIR POWERS ALWAYS END UP CONSUMING THEM...
THAT'S WHY NANCY'S BEEN SAVING THEM BY ERASING THEIR MEMORIES.
HOWEVER, THERE IS A RISK TO THAT!
AS NANCY USES HER POWER,
SHE ENDS UP BEING FORGOTTEN BY THE STUDENTS AROUND HER!!
FWISH
BUT STILL... SHE SAYS SHE'S THE ONLY ONE WHO CAN SAVE THE WITCHES, SO...
OH, NANCY, NANCY, SHE...
QUIVER
QUIVER
UH, YOU OKAY THERE?

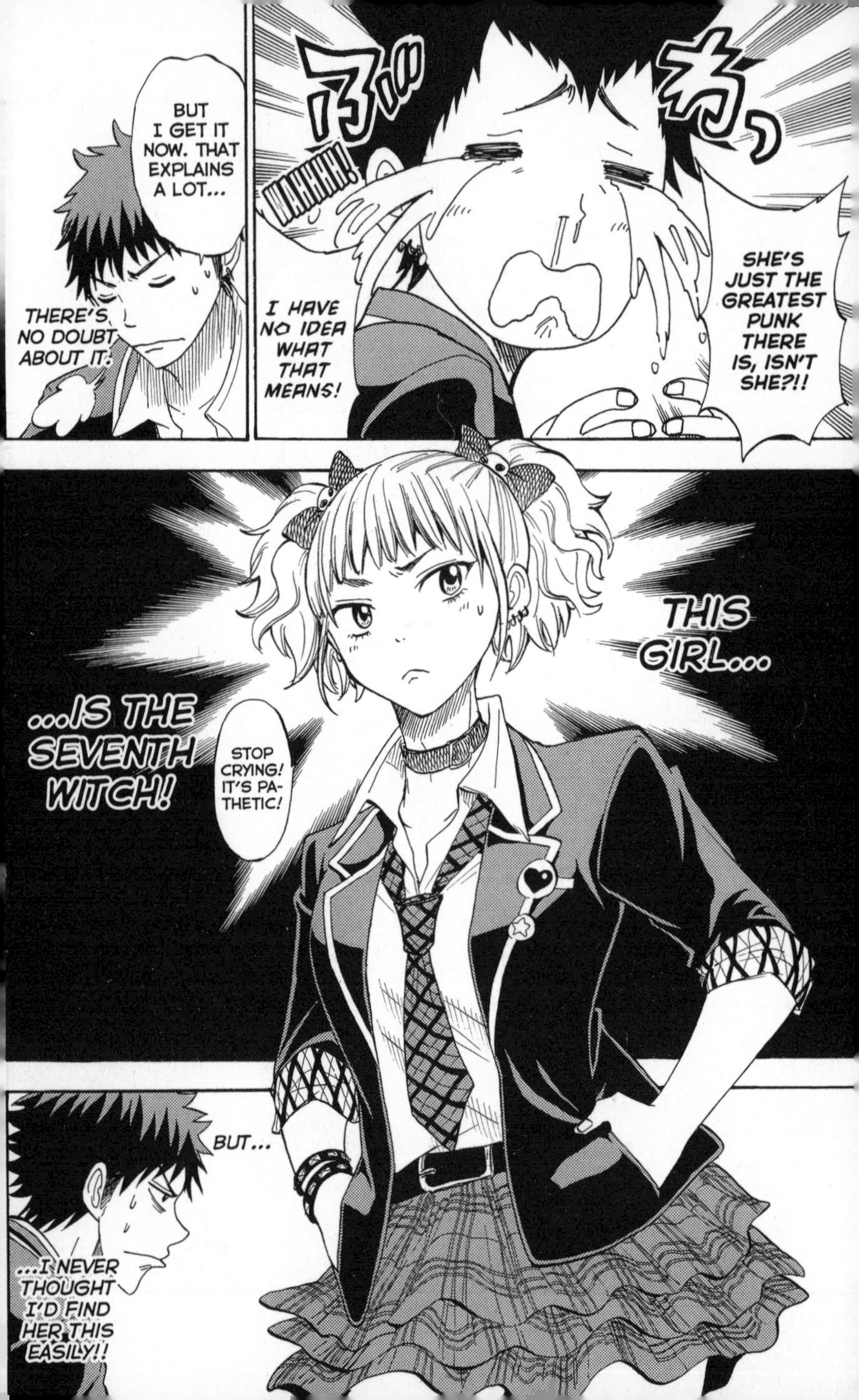
SHE'S JUST THE GREATEST PUNK THERE IS, ISN'T SHE?!!
I HAVE NO IDEA WHAT THAT MEANS!
BUT I GET IT NOW. THAT EXPLAINS A LOT...
THERE'S NO DOUBT ABOUT IT.
THIS GIRL...
...IS THE SEVENTH WITCH!
STOP CRYING! IT'S PA-THETIC!
BUT...
...I NEVER THOUGHT I'D FIND HER THIS EASILY!!

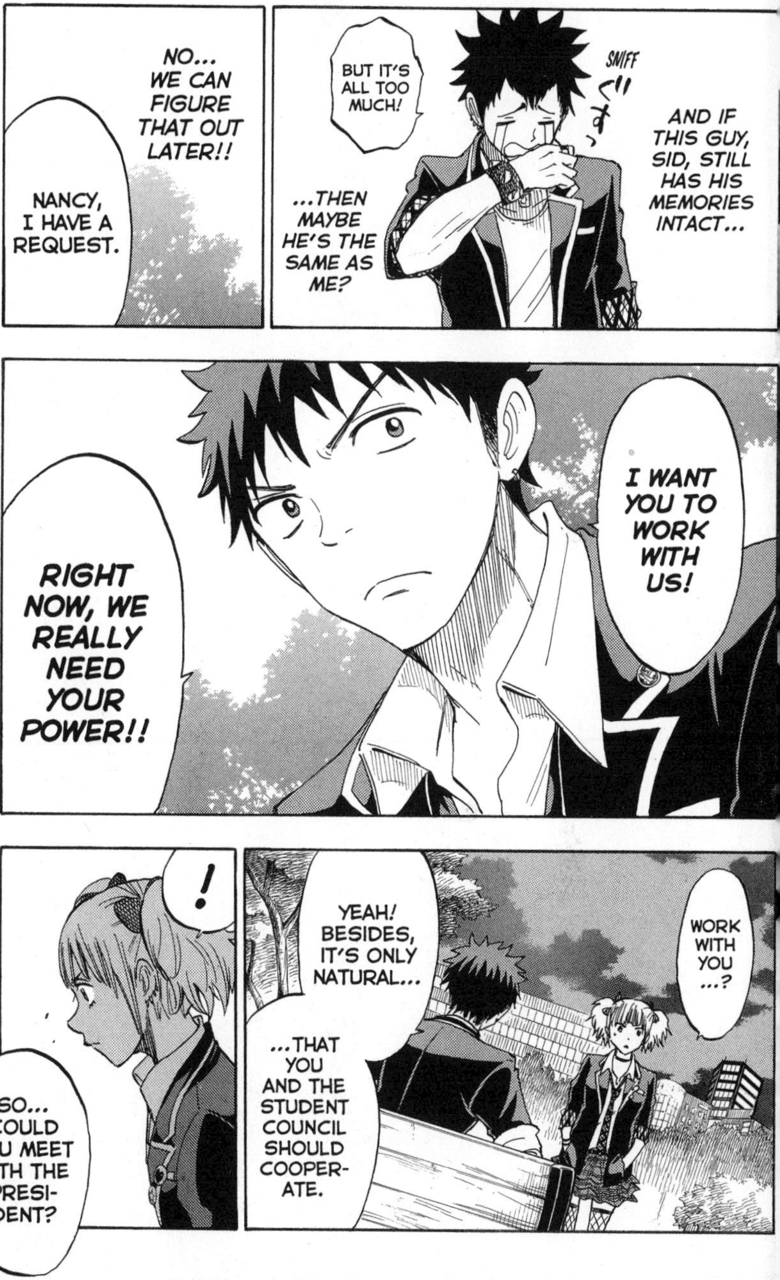
AND IF THIS GUY, SID, STILL HAS HIS MEMORIES INTACT...
SNIFF
ぐすっ
BUT IT'S ALL TOO MUCH!
...THEN MAYBE HE'S THE SAME AS ME?
NO... WE CAN FIGURE THAT OUT LATER!!
NANCY, I HAVE A REQUEST.
I WANT YOU TO WORK WITH US!
RIGHT NOW, WE REALLY NEED YOUR POWER!!
WORK WITH YOU ...?
YEAH! BESIDES, IT'S ONLY NATURAL...
...THAT YOU AND THE STUDENT COUNCIL SHOULD COOPER-ATE.
!
SO... COULD YOU MEET WITH THE PRESI-DENT?

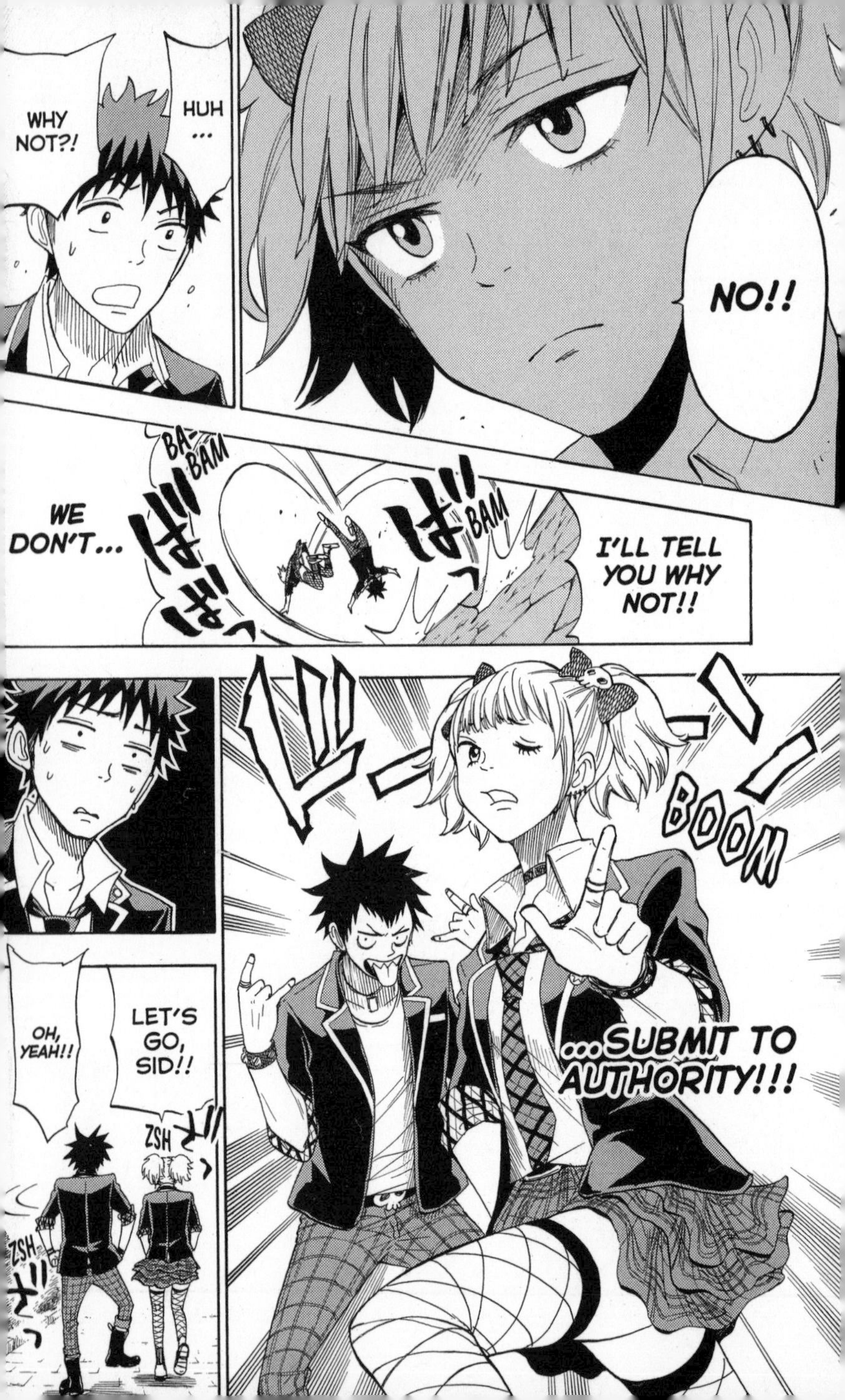
NO!!
HUH ...
WHY NOT?!
I'LL TELL YOU WHY NOT!!
BAM
BA-BAM
WE DON'T...
BOOM
...SUBMIT TO AUTHORITY!!!
LET'S GO, SID!!
OH, YEAH!!
ZSH
ZSH

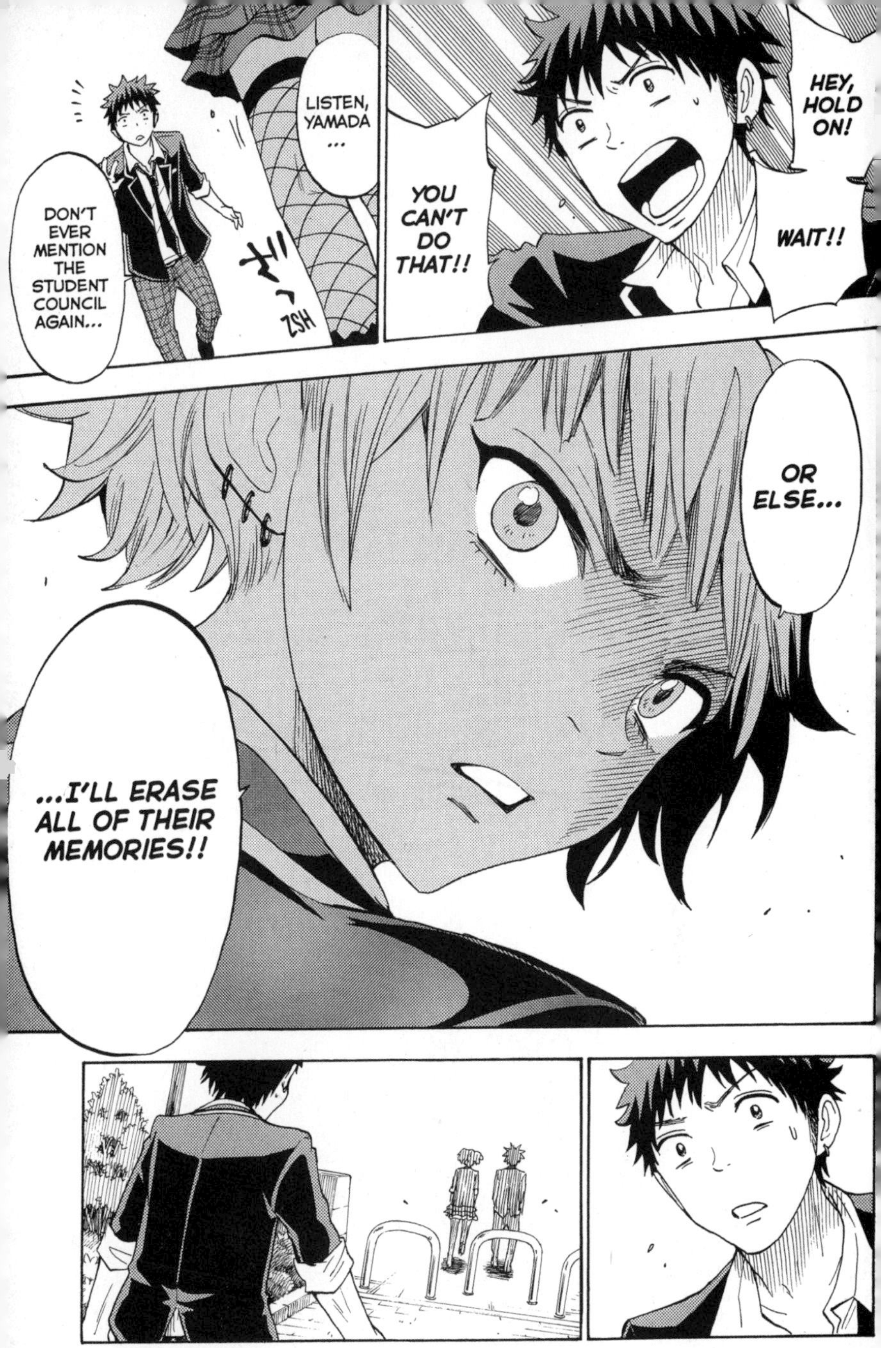
HEY, HOLD ON!
WAIT!!
YOU CAN'T DO THAT!!
LISTEN, YAMADA ...
ZSH
DON'T EVER MENTION THE STUDENT COUNCIL AGAIN...
OR ELSE...
...I'LL ERASE ALL OF THEIR MEMORIES!!

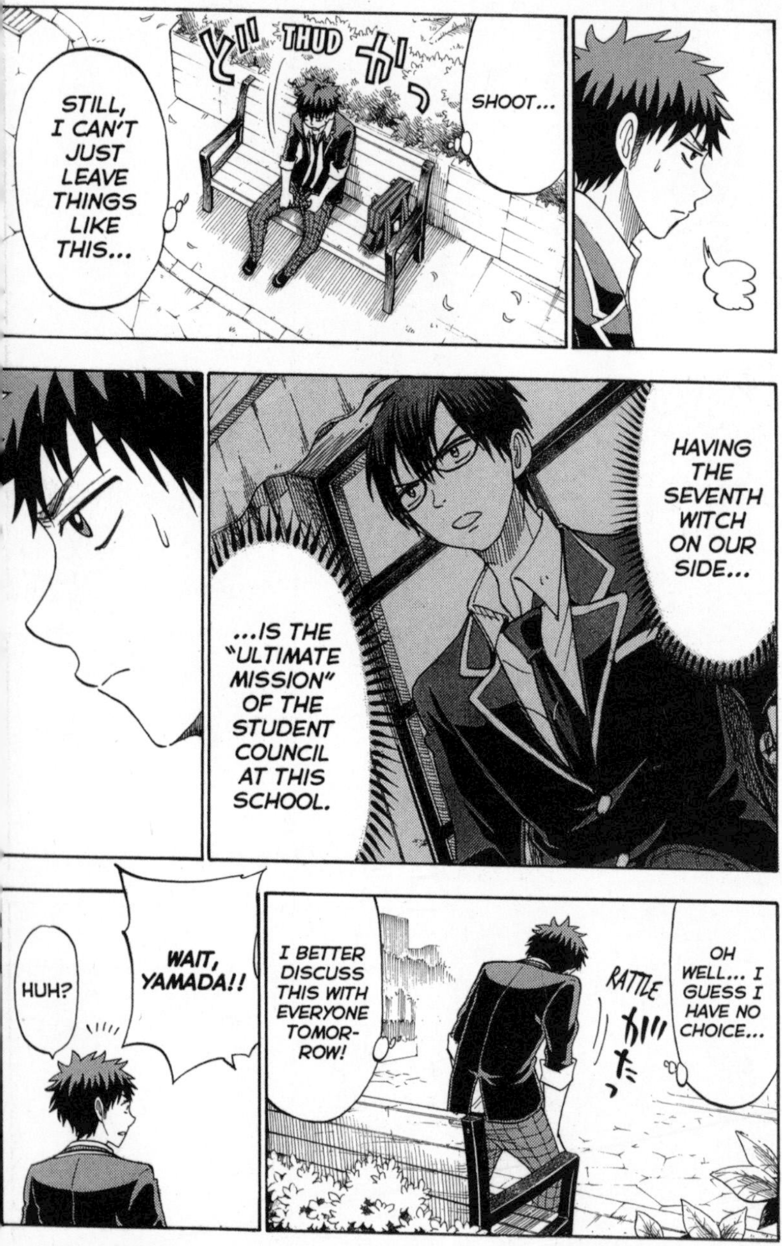
SHOOT...
THUD
STILL, I CAN'T JUST LEAVE THINGS LIKE THIS...
HAVING THE SEVENTH WITCH ON OUR SIDE...
...IS THE "ULTIMATE MISSION" OF THE STUDENT COUNCIL AT THIS SCHOOL.
OH WELL... I GUESS I HAVE NO CHOICE...
RATTLE
I BETTER DISCUSS THIS WITH EVERYONE TOMORROW!
WAIT, YAMADA!!
HUH?

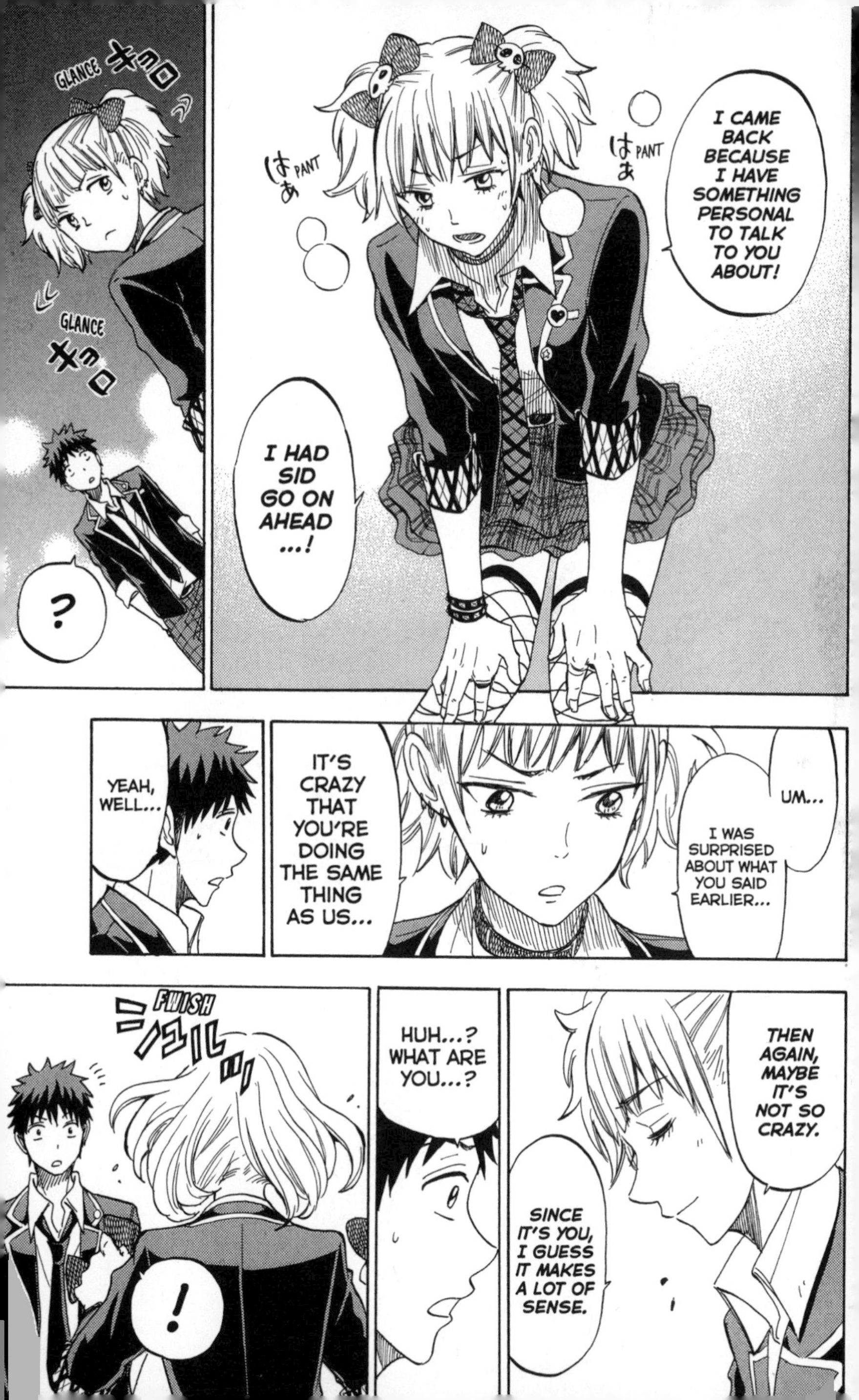
はあ PANT
はあ PANT
I CAME BACK BECAUSE I HAVE SOMETHING PERSONAL TO TALK TO YOU ABOUT!
I HAD SID GO ON AHEAD ...!
GLANCE キョロ
GLANCE キョロ
?
UM...
I WAS SURPRISED ABOUT WHAT YOU SAID EARLIER...
IT'S CRAZY THAT YOU'RE DOING THE SAME THING AS US...
YEAH, WELL...
THEN AGAIN, MAYBE IT'S NOT SO CRAZY.
SINCE IT'S YOU, I GUESS IT MAKES A LOT OF SENSE.
HUH...? WHAT ARE YOU...?
FWISH
!

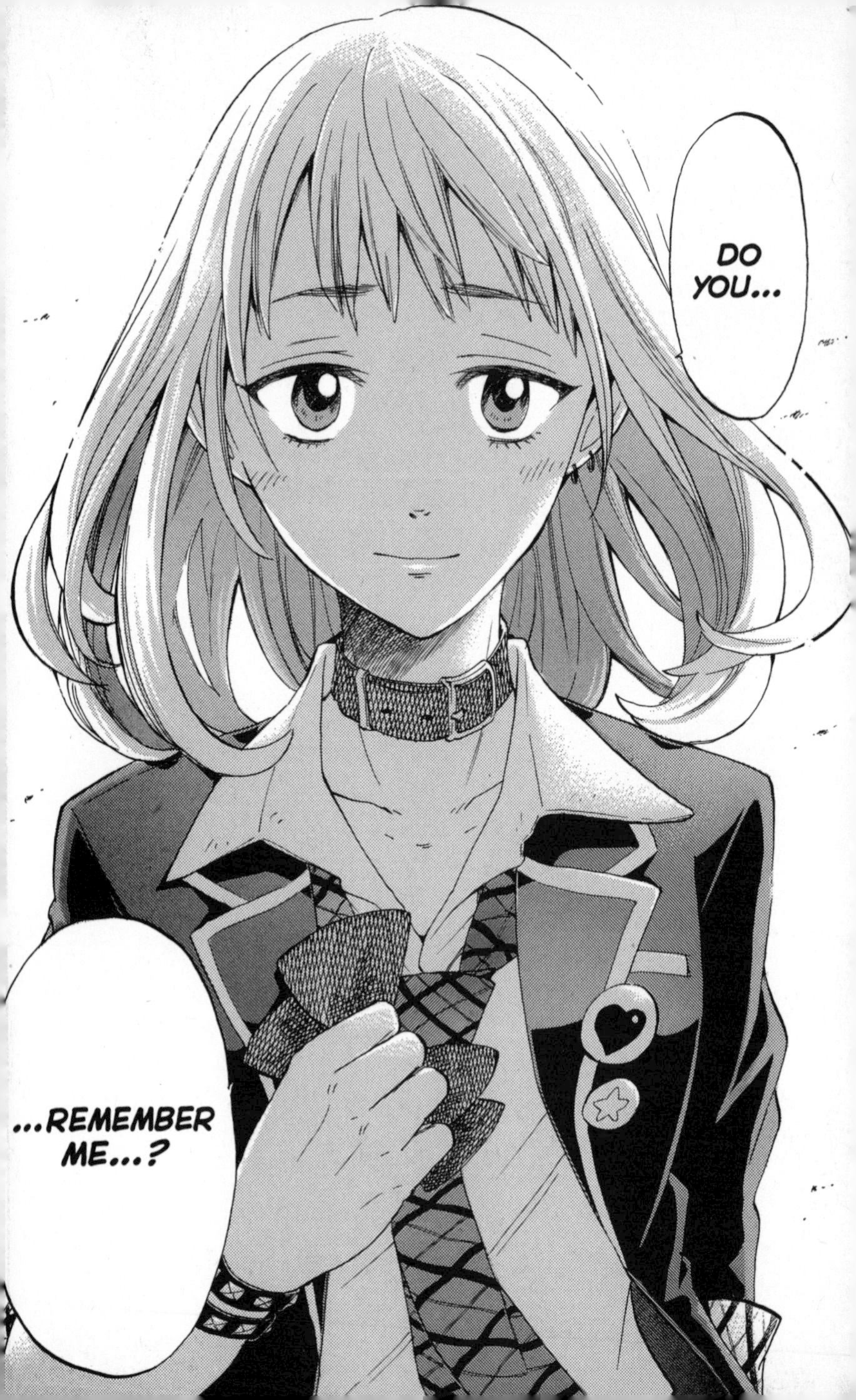
DO YOU...
...REMEMBER ME...?

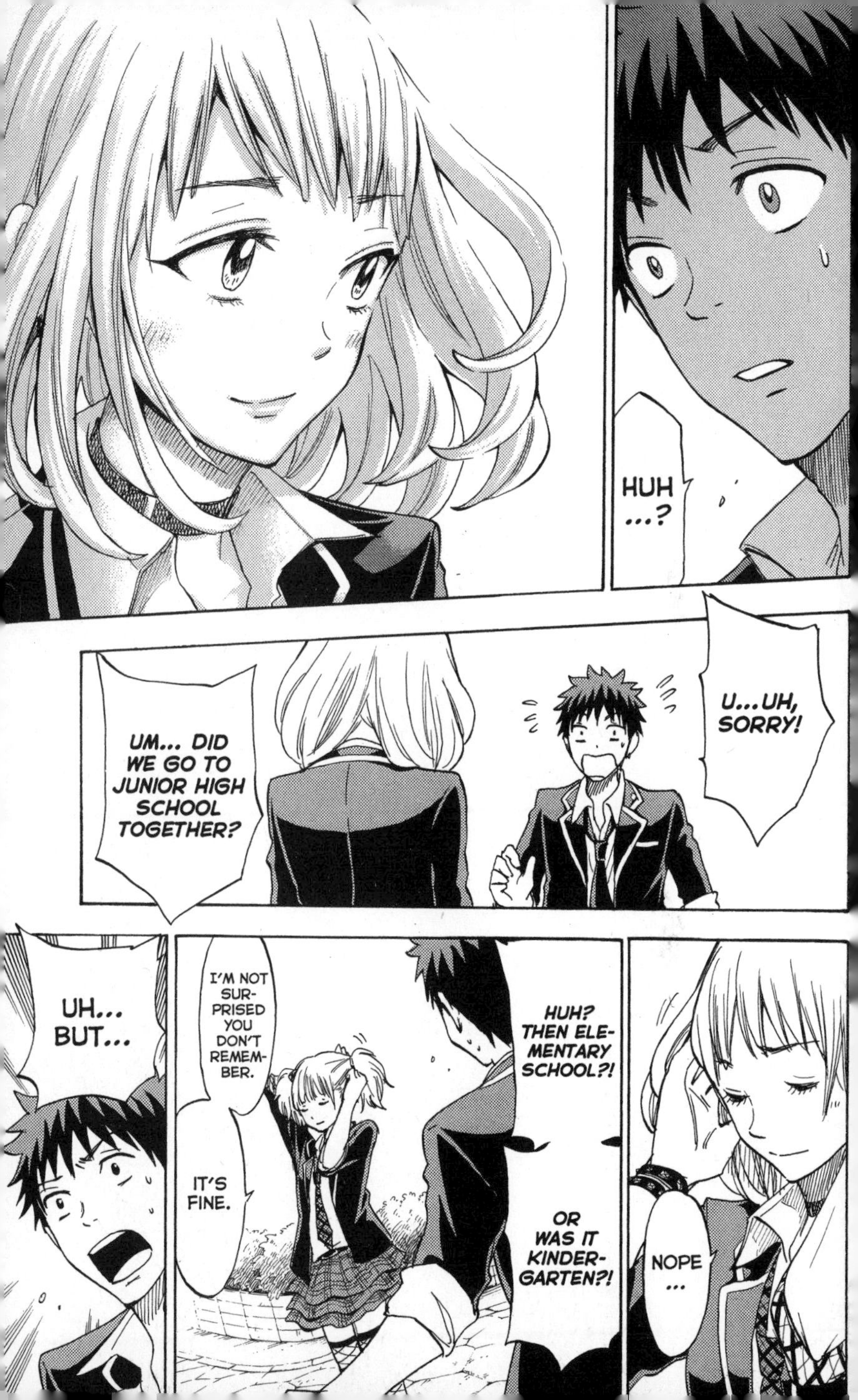
HUH ...?
U...UH, SORRY!
UM... DID WE GO TO JUNIOR HIGH SCHOOL TOGETHER?
HUH? THEN ELEMENTARY SCHOOL?!
OR WAS IT KINDERGARTEN?!
NOPE ...
I'M NOT SURPRISED YOU DON'T REMEMBER.
IT'S FINE.
UH... BUT...

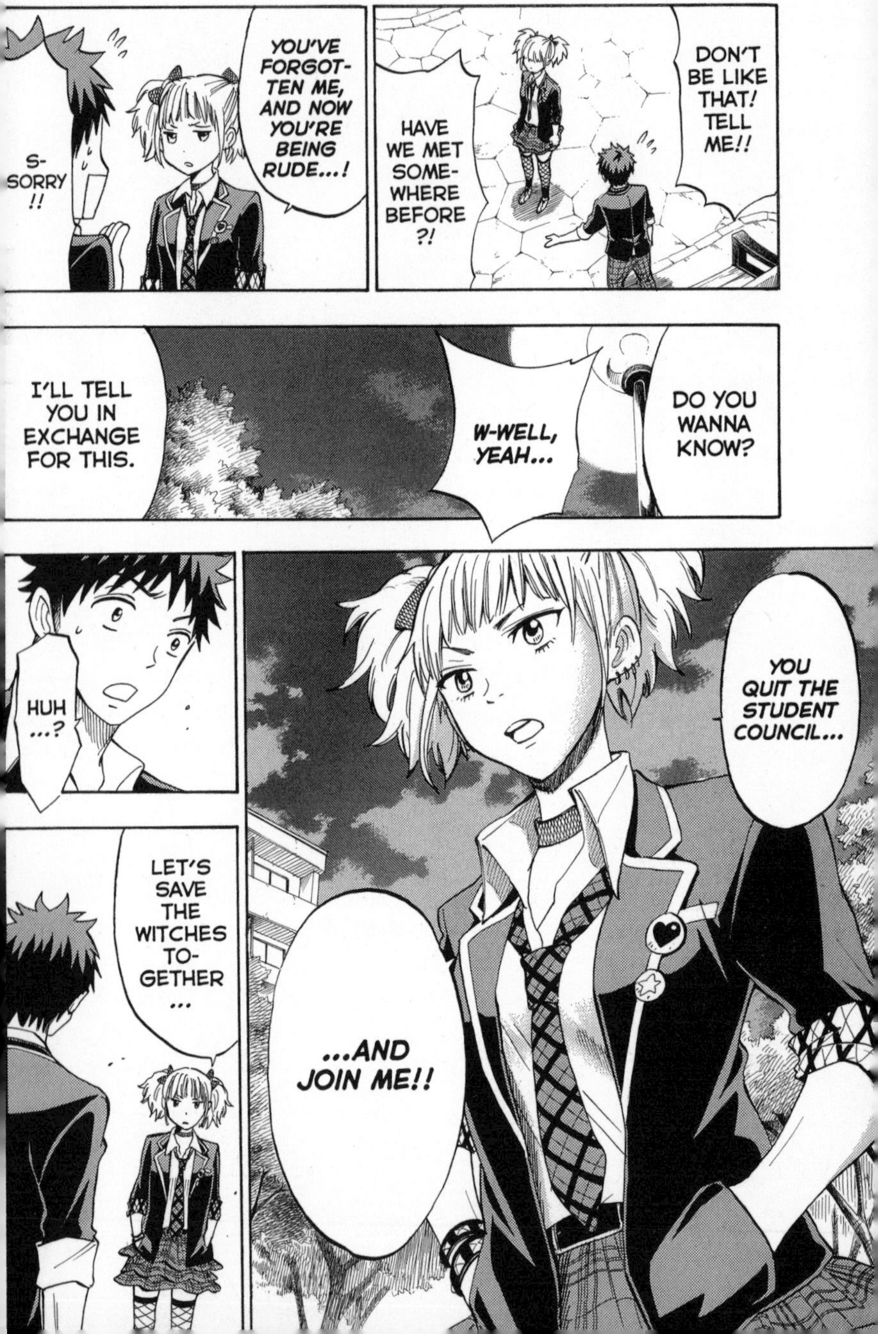
DON'T BE LIKE THAT! TELL ME!!
HAVE WE MET SOME-WHERE BEFORE ?!
YOU'VE FORGOT-TEN ME, AND NOW YOU'RE BEING RUDE...!
S-SORRY !!
DO YOU WANNA KNOW?
W-WELL, YEAH...
I'LL TELL YOU IN EXCHANGE FOR THIS.
YOU QUIT THE STUDENT COUNCIL...
...AND JOIN ME!!
HUH ...?
LET'S SAVE THE WITCHES TO-GETHER ...

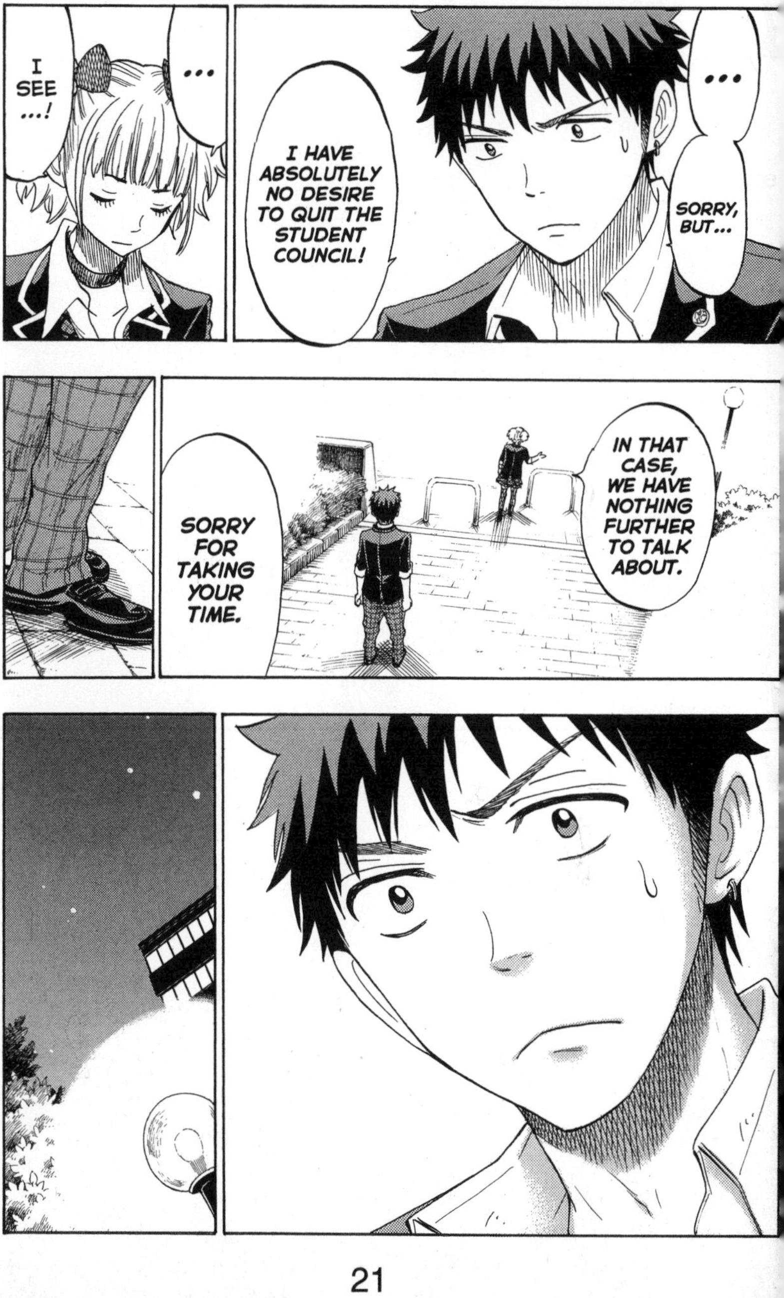
...
SORRY, BUT...
I HAVE ABSOLUTELY NO DESIRE TO QUIT THE STUDENT COUNCIL!
...
I SEE ...!
IN THAT CASE, WE HAVE NOTHING FURTHER TO TALK ABOUT.
SORRY FOR TAKING YOUR TIME.

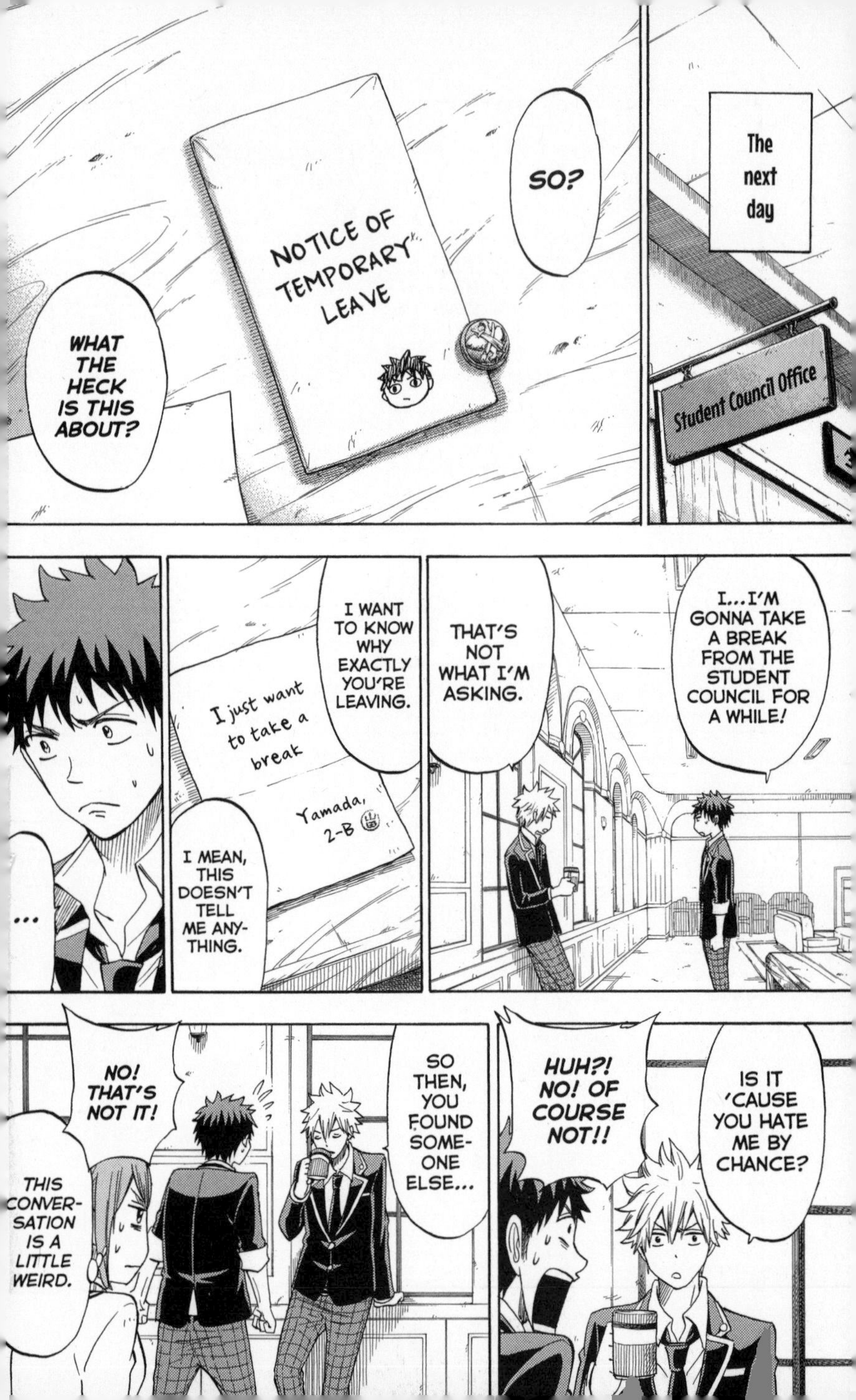

The next day
Student Council Office
SO?
NOTICE OF TEMPORARY LEAVE
WHAT THE HECK IS THIS ABOUT?
I...I'M GONNA TAKE A BREAK FROM THE STUDENT COUNCIL FOR A WHILE!
THAT'S NOT WHAT I'M ASKING.
I WANT TO KNOW WHY EXACTLY YOU'RE LEAVING.
I just want to take a break
Yamada, 2-B
I MEAN, THIS DOESN'T TELL ME ANY-THING.
...
IS IT 'CAUSE YOU HATE ME BY CHANCE?
HUH?! NO! OF COURSE NOT!!
SO THEN, YOU FOUND SOME-ONE ELSE...
NO! THAT'S NOT IT!
THIS CONVER-SATION IS A LITTLE WEIRD.

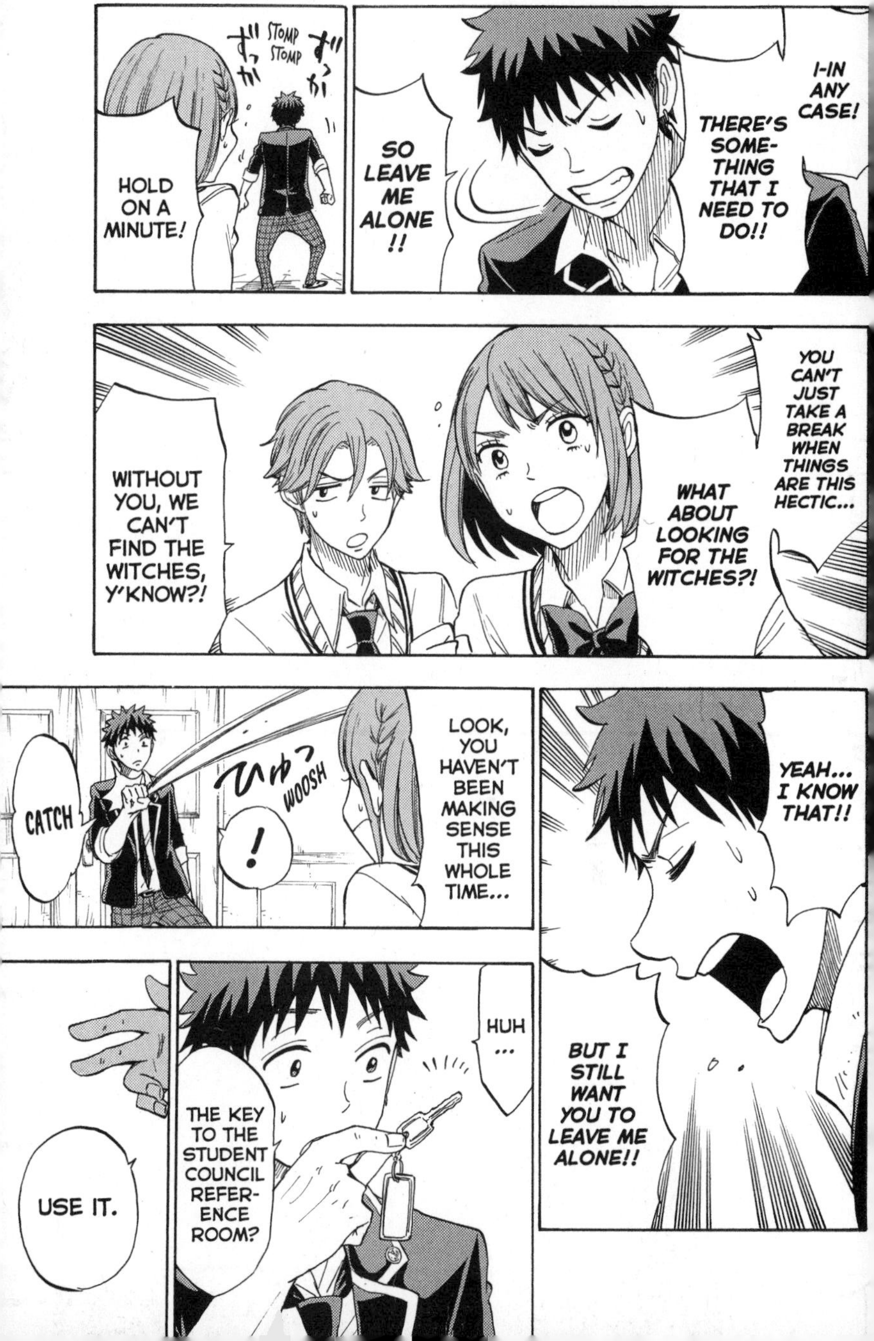
I-IN ANY CASE!
THERE'S SOME-THING THAT I NEED TO DO!!
SO LEAVE ME ALONE!!
STOMP STOMP
HOLD ON A MINUTE!
YOU CAN'T JUST TAKE A BREAK WHEN THINGS ARE THIS HECTIC...
WHAT ABOUT LOOKING FOR THE WITCHES?!
WITHOUT YOU, WE CAN'T FIND THE WITCHES, Y'KNOW?!
YEAH... I KNOW THAT!!
BUT I STILL WANT YOU TO LEAVE ME ALONE!!
LOOK, YOU HAVEN'T BEEN MAKING SENSE THIS WHOLE TIME...
ひゅっ WOOSH
!
CATCH
HUH...
THE KEY TO THE STUDENT COUNCIL REFERENCE ROOM?
USE IT.

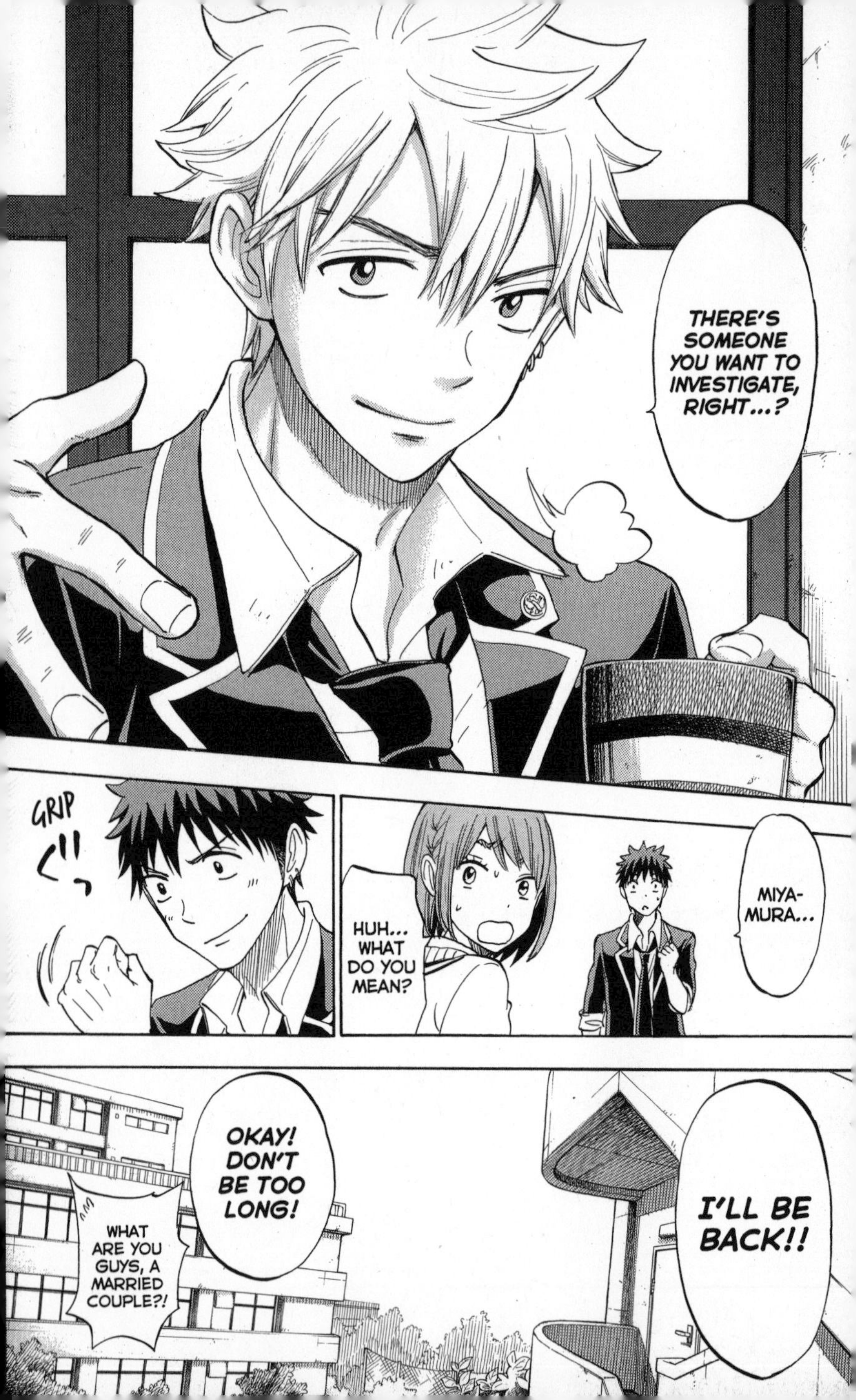
THERE'S SOMEONE YOU WANT TO INVESTIGATE, RIGHT...?
MIYA-MURA...
HUH... WHAT DO YOU MEAN?
GRIP
I'LL BE BACK!!
OKAY! DON'T BE TOO LONG!
WHAT ARE YOU GUYS, A MARRIED COUPLE?!

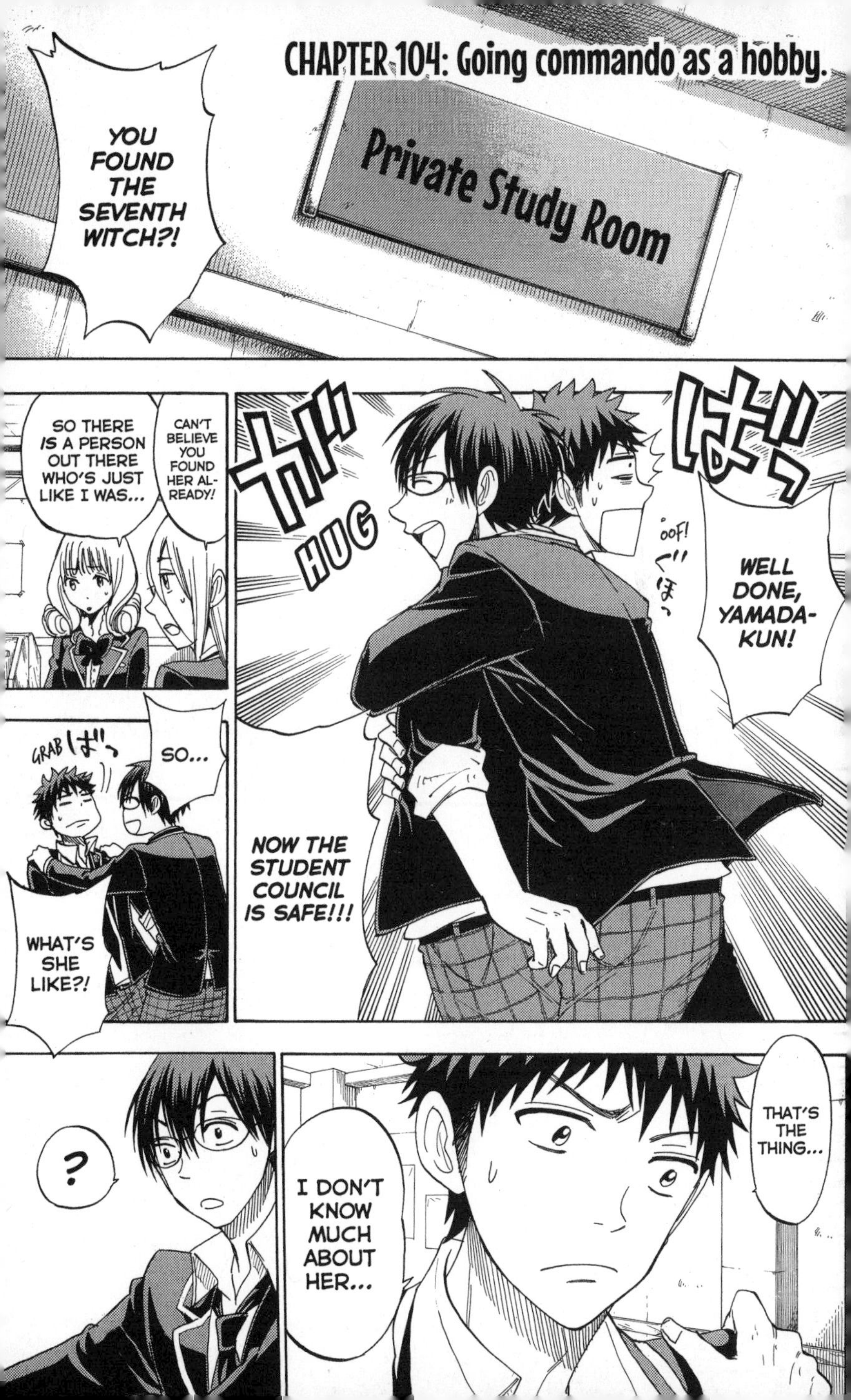
CHAPTER 104: Going commando as a hobby.
Private Study Room
YOU FOUND THE SEVENTH WITCH?!
はっ
WELL DONE, YAMADA-KUN!
ぐほっ OOF!
ガバ HUG
NOW THE STUDENT COUNCIL IS SAFE!!!
CAN'T BELIEVE YOU FOUND HER ALREADY!
SO THERE IS A PERSON OUT THERE WHO'S JUST LIKE I WAS...
SO...
ばっ GRAB
WHAT'S SHE LIKE?!
THAT'S THE THING...
I DON'T KNOW MUCH ABOUT HER...
?

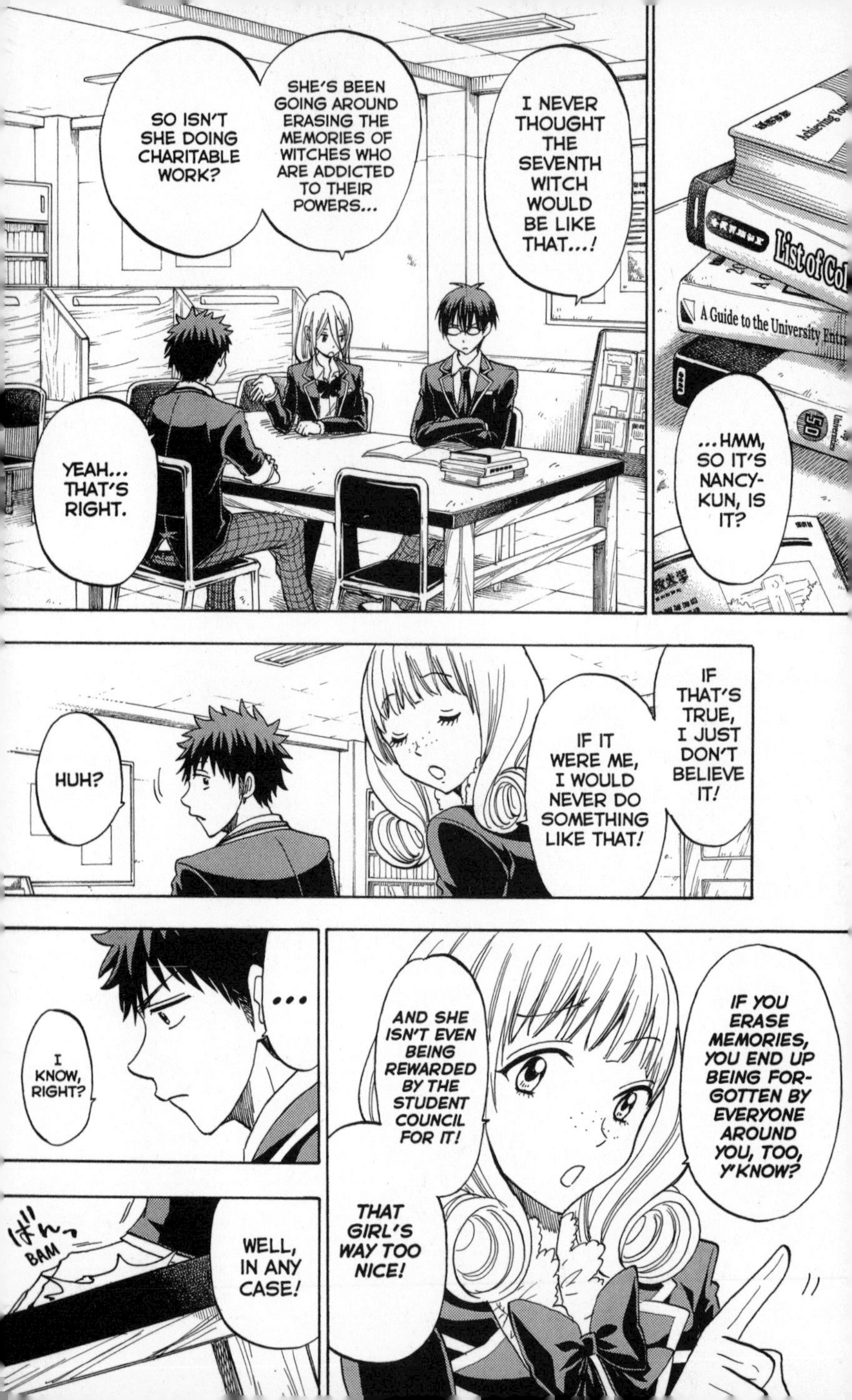
...HMM, SO IT'S NANCY-KUN, IS IT?
I NEVER THOUGHT THE SEVENTH WITCH WOULD BE LIKE THAT...!
SHE'S BEEN GOING AROUND ERASING THE MEMORIES OF WITCHES WHO ARE ADDICTED TO THEIR POWERS...
SO ISN'T SHE DOING CHARITABLE WORK?
YEAH... THAT'S RIGHT.
IF THAT'S TRUE, I JUST DON'T BELIEVE IT!
IF IT WERE ME, I WOULD NEVER DO SOMETHING LIKE THAT!
HUH?
IF YOU ERASE MEMORIES, YOU END UP BEING FOR-GOTTEN BY EVERYONE AROUND YOU, TOO, Y'KNOW?
AND SHE ISN'T EVEN BEING REWARDED BY THE STUDENT COUNCIL FOR IT!
THAT GIRL'S WAY TOO NICE!
...
I KNOW, RIGHT?
WELL, IN ANY CASE!
ばんっ
BAM

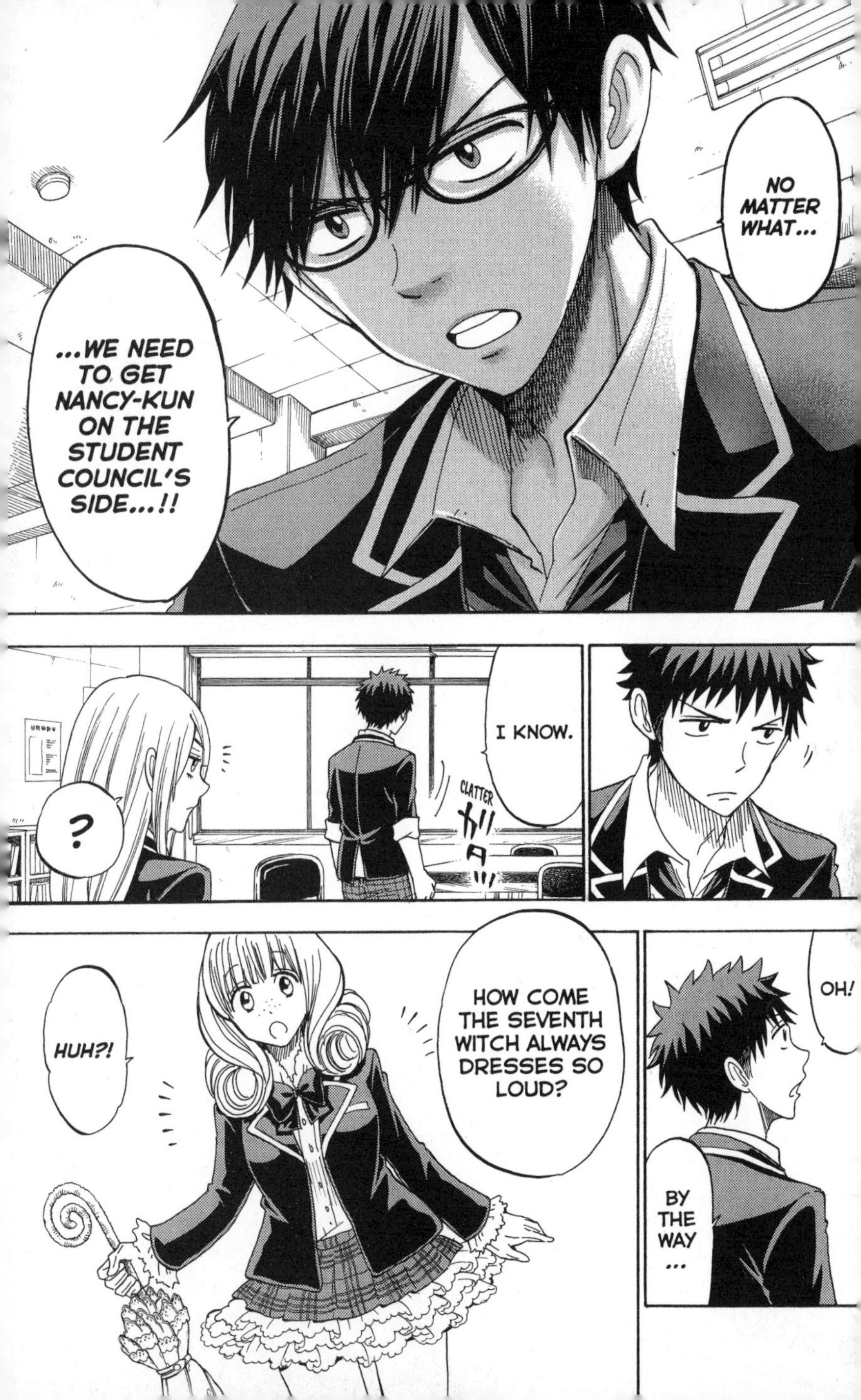
NO MATTER WHAT...
...WE NEED TO GET NANCY-KUN ON THE STUDENT COUNCIL'S SIDE...!!
I KNOW.
CLATTER
ガタ
?
OH!
BY THE WAY...
HOW COME THE SEVENTH WITCH ALWAYS DRESSES SO LOUD?
HUH?!

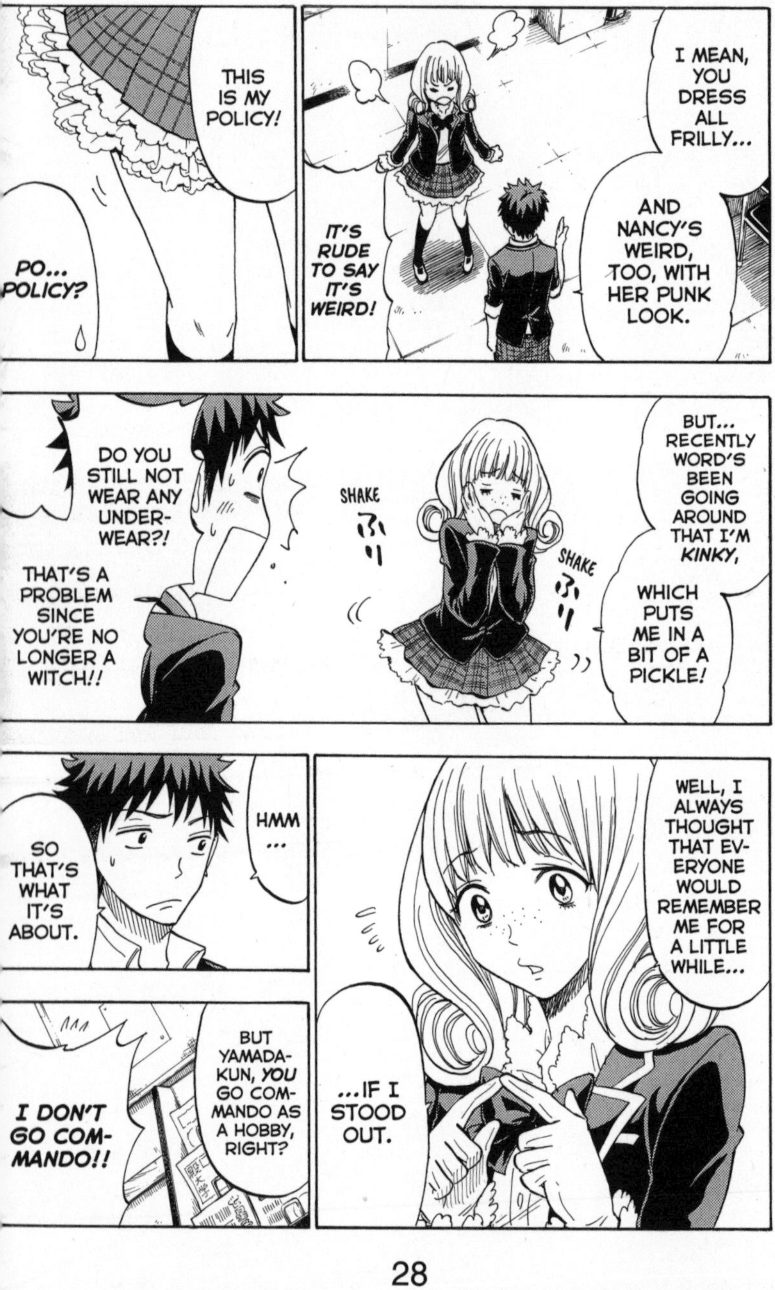
I MEAN, YOU DRESS ALL FRILLY...
AND NANCY'S WEIRD, TOO, WITH HER PUNK LOOK.
IT'S RUDE TO SAY IT'S WEIRD!
THIS IS MY POLICY!
PO... POLICY?
BUT... RECENTLY WORD'S BEEN GOING AROUND THAT I'M KINKY,
WHICH PUTS ME IN A BIT OF A PICKLE!
SHAKE ふり
SHAKE ふり
DO YOU STILL NOT WEAR ANY UNDER-WEAR?!
THAT'S A PROBLEM SINCE YOU'RE NO LONGER A WITCH!!
WELL, I ALWAYS THOUGHT THAT EV-ERYONE WOULD REMEMBER ME FOR A LITTLE WHILE...
...IF I STOOD OUT.
HMM...
SO THAT'S WHAT IT'S ABOUT.
BUT YAMADA-KUN, YOU GO COM-MANDO AS A HOBBY, RIGHT?
I DON'T GO COM-MANDO!!

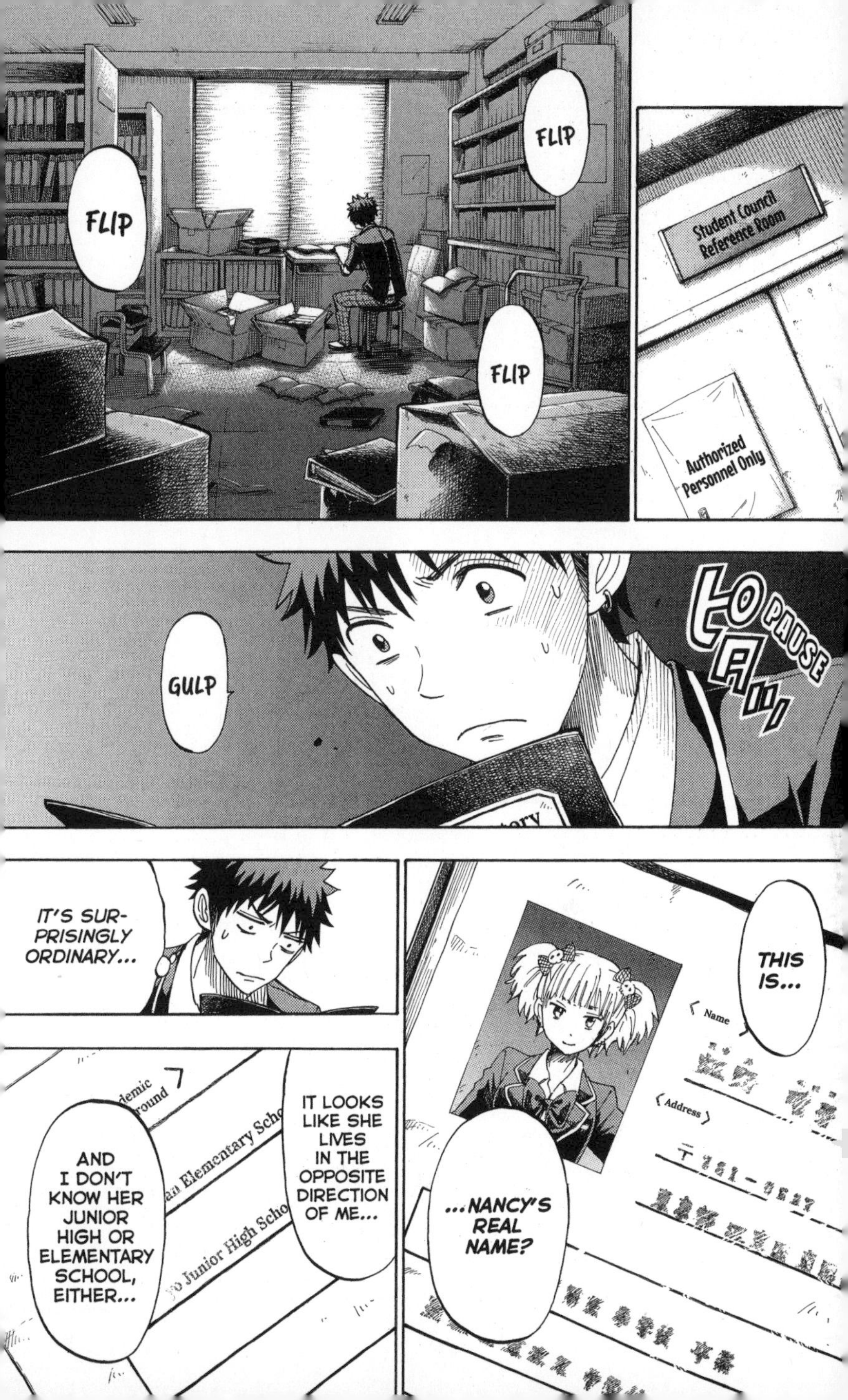
Student Council Reference Room
Authorized Personnel Only
FLIP
FLIP
FLIP
PAUSE
GULP
THIS IS...
Name
Address
...NANCY'S REAL NAME?
IT'S SUR-PRISINGLY ORDINARY...
IT LOOKS LIKE SHE LIVES IN THE OPPOSITE DIRECTION OF ME...
AND I DON'T KNOW HER JUNIOR HIGH OR ELEMENTARY SCHOOL, EITHER...

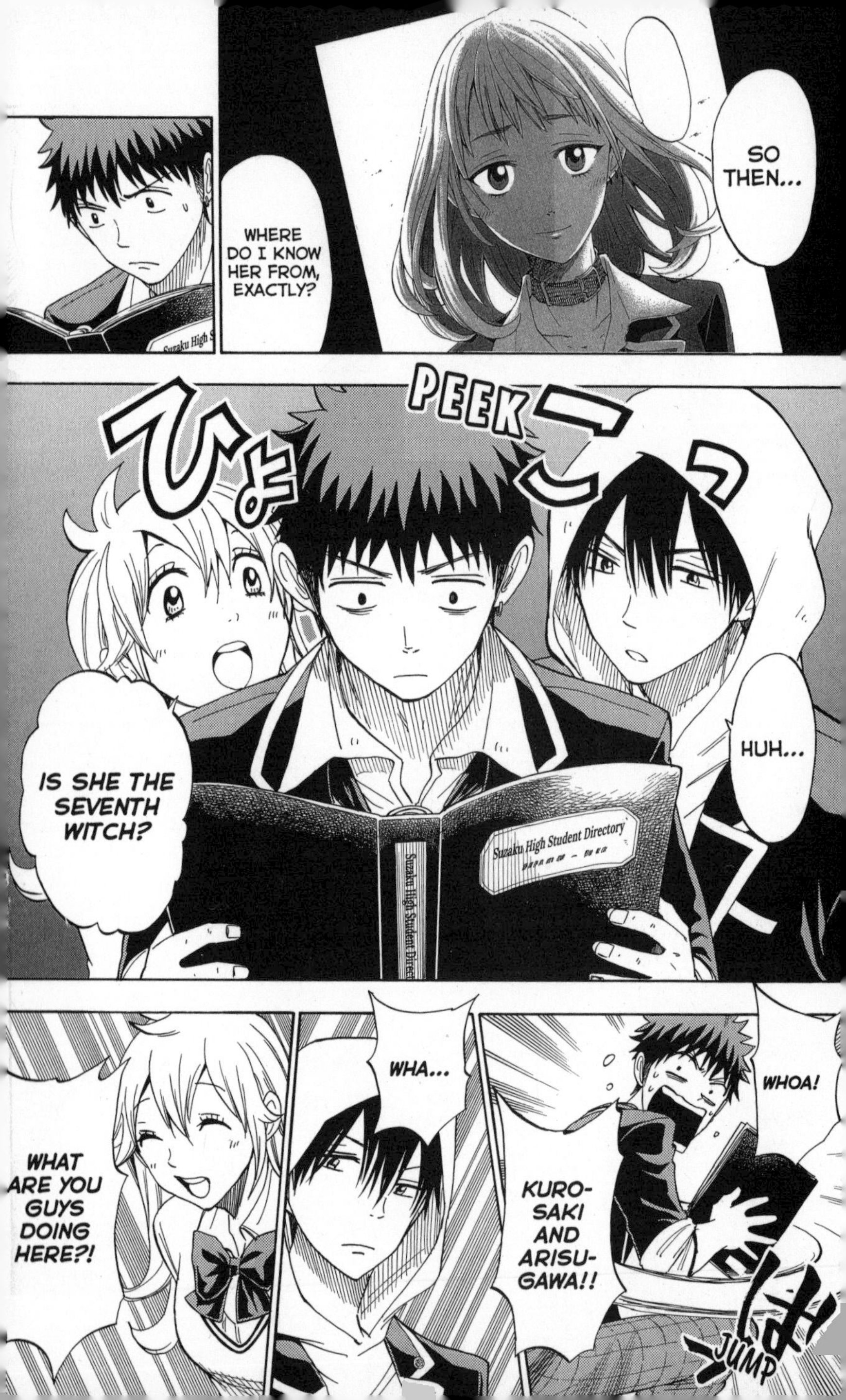
SO THEN...
WHERE DO I KNOW HER FROM, EXACTLY?
PEEK
ひょこっ
HUH...
IS SHE THE SEVENTH WITCH?
Suzaku High Student Directory
WHOA!
KURO-SAKI AND ARISU-GAWA!!
JUMP
WHA...
WHAT ARE YOU GUYS DOING HERE?!

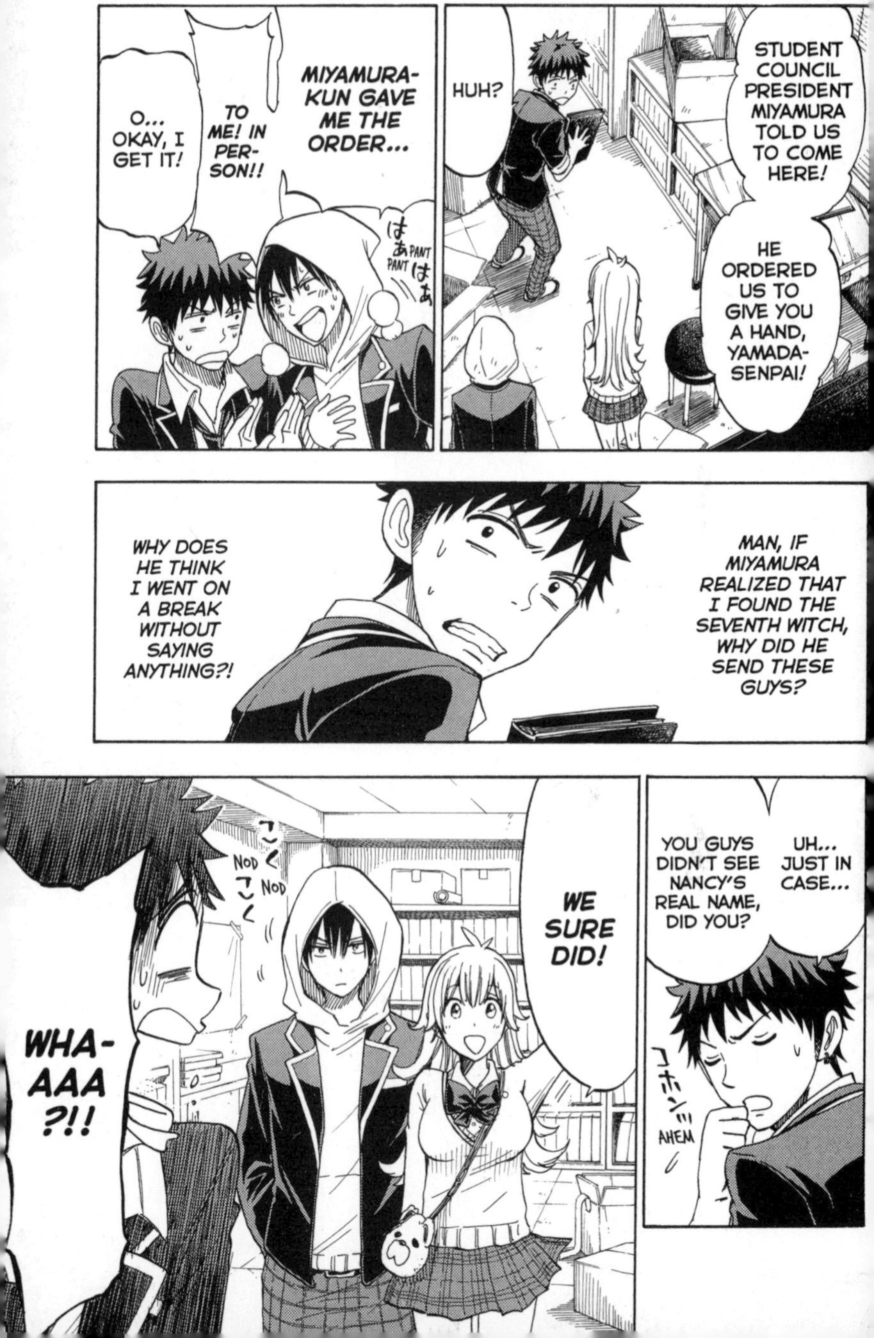
STUDENT COUNCIL PRESIDENT MIYAMURA TOLD US TO COME HERE!
HE ORDERED US TO GIVE YOU A HAND, YAMADA-SENPAI!
HUH?
MIYAMURA-KUN GAVE ME THE ORDER...
TO ME! IN PERSON!!
はあ はあ PANT PANT
O... OKAY, I GET IT!
MAN, IF MIYAMURA REALIZED THAT I FOUND THE SEVENTH WITCH, WHY DID HE SEND THESE GUYS?
WHY DOES HE THINK I WENT ON A BREAK WITHOUT SAYING ANYTHING?!
UH... JUST IN CASE...
YOU GUYS DIDN'T SEE NANCY'S REAL NAME, DID YOU?
コホンッ AHEM
WE SURE DID!
こく こく NOD NOD
WHA-AAA?!!

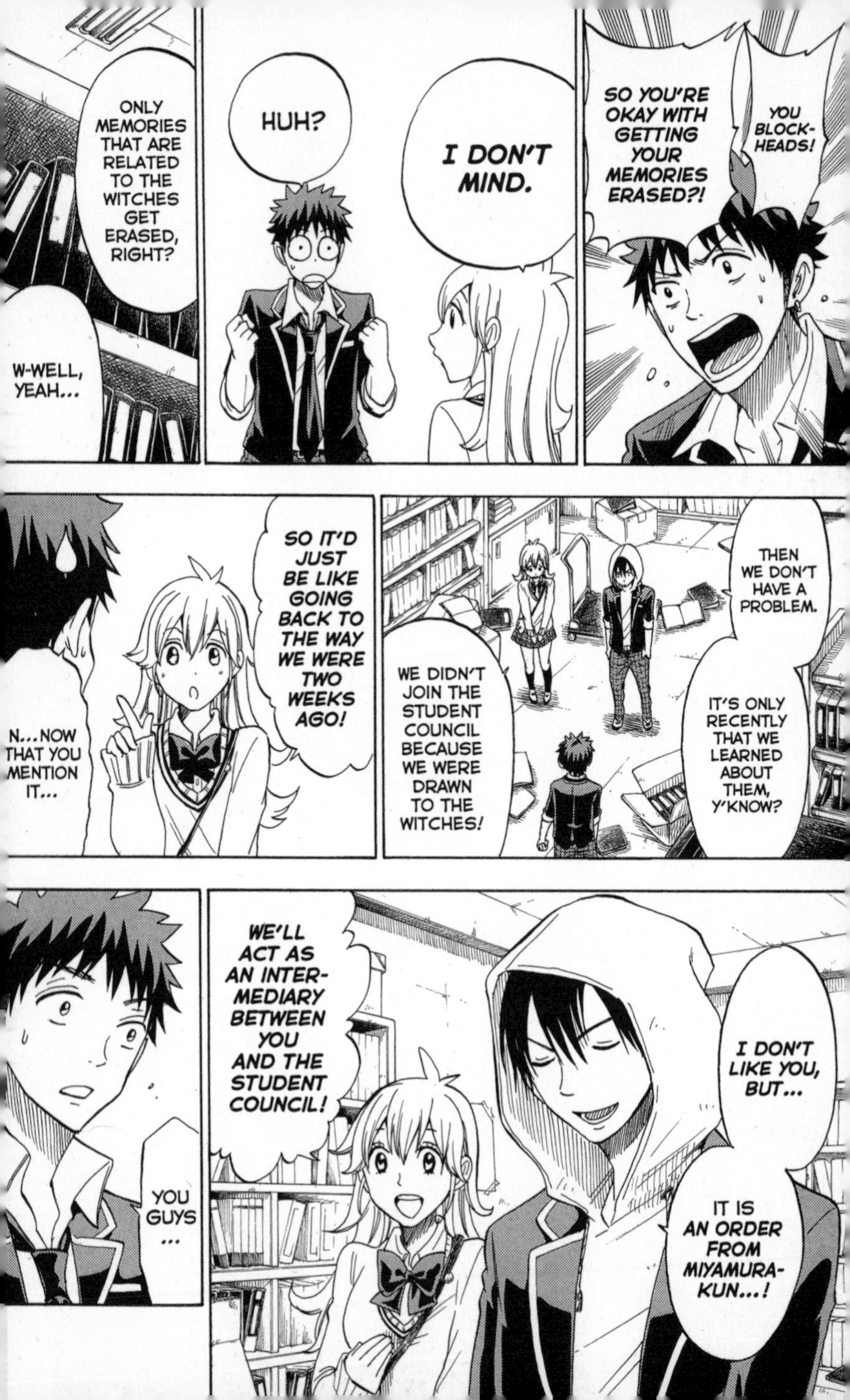
YOU BLOCKHEADS!
SO YOU'RE OKAY WITH GETTING YOUR MEMORIES ERASED?!
I DON'T MIND.
HUH?
ONLY MEMORIES THAT ARE RELATED TO THE WITCHES GET ERASED, RIGHT?
W-WELL, YEAH...
THEN WE DON'T HAVE A PROBLEM.
IT'S ONLY RECENTLY THAT WE LEARNED ABOUT THEM, Y'KNOW?
WE DIDN'T JOIN THE STUDENT COUNCIL BECAUSE WE WERE DRAWN TO THE WITCHES!
SO IT'D JUST BE LIKE GOING BACK TO THE WAY WE WERE TWO WEEKS AGO!
N...NOW THAT YOU MENTION IT...
I DON'T LIKE YOU, BUT...
IT IS AN ORDER FROM MIYAMURA-KUN...!
WE'LL ACT AS AN INTERMEDIARY BETWEEN YOU AND THE STUDENT COUNCIL!
YOU GUYS...

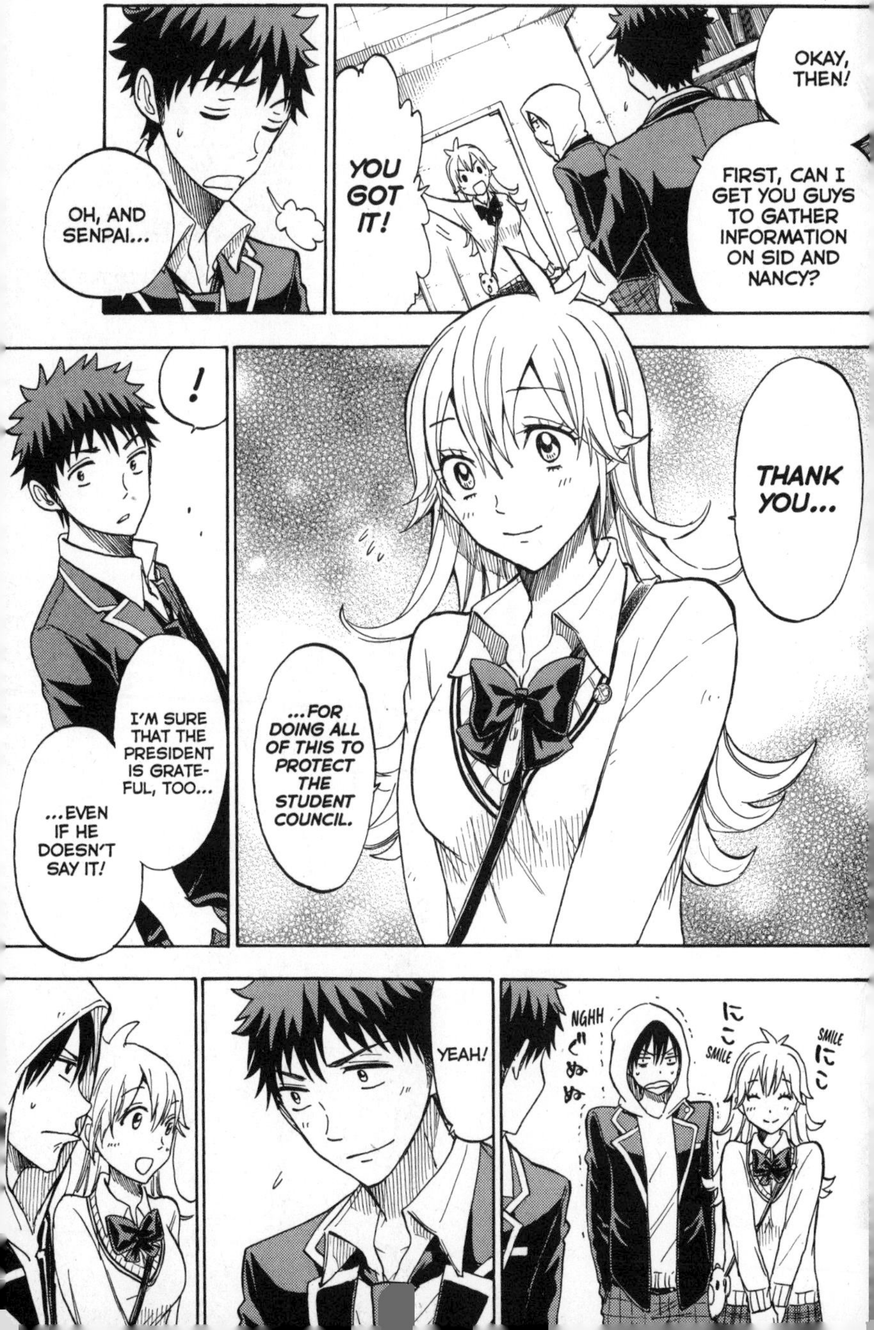
OKAY, THEN!
FIRST, CAN I GET YOU GUYS TO GATHER INFORMATION ON SID AND NANCY?
YOU GOT IT!
OH, AND SENPAI...
THANK YOU...
...FOR DOING ALL OF THIS TO PROTECT THE STUDENT COUNCIL.
!
I'M SURE THAT THE PRESIDENT IS GRATEFUL, TOO...
...EVEN IF HE DOESN'T SAY IT!
SMILE
にこ
SMILE
にこ
NGHH
ぐぬぬ
YEAH!

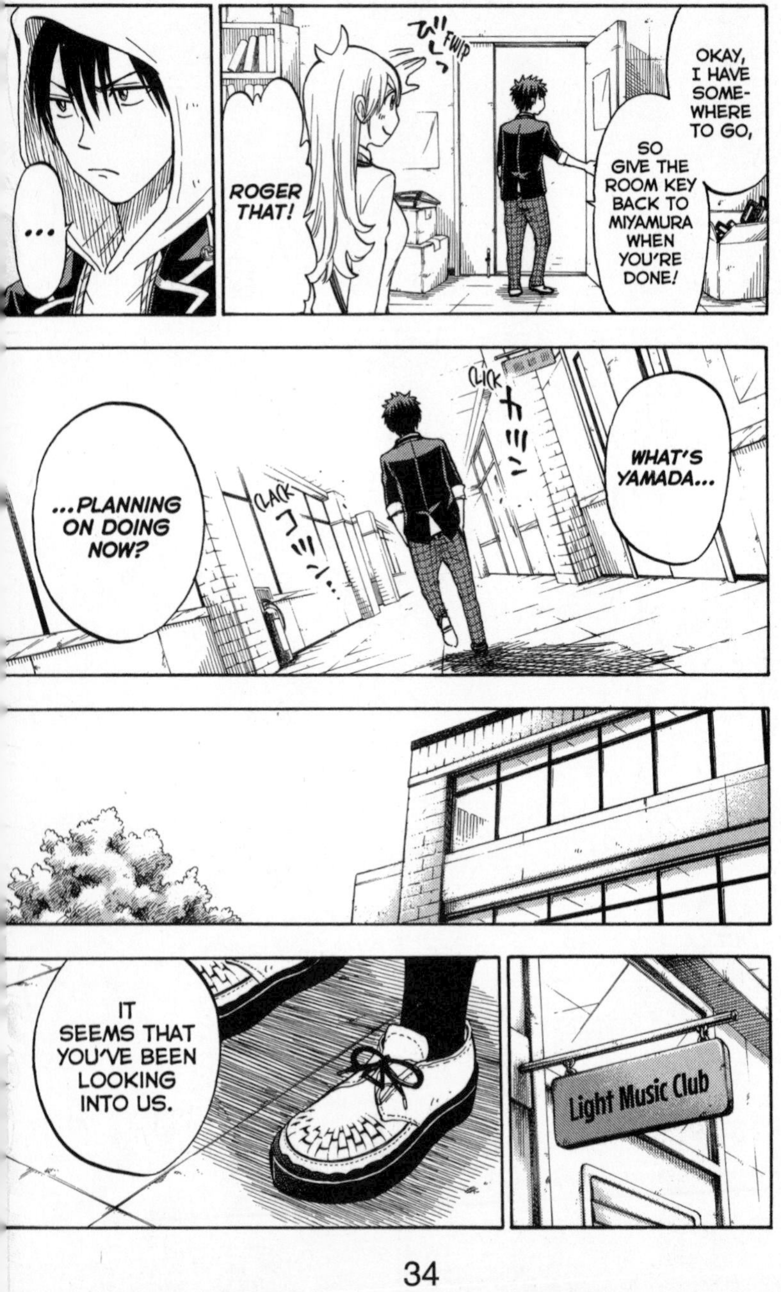
OKAY, I HAVE SOME-WHERE TO GO,
SO GIVE THE ROOM KEY BACK TO MIYAMURA WHEN YOU'RE DONE!
FWIP
ROGER THAT!
...
WHAT'S YAMADA...
CLICK
CLACK
...PLANNING ON DOING NOW?
Light Music Club
IT SEEMS THAT YOU'VE BEEN LOOKING INTO US.

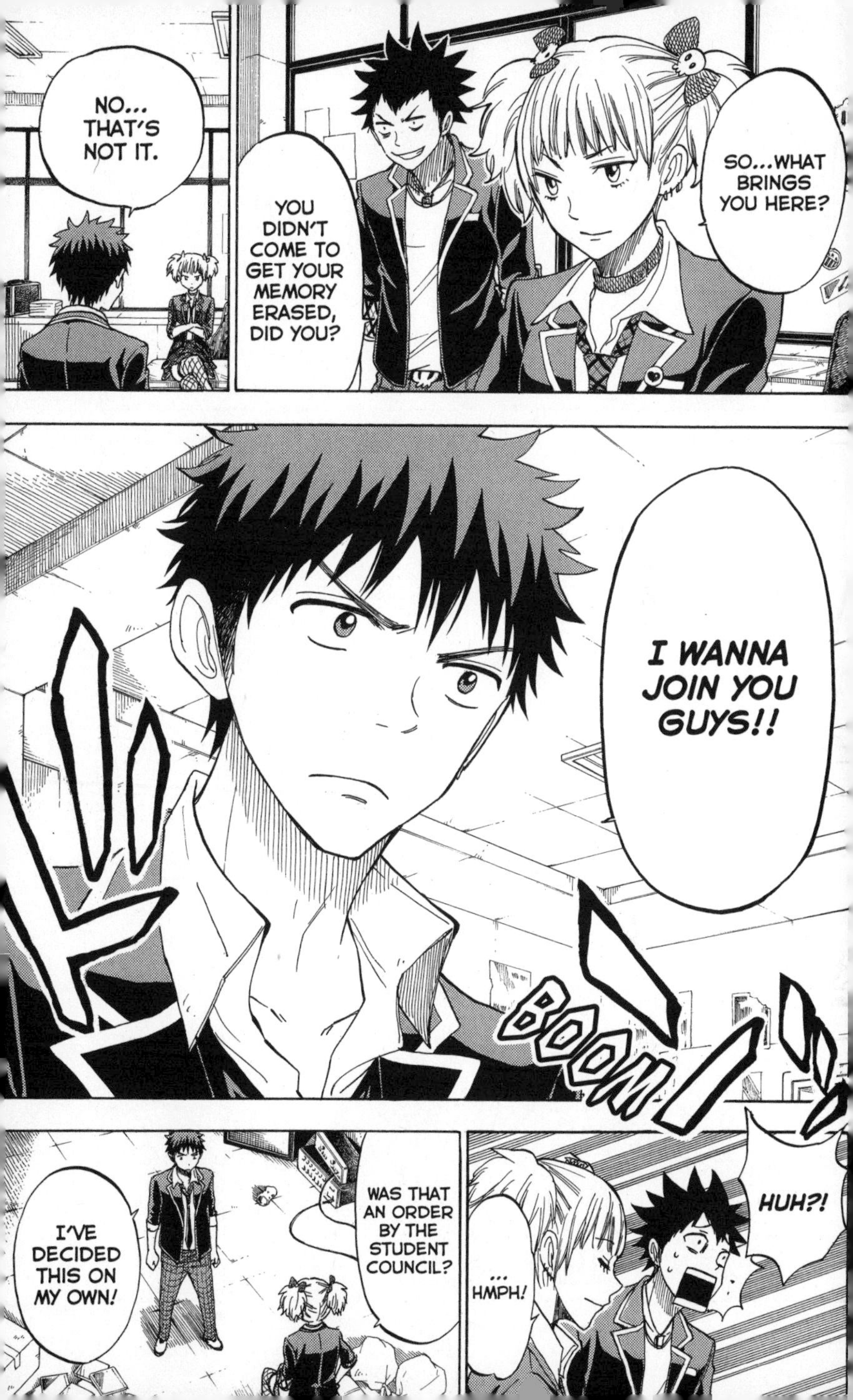
SO...WHAT BRINGS YOU HERE?
YOU DIDN'T COME TO GET YOUR MEMORY ERASED, DID YOU?
NO... THAT'S NOT IT.
I WANNA JOIN YOU GUYS!!
BOOM
HUH?!
...HMPH!
WAS THAT AN ORDER BY THE STUDENT COUNCIL?
I'VE DECIDED THIS ON MY OWN!

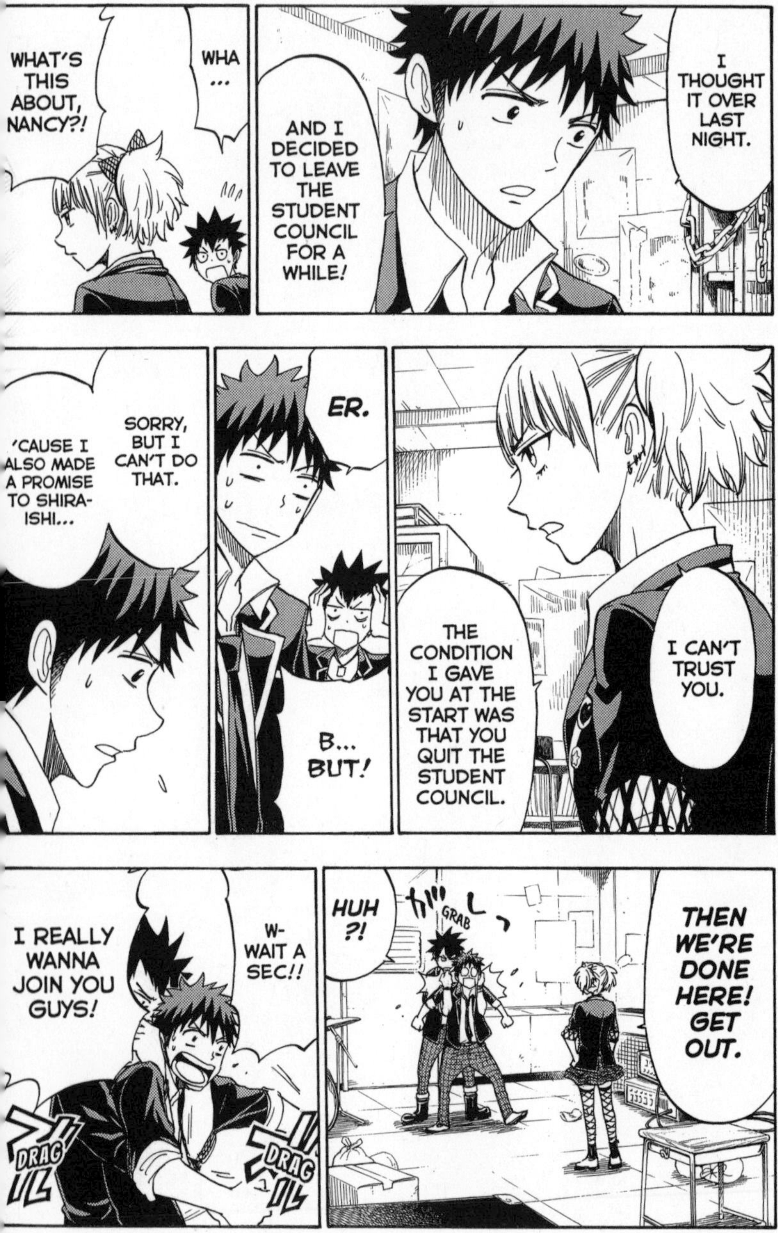
I THOUGHT IT OVER LAST NIGHT.
AND I DECIDED TO LEAVE THE STUDENT COUNCIL FOR A WHILE!
WHA...
WHAT'S THIS ABOUT, NANCY?!
I CAN'T TRUST YOU.
THE CONDITION I GAVE YOU AT THE START WAS THAT YOU QUIT THE STUDENT COUNCIL.
ER.
B... BUT!
SORRY, BUT I CAN'T DO THAT.
'CAUSE I ALSO MADE A PROMISE TO SHIRAISHI...
THEN WE'RE DONE HERE! GET OUT.
GRAB
HUH?!
W-WAIT A SEC!!
I REALLY WANNA JOIN YOU GUYS!
DRAG
DRAG

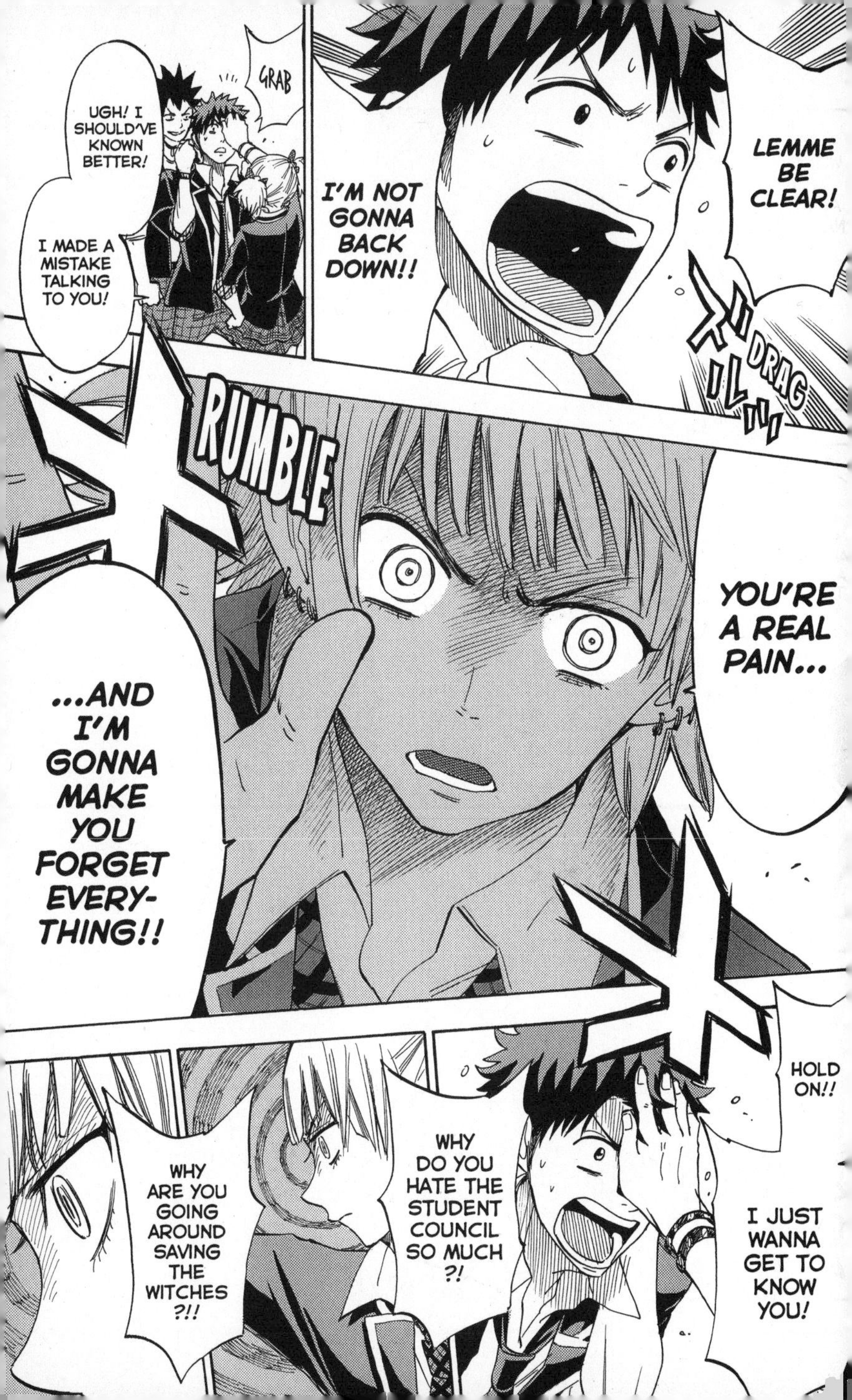
LEMME BE CLEAR!
I'M NOT GONNA BACK DOWN!!
DRAG
GRAB
UGH! I SHOULD'VE KNOWN BETTER!
I MADE A MISTAKE TALKING TO YOU!
RUMBLE
YOU'RE A REAL PAIN...
...AND I'M GONNA MAKE YOU FORGET EVERYTHING!!
HOLD ON!!
I JUST WANNA GET TO KNOW YOU!
WHY DO YOU HATE THE STUDENT COUNCIL SO MUCH?!
WHY ARE YOU GOING AROUND SAVING THE WITCHES?!!

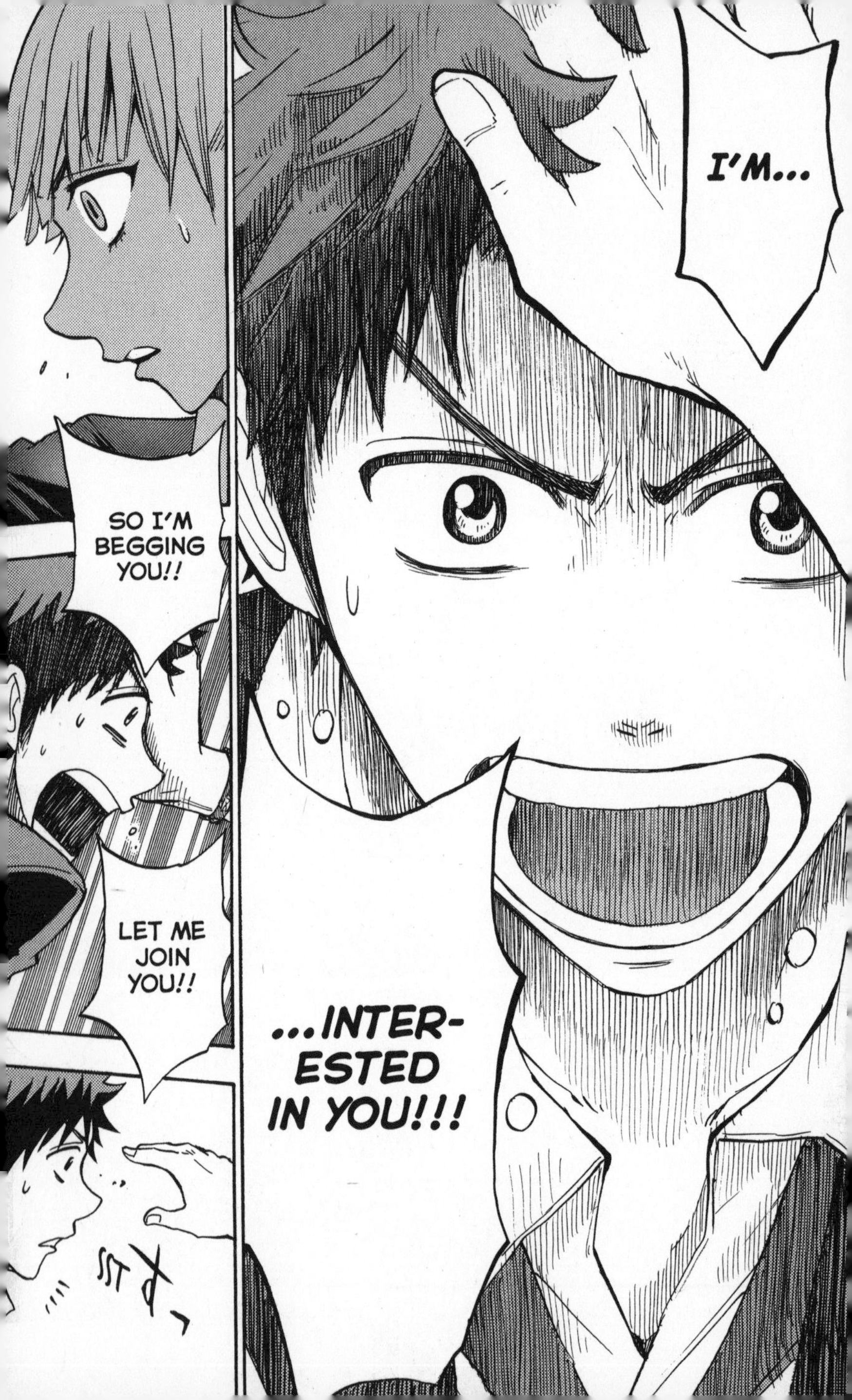
I'M...
...INTER-ESTED IN YOU!!!
SO I'M BEGGING YOU!!
LET ME JOIN YOU!!

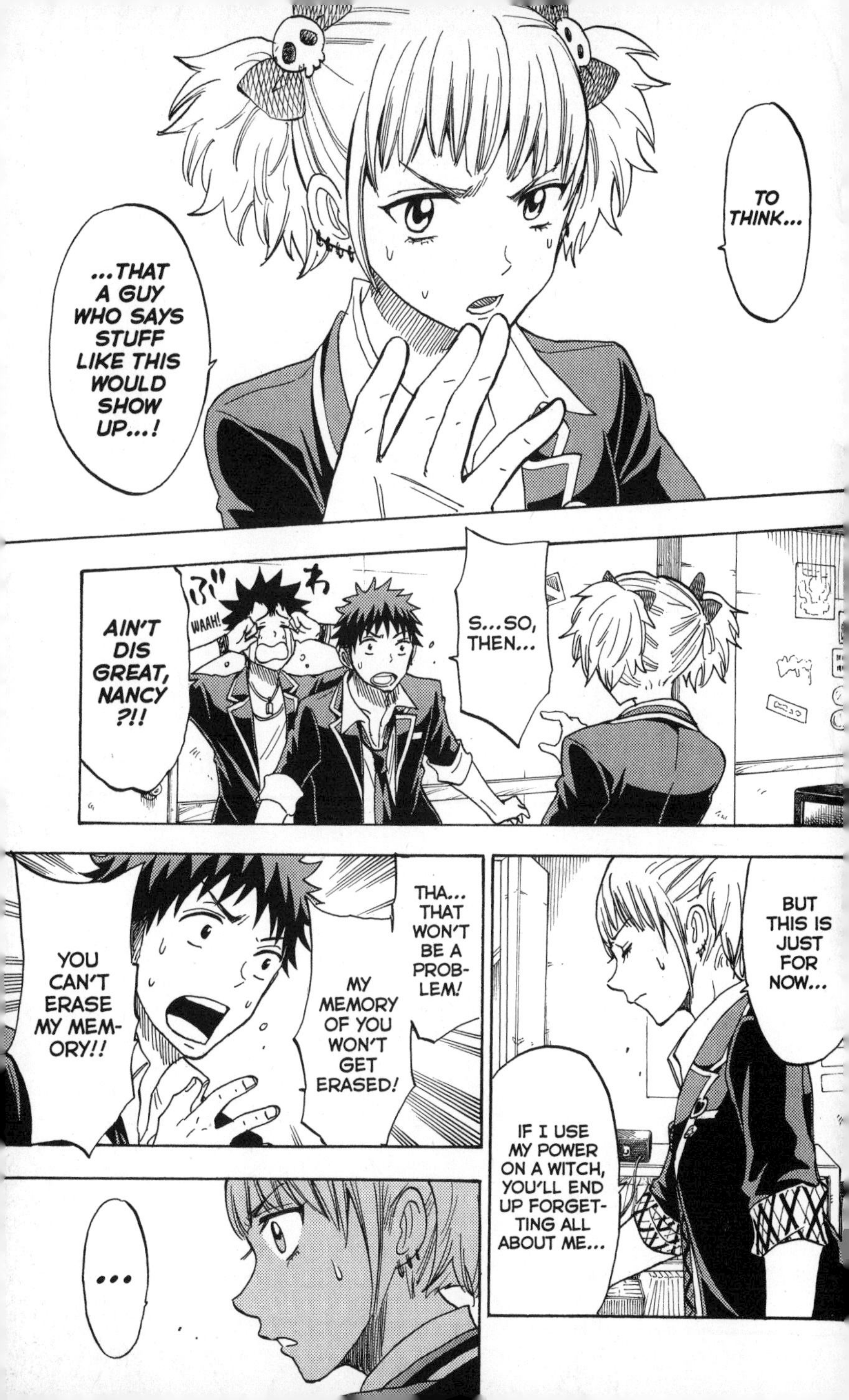
TO THINK...
...THAT A GUY WHO SAYS STUFF LIKE THIS WOULD SHOW UP...!
S...SO, THEN...
ぶわ
WAAH!
AIN'T DIS GREAT, NANCY?!!
BUT THIS IS JUST FOR NOW...
IF I USE MY POWER ON A WITCH, YOU'LL END UP FORGETTING ALL ABOUT ME...
THA... THAT WON'T BE A PROBLEM!
MY MEMORY OF YOU WON'T GET ERASED!
YOU CAN'T ERASE MY MEMORY!!
...

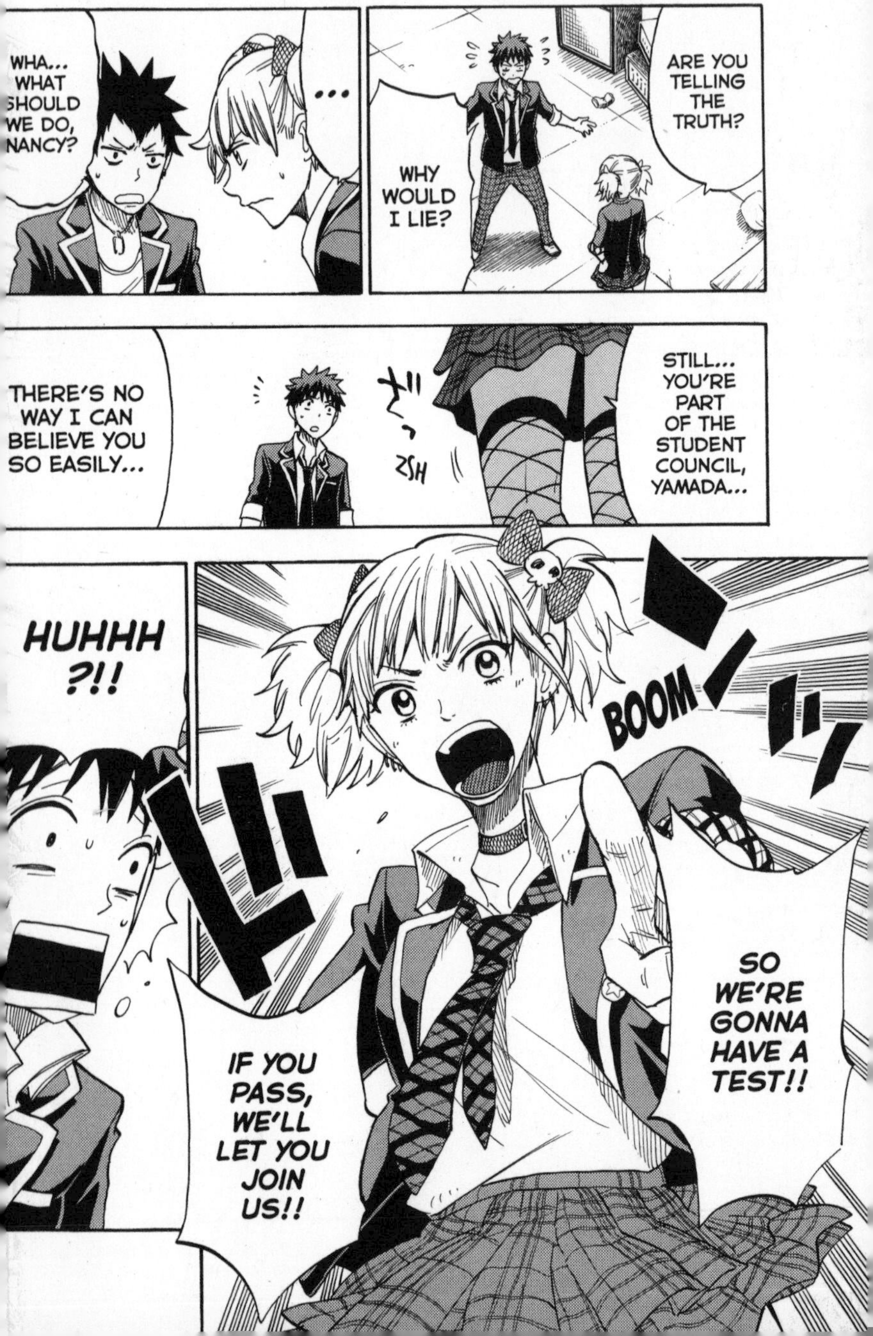
ARE YOU TELLING THE TRUTH?
WHY WOULD I LIE?
WHA... WHAT SHOULD WE DO, NANCY?
...
STILL... YOU'RE PART OF THE STUDENT COUNCIL, YAMADA...
ZSH
THERE'S NO WAY I CAN BELIEVE YOU SO EASILY...
SO WE'RE GONNA HAVE A TEST!!
BOOM
IF YOU PASS, WE'LL LET YOU JOIN US!!
HUHHH ?!!

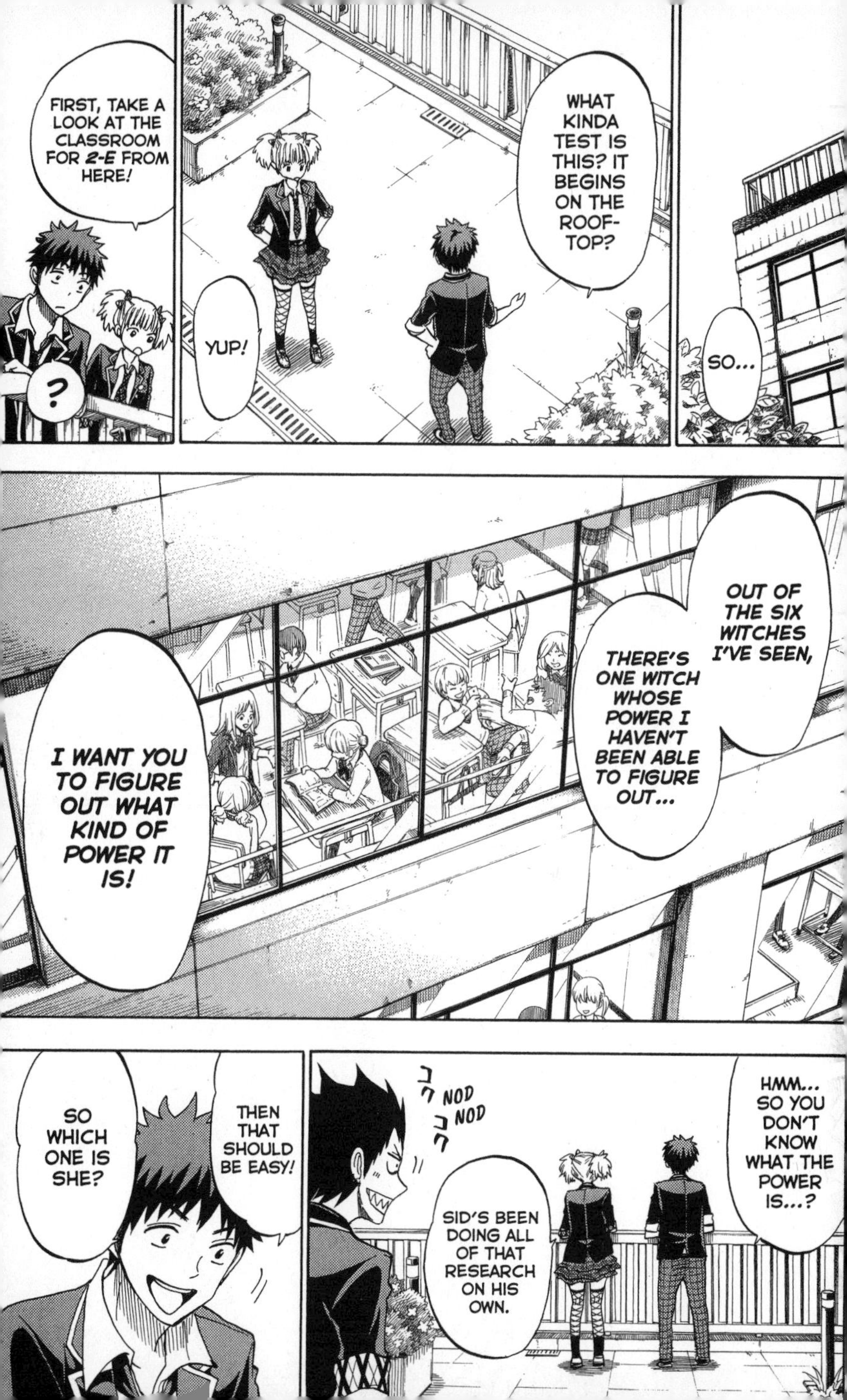
SO...
WHAT KINDA TEST IS THIS? IT BEGINS ON THE ROOF-TOP?
YUP!
FIRST, TAKE A LOOK AT THE CLASSROOM FOR 2-E FROM HERE!
?
OUT OF THE SIX WITCHES I'VE SEEN,
THERE'S ONE WITCH WHOSE POWER I HAVEN'T BEEN ABLE TO FIGURE OUT...
I WANT YOU TO FIGURE OUT WHAT KIND OF POWER IT IS!
HMM... SO YOU DON'T KNOW WHAT THE POWER IS...?
SID'S BEEN DOING ALL OF THAT RESEARCH ON HIS OWN.
コク コク NOD NOD
THEN THAT SHOULD BE EASY!
SO WHICH ONE IS SHE?

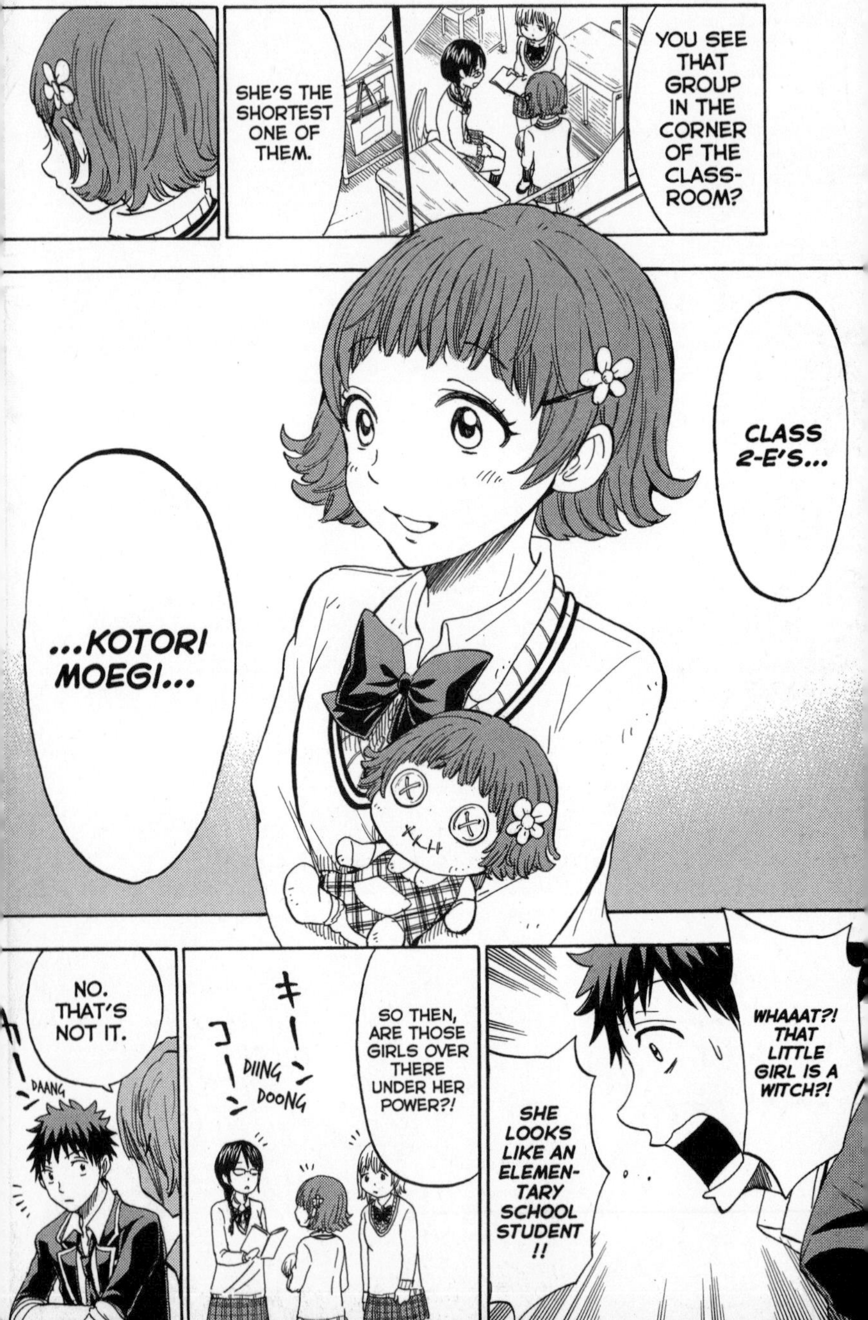
YOU SEE THAT GROUP IN THE CORNER OF THE CLASS-ROOM?
SHE'S THE SHORTEST ONE OF THEM.
CLASS 2-E'S...
...KOTORI MOEGI...
WHAAAT?! THAT LITTLE GIRL IS A WITCH?!
SHE LOOKS LIKE AN ELEMEN-TARY SCHOOL STUDENT !!
SO THEN, ARE THOSE GIRLS OVER THERE UNDER HER POWER?!
DIING DOONG
NO. THAT'S NOT IT.
DAANG

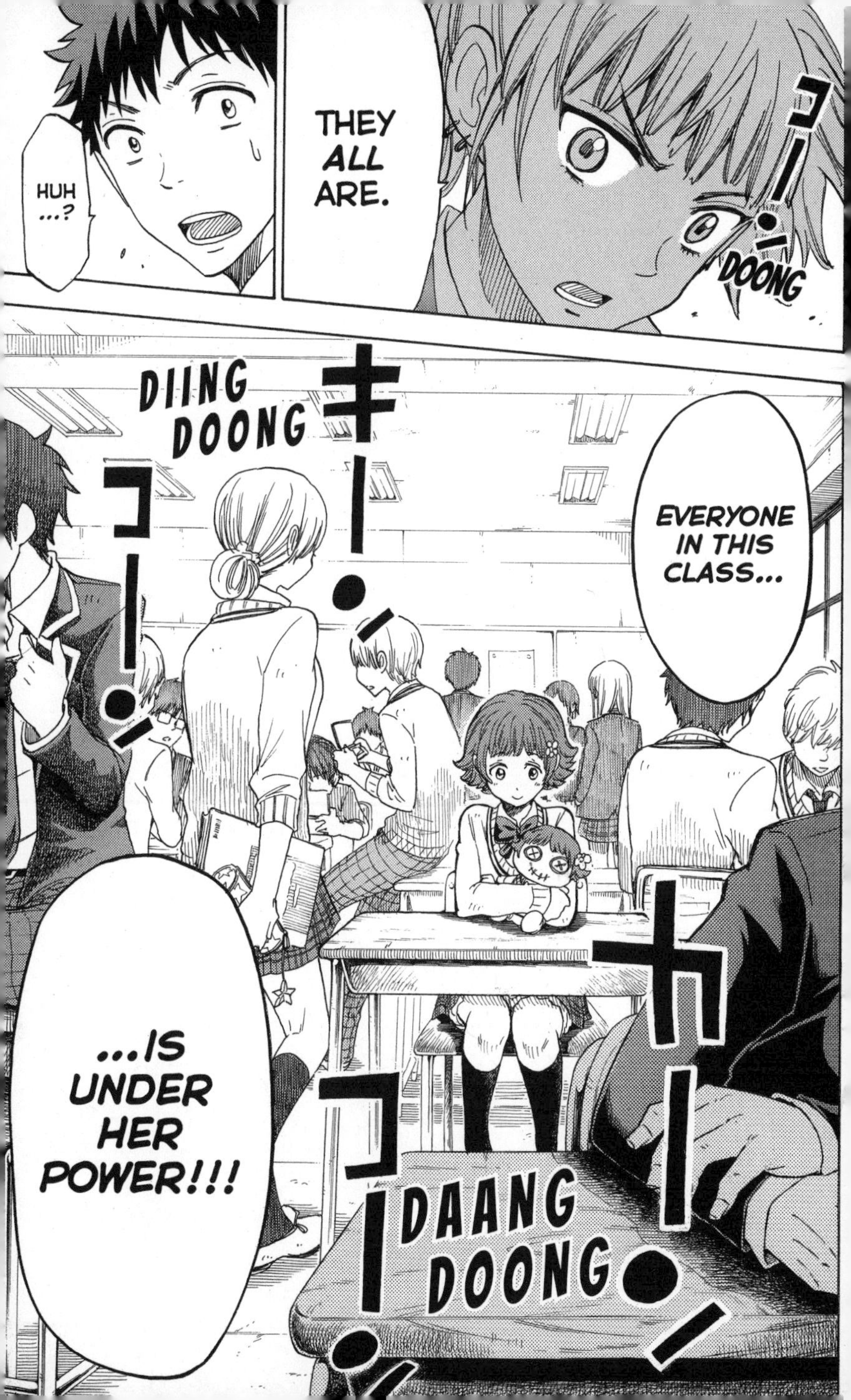
DOONG
THEY ALL ARE.
HUH ...?
EVERYONE IN THIS CLASS...
DIING DOONG
DAANG DOONG
...IS UNDER HER POWER!!!

Yamada-kun AND THE *Seven Witches*

"Yamada" is giving you a look that suggests he wishes to join you. Will you let him join you?

Yes
▶ No

CHAPTER 105: Sorry-sshi!

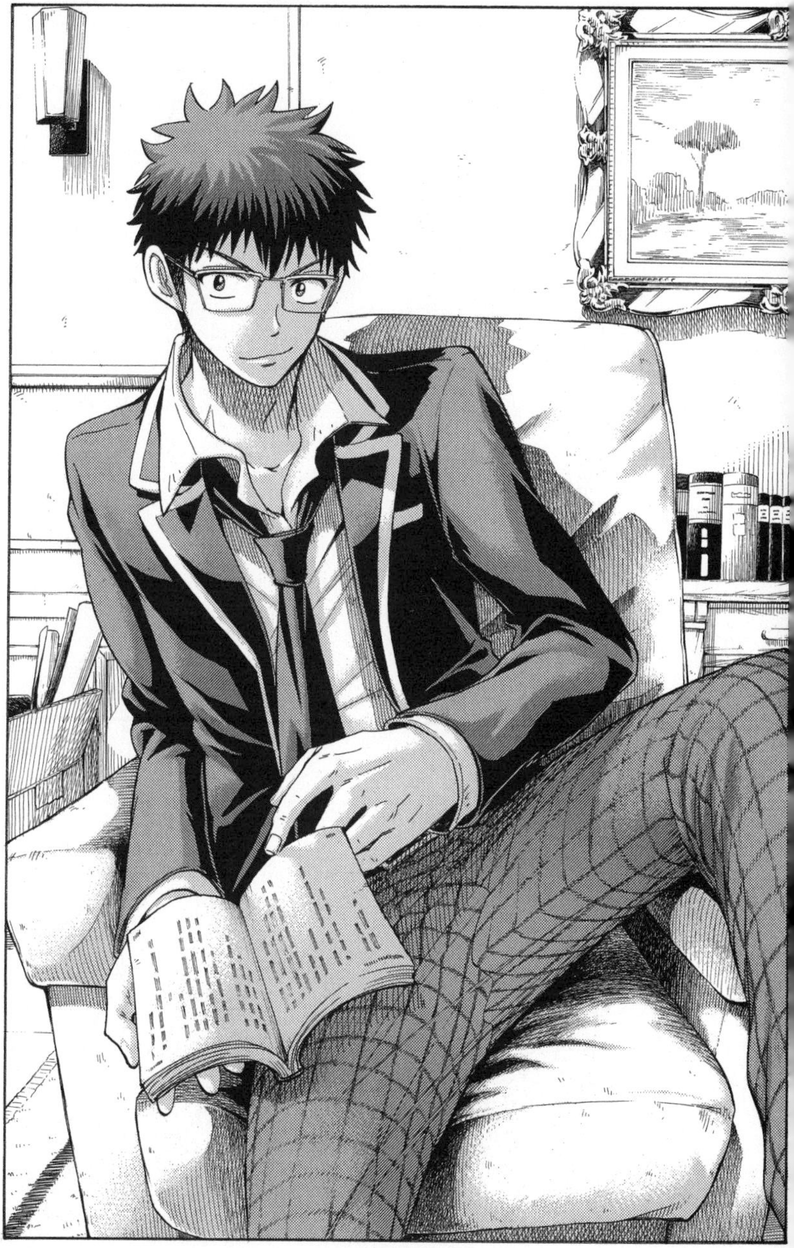

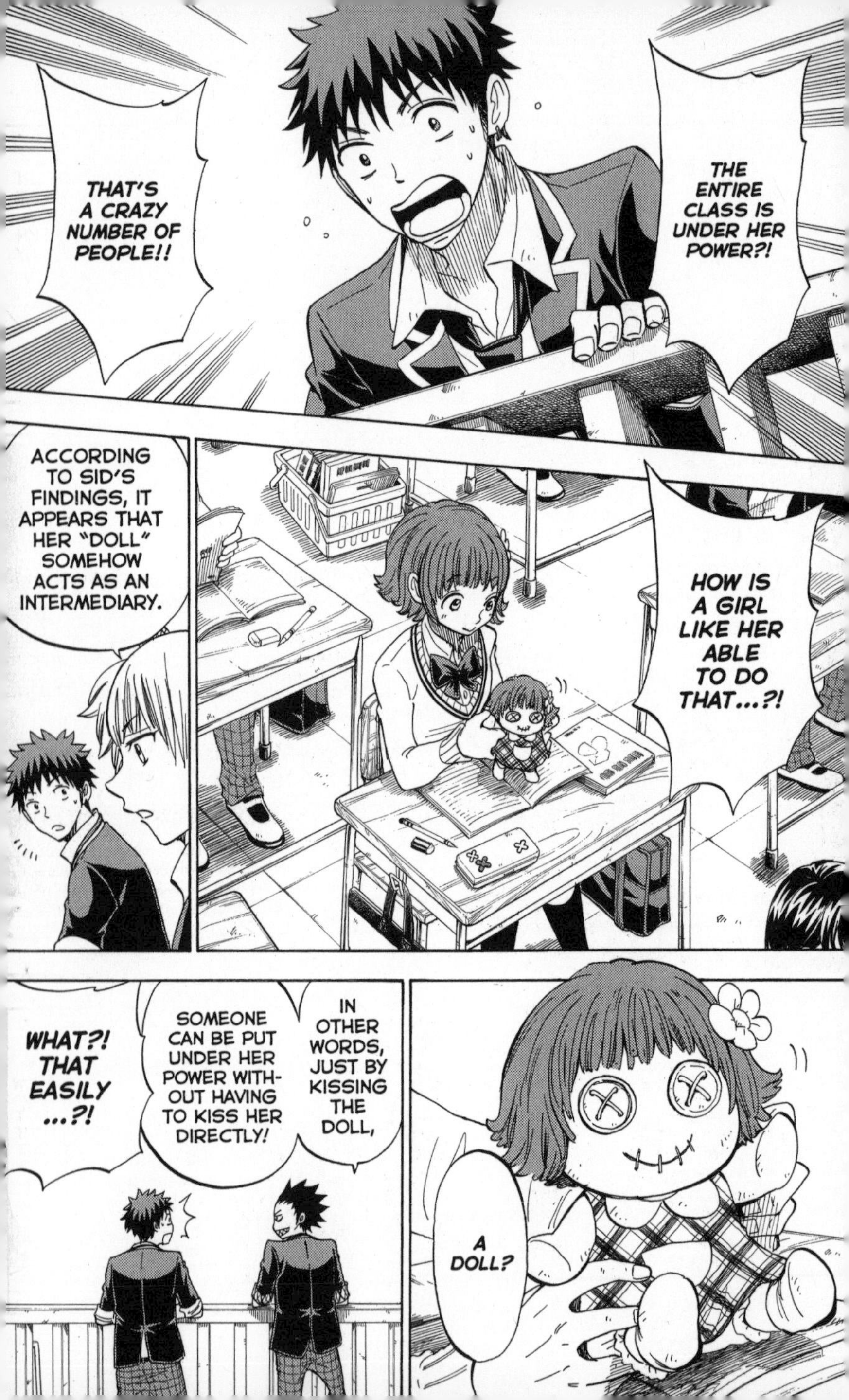
THE ENTIRE CLASS IS UNDER HER POWER?!
THAT'S A CRAZY NUMBER OF PEOPLE!!
HOW IS A GIRL LIKE HER ABLE TO DO THAT...?!
ACCORDING TO SID'S FINDINGS, IT APPEARS THAT HER "DOLL" SOMEHOW ACTS AS AN INTERMEDIARY.
A DOLL?
IN OTHER WORDS, JUST BY KISSING THE DOLL,
SOMEONE CAN BE PUT UNDER HER POWER WITH-OUT HAVING TO KISS HER DIRECTLY!
WHAT?! THAT EASILY ...?!

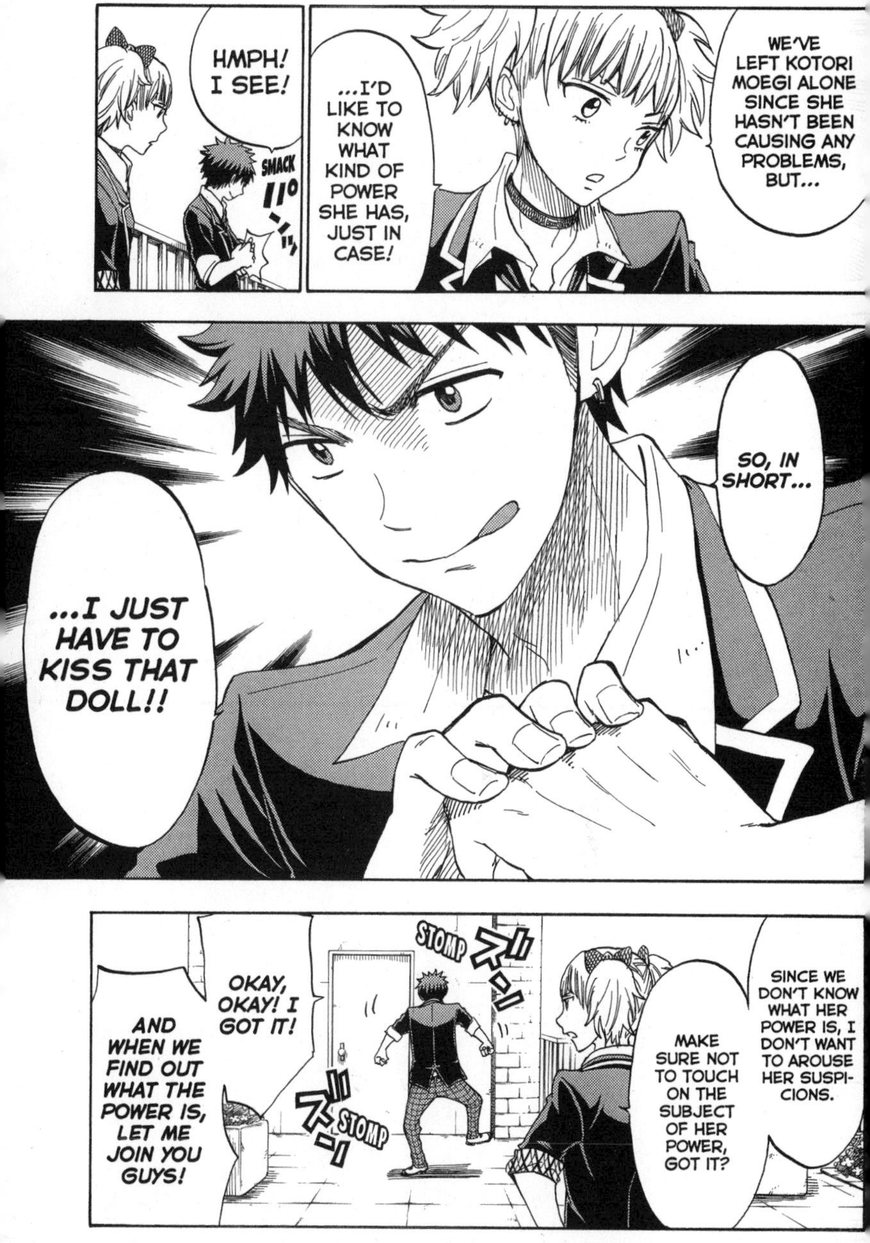
WE'VE LEFT KOTORI MOEGI ALONE SINCE SHE HASN'T BEEN CAUSING ANY PROBLEMS, BUT...
...I'D LIKE TO KNOW WHAT KIND OF POWER SHE HAS, JUST IN CASE!
HMPH! I SEE!
SMACK
SO, IN SHORT...
...I JUST HAVE TO KISS THAT DOLL!!
SINCE WE DON'T KNOW WHAT HER POWER IS, I DON'T WANT TO AROUSE HER SUSPICIONS.
MAKE SURE NOT TO TOUCH ON THE SUBJECT OF HER POWER, GOT IT?
STOMP
STOMP
OKAY, OKAY! I GOT IT!
AND WHEN WE FIND OUT WHAT THE POWER IS, LET ME JOIN YOU GUYS!

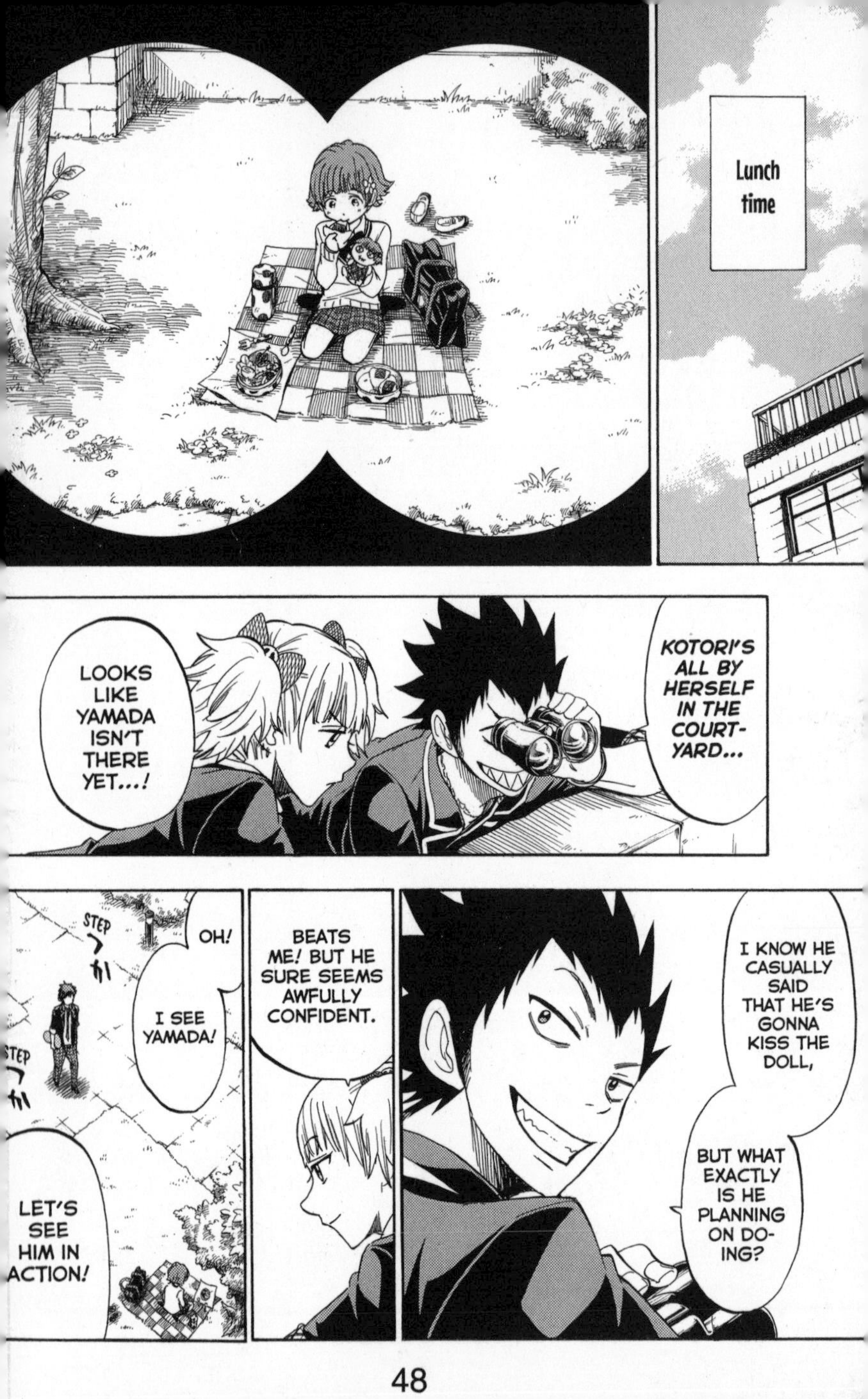
Lunch time
KOTORI'S ALL BY HERSELF IN THE COURT-YARD...
LOOKS LIKE YAMADA ISN'T THERE YET...!
I KNOW HE CASUALLY SAID THAT HE'S GONNA KISS THE DOLL,
BUT WHAT EXACTLY IS HE PLANNING ON DO-ING?
BEATS ME! BUT HE SURE SEEMS AWFULLY CONFIDENT.
OH!
I SEE YAMADA!
STEP
STEP
LET'S SEE HIM IN ACTION!

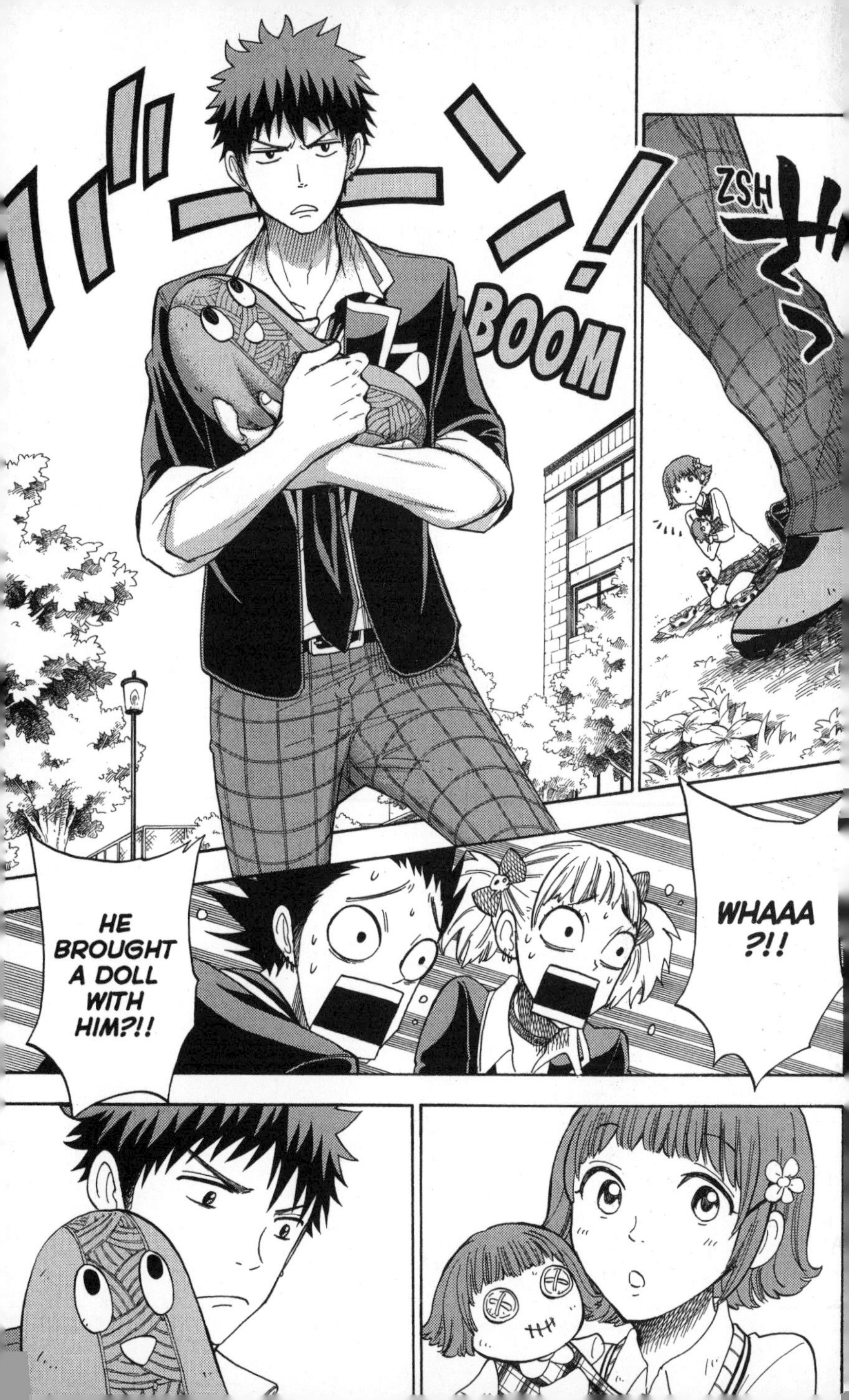
ZSH
BOOM
WHAAA ?!!
HE BROUGHT A DOLL WITH HIM?!!

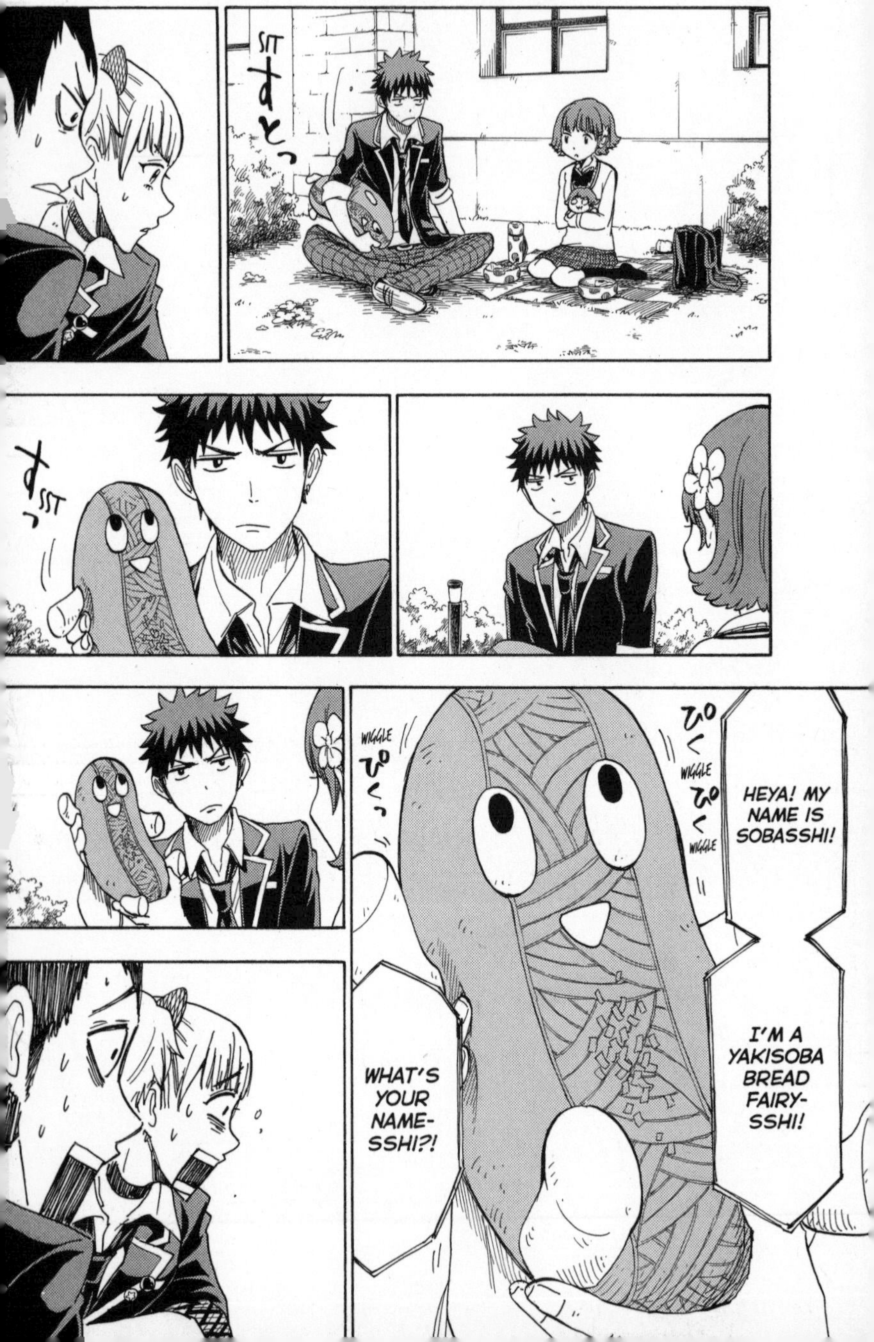
SIT
すとっ
すっ
SST
ぴく
WIGGLE
ぴく
WIGGLE
HEYA! MY NAME IS SOBASSHI!
I'M A YAKISOBA BREAD FAIRY-SSHI!
WIGGLE
ぴくっ
WHAT'S YOUR NAME-SSHI?!

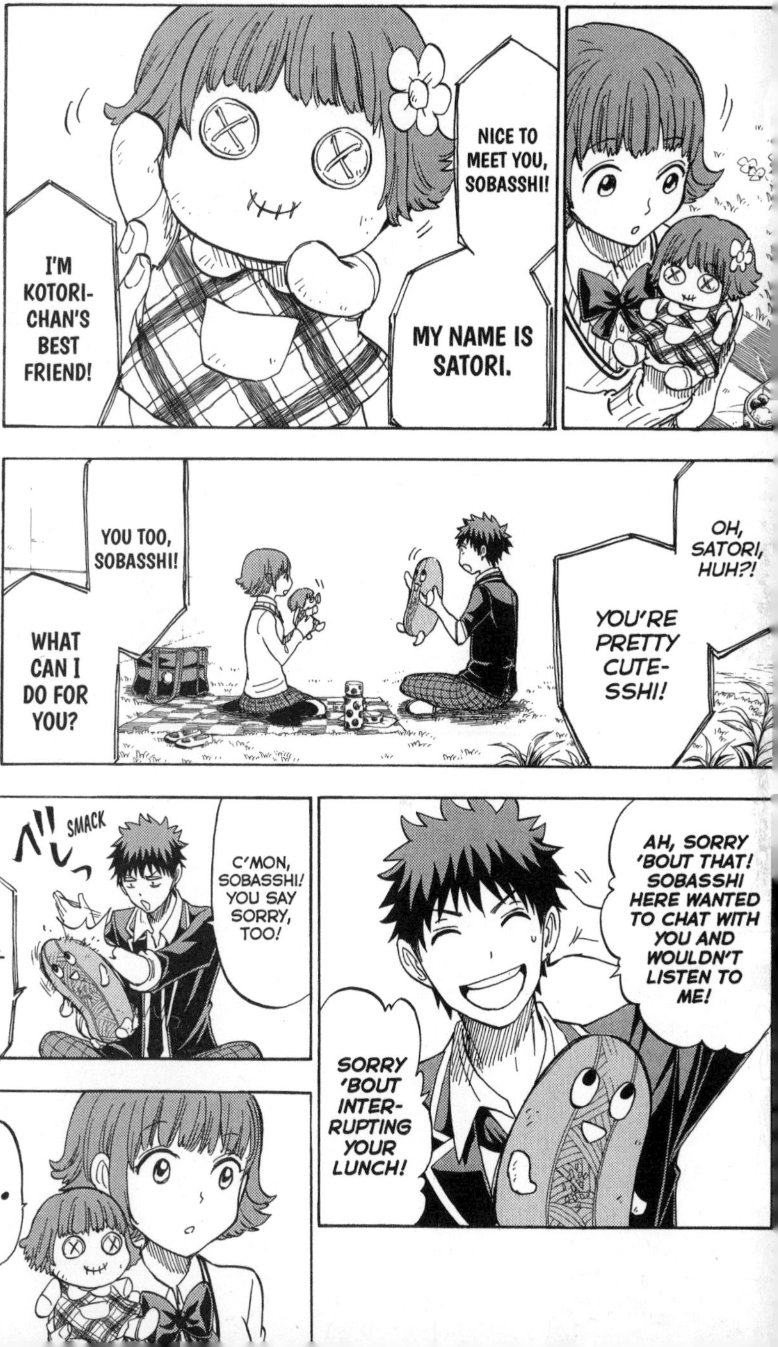
NICE TO MEET YOU, SOBASSHI!
MY NAME IS SATORI.
I'M KOTORI-CHAN'S BEST FRIEND!
OH, SATORI, HUH?!
YOU'RE PRETTY CUTE-SSHI!
YOU TOO, SOBASSHI!
WHAT CAN I DO FOR YOU?
AH, SORRY 'BOUT THAT! SOBASSHI HERE WANTED TO CHAT WITH YOU AND WOULDN'T LISTEN TO ME!
SORRY 'BOUT INTER-RUPTING YOUR LUNCH!
SMACK
C'MON, SOBASSHI! YOU SAY SORRY, TOO!
SORRY-SSHI!
...

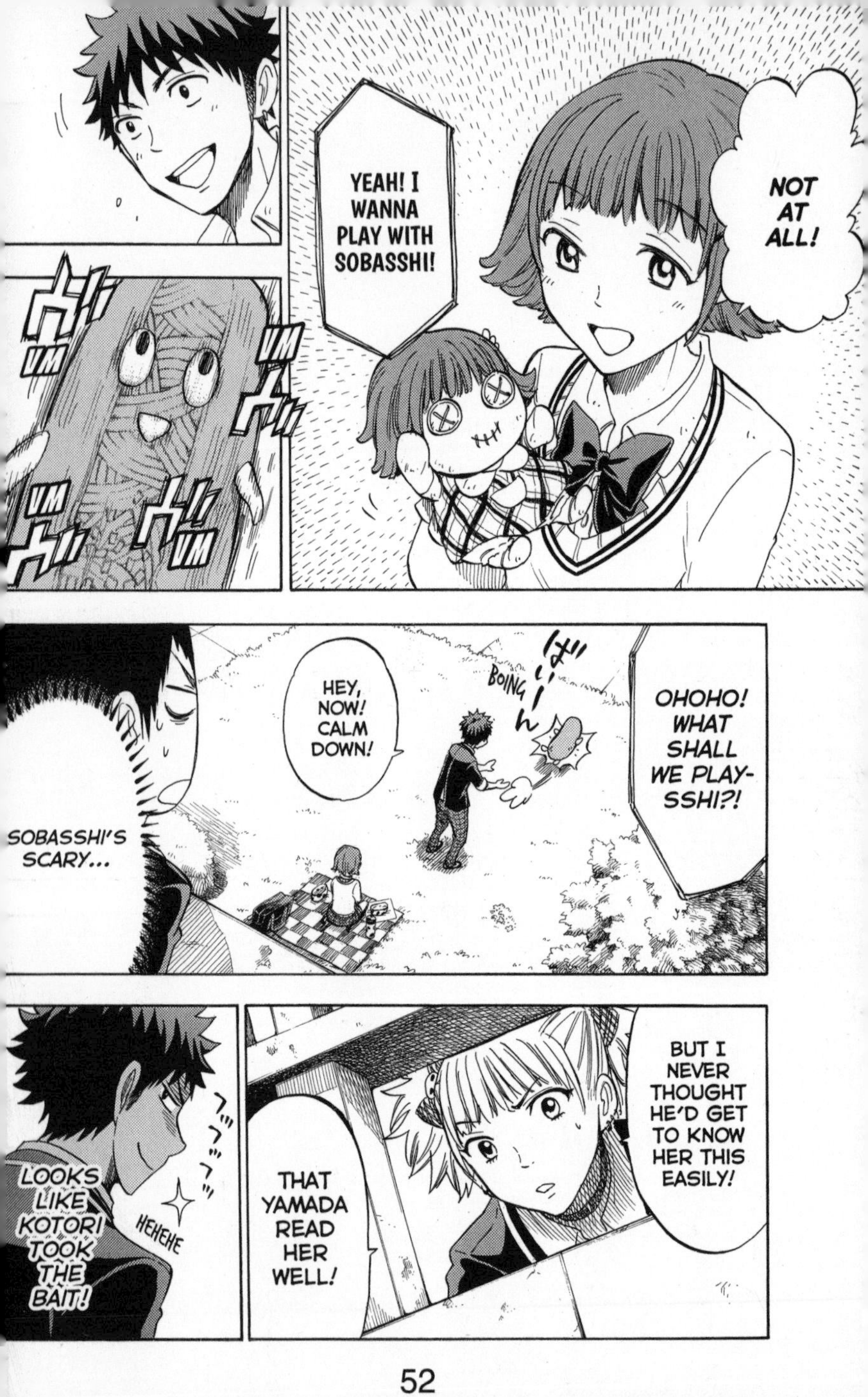
NOT AT ALL!
YEAH! I WANNA PLAY WITH SOBASSHI!
VM
VM
VM
VM
OHOHO! WHAT SHALL WE PLAY-SSHI?!
BOING
HEY, NOW! CALM DOWN!
SOBASSHI'S SCARY...
BUT I NEVER THOUGHT HE'D GET TO KNOW HER THIS EASILY!
THAT YAMADA READ HER WELL!
HEHEHE
LOOKS LIKE KOTORI TOOK THE BAIT!

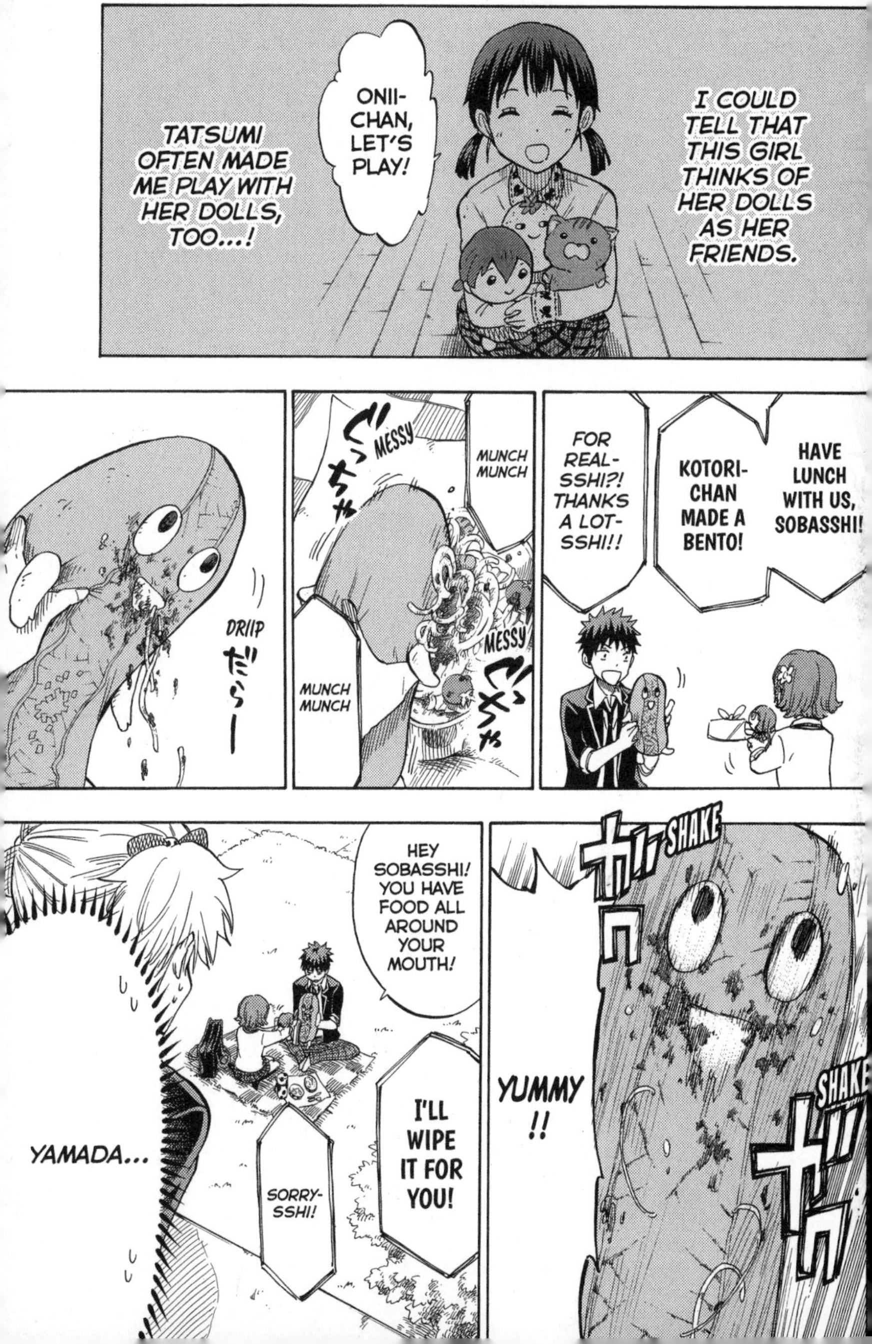

I COULD TELL THAT THIS GIRL THINKS OF HER DOLLS AS HER FRIENDS.
ONII-CHAN, LET'S PLAY!
TATSUMI OFTEN MADE ME PLAY WITH HER DOLLS, TOO...!
HAVE LUNCH WITH US, SOBASSHI!
KOTORI-CHAN MADE A BENTO!
FOR REAL-SSHI?! THANKS A LOT-SSHI!!
MUNCH MUNCH
MESSY
MESSY
MUNCH MUNCH
DRIIP
SHAKE
YUMMY!!
SHAKE
HEY SOBASSHI! YOU HAVE FOOD ALL AROUND YOUR MOUTH!
I'LL WIPE IT FOR YOU!
SORRY-SSHI!
YAMADA...

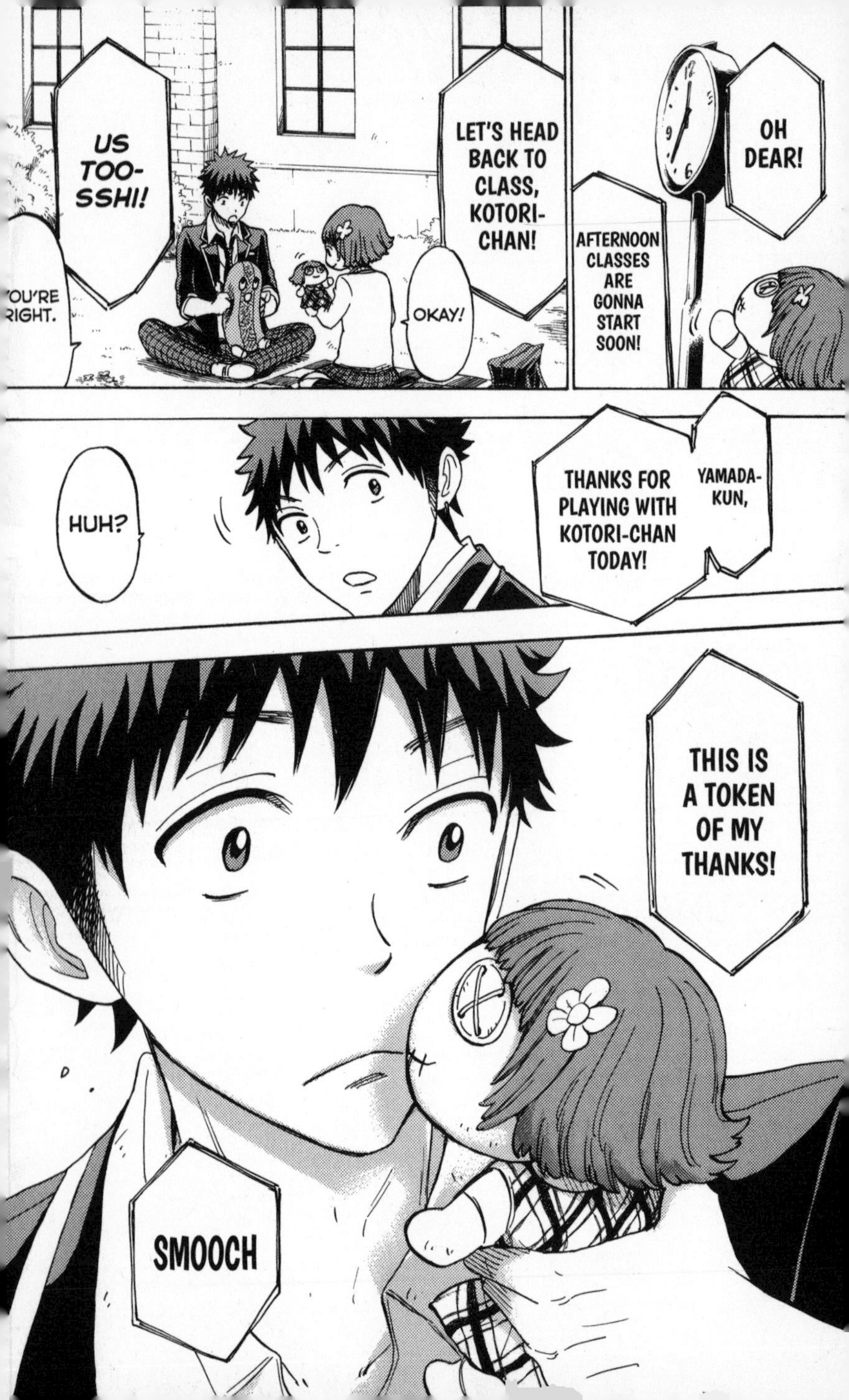
OH DEAR!
AFTERNOON CLASSES ARE GONNA START SOON!
LET'S HEAD BACK TO CLASS, KOTORI-CHAN!
OKAY!
US TOO-SSHI!
OU'RE RIGHT.
YAMADA-KUN,
THANKS FOR PLAYING WITH KOTORI-CHAN TODAY!
HUH?
THIS IS A TOKEN OF MY THANKS!
SMOOCH

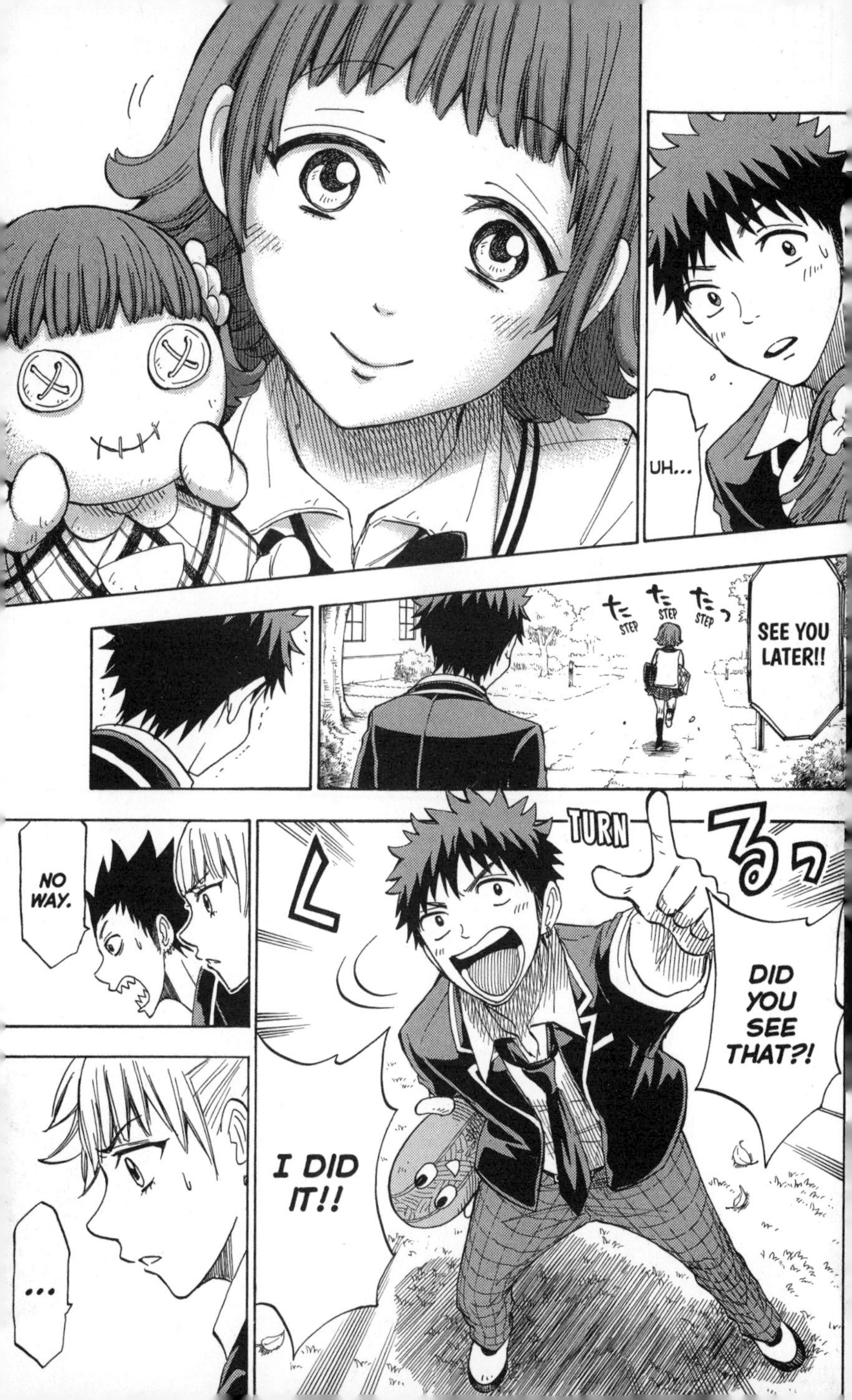
UH...
SEE YOU LATER!!
たっ STEP
た STEP
た STEP
TURN
るっ
DID YOU SEE THAT?!
I DID IT!!
NO WAY.
...

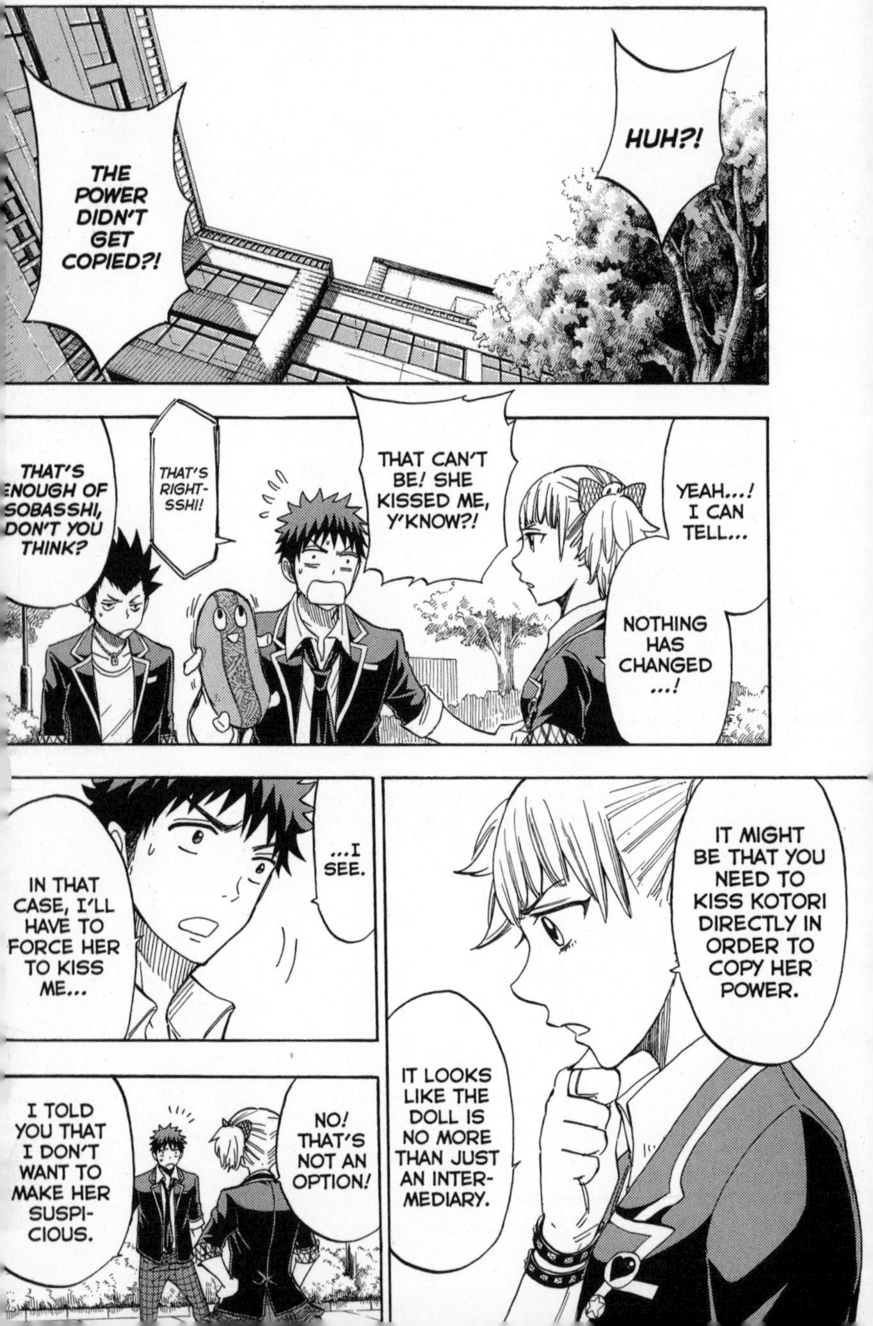
HUH?!
THE POWER DIDN'T GET COPIED?!
YEAH...! I CAN TELL...
NOTHING HAS CHANGED ...!
THAT CAN'T BE! SHE KISSED ME, Y'KNOW?!
THAT'S RIGHT-SSHI!
THAT'S ENOUGH OF SOBASSHI, DON'T YOU THINK?
IT MIGHT BE THAT YOU NEED TO KISS KOTORI DIRECTLY IN ORDER TO COPY HER POWER.
IT LOOKS LIKE THE DOLL IS NO MORE THAN JUST AN INTER-MEDIARY.
...I SEE.
IN THAT CASE, I'LL HAVE TO FORCE HER TO KISS ME...
NO! THAT'S NOT AN OPTION!
I TOLD YOU THAT I DON'T WANT TO MAKE HER SUSPI-CIOUS.

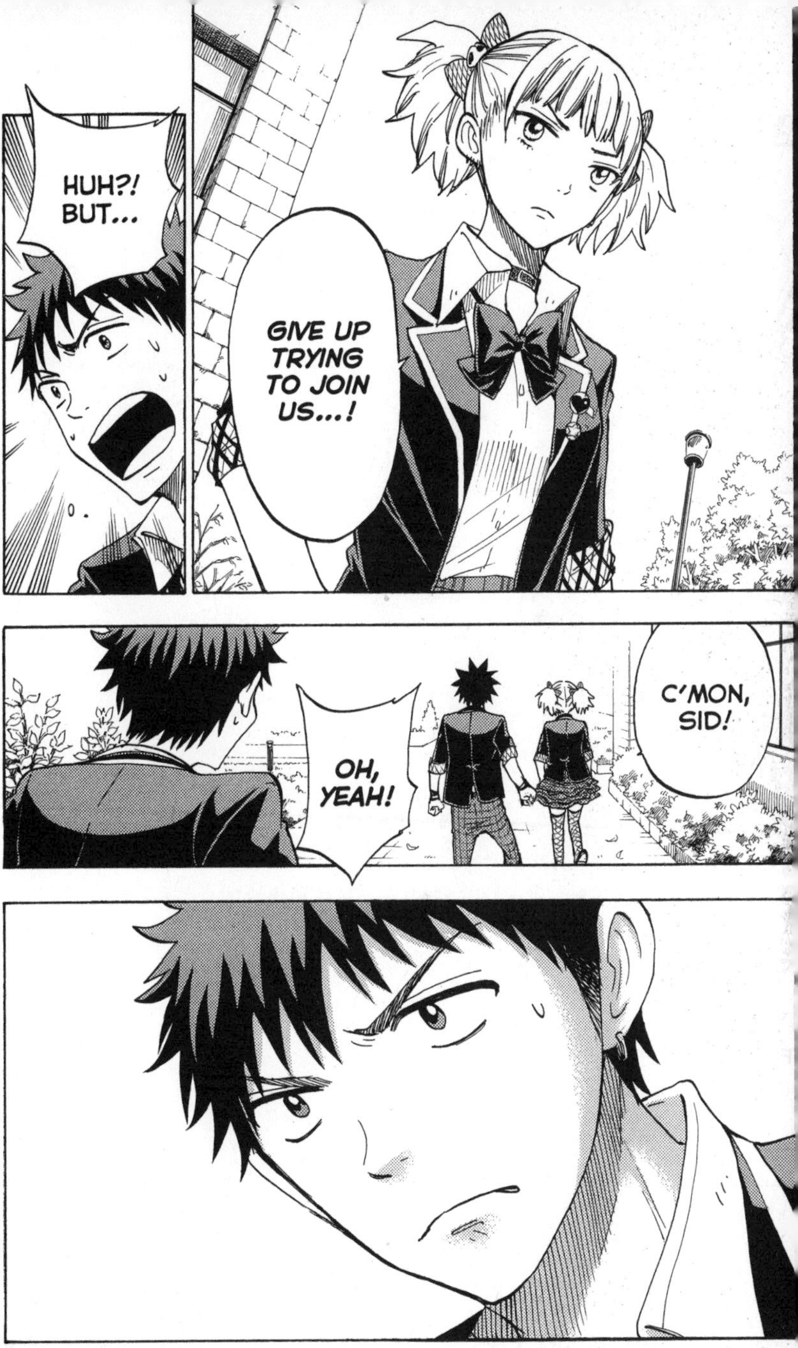
GIVE UP TRYING TO JOIN US...!
HUH?! BUT...
C'MON, SID!
OH, YEAH!

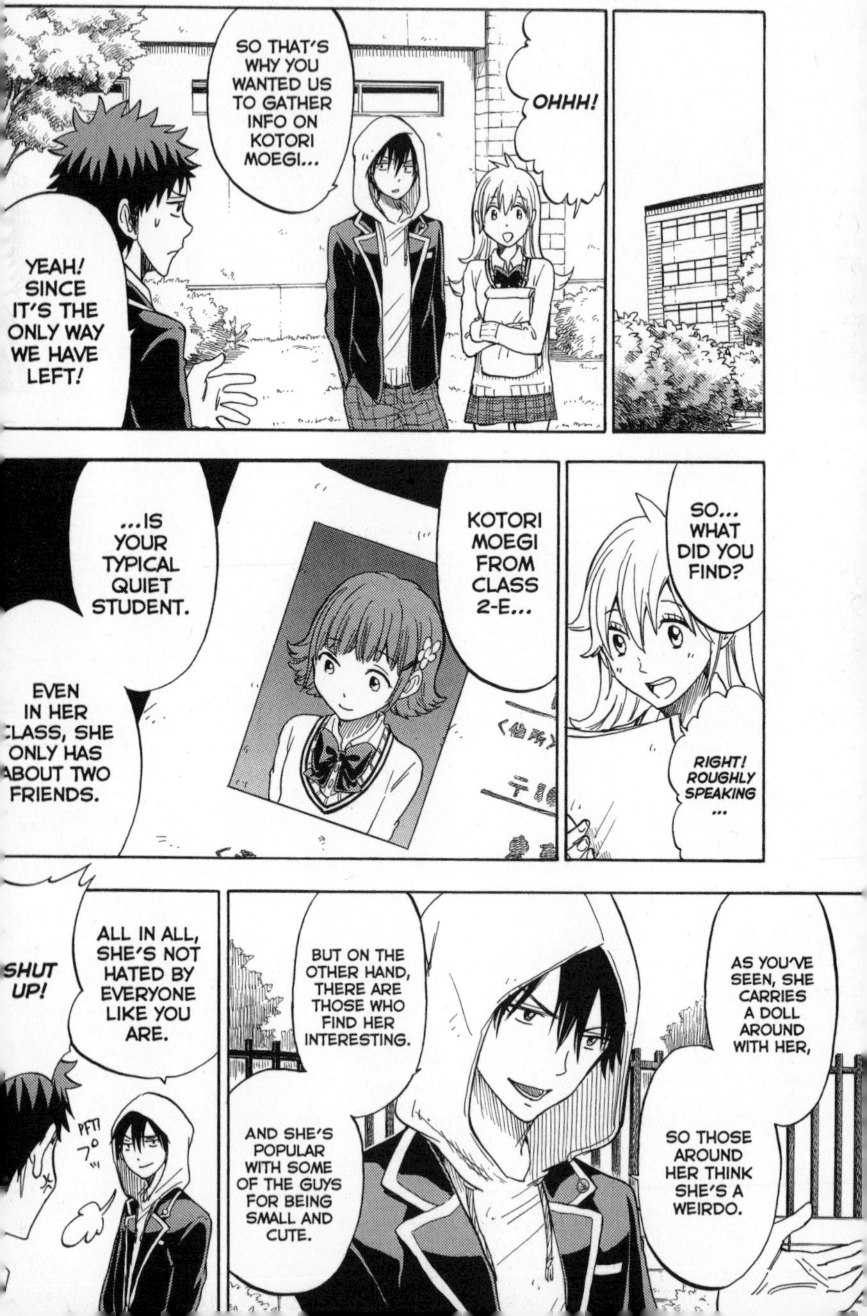
OHHH!
SO THAT'S WHY YOU WANTED US TO GATHER INFO ON KOTORI MOEGI...
YEAH! SINCE IT'S THE ONLY WAY WE HAVE LEFT!
SO... WHAT DID YOU FIND?
RIGHT! ROUGHLY SPEAKING...
KOTORI MOEGI FROM CLASS 2-E...
...IS YOUR TYPICAL QUIET STUDENT.
EVEN IN HER CLASS, SHE ONLY HAS ABOUT TWO FRIENDS.
AS YOU'VE SEEN, SHE CARRIES A DOLL AROUND WITH HER,
SO THOSE AROUND HER THINK SHE'S A WEIRDO.
BUT ON THE OTHER HAND, THERE ARE THOSE WHO FIND HER INTERESTING.
AND SHE'S POPULAR WITH SOME OF THE GUYS FOR BEING SMALL AND CUTE.
ALL IN ALL, SHE'S NOT HATED BY EVERYONE LIKE YOU ARE.
SHUT UP!
PFT!

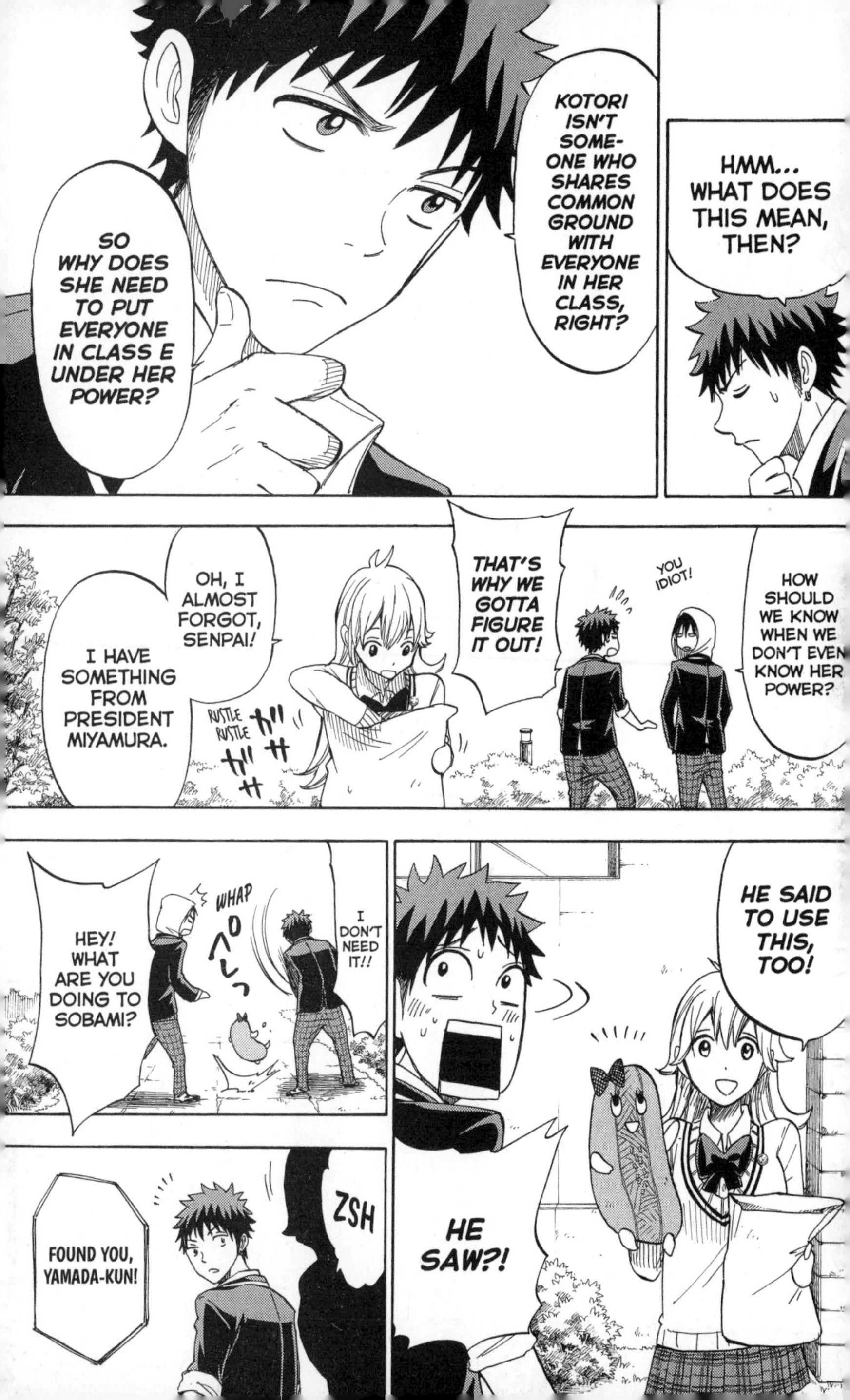
HMM... WHAT DOES THIS MEAN, THEN?
KOTORI ISN'T SOME-ONE WHO SHARES COMMON GROUND WITH EVERYONE IN HER CLASS, RIGHT?
SO WHY DOES SHE NEED TO PUT EVERYONE IN CLASS E UNDER HER POWER?
HOW SHOULD WE KNOW WHEN WE DON'T EVEN KNOW HER POWER?
YOU IDIOT!
THAT'S WHY WE GOTTA FIGURE IT OUT!
OH, I ALMOST FORGOT, SENPAI!
I HAVE SOMETHING FROM PRESIDENT MIYAMURA.
RUSTLE RUSTLE
HE SAID TO USE THIS, TOO!
HE SAW?!
I DON'T NEED IT!!
WHAP
HEY! WHAT ARE YOU DOING TO SOBAMI?
ZSH
FOUND YOU, YAMADA-KUN!

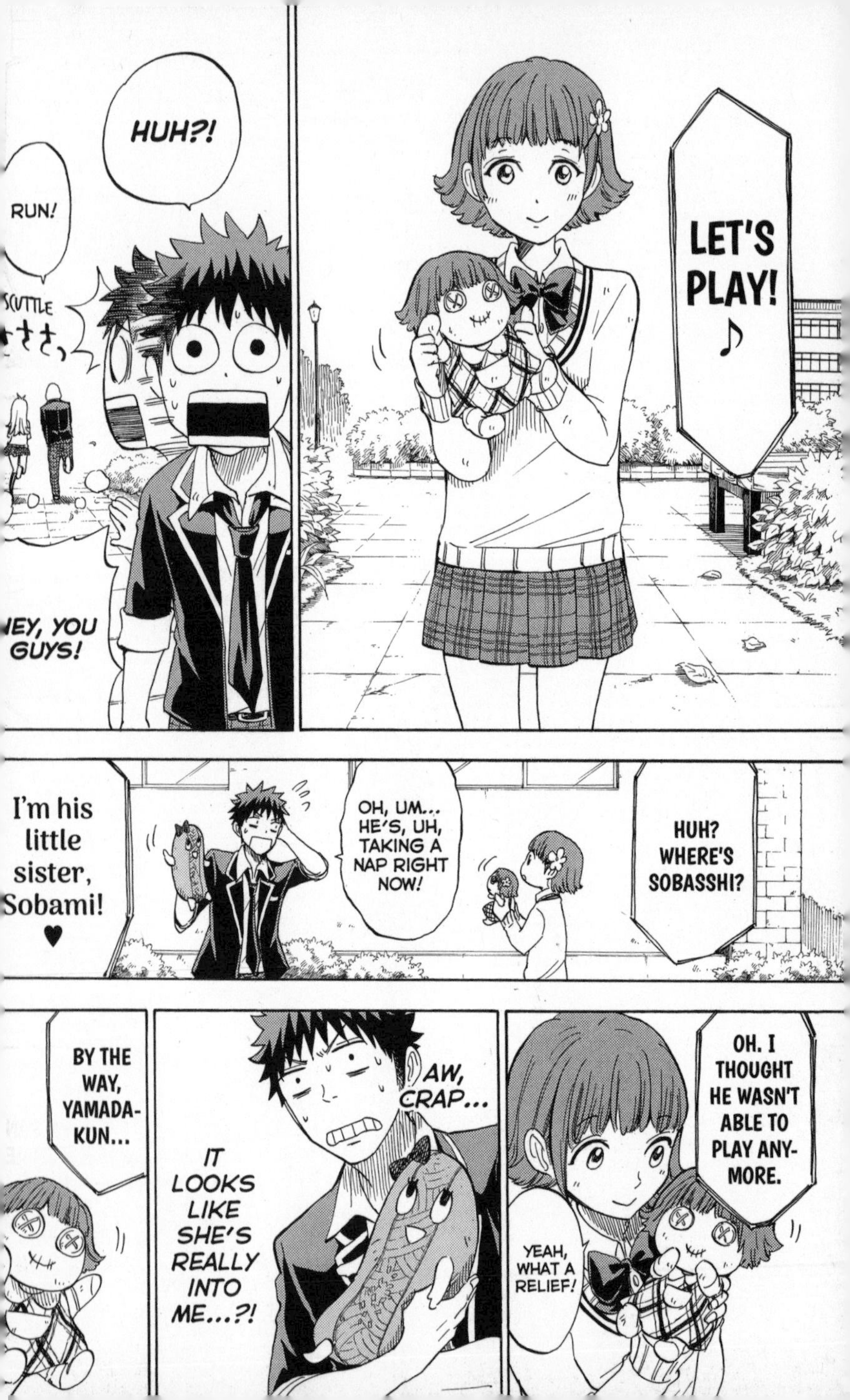
LET'S PLAY! ♪
HUH?!
RUN!
SCUTTLE
EY, YOU GUYS!
HUH? WHERE'S SOBASSHI?
OH, UM... HE'S, UH, TAKING A NAP RIGHT NOW!
I'm his little sister, Sobami! ♥
OH. I THOUGHT HE WASN'T ABLE TO PLAY ANY-MORE.
YEAH, WHAT A RELIEF!
AW, CRAP...
IT LOOKS LIKE SHE'S REALLY INTO ME...?!
BY THE WAY, YAMADA-KUN...

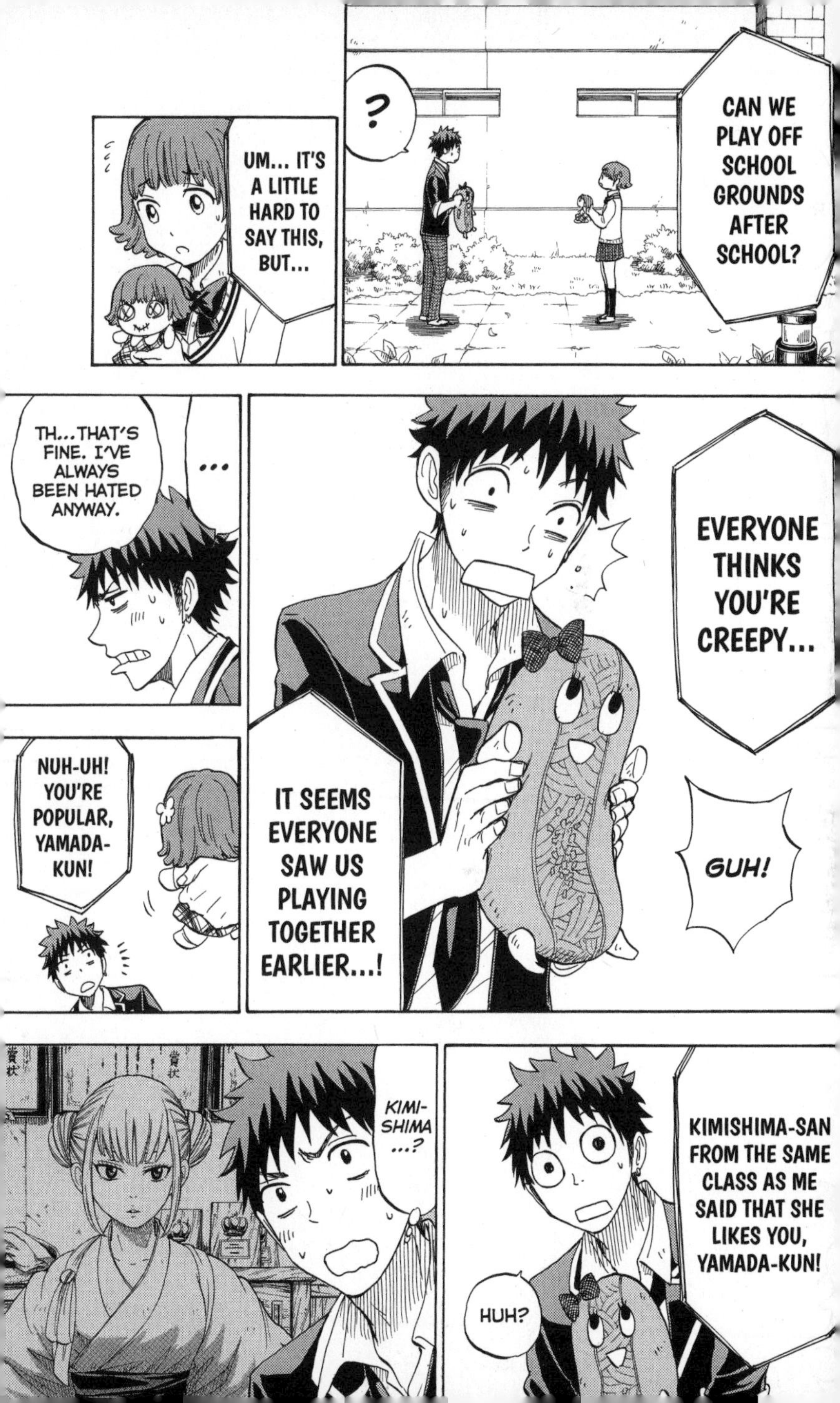

CAN WE PLAY OFF SCHOOL GROUNDS AFTER SCHOOL?
?
UM... IT'S A LITTLE HARD TO SAY THIS, BUT...
EVERYONE THINKS YOU'RE CREEPY...
GUH!
IT SEEMS EVERYONE SAW US PLAYING TOGETHER EARLIER...!
...
TH...THAT'S FINE. I'VE ALWAYS BEEN HATED ANYWAY.
NUH-UH! YOU'RE POPULAR, YAMADA-KUN!
KIMISHIMA-SAN FROM THE SAME CLASS AS ME SAID THAT SHE LIKES YOU, YAMADA-KUN!
HUH?
KIMI-SHIMA...?

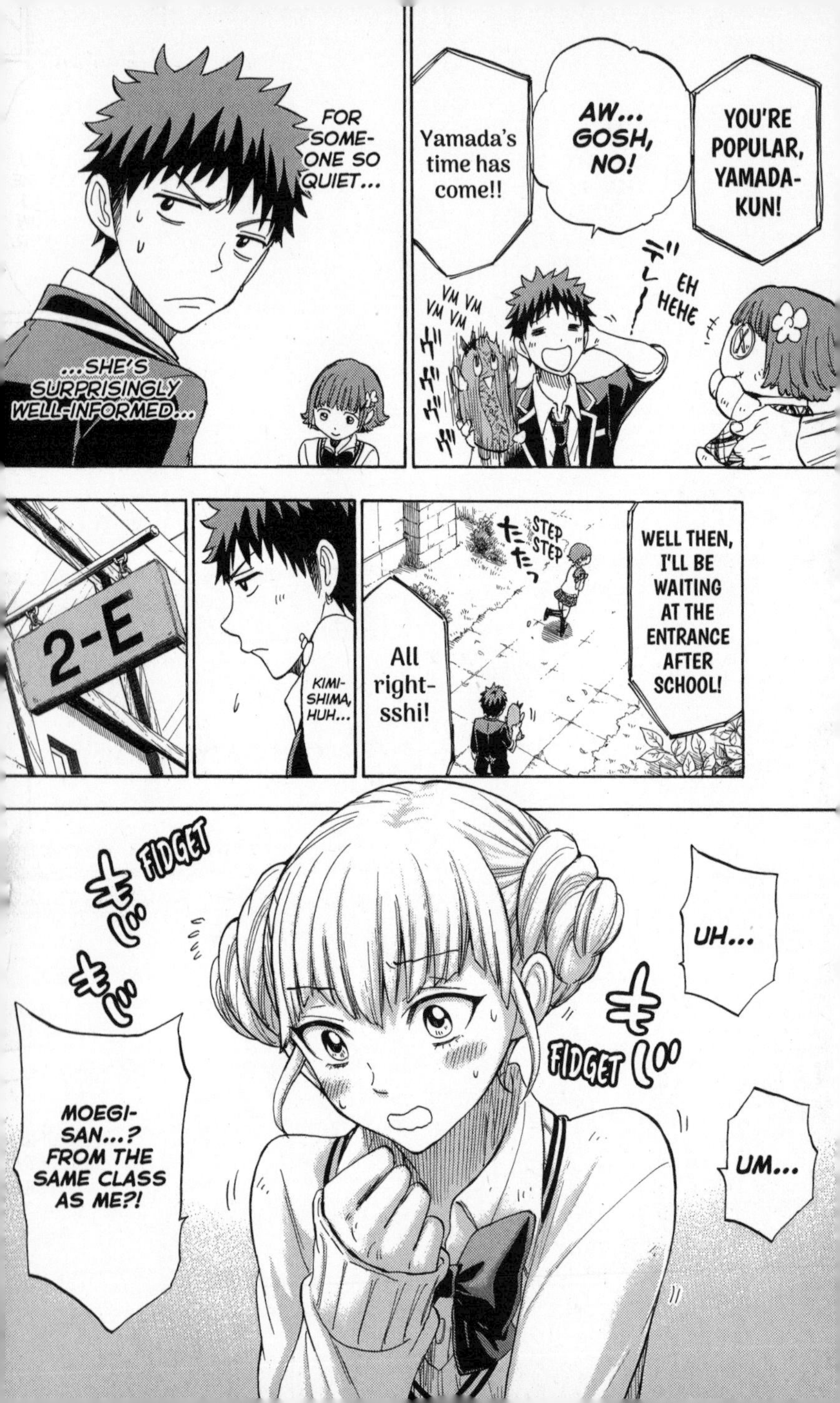
YOU'RE POPULAR, YAMADA-KUN!
AW... GOSH, NO!
Yamada's time has come!!
EH HEHE
VM VM VM VM
FOR SOME-ONE SO QUIET...
...SHE'S SURPRISINGLY WELL-INFORMED...
WELL THEN, I'LL BE WAITING AT THE ENTRANCE AFTER SCHOOL!
STEP STEP
All right-sshi!
KIMI-SHIMA, HUH...
2-E
UH...
UM...
FIDGET
MOEGI-SAN...? FROM THE SAME CLASS AS ME?!
FIDGET

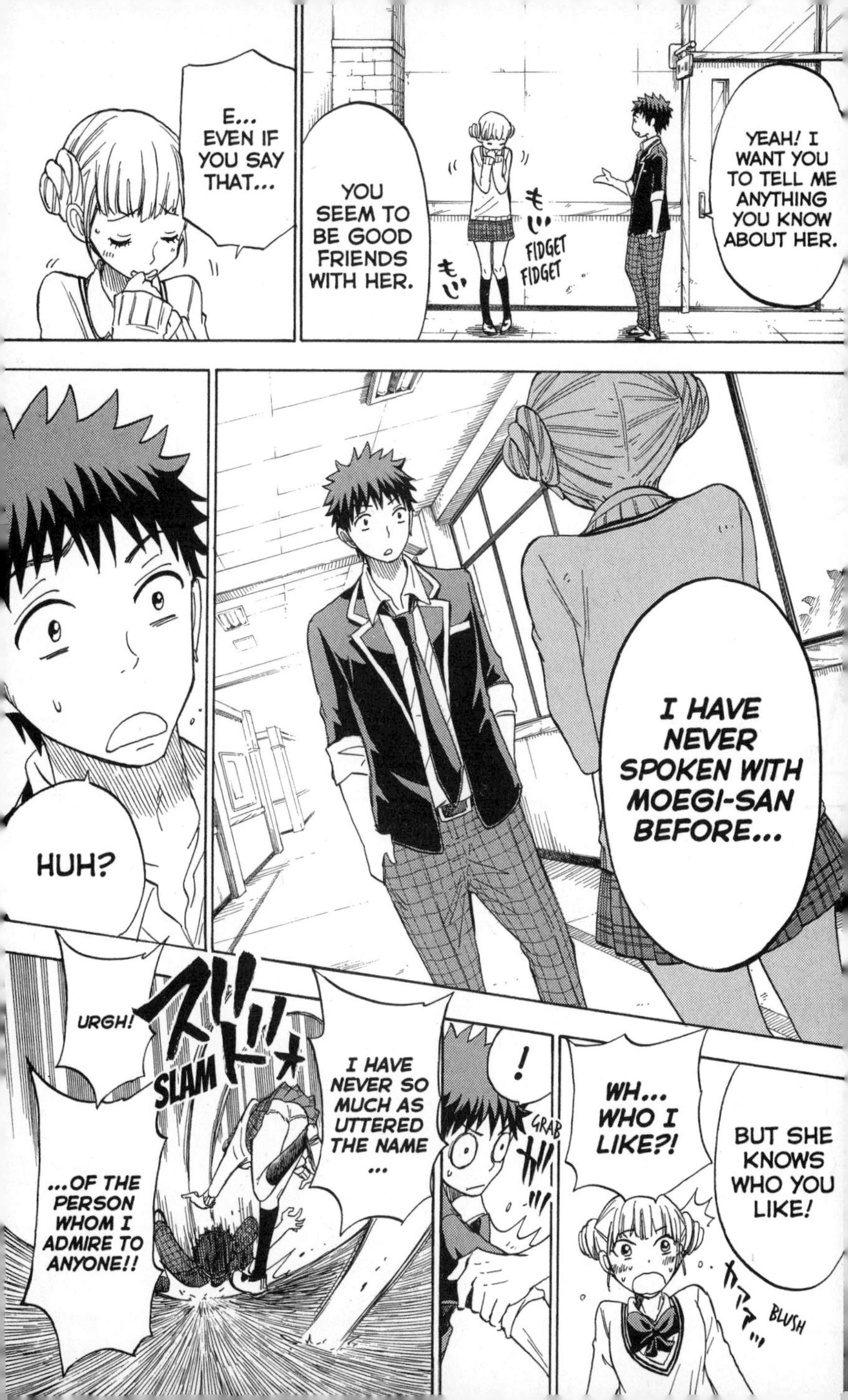
YEAH! I WANT YOU TO TELL ME ANYTHING YOU KNOW ABOUT HER.
YOU SEEM TO BE GOOD FRIENDS WITH HER.
もじ もじ
FIDGET FIDGET
E... EVEN IF YOU SAY THAT...
I HAVE NEVER SPOKEN WITH MOEGI-SAN BEFORE...
HUH?
BUT SHE KNOWS WHO YOU LIKE!
BLUSH
WH... WHO I LIKE?!
!
GRAB
I HAVE NEVER SO MUCH AS UTTERED THE NAME...
...OF THE PERSON WHOM I ADMIRE TO ANYONE!!
SLAM
URGH!

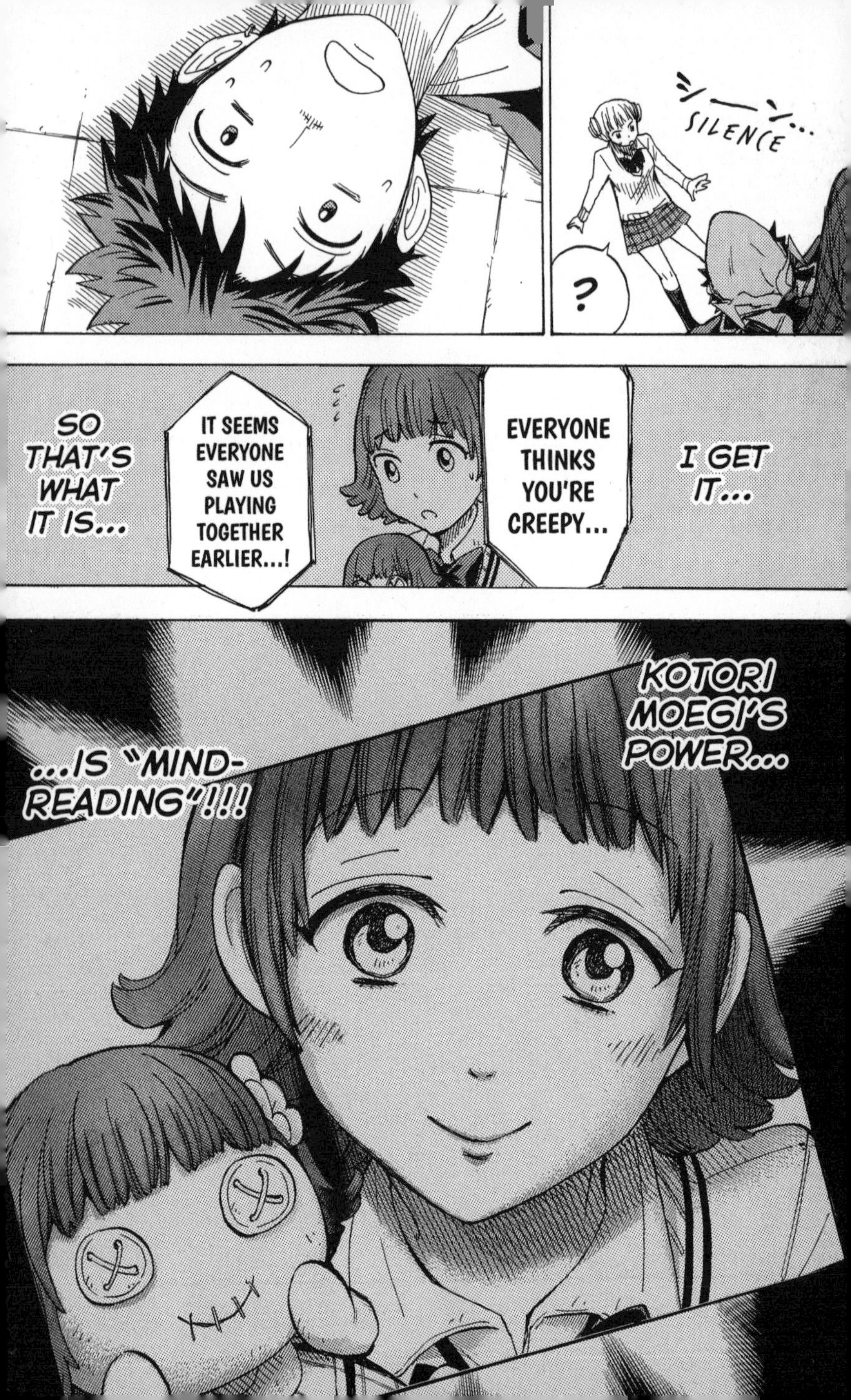
SILENCE
?
I GET IT...
EVERYONE THINKS YOU'RE CREEPY...
IT SEEMS EVERYONE SAW US PLAYING TOGETHER EARLIER...!
SO THAT'S WHAT IT IS...
KOTORI MOEGI'S POWER...
...IS "MIND-READING"!!!

CHAPTER 106: She's got a dirty mind.

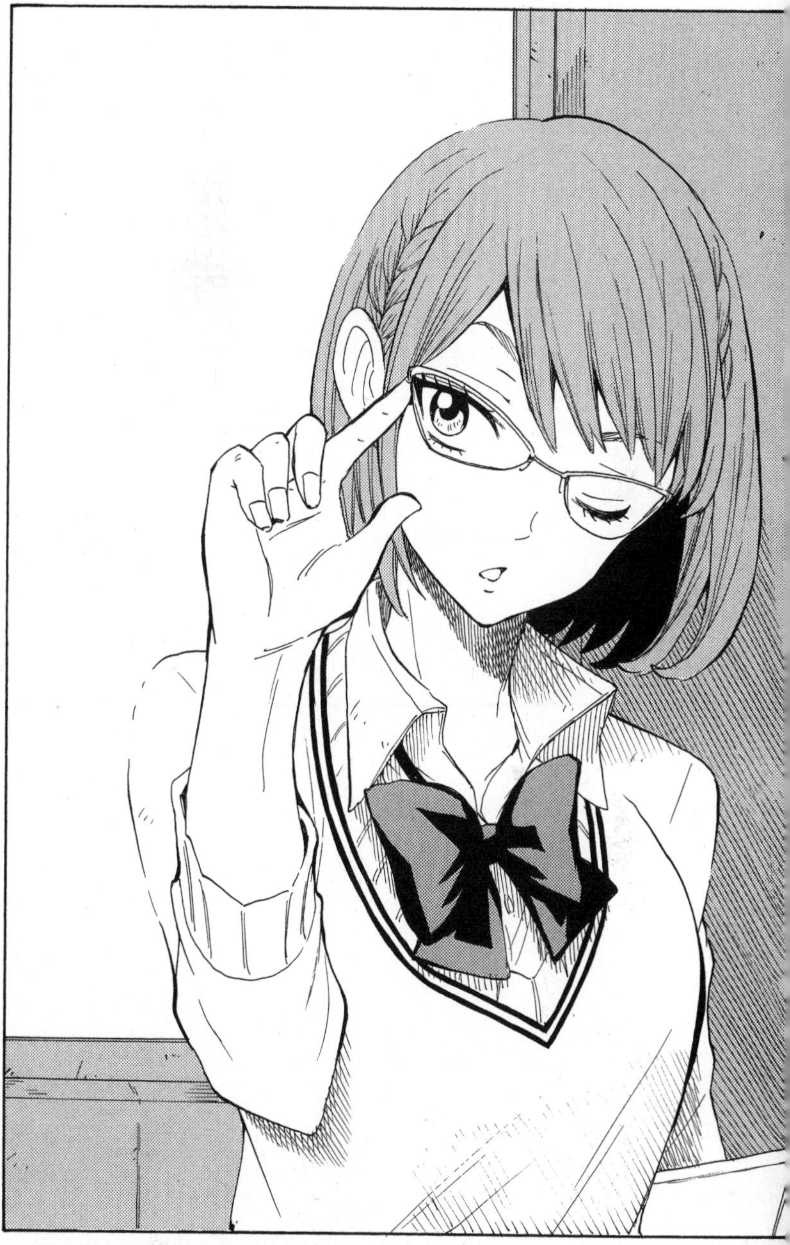

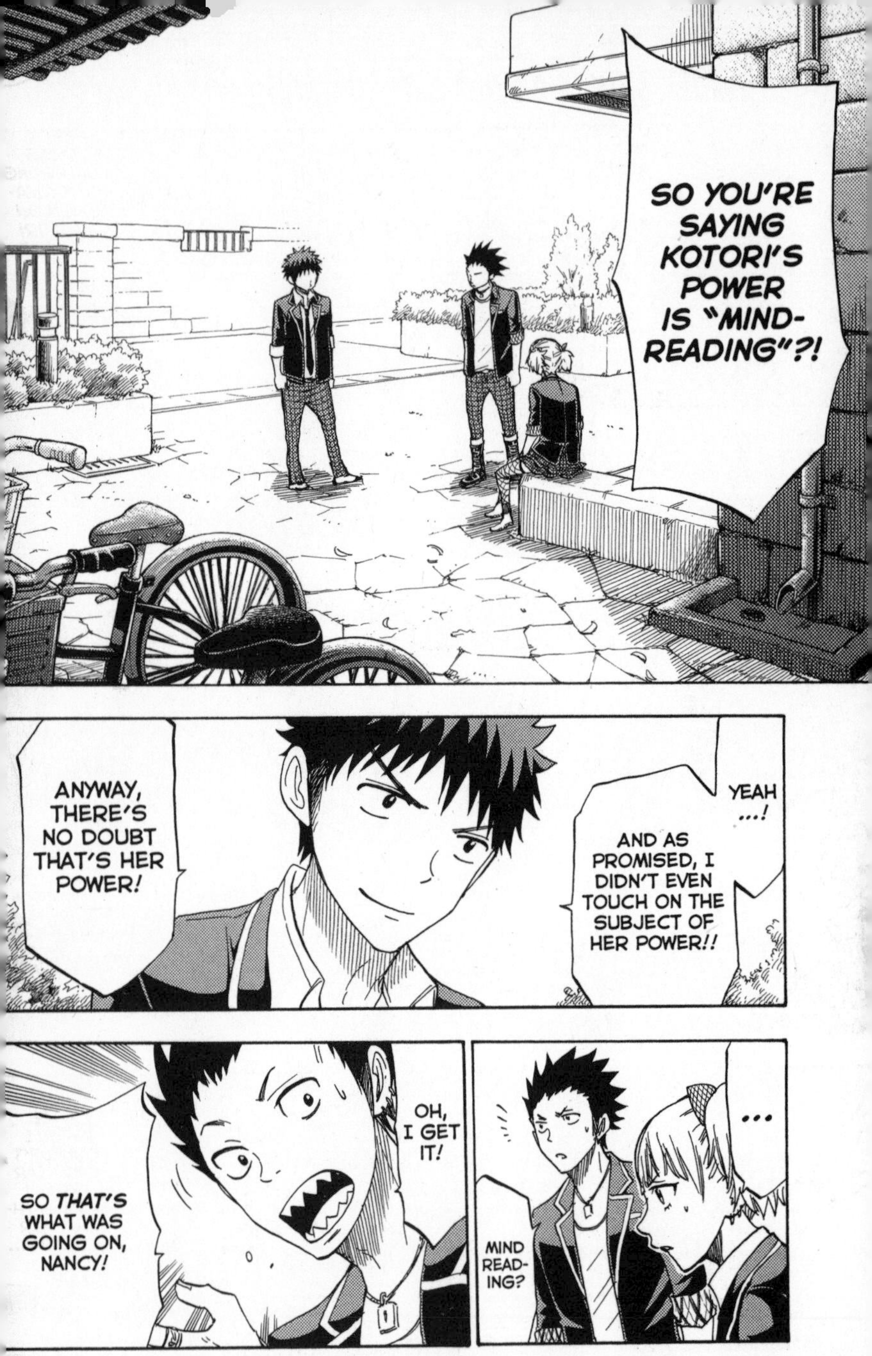
SO YOU'RE SAYING KOTORI'S POWER IS "MIND-READING"?!
YEAH ...!
AND AS PROMISED, I DIDN'T EVEN TOUCH ON THE SUBJECT OF HER POWER!!
ANYWAY, THERE'S NO DOUBT THAT'S HER POWER!
...
MIND READ-ING?
OH, I GET IT!
SO *THAT'S* WHAT WAS GOING ON, NANCY!

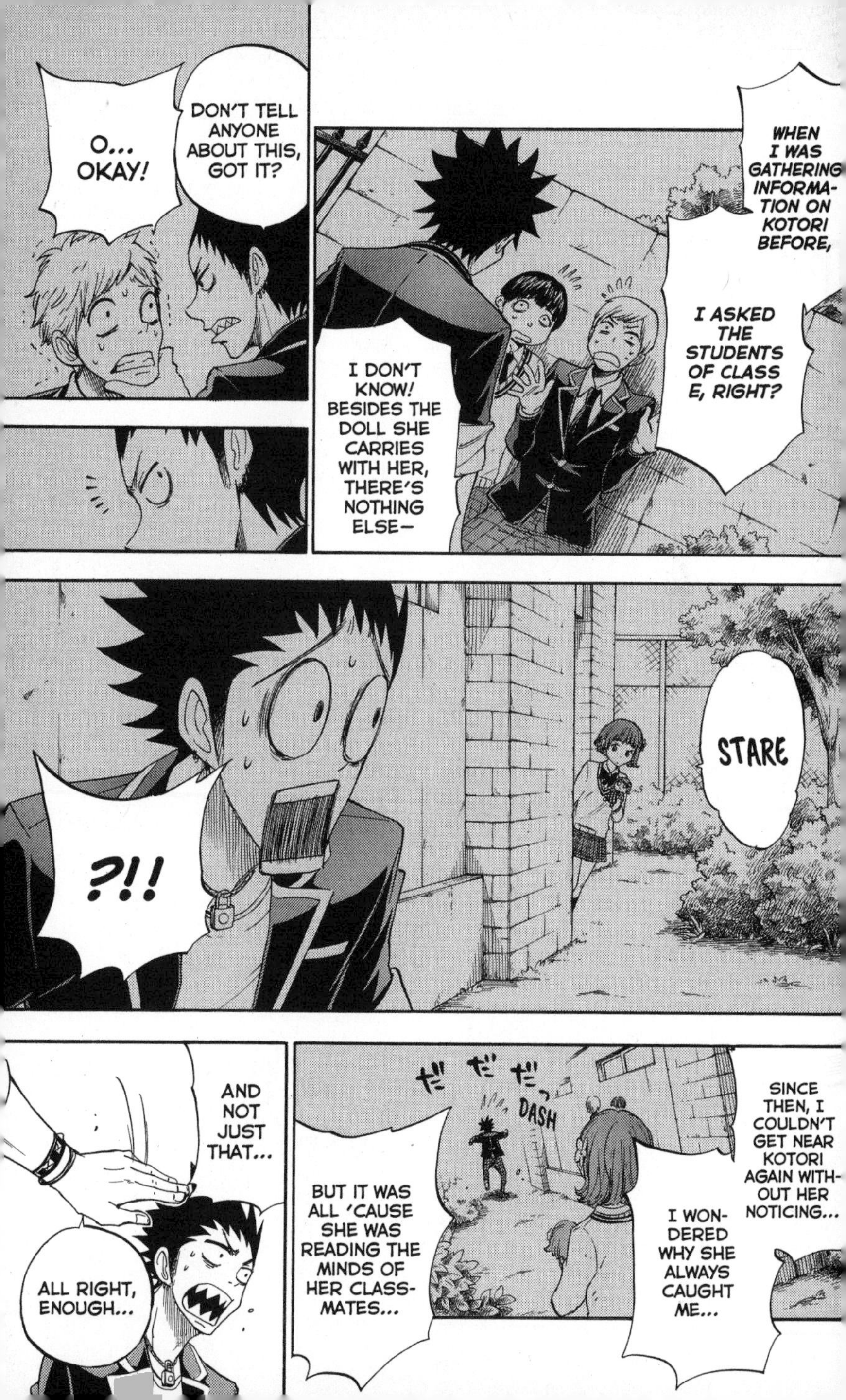
DON'T TELL ANYONE ABOUT THIS, GOT IT?
O... OKAY!
WHEN I WAS GATHERING INFORMATION ON KOTORI BEFORE,
I ASKED THE STUDENTS OF CLASS E, RIGHT?
I DON'T KNOW! BESIDES THE DOLL SHE CARRIES WITH HER, THERE'S NOTHING ELSE—
STARE
?!!
SINCE THEN, I COULDN'T GET NEAR KOTORI AGAIN WITHOUT HER NOTICING...
I WONDERED WHY SHE ALWAYS CAUGHT ME...
DASH
BUT IT WAS ALL 'CAUSE SHE WAS READING THE MINDS OF HER CLASSMATES...
AND NOT JUST THAT...
ALL RIGHT, ENOUGH...

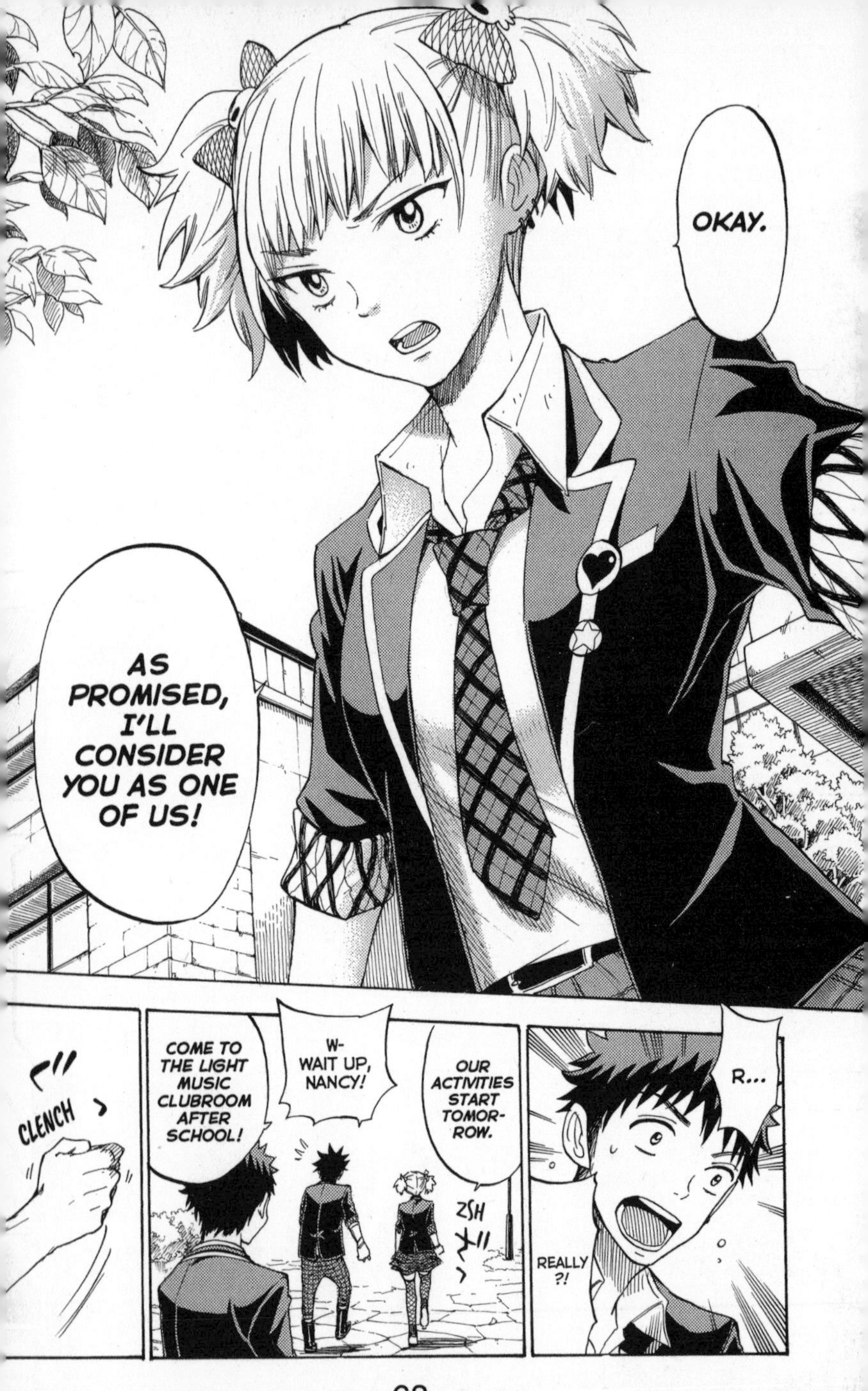
OKAY.
AS PROMISED, I'LL CONSIDER YOU AS ONE OF US!
R...
REALLY ?!
OUR ACTIVITIES START TOMOR-ROW.
W- WAIT UP, NANCY!
COME TO THE LIGHT MUSIC CLUBROOM AFTER SCHOOL!
ZSH
CLENCH

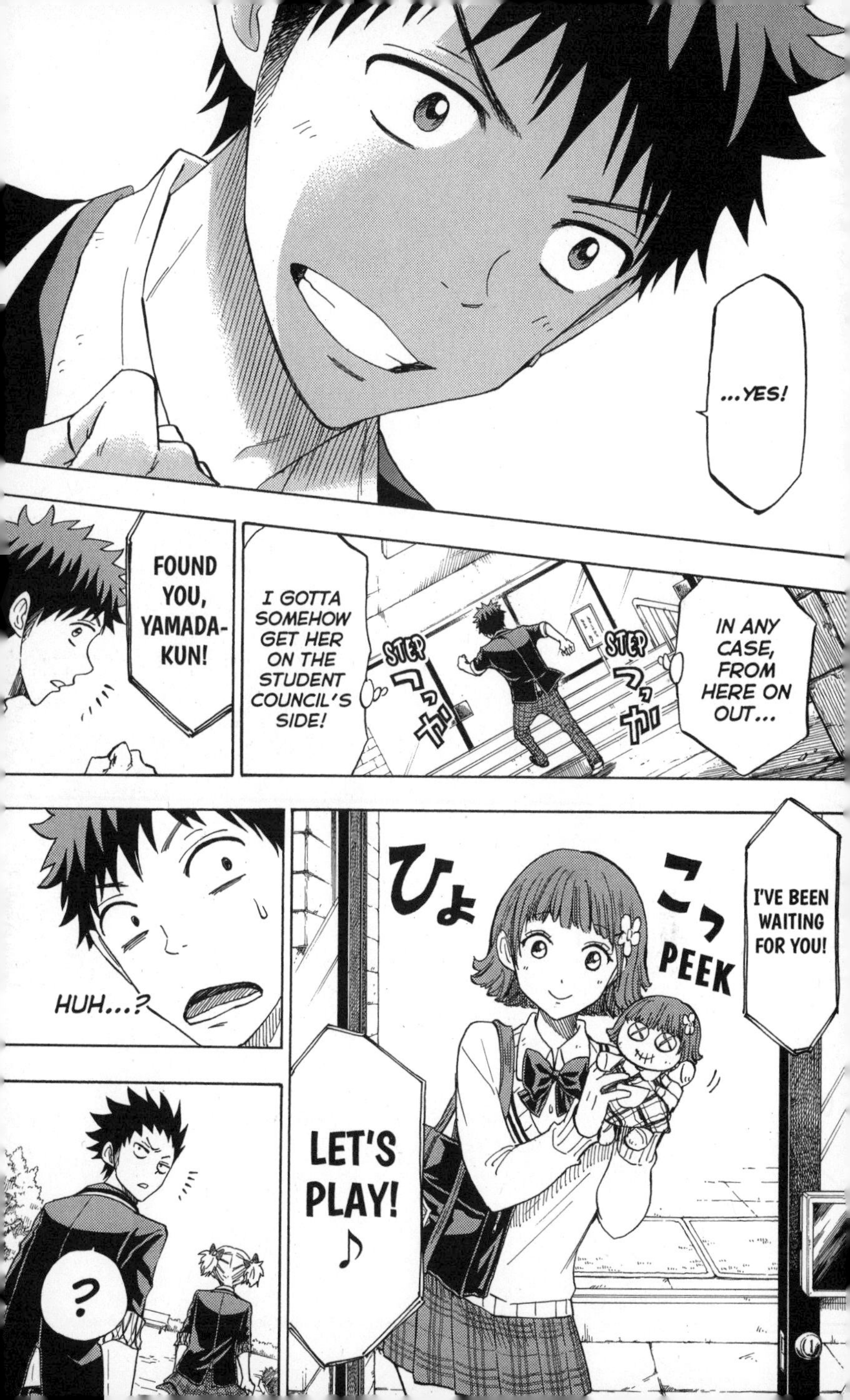
...YES!
IN ANY CASE, FROM HERE ON OUT...
STEP
STEP
I GOTTA SOMEHOW GET HER ON THE STUDENT COUNCIL'S SIDE!
FOUND YOU, YAMADA-KUN!
I'VE BEEN WAITING FOR YOU!
ひょこっ
PEEK
LET'S PLAY! ♪
HUH...?
?

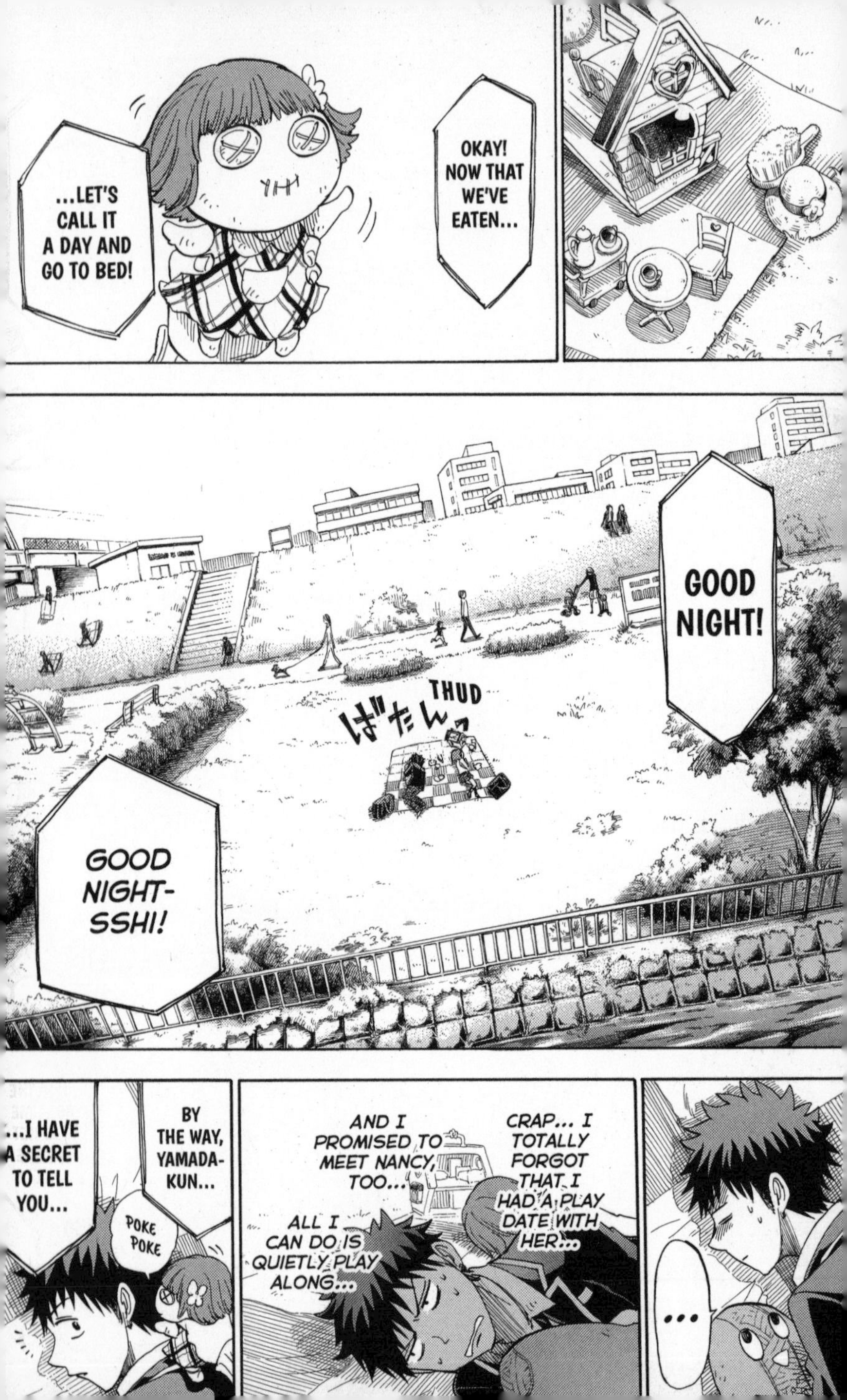
OKAY! NOW THAT WE'VE EATEN...
...LET'S CALL IT A DAY AND GO TO BED!
GOOD NIGHT!
ばたん
THUD
GOOD NIGHT-SSHI!
...
CRAP... I TOTALLY FORGOT THAT I HAD A PLAY DATE WITH HER...
AND I PROMISED TO MEET NANCY, TOO...
ALL I CAN DO IS QUIETLY PLAY ALONG...
BY THE WAY, YAMADA-KUN...
...I HAVE A SECRET TO TELL YOU...
POKE POKE

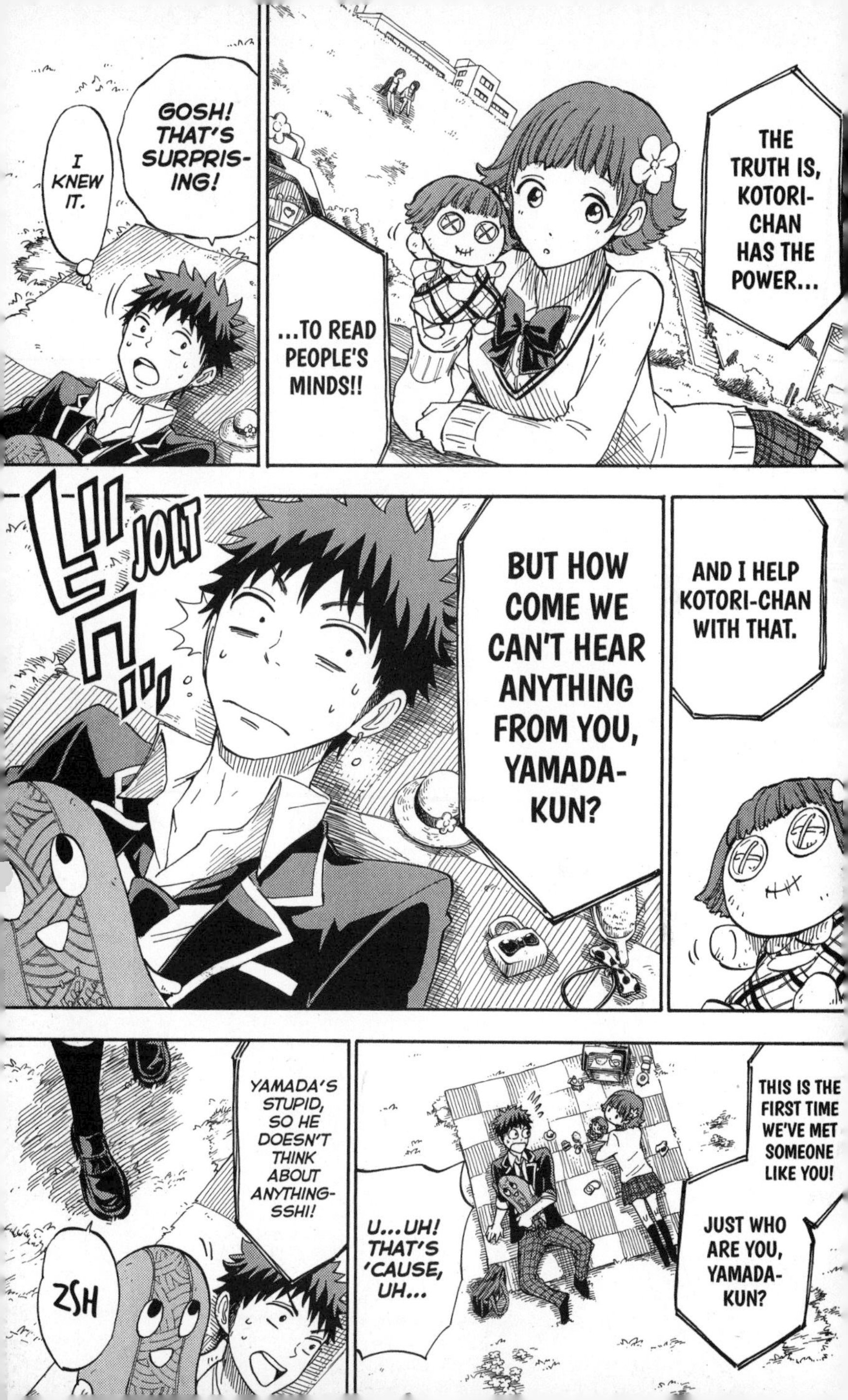
THE TRUTH IS, KOTORI-CHAN HAS THE POWER...
...TO READ PEOPLE'S MINDS!!
GOSH! THAT'S SURPRIS-ING!
I KNEW IT.
AND I HELP KOTORI-CHAN WITH THAT.
BUT HOW COME WE CAN'T HEAR ANYTHING FROM YOU, YAMADA-KUN?
JOLT
THIS IS THE FIRST TIME WE'VE MET SOMEONE LIKE YOU!
JUST WHO ARE YOU, YAMADA-KUN?
U...UH! THAT'S 'CAUSE, UH...
YAMADA'S STUPID, SO HE DOESN'T THINK ABOUT ANYTHING-SSHI!
ZSH

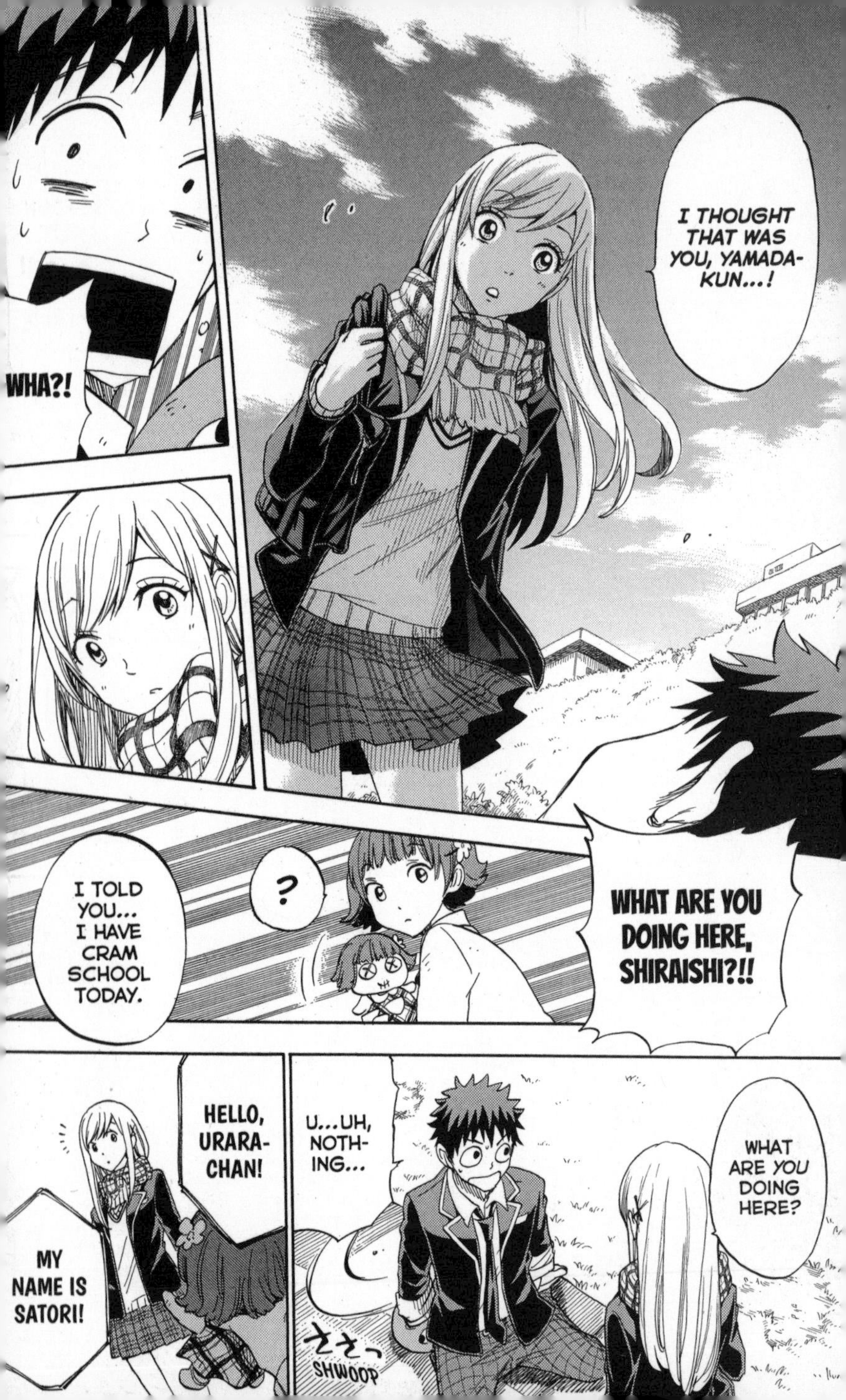
I THOUGHT THAT WAS YOU, YAMADA-KUN...!
WHA?!
WHAT ARE YOU DOING HERE, SHIRAISHI?!!
?
I TOLD YOU... I HAVE CRAM SCHOOL TODAY.
WHAT ARE YOU DOING HERE?
U...UH, NOTHING...
そそっ
SHWOOP
HELLO, URARA-CHAN!
MY NAME IS SATORI!

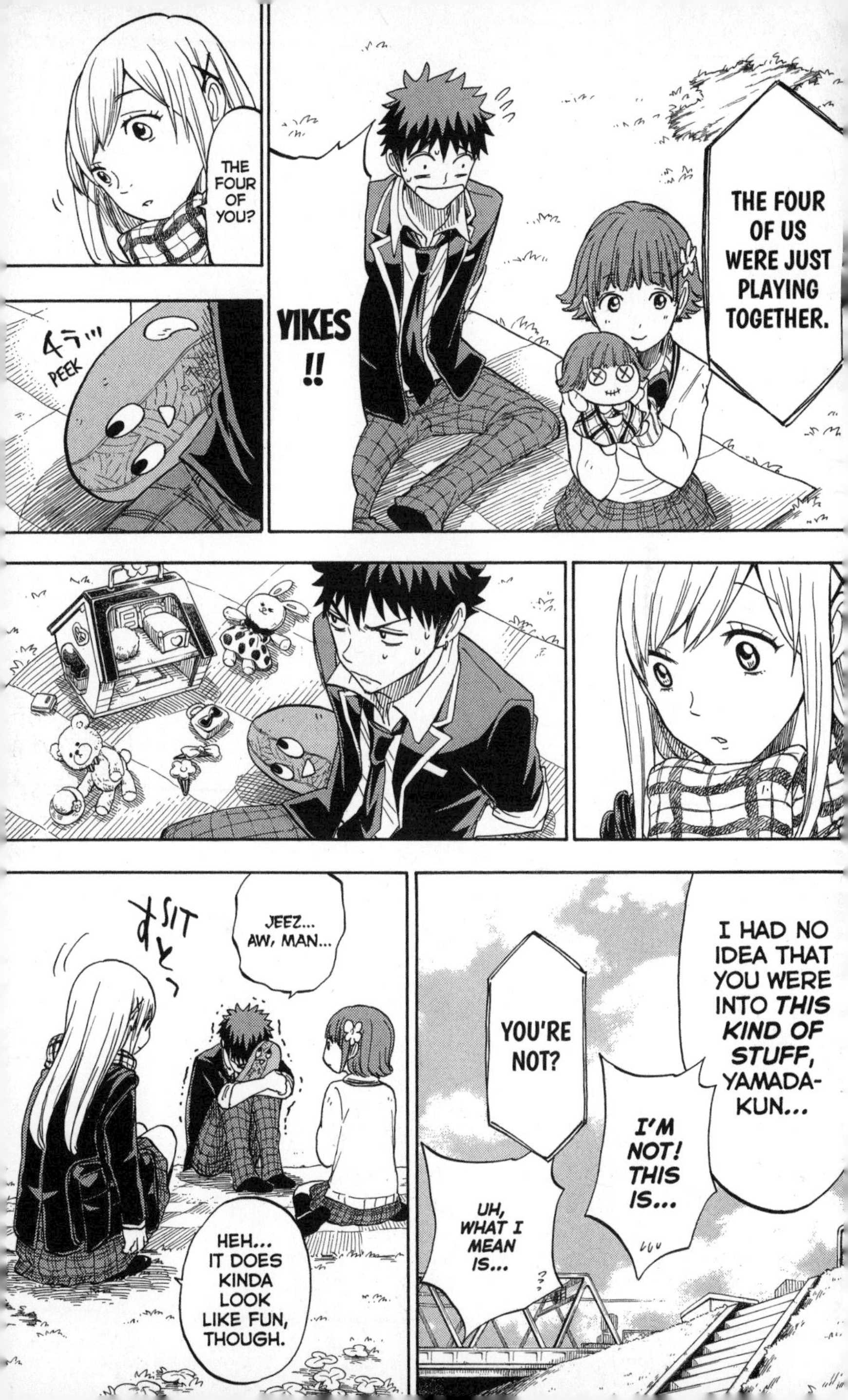
THE FOUR OF US WERE JUST PLAYING TOGETHER.
YIKES!!
THE FOUR OF YOU?
イラッ
PEEK
I HAD NO IDEA THAT YOU WERE INTO *THIS KIND OF STUFF*, YAMADA-KUN...
I'M NOT! THIS IS...
YOU'RE NOT?
UH, WHAT I MEAN IS...
JEEZ... AW, MAN...
すとっ
SIT
HEH... IT DOES KINDA LOOK LIKE FUN, THOUGH.

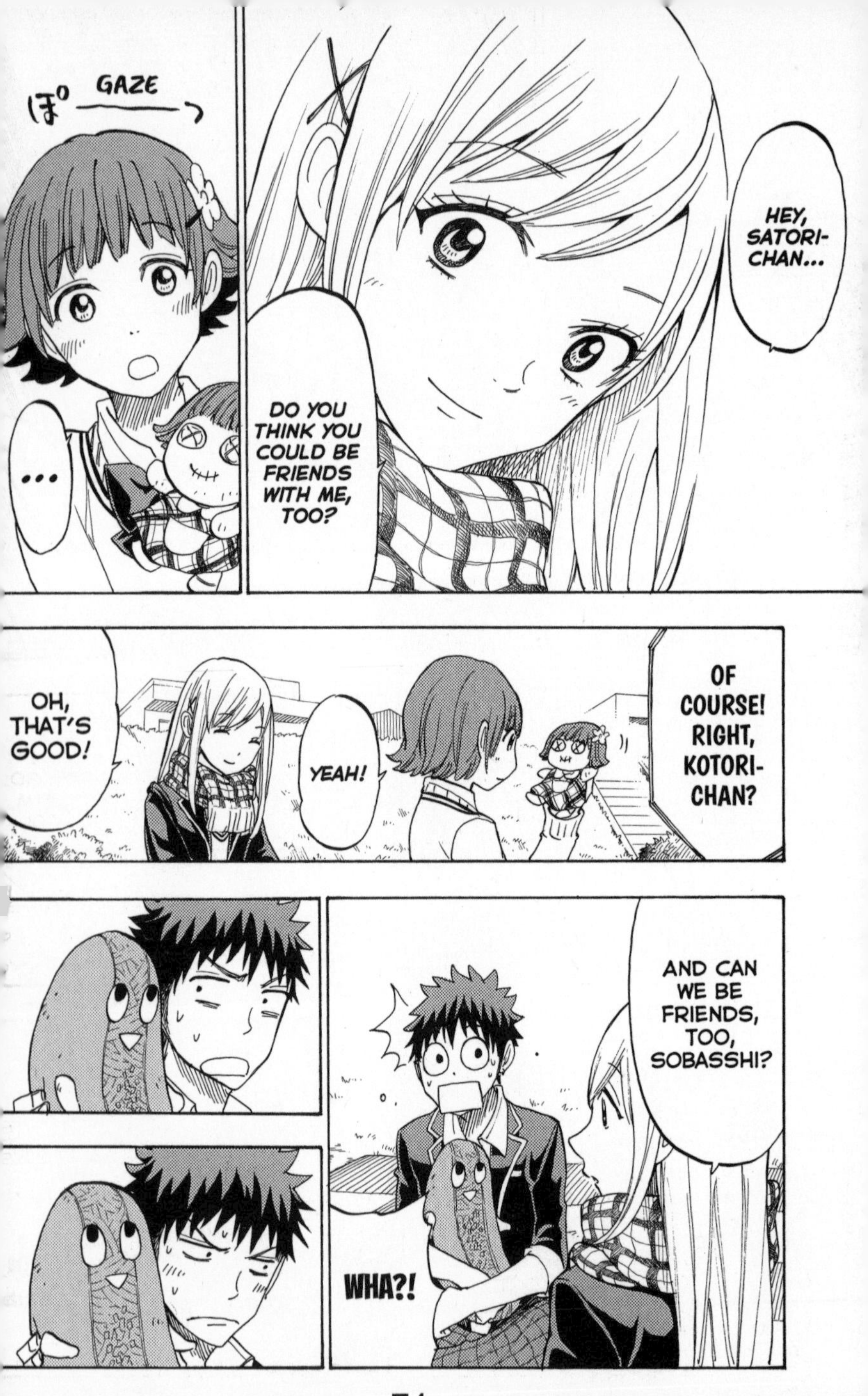
HEY, SATORI-CHAN...
DO YOU THINK YOU COULD BE FRIENDS WITH ME, TOO?
ぽ
GAZE
...
OF COURSE! RIGHT, KOTORI-CHAN?
YEAH!
OH, THAT'S GOOD!
AND CAN WE BE FRIENDS, TOO, SOBASSHI?
WHA?!

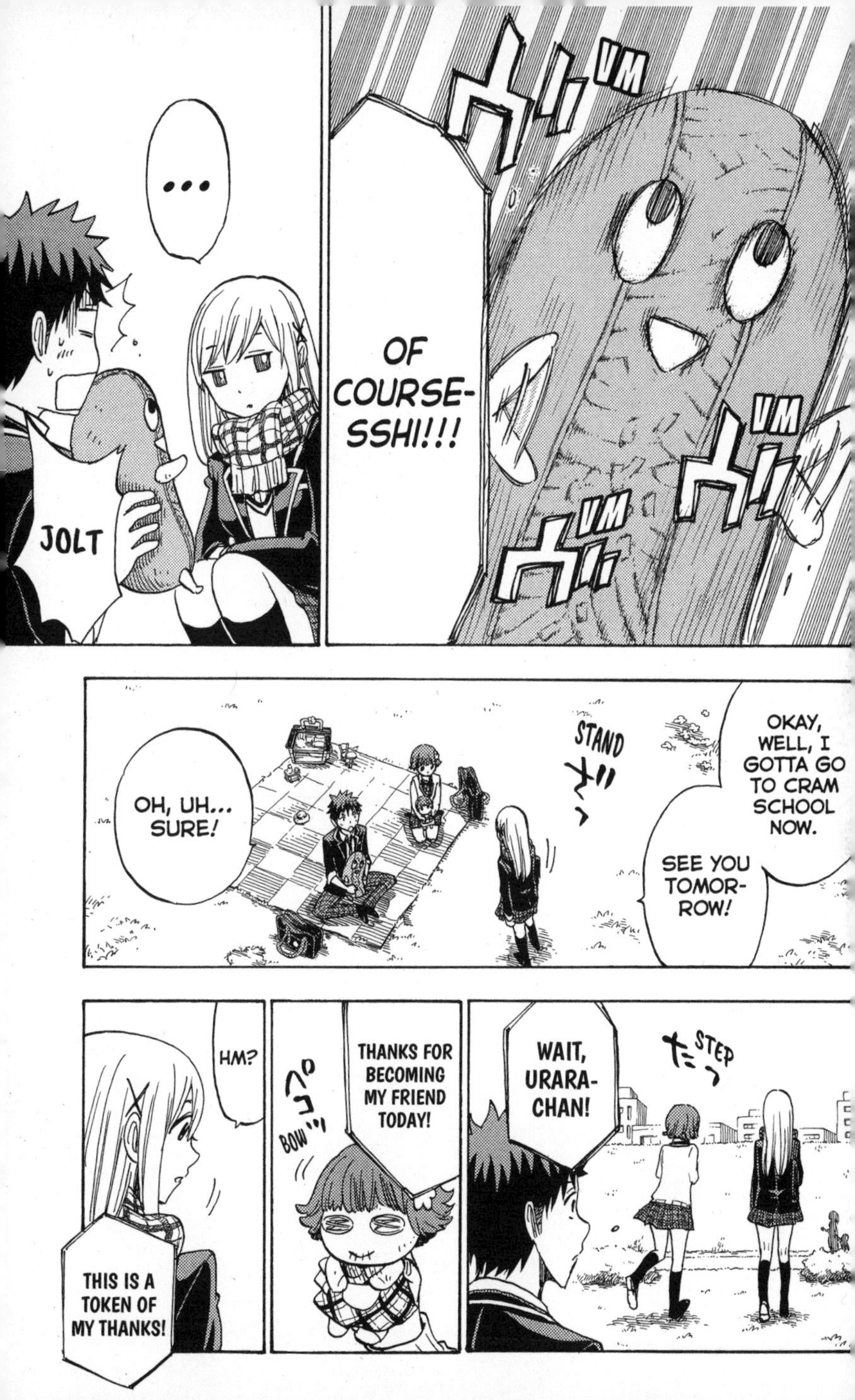
VM
OF COURSE-SSHI!!!
VM
VM
...
JOLT
OKAY, WELL, I GOTTA GO TO CRAM SCHOOL NOW.
SEE YOU TOMOR-ROW!
STAND
OH, UH... SURE!
STEP
WAIT, URARA-CHAN!
THANKS FOR BECOMING MY FRIEND TODAY!
BOW
HM?
THIS IS A TOKEN OF MY THANKS!

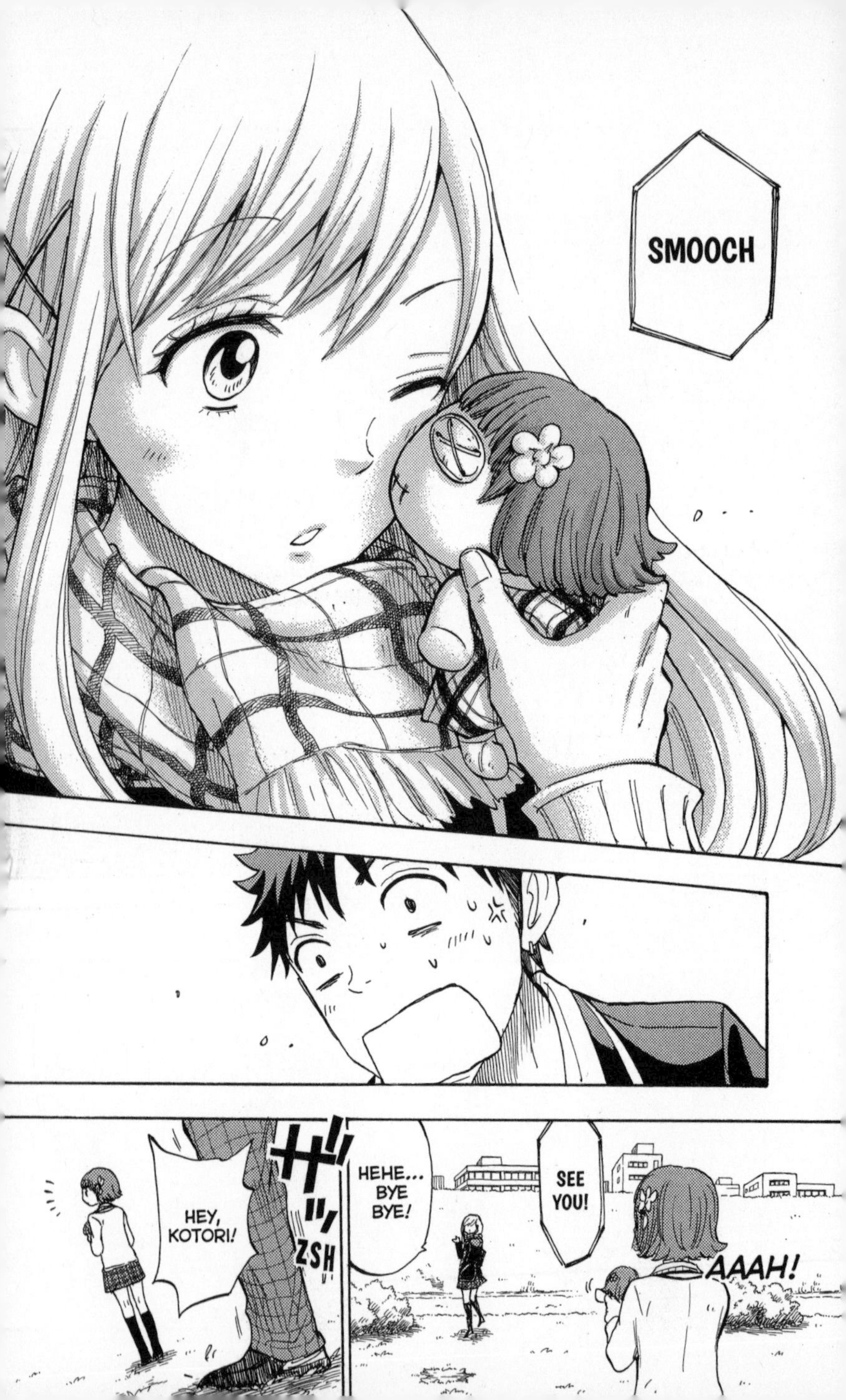
SMOOCH
SEE YOU!
HEHE... BYE BYE!
AAAH!
ZSH
HEY, KOTORI!

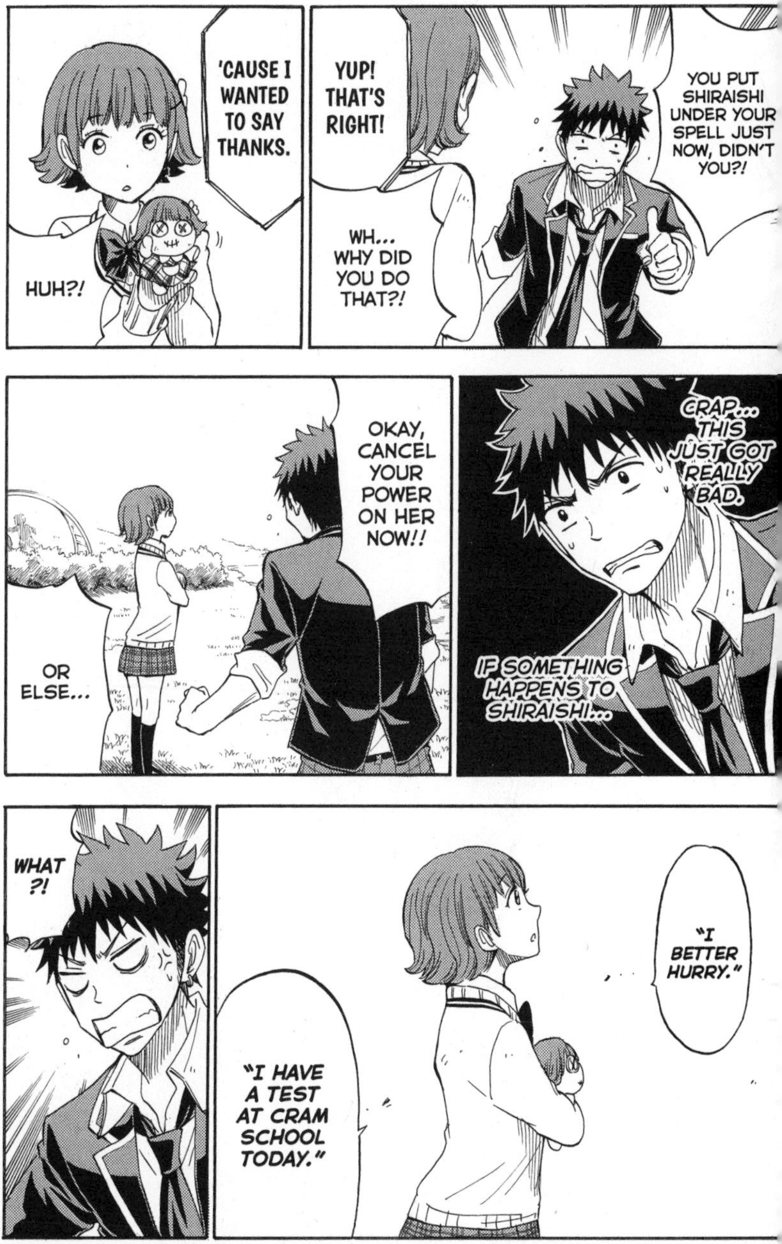
YOU PUT SHIRAISHI UNDER YOUR SPELL JUST NOW, DIDN'T YOU?!
YUP! THAT'S RIGHT!
WH... WHY DID YOU DO THAT?!
'CAUSE I WANTED TO SAY THANKS.
HUH?!
CRAP... THIS JUST GOT REALLY BAD.
IF SOMETHING HAPPENS TO SHIRAISHI...
OKAY, CANCEL YOUR POWER ON HER NOW!!
OR ELSE...
"I BETTER HURRY."
"I HAVE A TEST AT CRAM SCHOOL TODAY."
WHAT?!

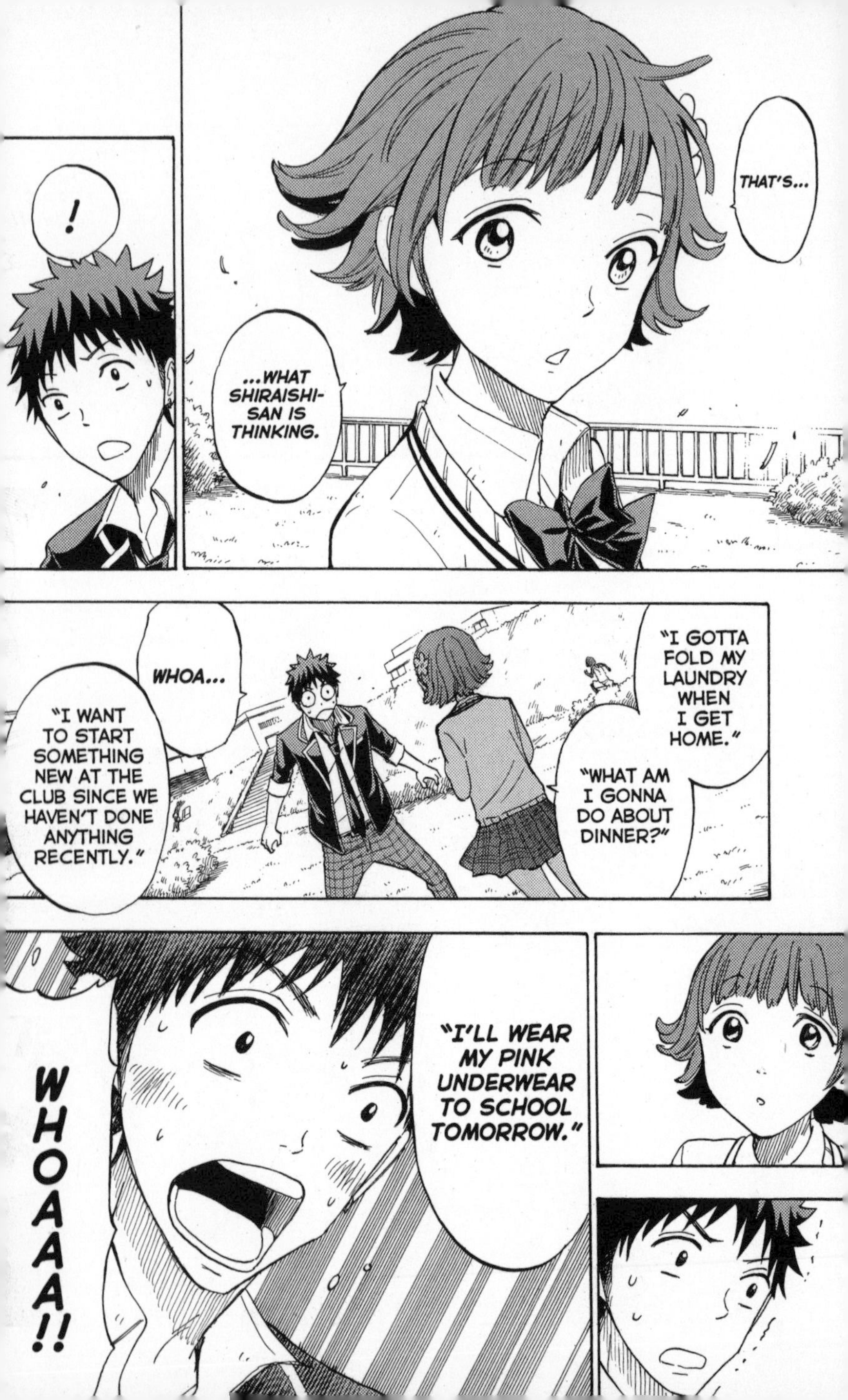
THAT'S...
...WHAT SHIRAISHI-SAN IS THINKING.
!
"I GOTTA FOLD MY LAUNDRY WHEN I GET HOME."
"WHAT AM I GONNA DO ABOUT DINNER?"
WHOA...
"I WANT TO START SOMETHING NEW AT THE CLUB SINCE WE HAVEN'T DONE ANYTHING RECENTLY."
"I'LL WEAR MY PINK UNDERWEAR TO SCHOOL TOMORROW."
WHOAAAA!!

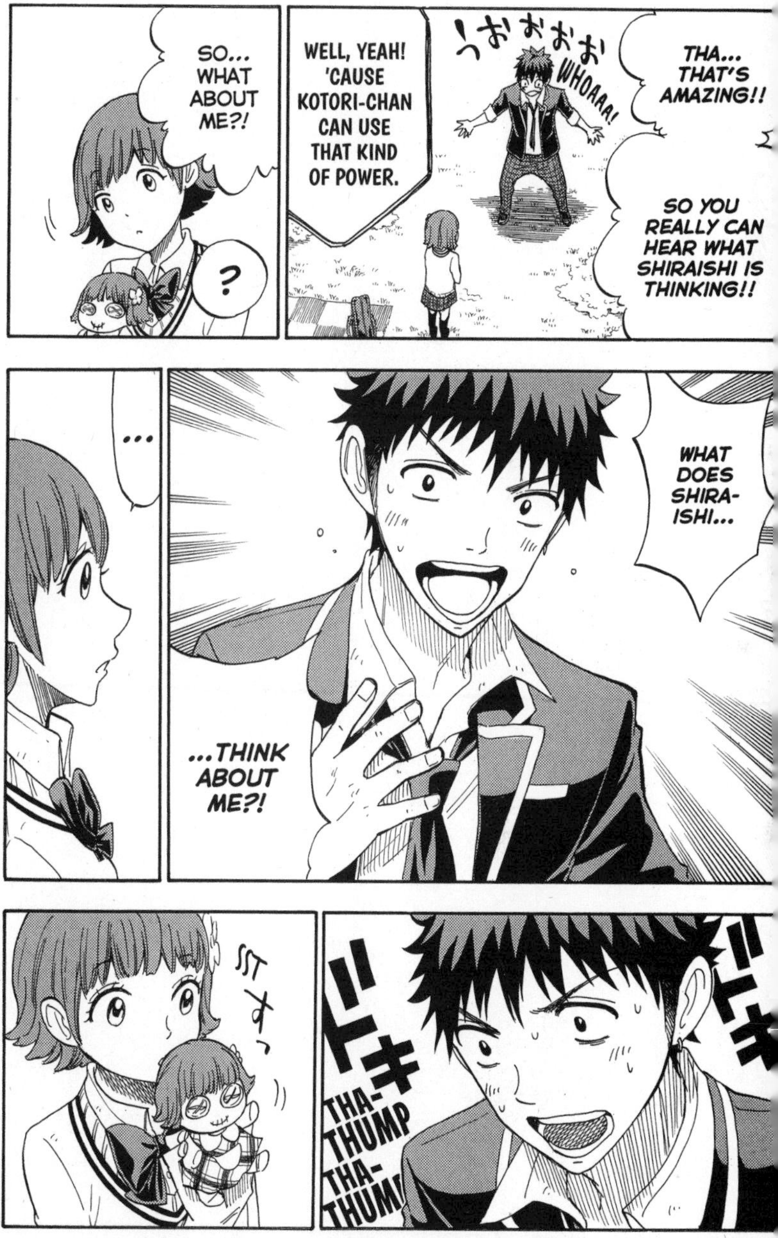
THA... THAT'S AMAZING!!
SO YOU REALLY CAN HEAR WHAT SHIRAISHI IS THINKING!!
うおおおお
WHOAAA!
WELL, YEAH! 'CAUSE KOTORI-CHAN CAN USE THAT KIND OF POWER.
SO... WHAT ABOUT ME?!
?
WHAT DOES SHIRA-ISHI...
...THINK ABOUT ME?!
...
ドキ
ドキ
THA-THUMP THA-THUMP
すっ
SST

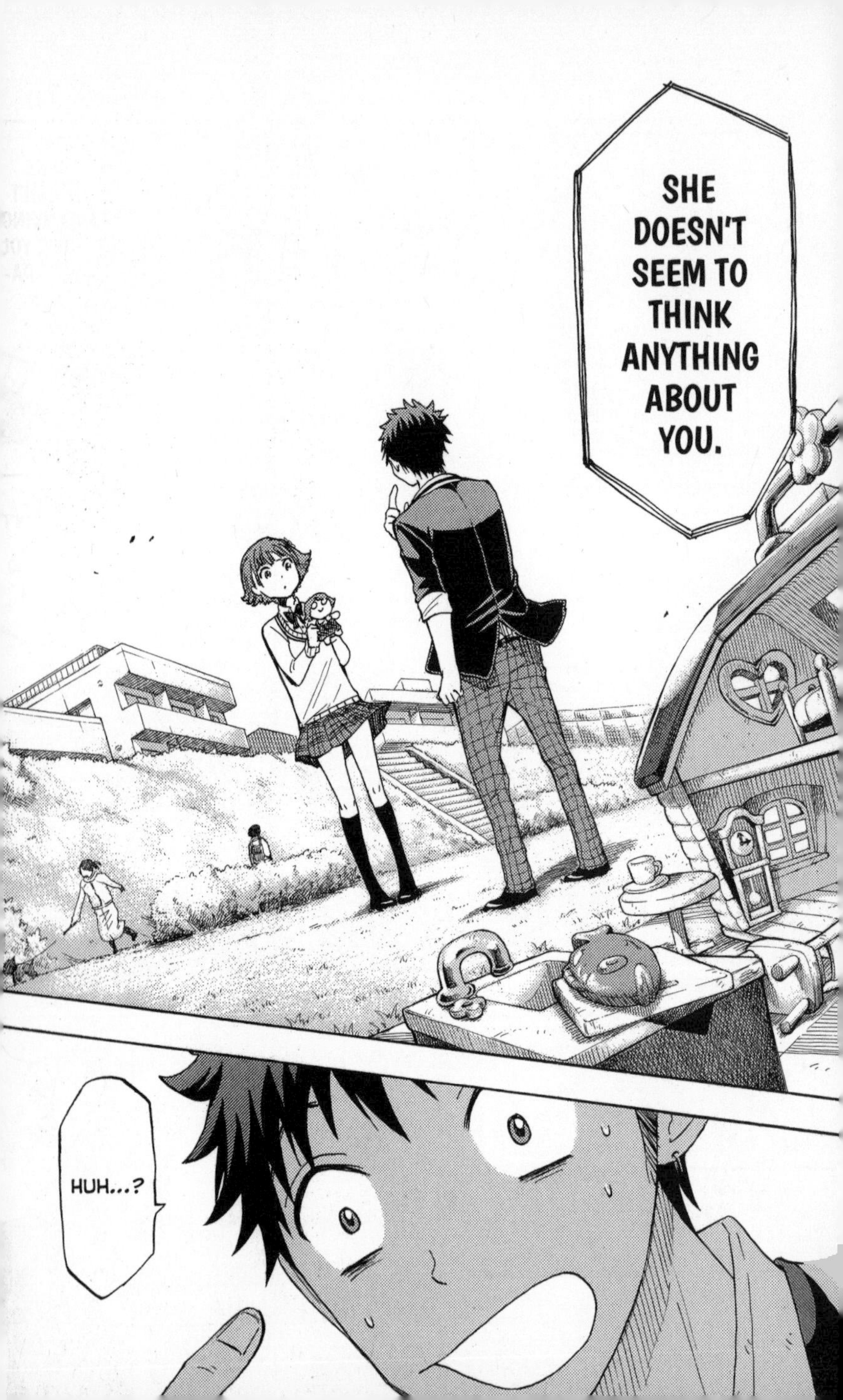
SHE DOESN'T SEEM TO THINK ANYTHING ABOUT YOU.
HUH...?

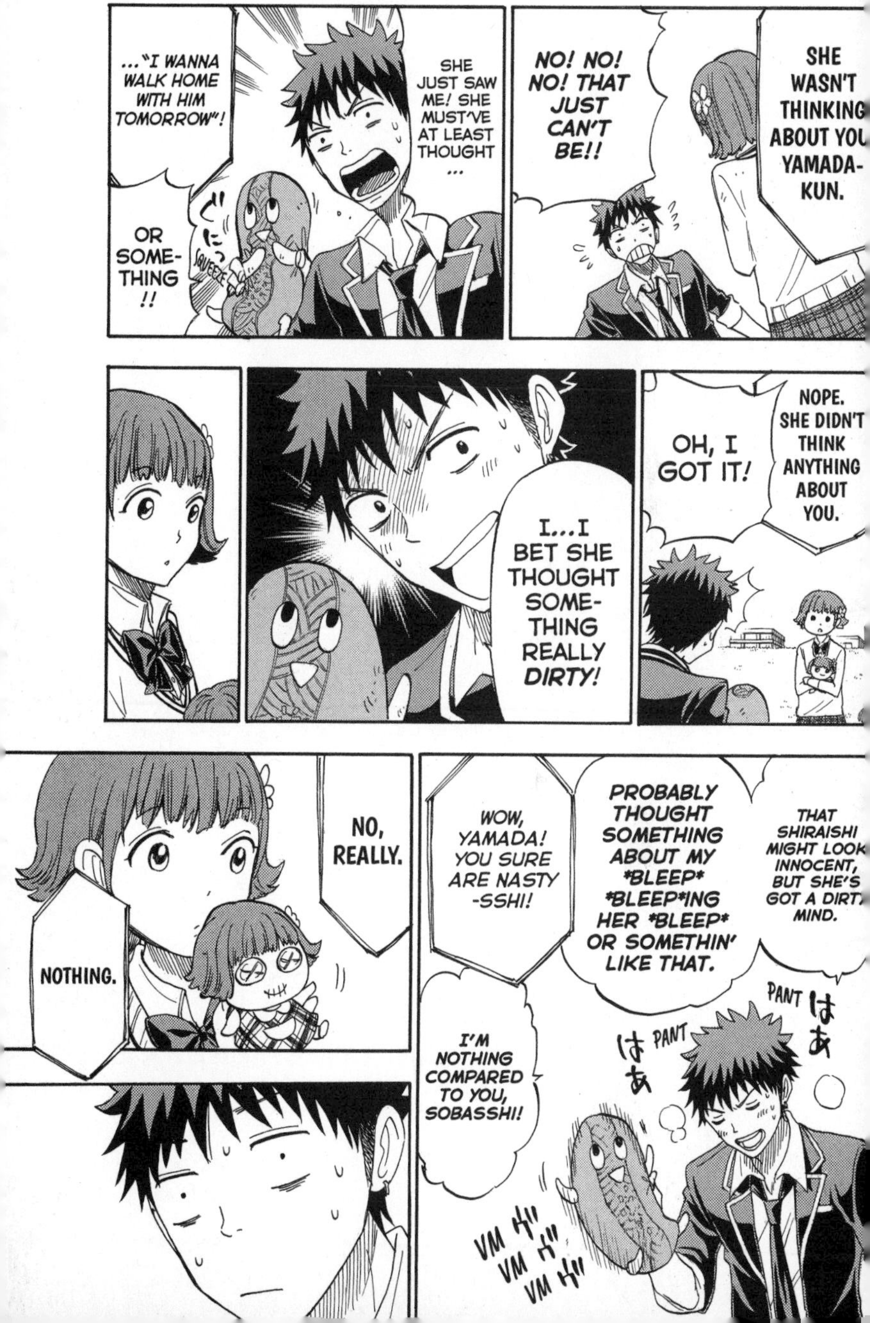
SHE WASN'T THINKING ABOUT YOU YAMADA-KUN.
NO! NO! NO! THAT JUST CAN'T BE!!
SHE JUST SAW ME! SHE MUST'VE AT LEAST THOUGHT ...
..."I WANNA WALK HOME WITH HIM TOMORROW"!
OR SOME-THING !!
ぐにっ SQUEEZE
NOPE. SHE DIDN'T THINK ANYTHING ABOUT YOU.
OH, I GOT IT!
I...I BET SHE THOUGHT SOME-THING REALLY DIRTY!
THAT SHIRAISHI MIGHT LOOK INNOCENT, BUT SHE'S GOT A DIRT MIND.
PROBABLY THOUGHT SOMETHING ABOUT MY *BLEEP* *BLEEP*ING HER *BLEEP* OR SOMETHIN' LIKE THAT.
WOW, YAMADA! YOU SURE ARE NASTY -SSHI!
I'M NOTHING COMPARED TO YOU, SOBASSHI!
PANT はあ
PANT はあ
VM ヴ VM ヴ VM ヴ
NO, REALLY.
NOTHING.

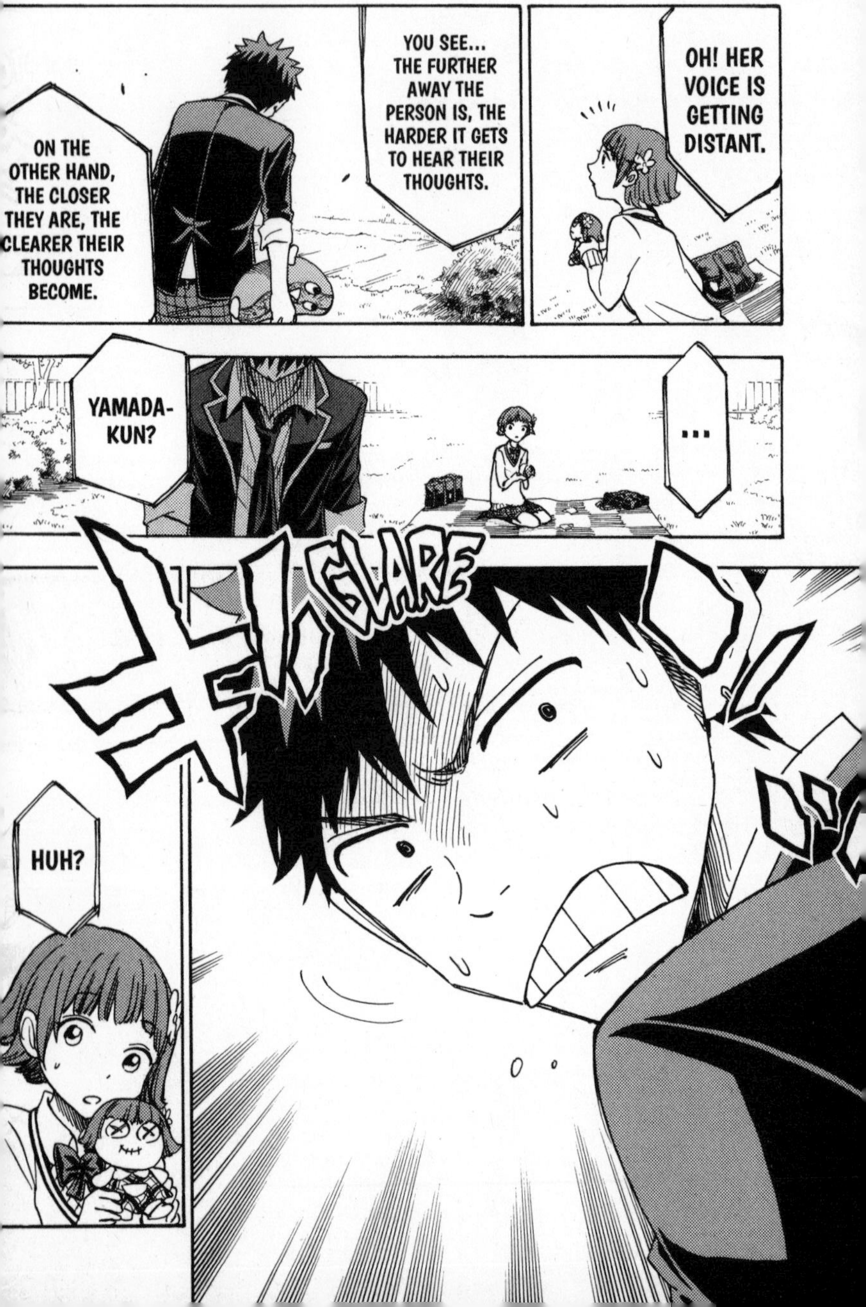
OH! HER VOICE IS GETTING DISTANT.
YOU SEE... THE FURTHER AWAY THE PERSON IS, THE HARDER IT GETS TO HEAR THEIR THOUGHTS.
ON THE OTHER HAND, THE CLOSER THEY ARE, THE CLEARER THEIR THOUGHTS BECOME.
...
YAMADA-KUN?
GLARE
HUH?

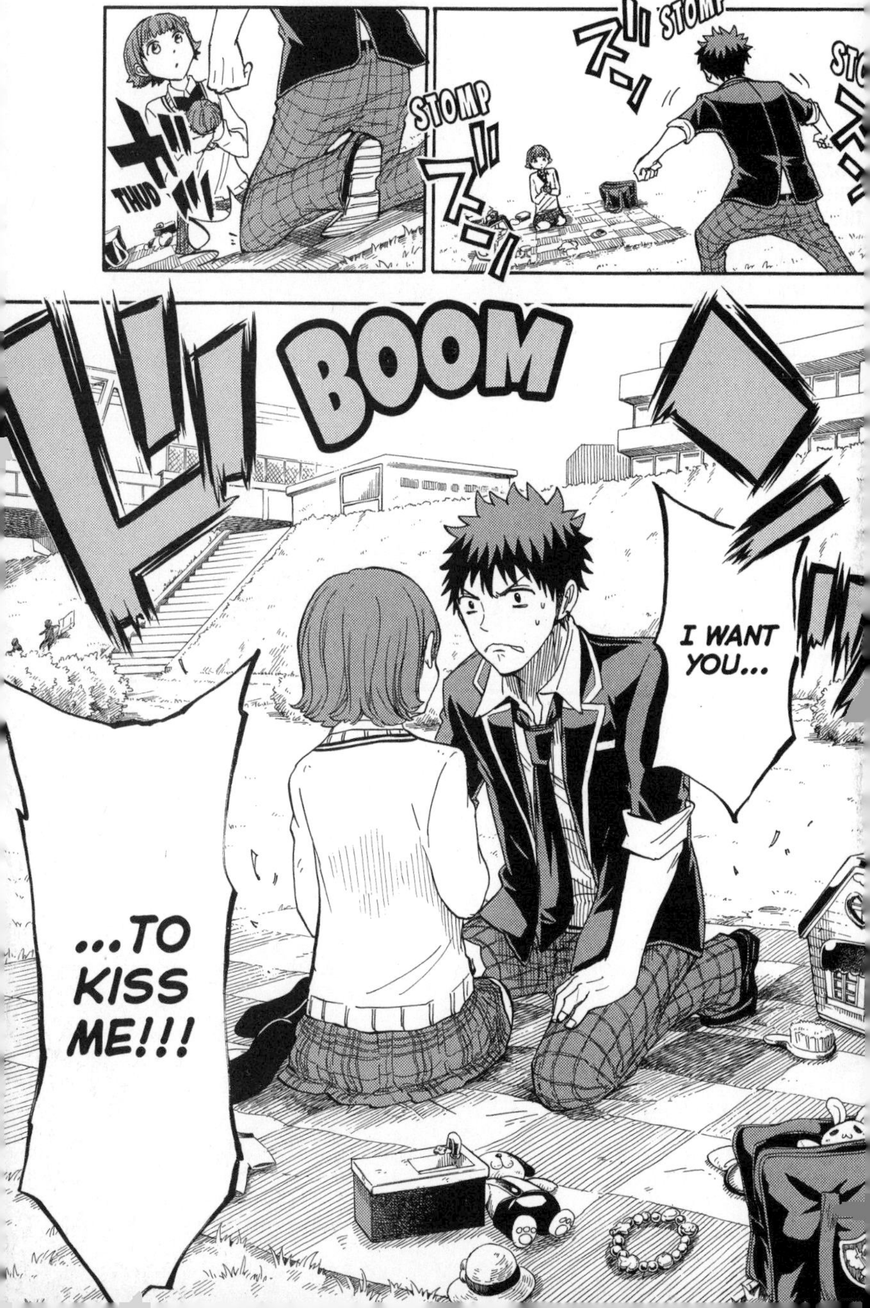
STOMP
STOMP
THUD
BOOM
I WANT YOU...
...TO KISS ME!!!

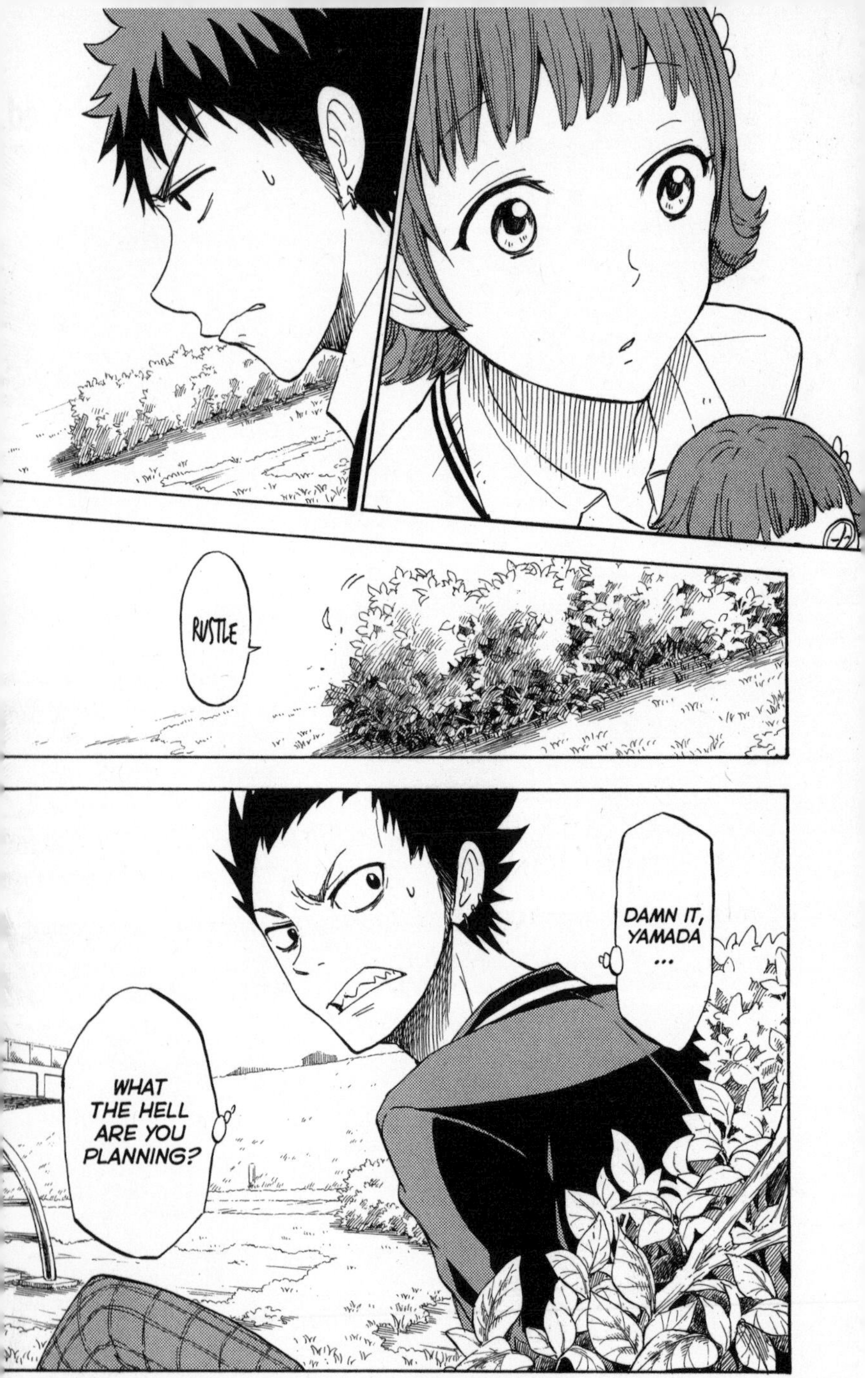
RUSTLE
DAMN IT, YAMADA ...
WHAT THE HELL ARE YOU PLANNING?

CHAPTER 107: He looks bored.

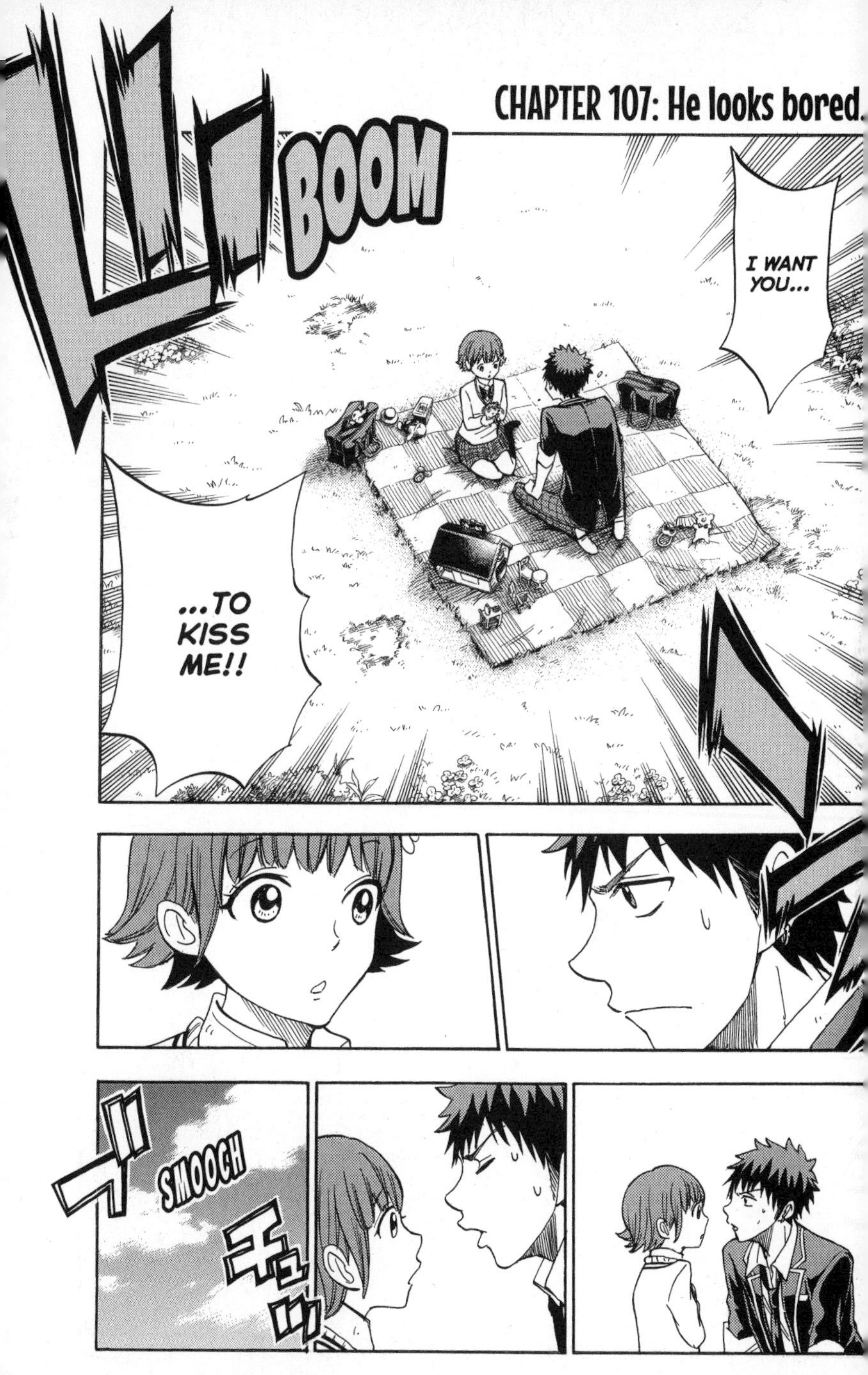
BOOM
I WANT YOU...
...TO KISS ME!!
SMOOCH

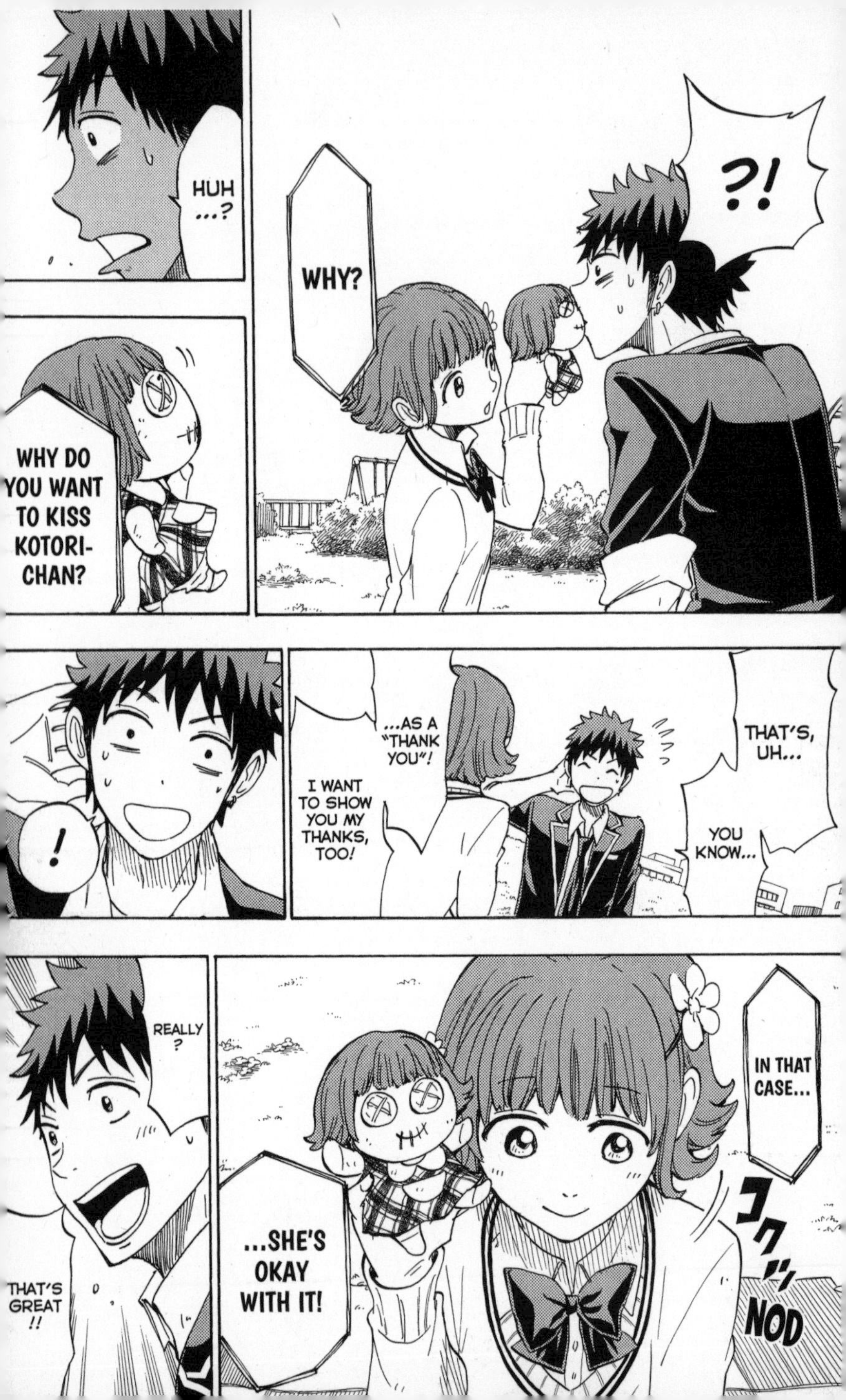

?!
WHY?
HUH...?
WHY DO YOU WANT TO KISS KOTORI-CHAN?
THAT'S, UH...
YOU KNOW...
...AS A "THANK YOU"!
I WANT TO SHOW YOU MY THANKS, TOO!
!
IN THAT CASE...
コクッ
NOD
...SHE'S OKAY WITH IT!
REALLY?
THAT'S GREAT!!

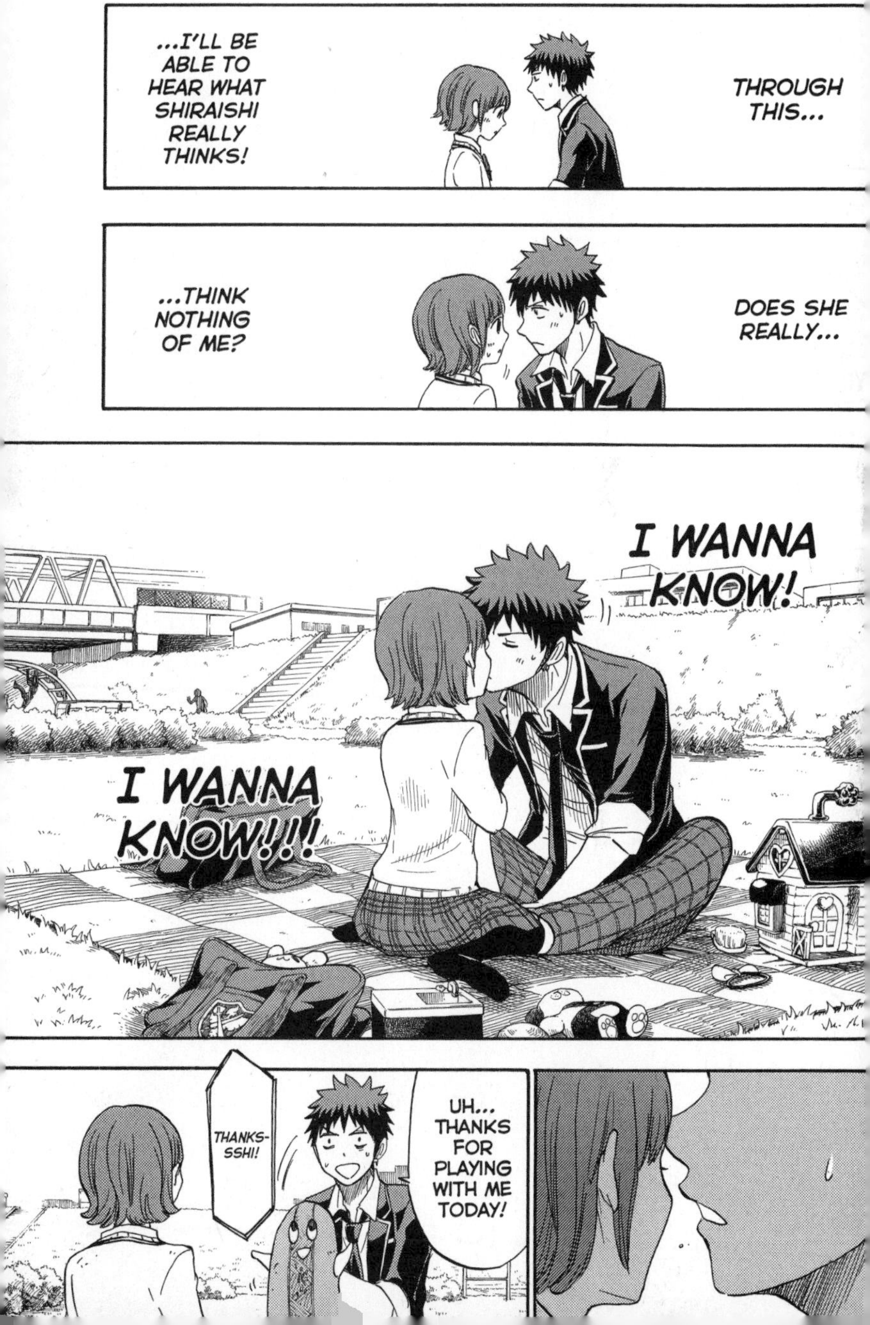
THROUGH THIS...
...I'LL BE ABLE TO HEAR WHAT SHIRAISHI REALLY THINKS!
DOES SHE REALLY...
...THINK NOTHING OF ME?
I WANNA KNOW!
I WANNA KNOW!!!
UH... THANKS FOR PLAYING WITH ME TODAY!
THANKS-SSHI!

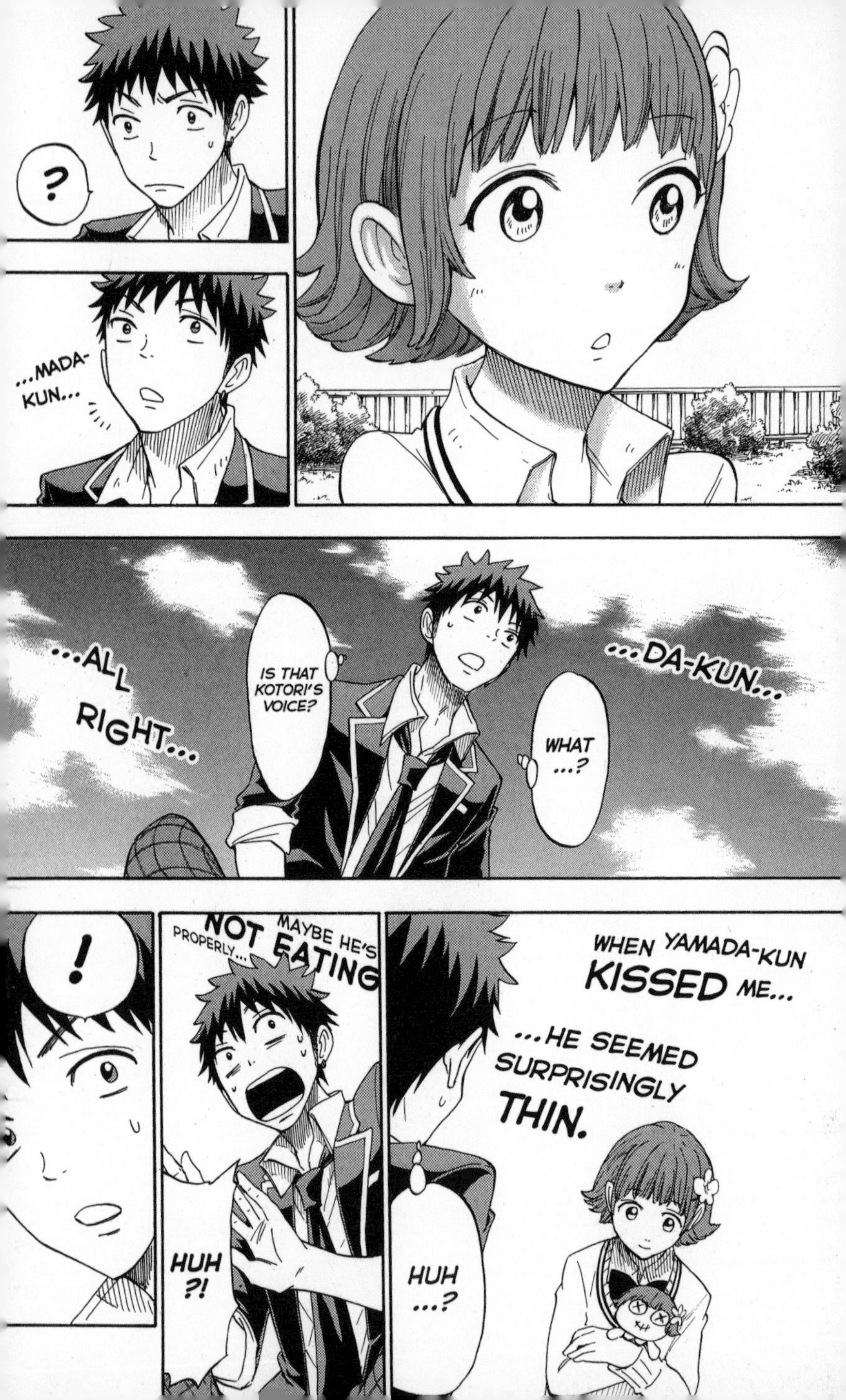
?
...MADA-KUN...
...DA-KUN...
WHAT ...?
IS THAT KOTORI'S VOICE?
...ALL RIGHT...
WHEN YAMADA-KUN KISSED ME...
...HE SEEMED SURPRISINGLY THIN.
HUH ...?
MAYBE HE'S NOT EATING PROPERLY...
HUH ?!
!

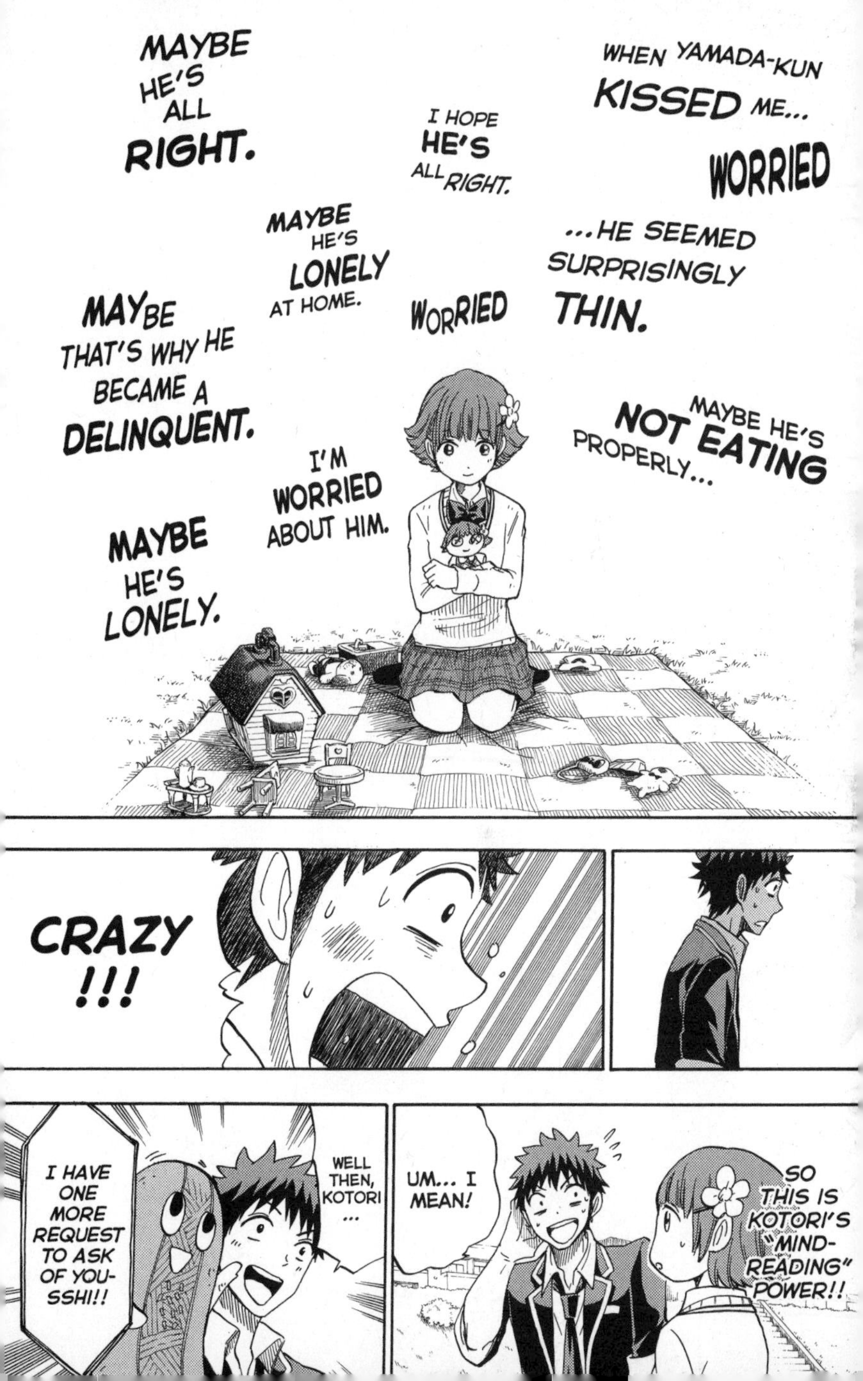
WHEN YAMADA-KUN KISSED ME...
WORRIED
I HOPE HE'S ALL RIGHT.
MAYBE HE'S ALL RIGHT.
...HE SEEMED SURPRISINGLY THIN.
WORRIED
MAYBE HE'S LONELY AT HOME.
MAYBE THAT'S WHY HE BECAME A DELINQUENT.
MAYBE HE'S NOT EATING PROPERLY...
I'M WORRIED ABOUT HIM.
MAYBE HE'S LONELY.
CRAZY !!!
SO THIS IS KOTORI'S "MIND-READING" POWER!!
UM... I MEAN!
WELL THEN, KOTORI ...
I HAVE ONE MORE REQUEST TO ASK OF YOU-SSHI!!

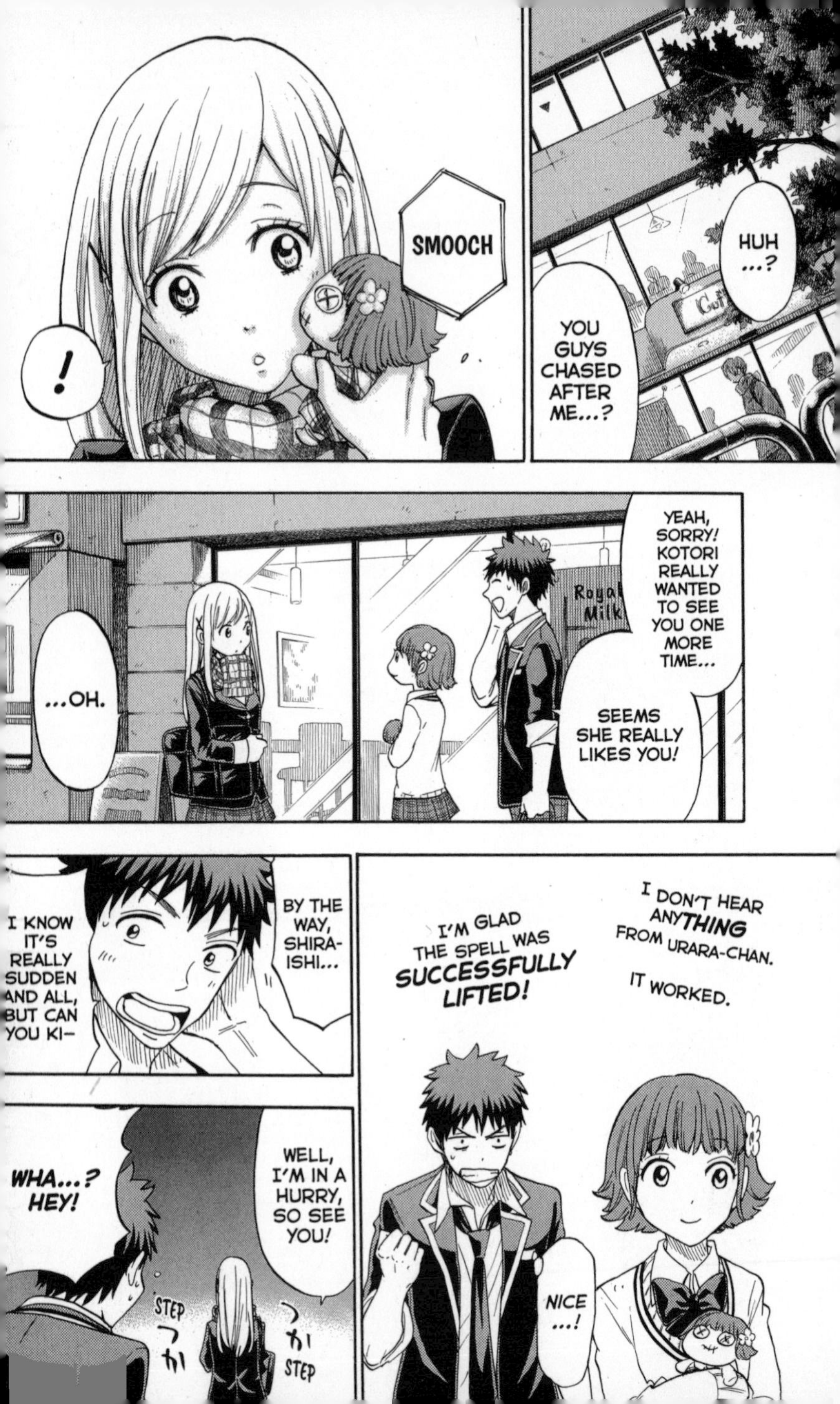
HUH ...?
YOU GUYS CHASED AFTER ME...?
SMOOCH
!
YEAH, SORRY! KOTORI REALLY WANTED TO SEE YOU ONE MORE TIME...
SEEMS SHE REALLY LIKES YOU!
...OH.
I DON'T HEAR ANY*THING* FROM URARA-CHAN.
IT WORKED.
I'M GLAD THE SPELL WAS **SUCCESSFULLY LIFTED!**
NICE ...!
BY THE WAY, SHIRA-ISHI...
I KNOW IT'S REALLY SUDDEN AND ALL, BUT CAN YOU KI–
WELL, I'M IN A HURRY, SO SEE YOU!
WHA...? HEY!
つか STEP
STEP つか

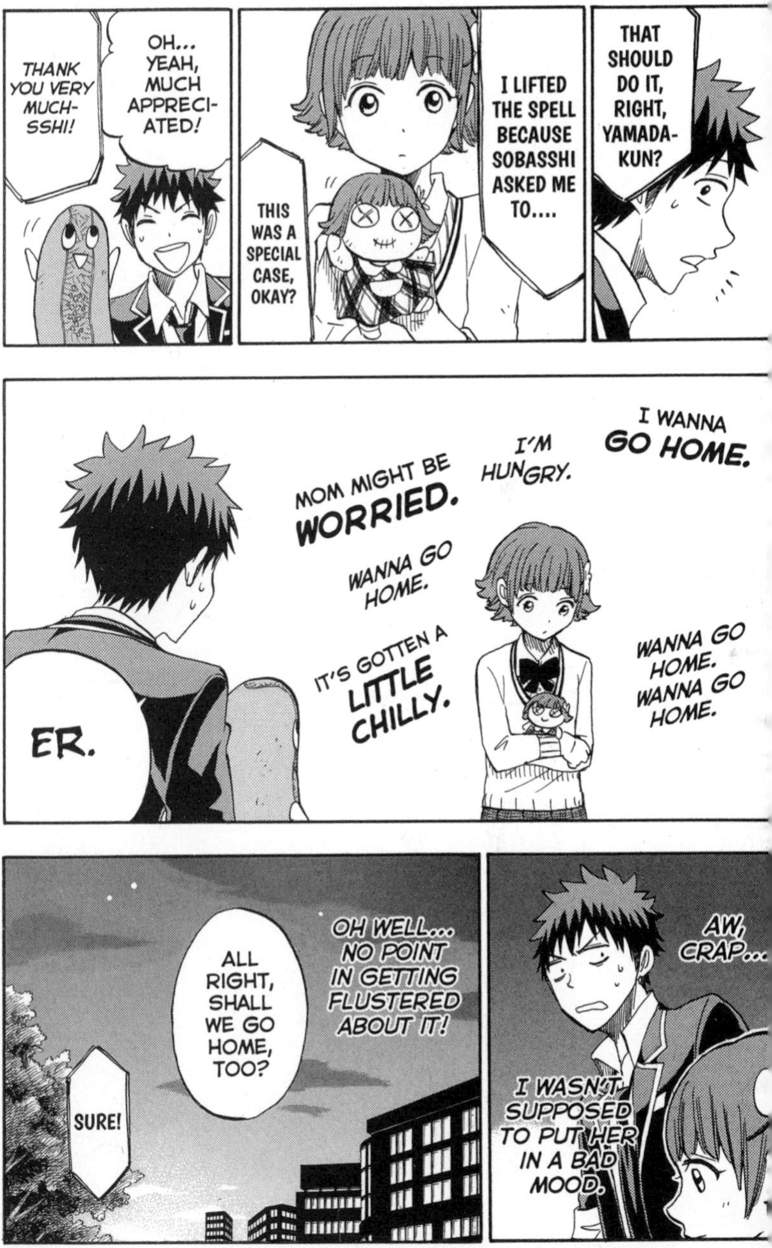
THAT SHOULD DO IT, RIGHT, YAMADA-KUN?
I LIFTED THE SPELL BECAUSE SOBASSHI ASKED ME TO....
THIS WAS A SPECIAL CASE, OKAY?
OH... YEAH, MUCH APPRECIATED!
THANK YOU VERY MUCH-SSHI!
I WANNA GO HOME.
I'M HUNGRY.
MOM MIGHT BE WORRIED.
WANNA GO HOME.
WANNA GO HOME. WANNA GO HOME.
IT'S GOTTEN A LITTLE CHILLY.
ER.
AW, CRAP...
I WASN'T SUPPOSED TO PUT HER IN A BAD MOOD.
OH WELL... NO POINT IN GETTING FLUSTERED ABOUT IT!
ALL RIGHT, SHALL WE GO HOME, TOO?
SURE!

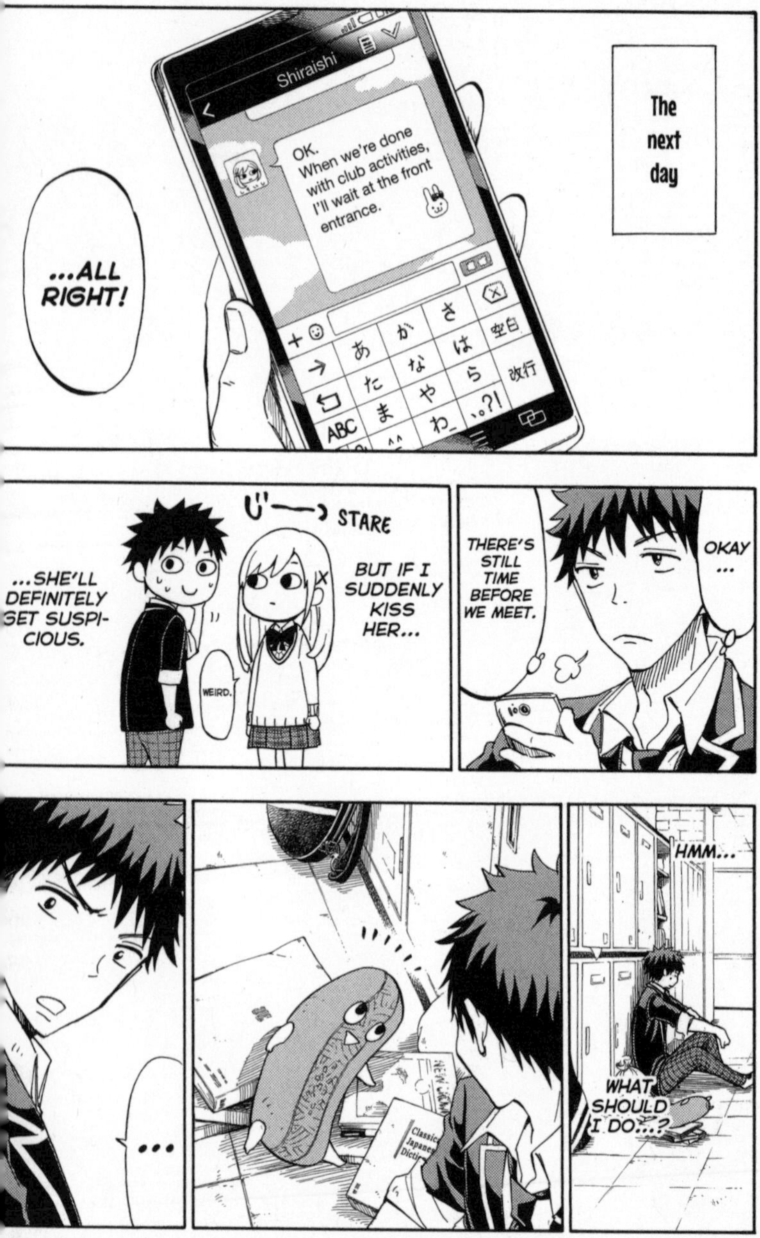
The next day
Shiraishi
OK.
When we're done with club activities, I'll wait at the front entrance.
...ALL RIGHT!
OKAY...
THERE'S STILL TIME BEFORE WE MEET.
BUT IF I SUDDENLY KISS HER...
じーっ STARE
...SHE'LL DEFINITELY GET SUSPICIOUS.
WEIRD.
HMM...
WHAT SHOULD I DO...?
...

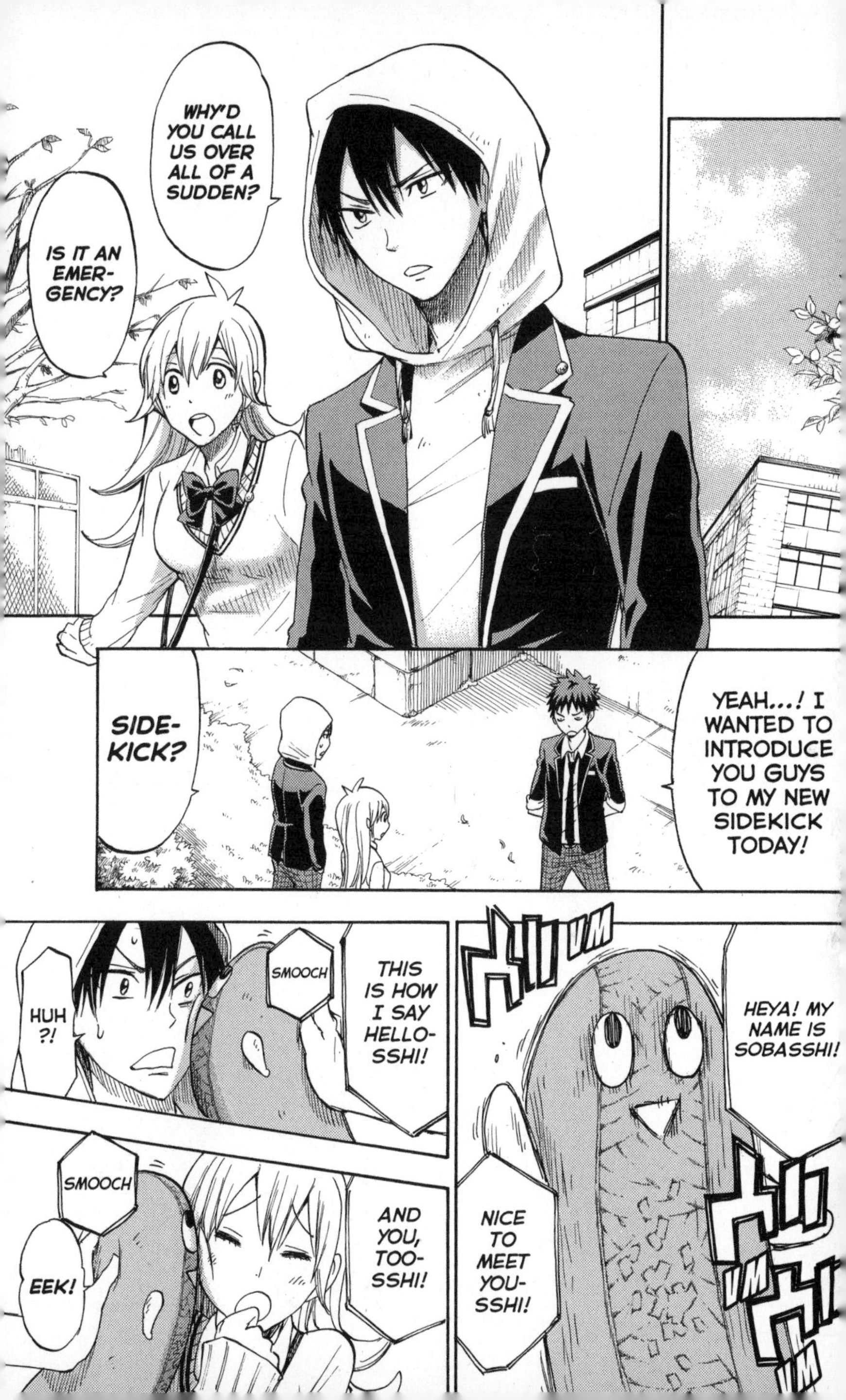
WHY'D YOU CALL US OVER ALL OF A SUDDEN?
IS IT AN EMERGENCY?
YEAH...! I WANTED TO INTRODUCE YOU GUYS TO MY NEW SIDEKICK TODAY!
SIDE-KICK?
HEYA! MY NAME IS SOBASSHI!
NICE TO MEET YOU-SSHI!
THIS IS HOW I SAY HELLO-SSHI!
SMOOCH
HUH?!
AND YOU, TOO-SSHI!
SMOOCH
EEK!

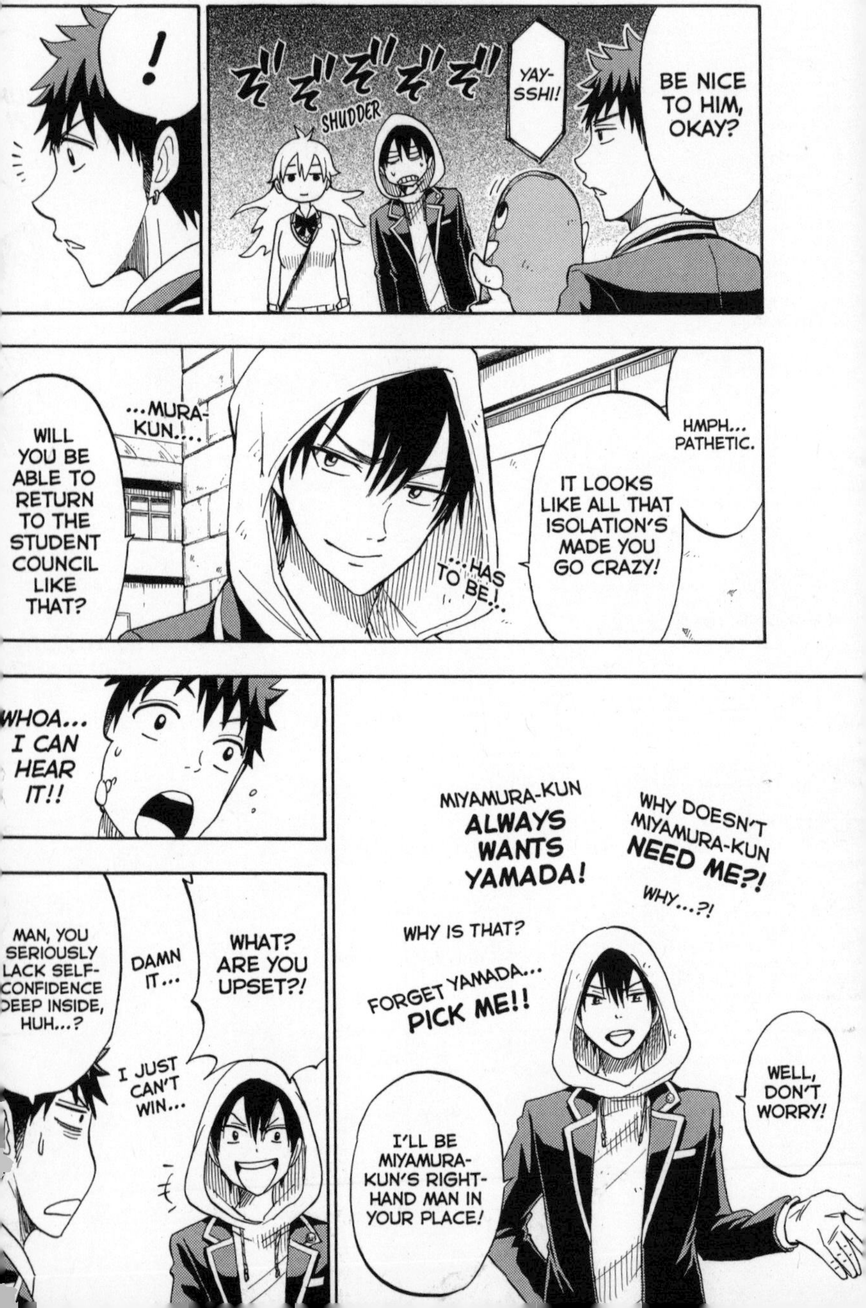
BE NICE TO HIM, OKAY?
YAY-SSHI!
ぞぞぞぞぞ
SHUDDER
!
HMPH... PATHETIC.
IT LOOKS LIKE ALL THAT ISOLATION'S MADE YOU GO CRAZY!
...HAS TO BE...
...MURA-KUN...
WILL YOU BE ABLE TO RETURN TO THE STUDENT COUNCIL LIKE THAT?
WHY DOESN'T MIYAMURA-KUN NEED ME?!
MIYAMURA-KUN ALWAYS WANTS YAMADA!
WHY...?!
WHY IS THAT?
FORGET YAMADA... PICK ME!!
WELL, DON'T WORRY!
I'LL BE MIYAMURA-KUN'S RIGHT-HAND MAN IN YOUR PLACE!
WHOA... I CAN HEAR IT!!
WHAT? ARE YOU UPSET?!
DAMN IT...
I JUST CAN'T WIN...
MAN, YOU SERIOUSLY LACK SELF-CONFIDENCE DEEP INSIDE, HUH...?

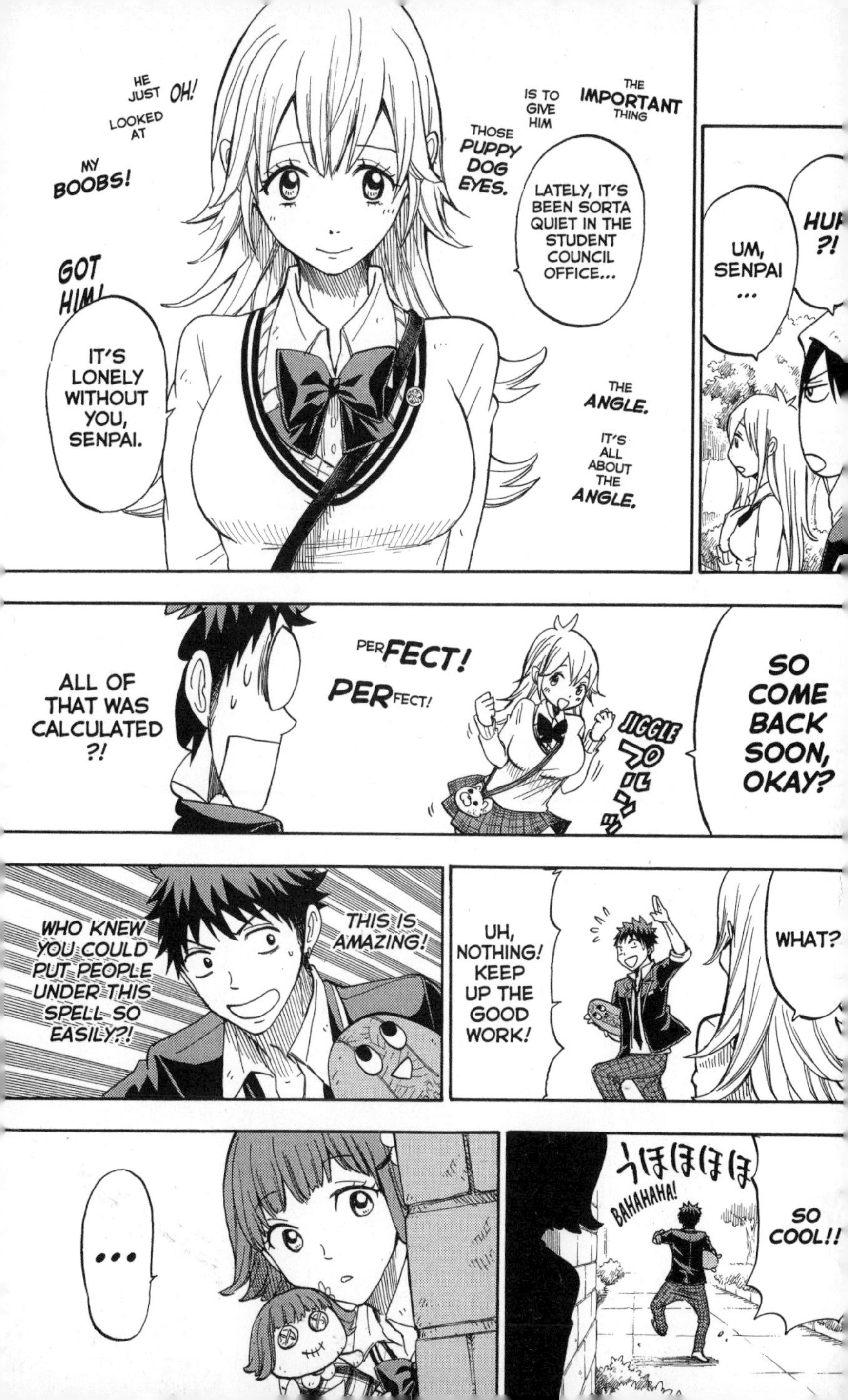

HU ?!
UM, SENPAI...
THE IMPORTANT THING IS TO GIVE HIM THOSE PUPPY DOG EYES.
LATELY, IT'S BEEN SORTA QUIET IN THE STUDENT COUNCIL OFFICE...
OH! HE JUST LOOKED AT MY BOOBS!
THE ANGLE. IT'S ALL ABOUT THE ANGLE.
GOT HIM!
IT'S LONELY WITHOUT YOU, SENPAI.
SO COME BACK SOON, OKAY?
JIGGLE
PERFECT!
PERFECT!
ALL OF THAT WAS CALCULATED ?!
WHAT?
UH, NOTHING! KEEP UP THE GOOD WORK!
THIS IS AMAZING!
WHO KNEW YOU COULD PUT PEOPLE UNDER THIS SPELL SO EASILY?!
SO COOL!!
うほほほほ
BAHAHAHA!
...

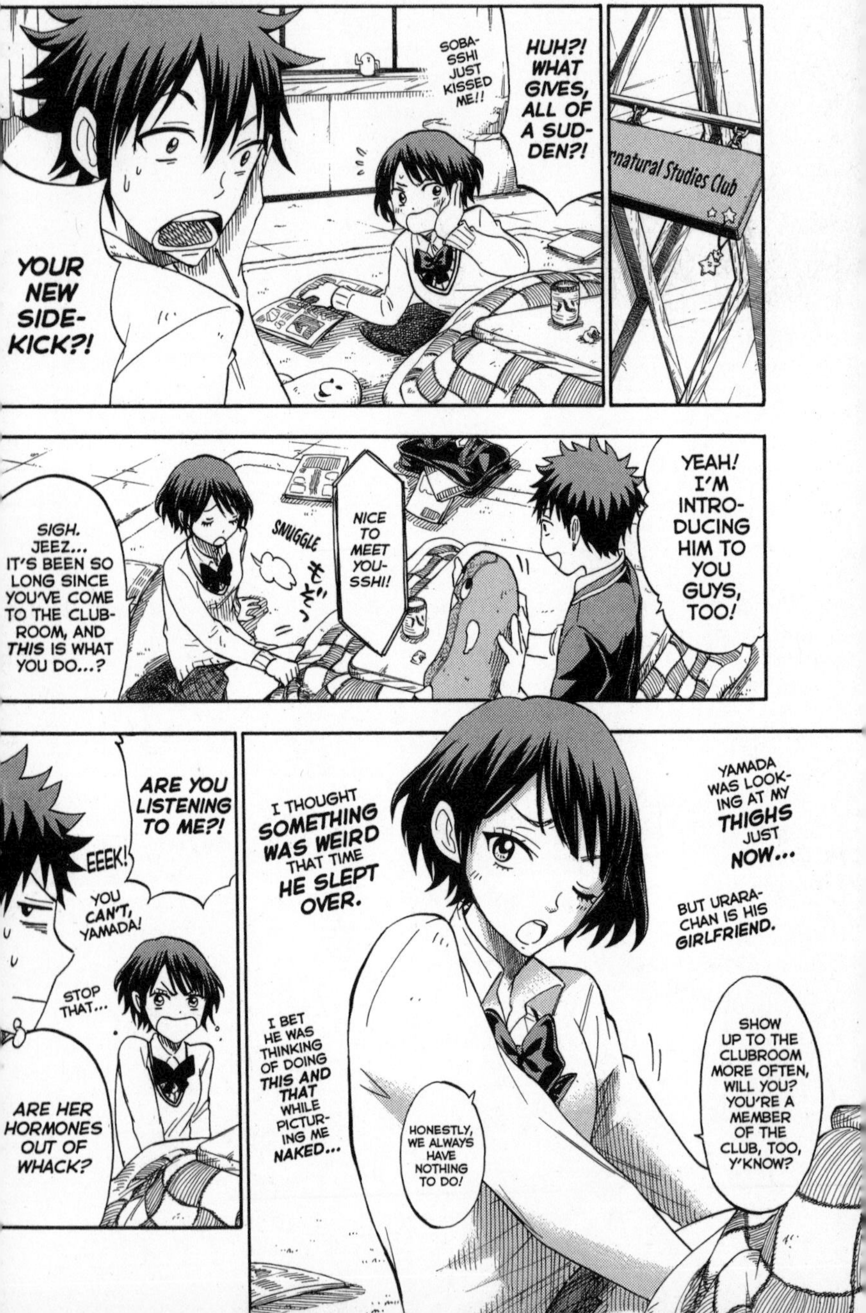
rnatural Studies Club
HUH?! WHAT GIVES, ALL OF A SUDDEN?!
SOBA-SSHI JUST KISSED ME!!
YOUR NEW SIDE-KICK?!
YEAH! I'M INTRODUCING HIM TO YOU GUYS, TOO!
NICE TO MEET YOU-SSHI!
SNUGGLE
SIGH. JEEZ... IT'S BEEN SO LONG SINCE YOU'VE COME TO THE CLUB-ROOM, AND THIS IS WHAT YOU DO...?
YAMADA WAS LOOK-ING AT MY THIGHS JUST NOW...
BUT URARA-CHAN IS HIS GIRLFRIEND.
I THOUGHT SOMETHING WAS WEIRD THAT TIME HE SLEPT OVER.
SHOW UP TO THE CLUBROOM MORE OFTEN, WILL YOU? YOU'RE A MEMBER OF THE CLUB, TOO, Y'KNOW?
HONESTLY, WE ALWAYS HAVE NOTHING TO DO!
I BET HE WAS THINKING OF DOING THIS AND THAT WHILE PICTUR-ING ME NAKED...
ARE YOU LISTENING TO ME?!
EEEK!
YOU CAN'T, YAMADA!
STOP THAT...
ARE HER HORMONES OUT OF WHACK?

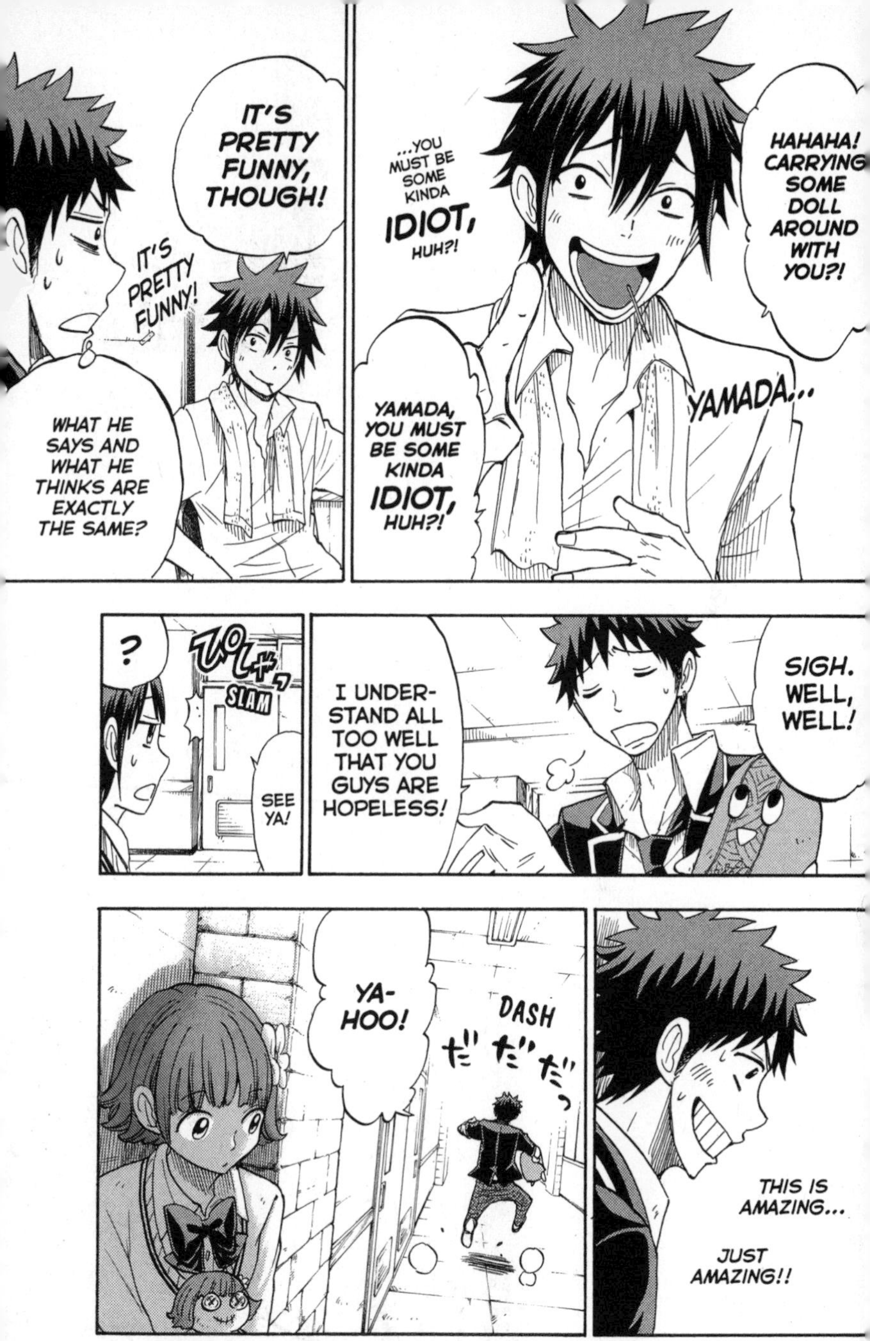

HAHAHA! CARRYING SOME DOLL AROUND WITH YOU?!
...YOU MUST BE SOME KINDA IDIOT, HUH?!
YAMADA...
YAMADA, YOU MUST BE SOME KINDA IDIOT, HUH?!
IT'S PRETTY FUNNY, THOUGH!
IT'S PRETTY FUNNY!
WHAT HE SAYS AND WHAT HE THINKS ARE EXACTLY THE SAME?
SIGH. WELL, WELL!
I UNDER-STAND ALL TOO WELL THAT YOU GUYS ARE HOPELESS!
ぴしゃっ
SLAM
?
SEE YA!
THIS IS AMAZING...
JUST AMAZING!!
YA-HOO!
DASH
だだだっ

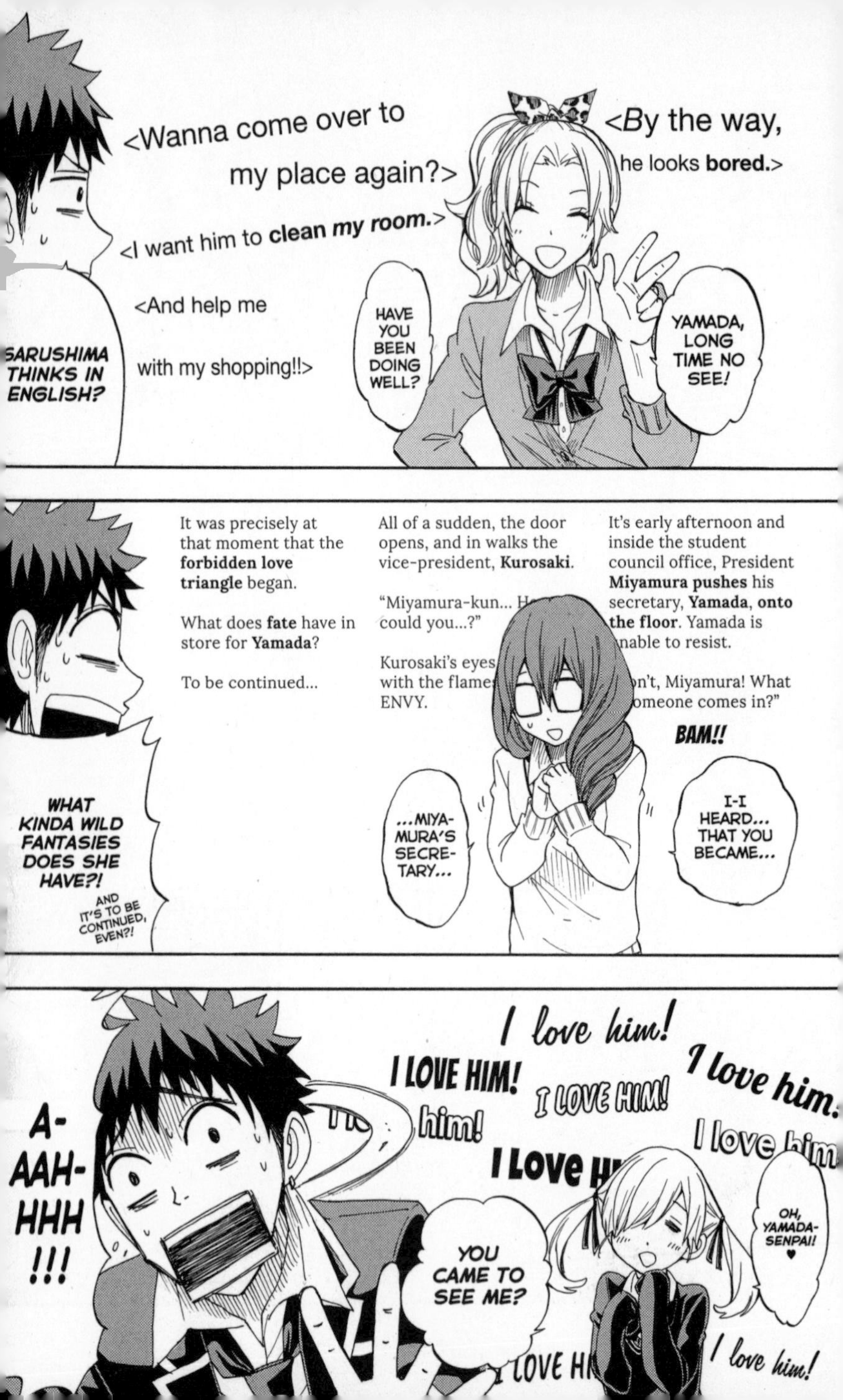

YAMADA, LONG TIME NO SEE!
<By the way, he looks **bored.**>
HAVE YOU BEEN DOING WELL?
<Wanna come over to my place again?>
<I want him to **clean my room.**>
<And help me with my shopping!!>
SARUSHIMA THINKS IN ENGLISH?
It's early afternoon and inside the student council office, President **Miyamura pushes** his secretary, **Yamada, onto the floor**. Yamada is nable to resist.
n't, Miyamura! What omeone comes in?"
BAM!!
I-I HEARD... THAT YOU BECAME...
...MIYAMURA'S SECRETARY...
All of a sudden, the door opens, and in walks the vice-president, **Kurosaki**.
"Miyamura-kun... H could you...?"
Kurosaki's eyes with the flame ENVY.
It was precisely at that moment that the **forbidden love triangle** began.
What does **fate** have in store for **Yamada**?
To be continued...
WHAT KINDA WILD FANTASIES DOES SHE HAVE?!
AND IT'S TO BE CONTINUED, EVEN?!
OH, YAMADA-SENPAI! ♥
I love him!
I love him.
I LOVE HIM!
I love him
I LOVE HIM!
him!
I Love H
YOU CAME TO SEE ME?
I love him!
LOVE H
A-AAH-HHH!!!

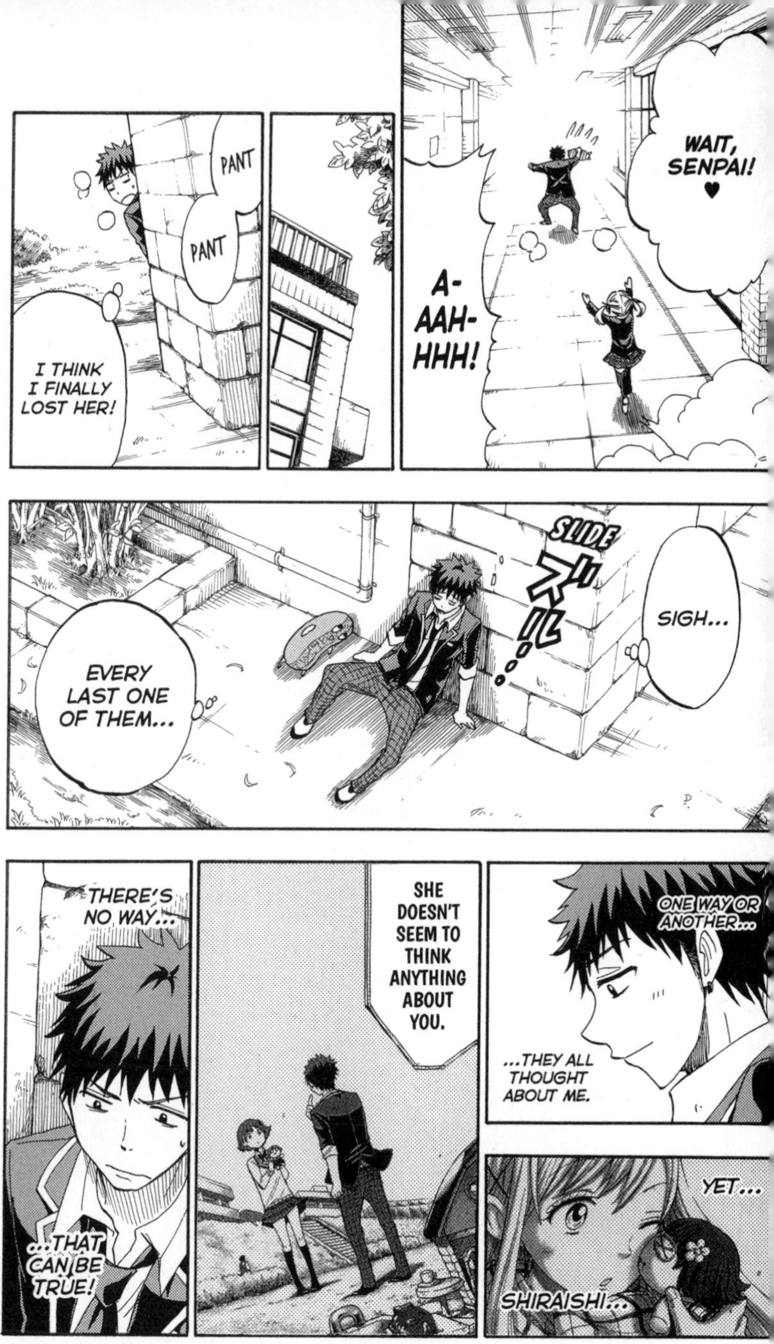
WAIT, SENPAI! ♥
A-AAH-HHH!
PANT
PANT
I THINK I FINALLY LOST HER!
SLIDE
SIGH...
EVERY LAST ONE OF THEM...
ONE WAY OR ANOTHER...
...THEY ALL THOUGHT ABOUT ME.
YET...
SHIRAISHI...
SHE DOESN'T SEEM TO THINK ANYTHING ABOUT YOU.
THERE'S NO WAY...
...THAT CAN BE TRUE!

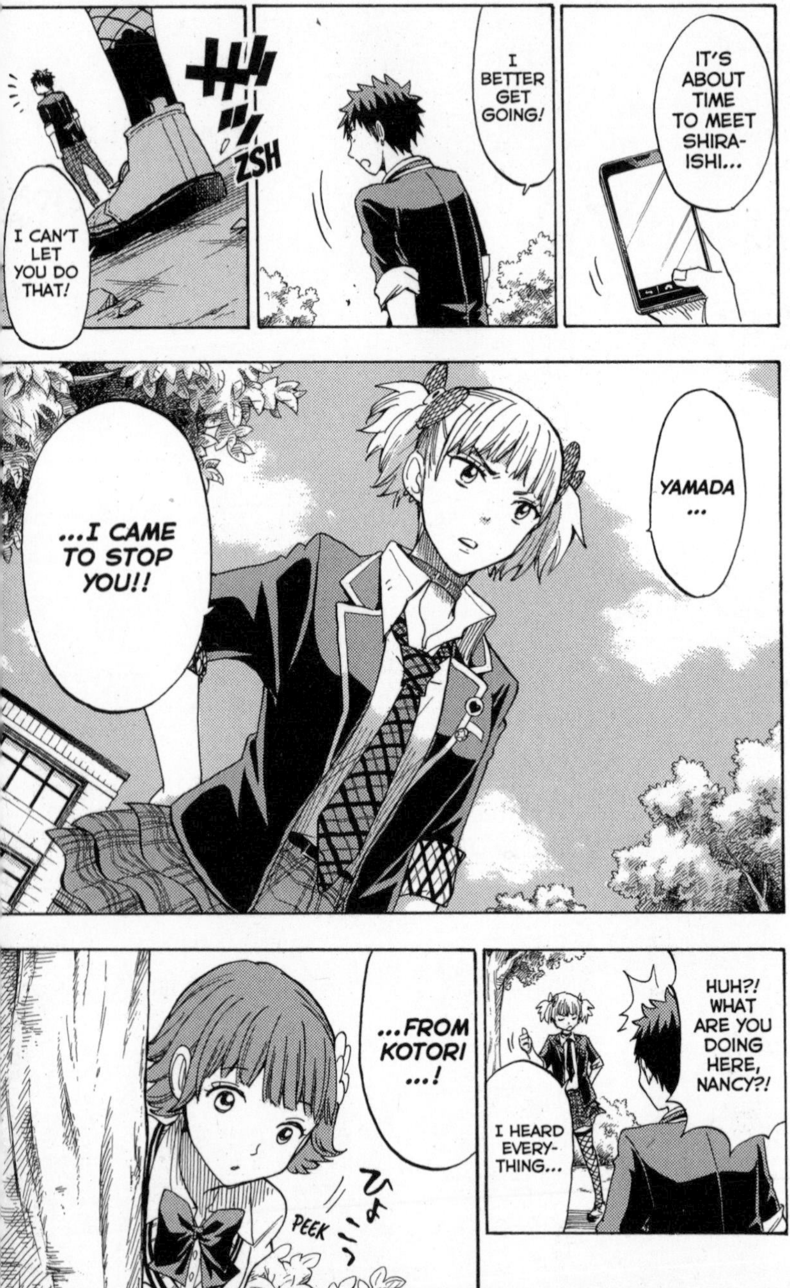
IT'S ABOUT TIME TO MEET SHIRA-ISHI...
I BETTER GET GOING!
ZSH
I CAN'T LET YOU DO THAT!
YAMADA...
...I CAME TO STOP YOU!!
HUH?! WHAT ARE YOU DOING HERE, NANCY?!
I HEARD EVERY-THING...
...FROM KOTORI...!
ひょこっ
PEEK

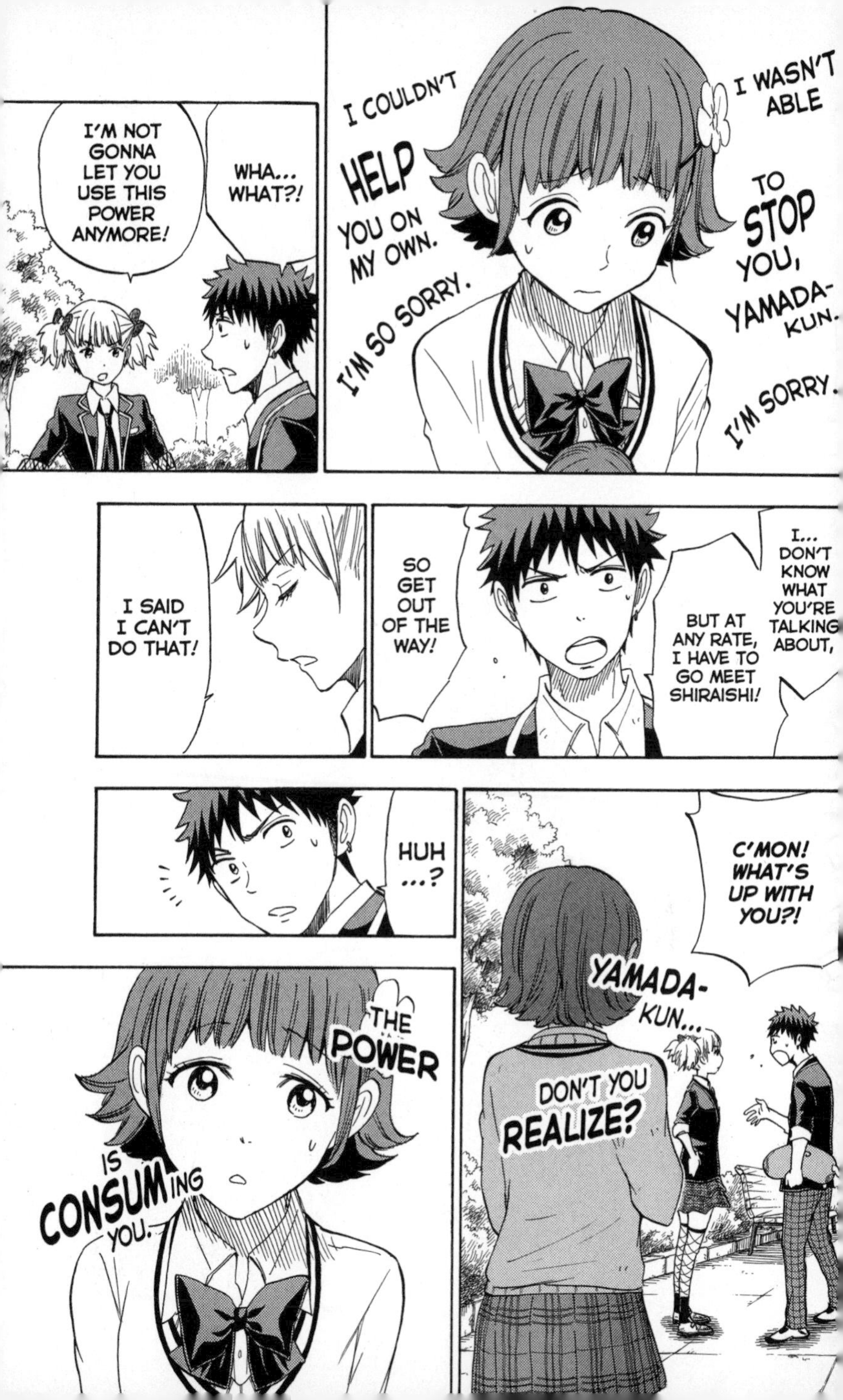
I WASN'T ABLE TO STOP YOU, YAMADA-KUN.
I'M SORRY.
I COULDN'T HELP YOU ON MY OWN.
I'M SO SORRY.
WHA... WHAT?!
I'M NOT GONNA LET YOU USE THIS POWER ANYMORE!
I... DON'T KNOW WHAT YOU'RE TALKING ABOUT,
BUT AT ANY RATE, I HAVE TO GO MEET SHIRAISHI!
SO GET OUT OF THE WAY!
I SAID I CAN'T DO THAT!
C'MON! WHAT'S UP WITH YOU?!
YAMADA-KUN...
DON'T YOU REALIZE?
HUH ...?
THE POWER
IS CONSUMING YOU.

I gotta know.
WHA...
Shiraishi...
re's no way...
I gotta know.
I wanna know.
Could she
I wanna know.
I gotta know.
Shiraishi...
I gotta know.
hiraishi
ta
WHAT ARE YOU TALKING ABOUT...?

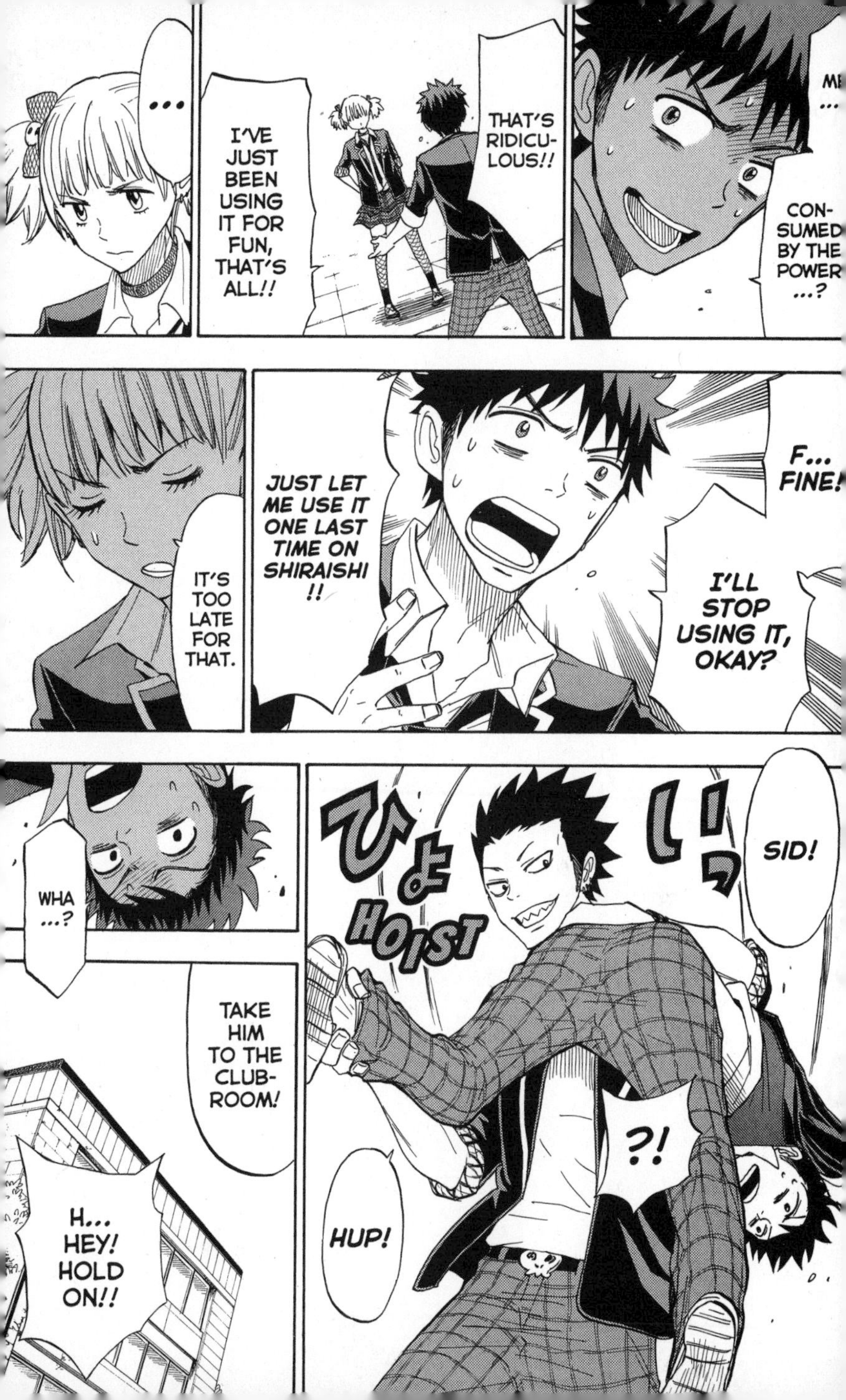
CON-SUMED BY THE POWER ...?
THAT'S RIDICU-LOUS!!
I'VE JUST BEEN USING IT FOR FUN, THAT'S ALL!!
...
F... FINE!
I'LL STOP USING IT, OKAY?
JUST LET ME USE IT ONE LAST TIME ON SHIRAISHI !!
IT'S TOO LATE FOR THAT.
SID!
ひょい
HOIST
?!
HUP!
WHA ...?
TAKE HIM TO THE CLUB-ROOM!
H... HEY! HOLD ON!!

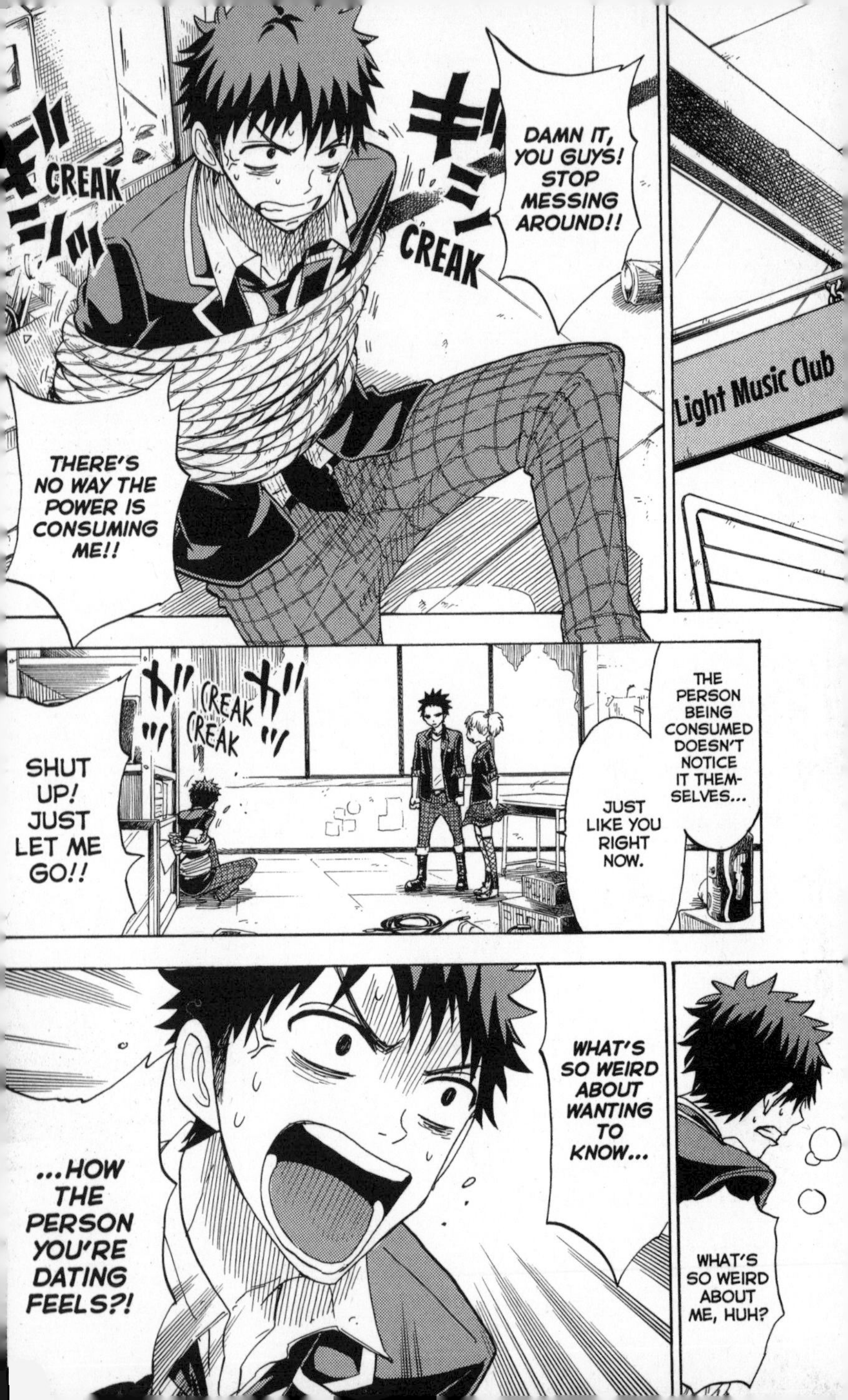
DAMN IT, YOU GUYS! STOP MESSING AROUND!!
Light Music Club
CREAK
CREAK
THERE'S NO WAY THE POWER IS CONSUMING ME!!
THE PERSON BEING CONSUMED DOESN'T NOTICE IT THEM-SELVES...
JUST LIKE YOU RIGHT NOW.
CREAK CREAK
SHUT UP! JUST LET ME GO!!
WHAT'S SO WEIRD ABOUT ME, HUH?
WHAT'S SO WEIRD ABOUT WANTING TO KNOW...
...HOW THE PERSON YOU'RE DATING FEELS?!

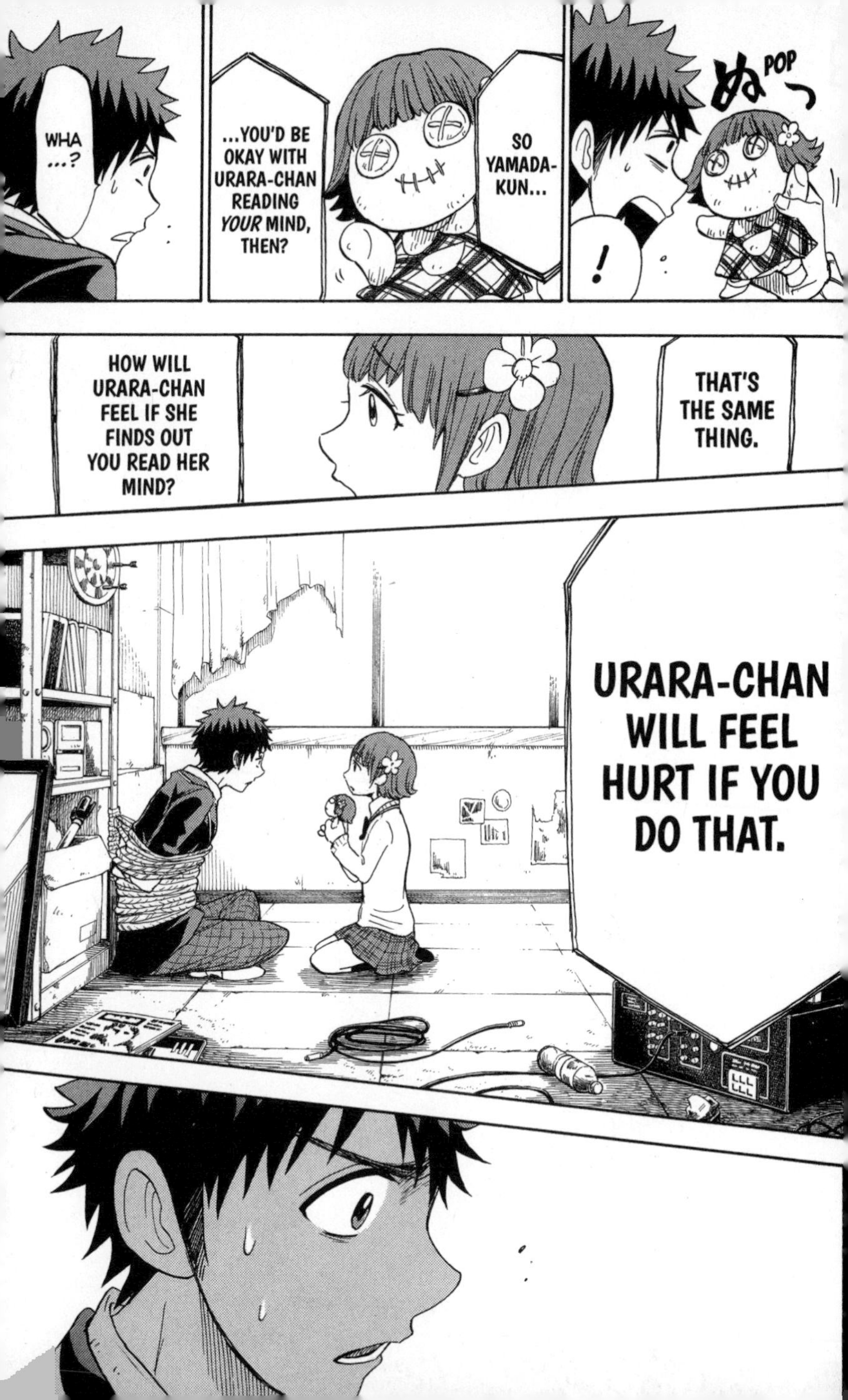
ぬ POP
!
SO YAMADA-KUN...
...YOU'D BE OKAY WITH URARA-CHAN READING *YOUR* MIND, THEN?
WHA ...?
THAT'S THE SAME THING.
HOW WILL URARA-CHAN FEEL IF SHE FINDS OUT YOU READ HER MIND?
URARA-CHAN WILL FEEL HURT IF YOU DO THAT.

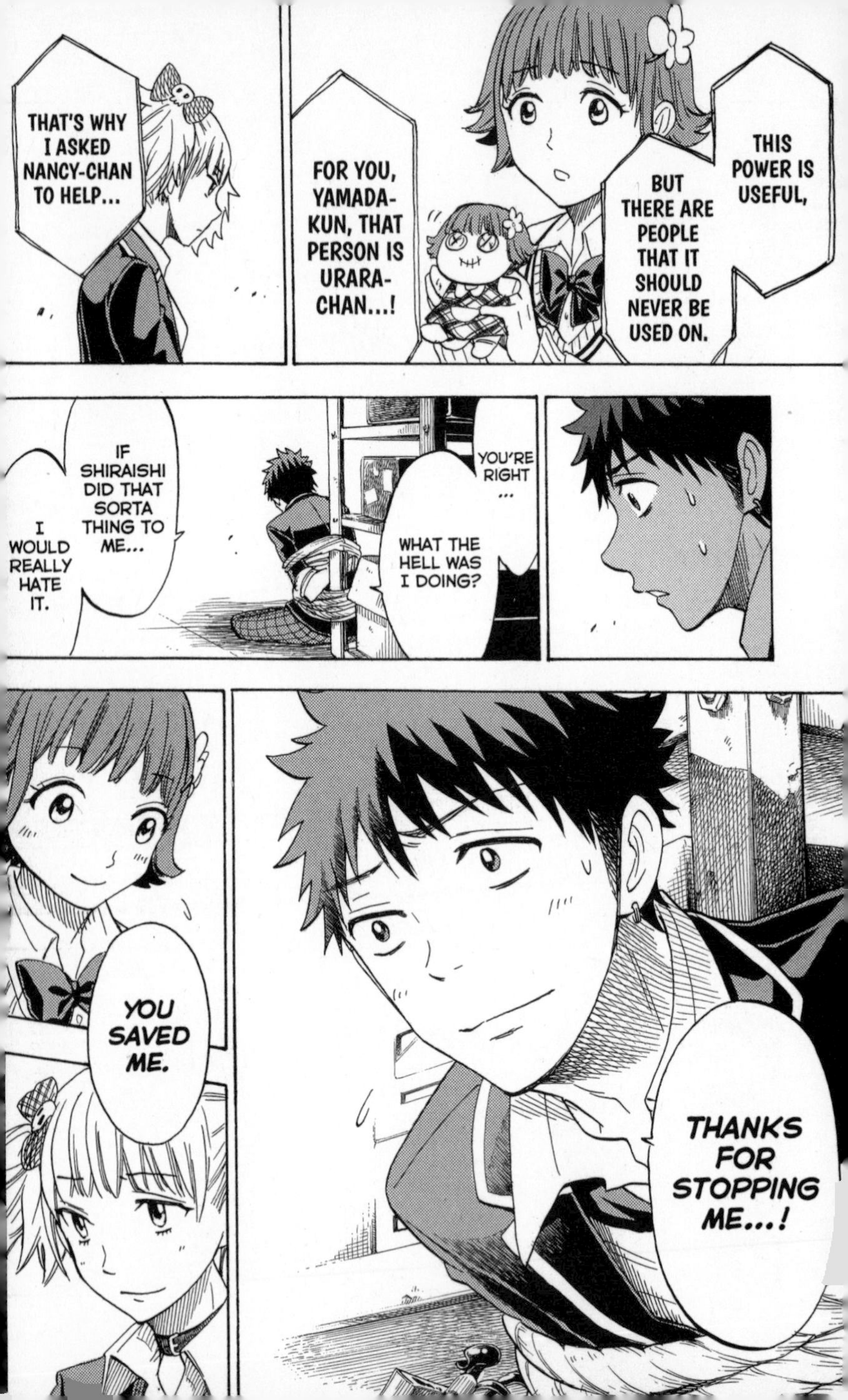
THIS POWER IS USEFUL,
BUT THERE ARE PEOPLE THAT IT SHOULD NEVER BE USED ON.
FOR YOU, YAMADA-KUN, THAT PERSON IS URARA-CHAN...!
THAT'S WHY I ASKED NANCY-CHAN TO HELP...
YOU'RE RIGHT ...
WHAT THE HELL WAS I DOING?
IF SHIRAISHI DID THAT SORTA THING TO ME...
I WOULD REALLY HATE IT.
THANKS FOR STOPPING ME...!
YOU SAVED ME.

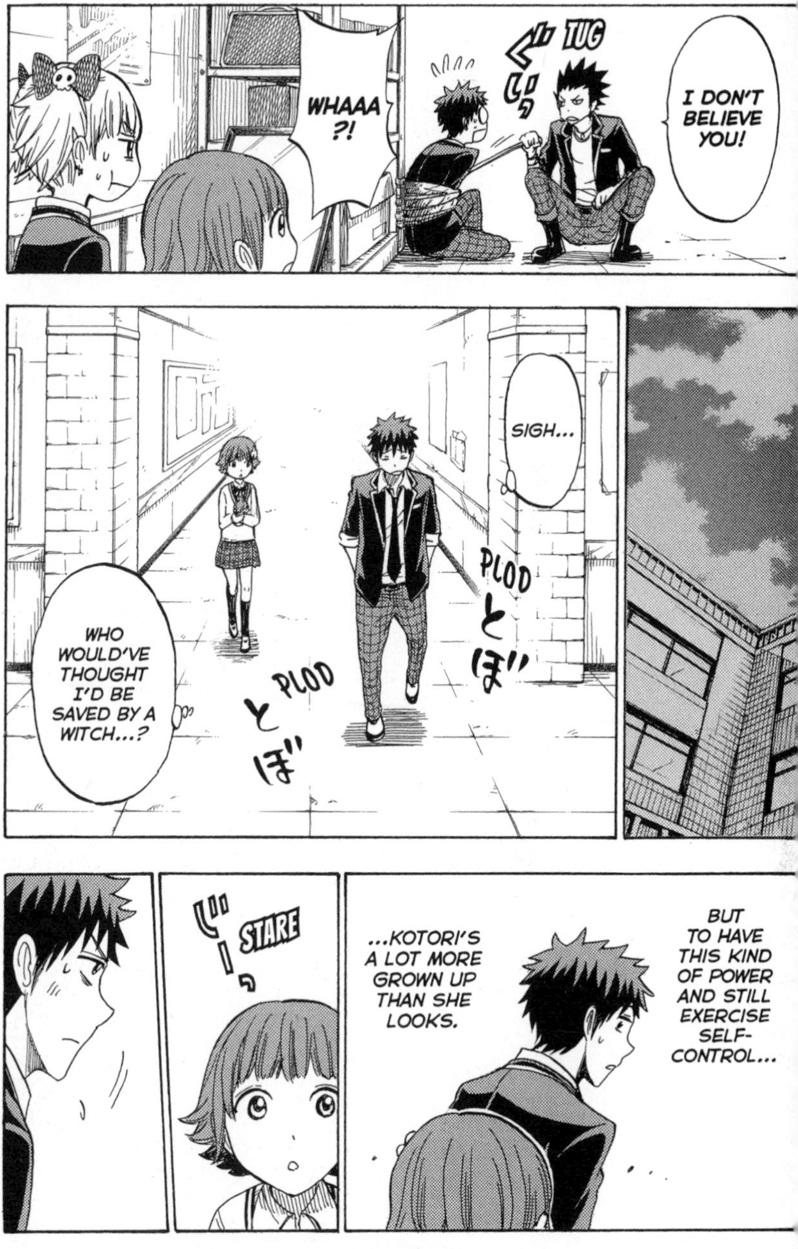
I DON'T BELIEVE YOU!
TUG
WHAAA ?!
SIGH...
PLOD
とぼ
PLOD
とぼ
WHO WOULD'VE THOUGHT I'D BE SAVED BY A WITCH...?
BUT TO HAVE THIS KIND OF POWER AND STILL EXERCISE SELF-CONTROL...
...KOTORI'S A LOT MORE GROWN UP THAN SHE LOOKS.
STARE

OH, CRAP!

I TOTALLY FORGOT ABOUT MY PROMISE TO WALK HOME WITH SHIRAISHI!

PAUSE

AH!

RUMBLE RUMBLE RUMBLE

RUMBLE

RUMBLE

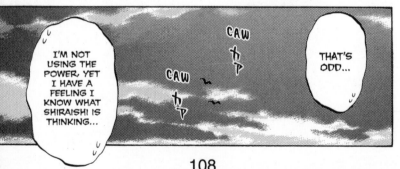

I'M NOT USING THE POWER, YET I HAVE A FEELING I KNOW WHAT SHIRAISHI IS THINKING...

CAW

CAW

THAT'S ODD...

CHAPTER 108: A sorta bittersweet alliance.

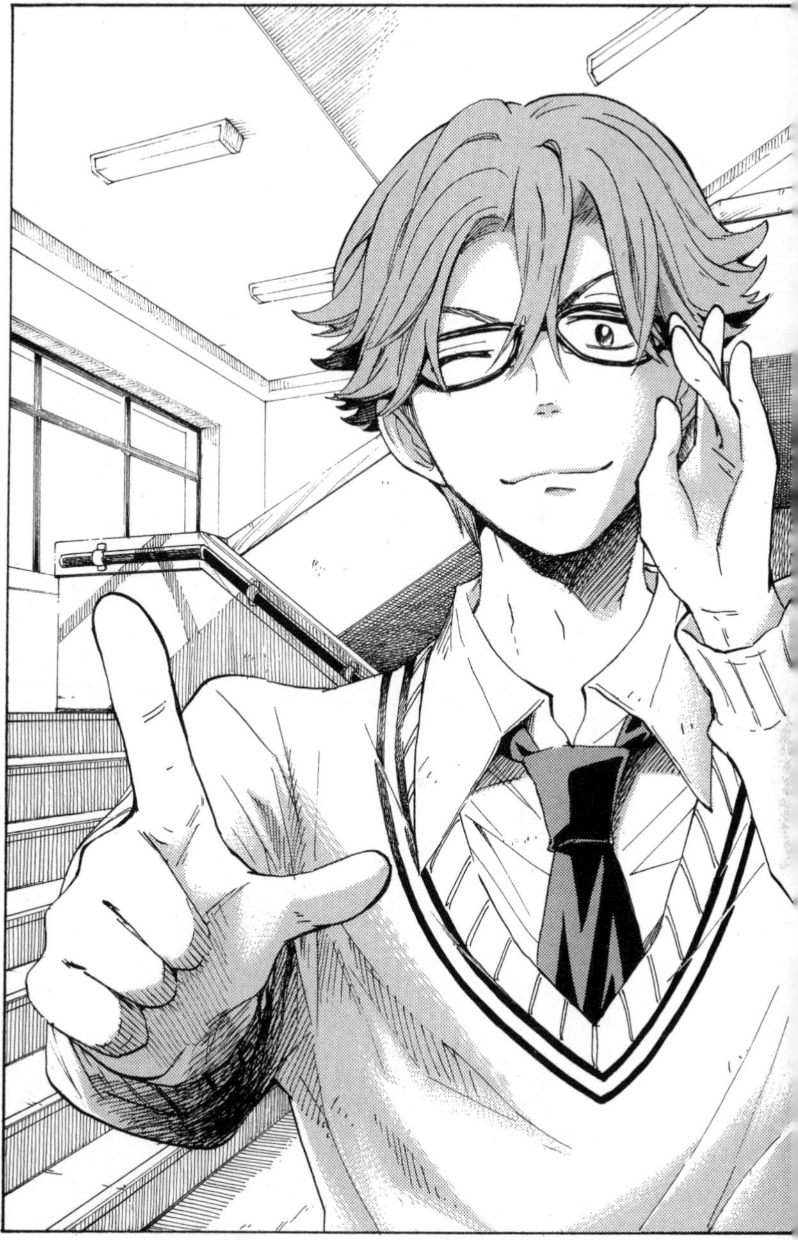

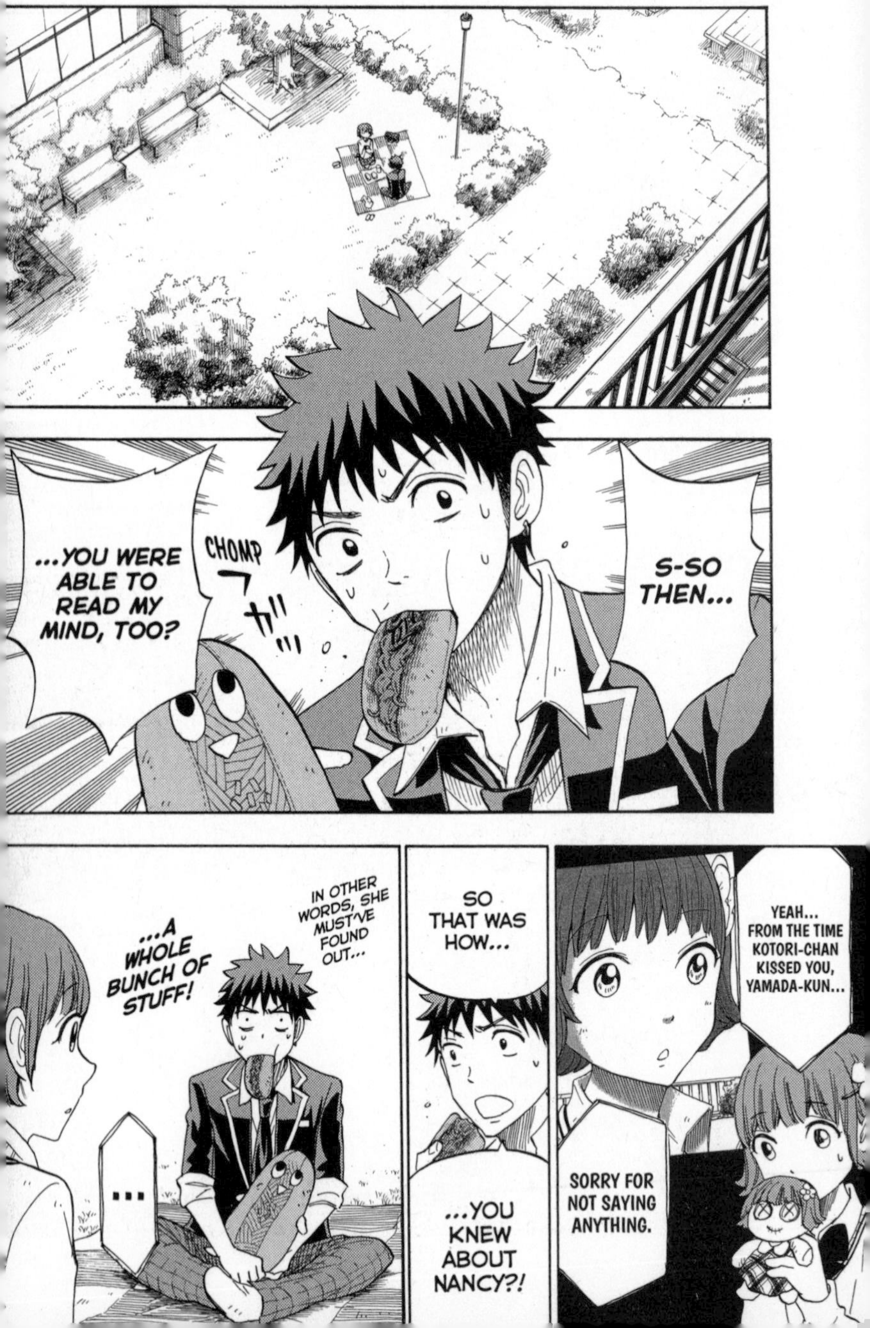
S-SO THEN...
CHOMP
...YOU WERE ABLE TO READ MY MIND, TOO?
YEAH... FROM THE TIME KOTORI-CHAN KISSED YOU, YAMADA-KUN...
SORRY FOR NOT SAYING ANYTHING.
SO THAT WAS HOW...
...YOU KNEW ABOUT NANCY?!
IN OTHER WORDS, SHE MUST'VE FOUND OUT...
...A WHOLE BUNCH OF STUFF!
...

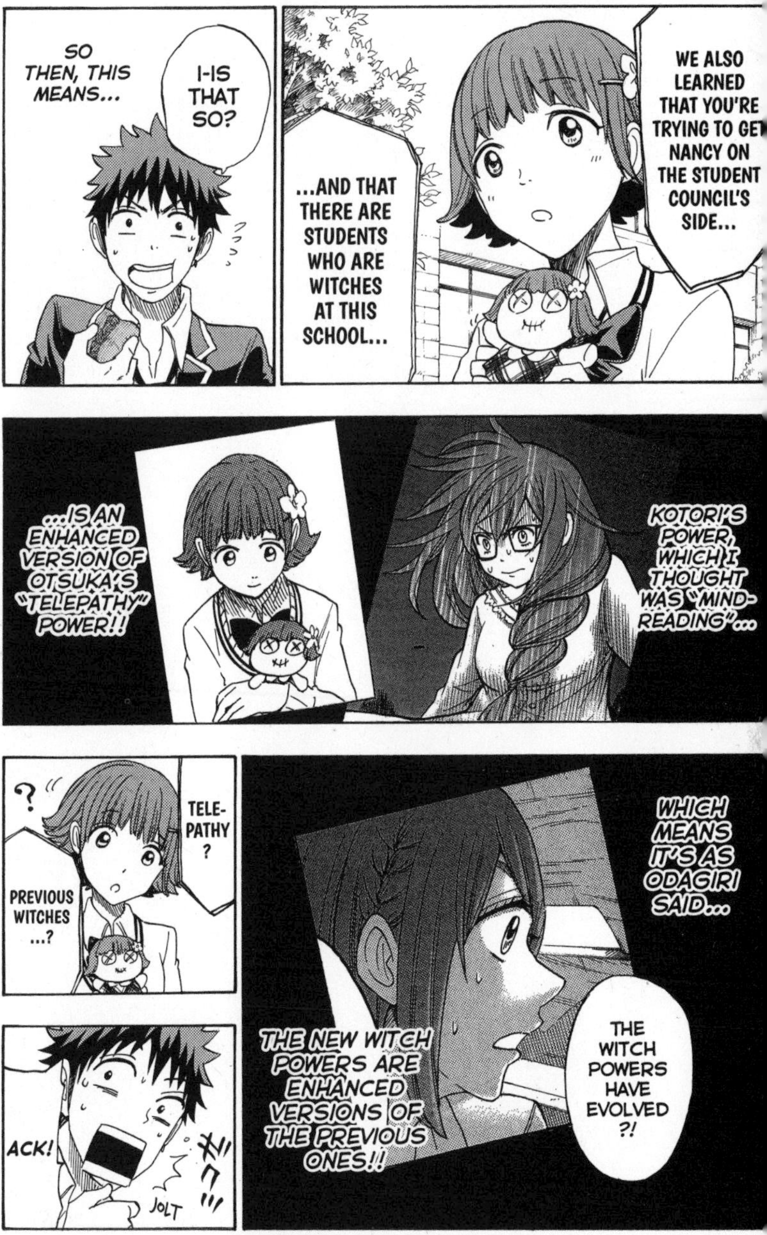
WE ALSO LEARNED THAT YOU'RE TRYING TO GET NANCY ON THE STUDENT COUNCIL'S SIDE...
...AND THAT THERE ARE STUDENTS WHO ARE WITCHES AT THIS SCHOOL...
I-IS THAT SO?
SO THEN, THIS MEANS...
KOTORI'S POWER, WHICH I THOUGHT WAS "MIND-READING"...
...IS AN ENHANCED VERSION OF OTSUKA'S "TELEPATHY" POWER!!
WHICH MEANS IT'S AS ODAGIRI SAID...
THE WITCH POWERS HAVE EVOLVED?!
THE NEW WITCH POWERS ARE ENHANCED VERSIONS OF THE PREVIOUS ONES!!
TELE-PATHY?
PREVIOUS WITCHES...?
JOLT
ACK!

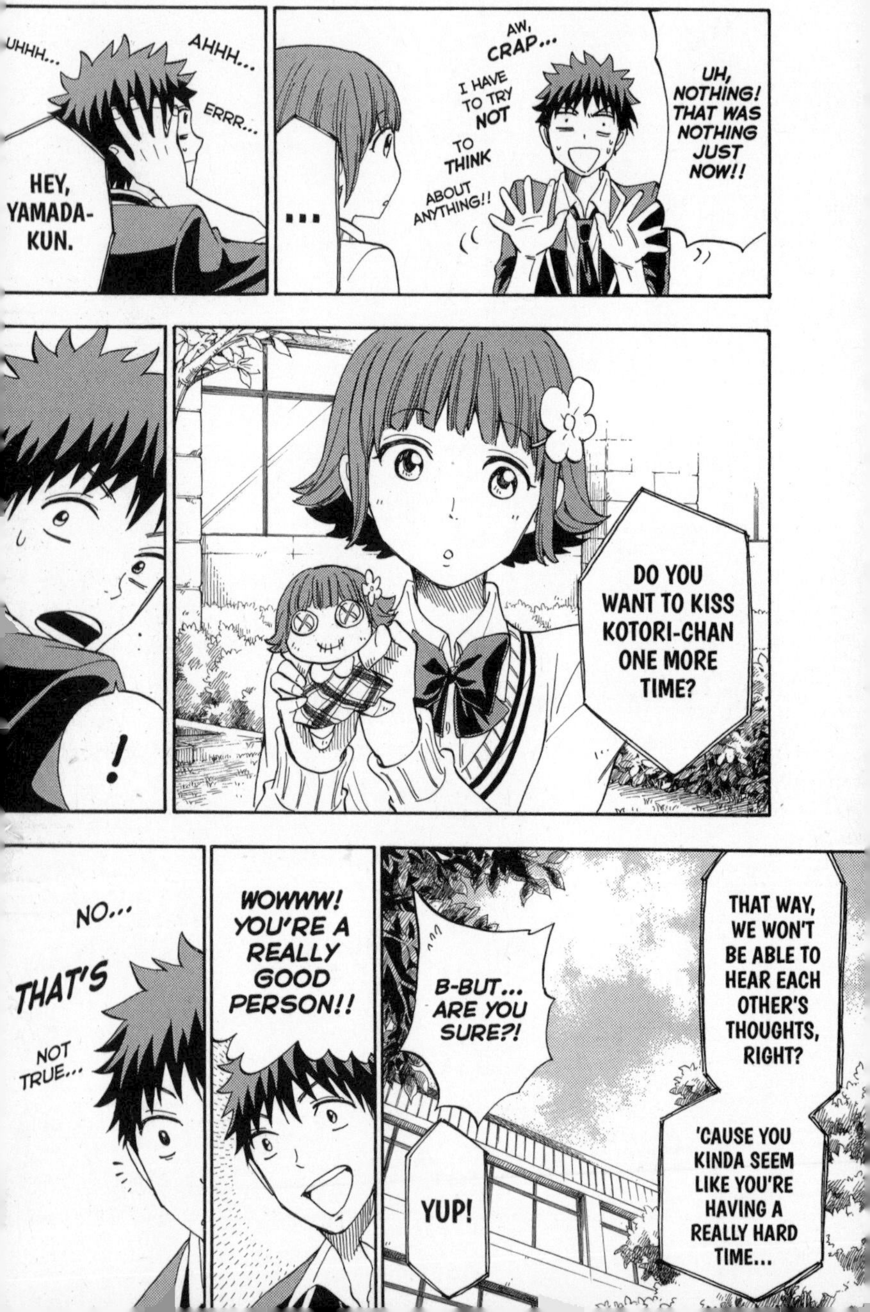
UH, NOTHING! THAT WAS NOTHING JUST NOW!!
AW, CRAP... I HAVE TO TRY NOT TO THINK ABOUT ANYTHING!!
...
AHHH...
ERRR...
UHHH...
HEY, YAMADA-KUN.
DO YOU WANT TO KISS KOTORI-CHAN ONE MORE TIME?
!
THAT WAY, WE WON'T BE ABLE TO HEAR EACH OTHER'S THOUGHTS, RIGHT?
'CAUSE YOU KINDA SEEM LIKE YOU'RE HAVING A REALLY HARD TIME...
B-BUT... ARE YOU SURE?!
YUP!
WOWWW! YOU'RE A REALLY GOOD PERSON!!
NO... THAT'S NOT TRUE...

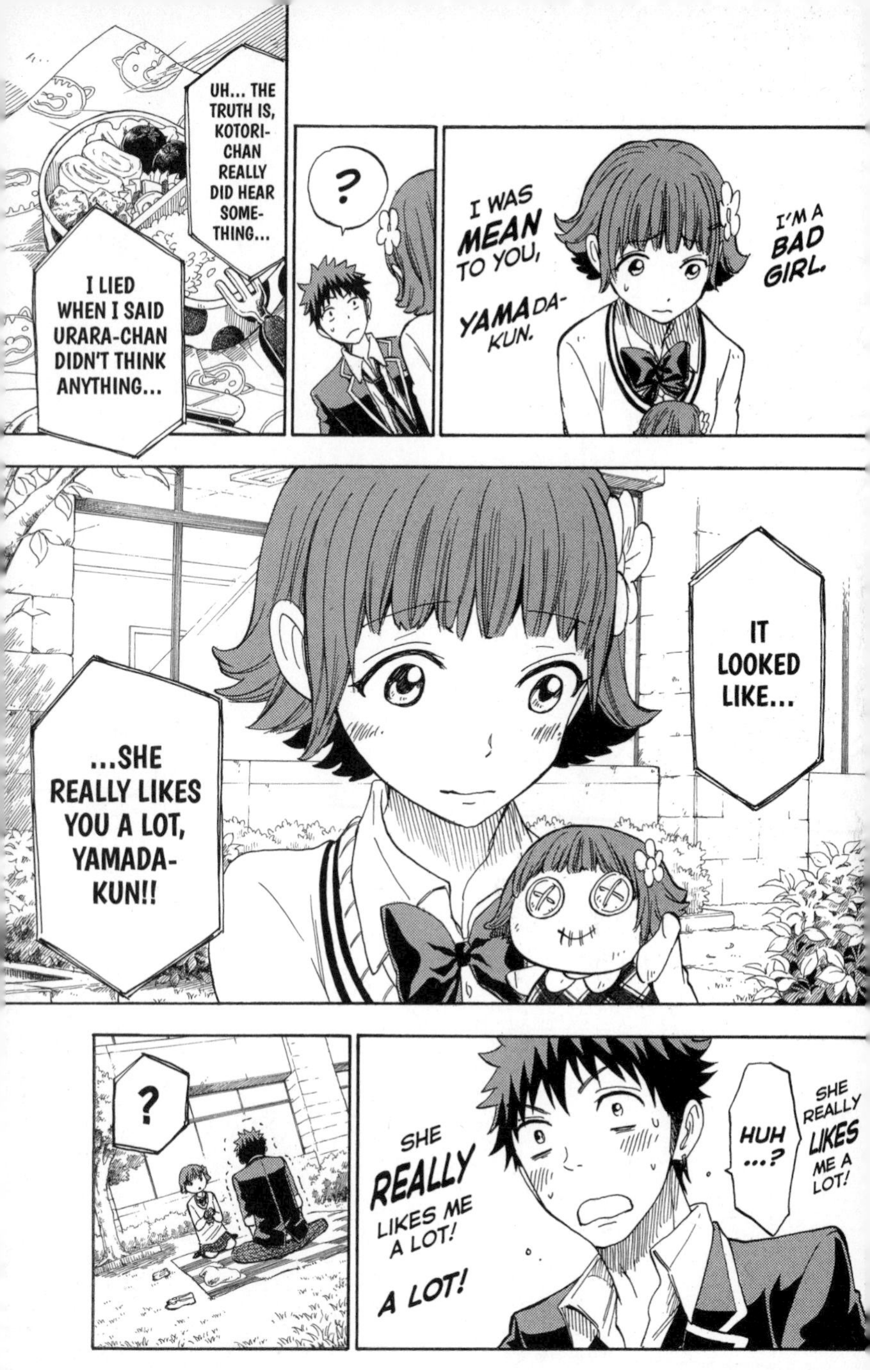
I'M A BAD GIRL.
I WAS MEAN TO YOU, YAMADA-KUN.
?
UH... THE TRUTH IS, KOTORI-CHAN REALLY DID HEAR SOME-THING...
I LIED WHEN I SAID URARA-CHAN DIDN'T THINK ANYTHING...
IT LOOKED LIKE...
...SHE REALLY LIKES YOU A LOT, YAMADA-KUN!!
SHE REALLY LIKES ME A LOT!
HUH ...?
SHE REALLY LIKES ME A LOT!
A LOT!
?

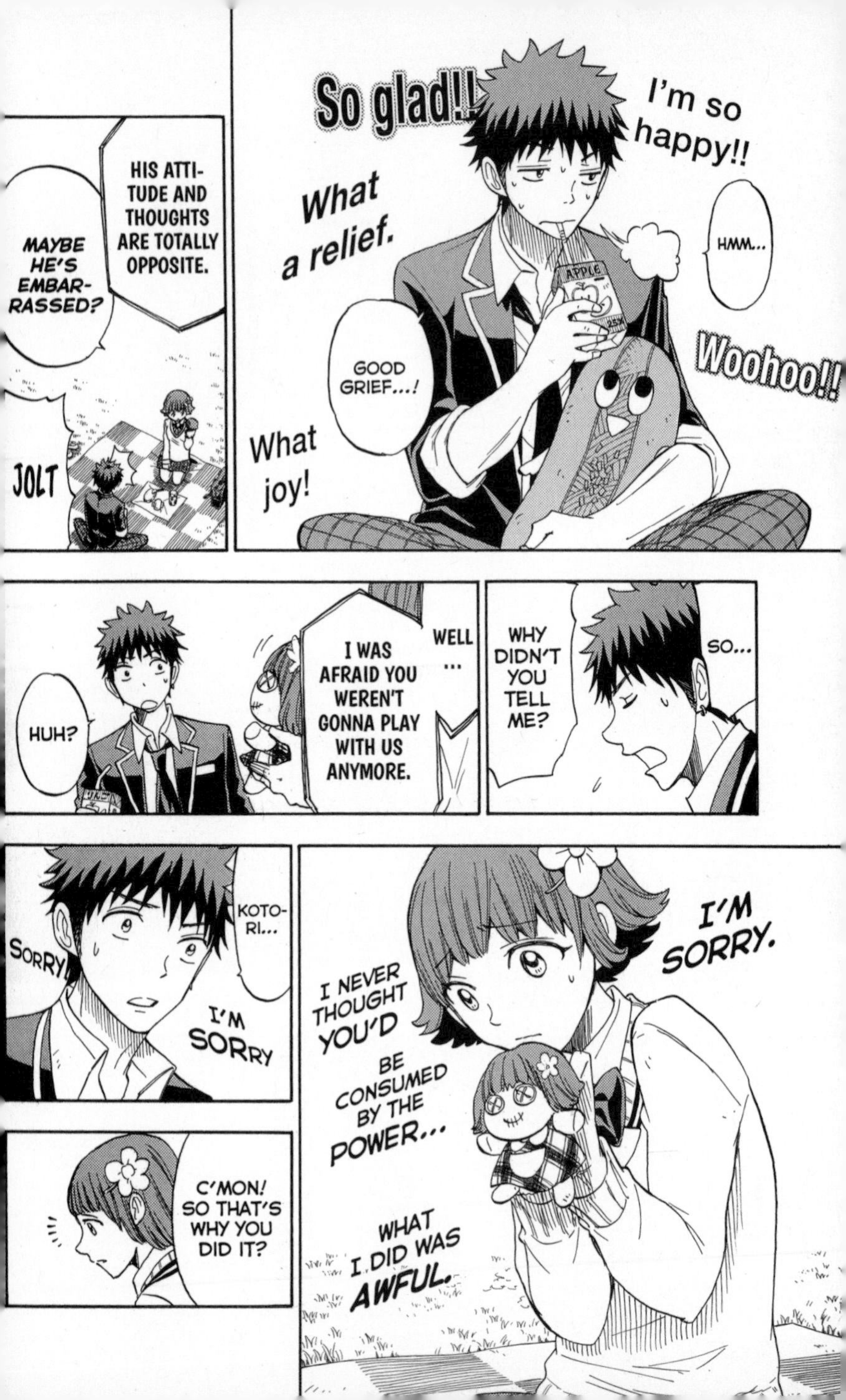
So glad!!
I'm so happy!!
HMM...
What a relief.
Woohoo!!
GOOD GRIEF...!
What joy!
HIS ATTI-TUDE AND THOUGHTS ARE TOTALLY OPPOSITE.
MAYBE HE'S EMBAR-RASSED?
JOLT
SO...
WHY DIDN'T YOU TELL ME?
WELL ...
I WAS AFRAID YOU WEREN'T GONNA PLAY WITH US ANYMORE.
HUH?
I'M SORRY.
I NEVER THOUGHT YOU'D BE CONSUMED BY THE POWER...
WHAT I DID WAS AWFUL.
KOTO-RI...
I'M SORRY
SORRY
C'MON! SO THAT'S WHY YOU DID IT?

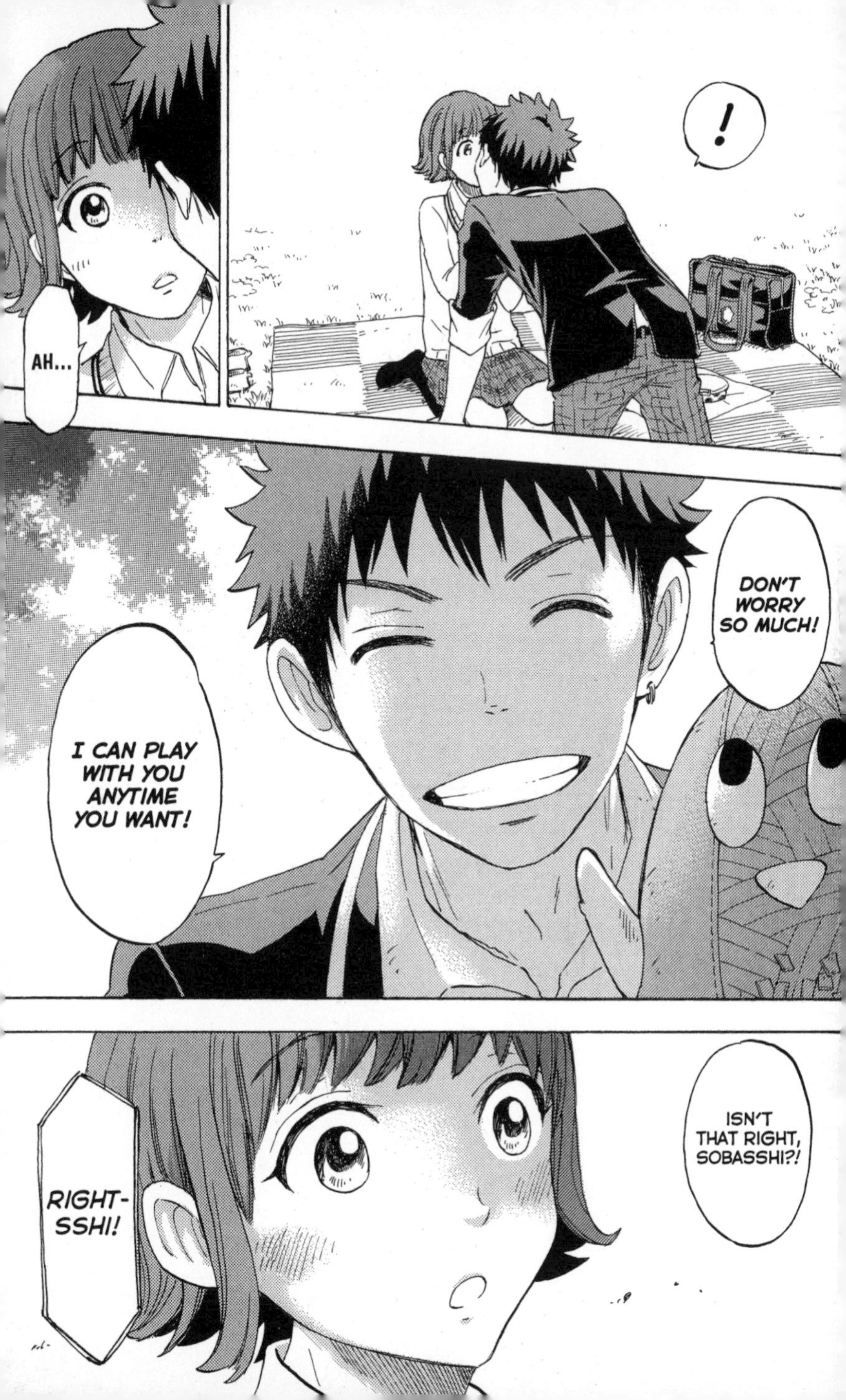
!
AH...
DON'T WORRY SO MUCH!
I CAN PLAY WITH YOU ANYTIME YOU WANT!
ISN'T THAT RIGHT, SOBASSHI?!
RIGHT-SSHI!

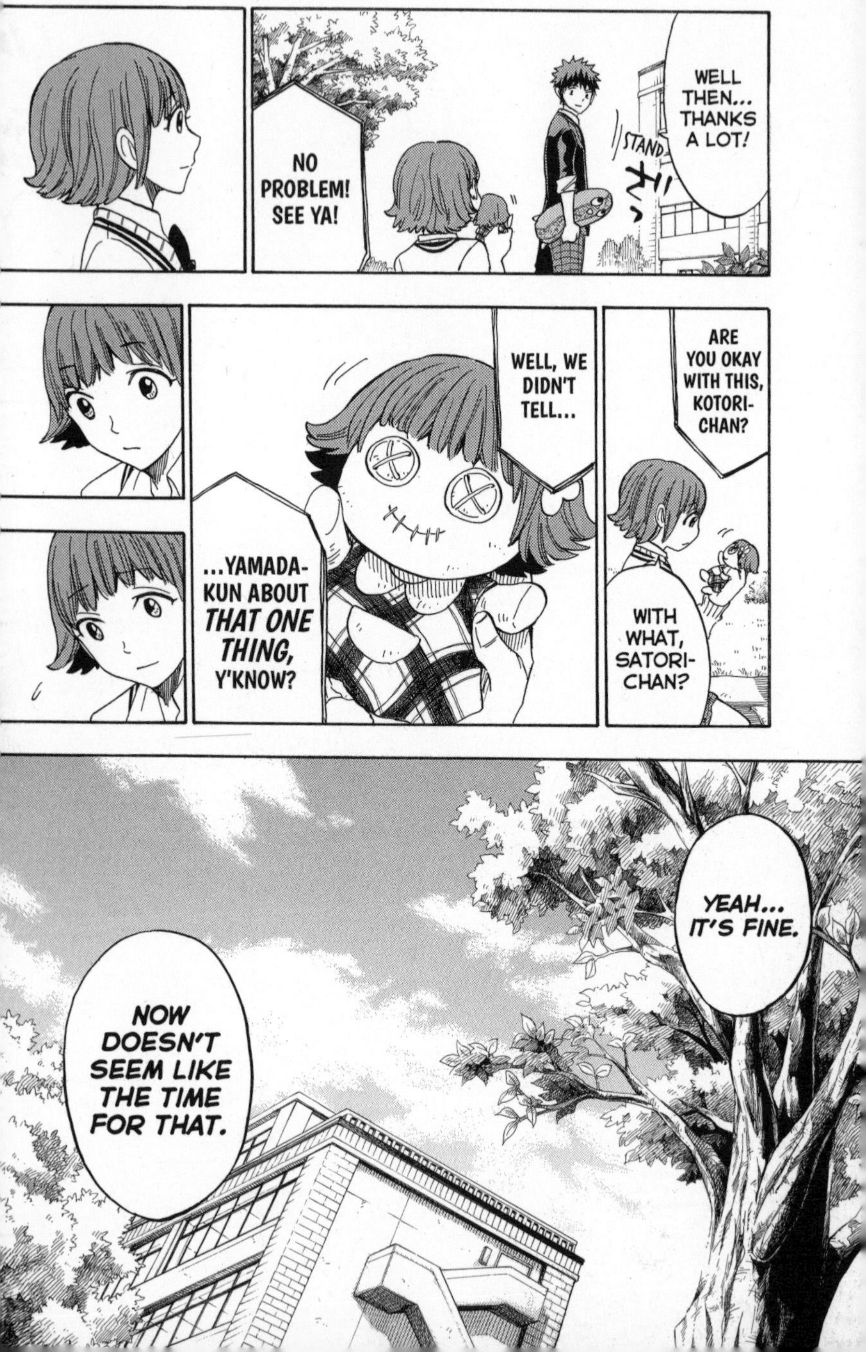
WELL THEN... THANKS A LOT!
STAND
NO PROBLEM! SEE YA!
ARE YOU OKAY WITH THIS, KOTORI-CHAN?
WITH WHAT, SATORI-CHAN?
WELL, WE DIDN'T TELL...
...YAMADA-KUN ABOUT *THAT ONE THING,* Y'KNOW?
YEAH... IT'S FINE.
NOW DOESN'T SEEM LIKE THE TIME FOR THAT.

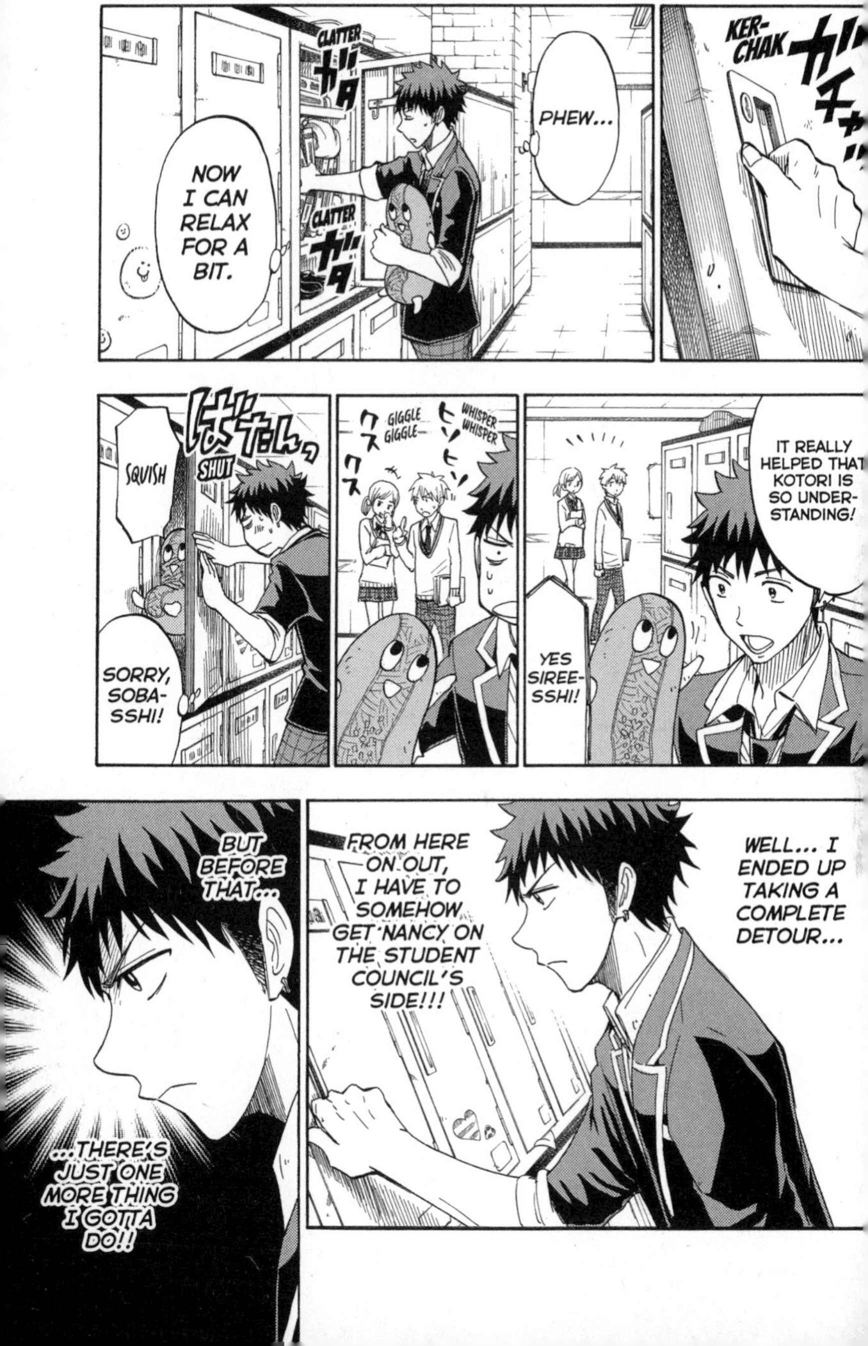
KER-CHAK
カチャ
PHEW...
CLATTER
ガタ
CLATTER
ガタ
NOW I CAN RELAX FOR A BIT.
IT REALLY HELPED THAT KOTORI IS SO UNDER-STANDING!
YES SIREE-SSHI!
WHISPER WHISPER
ヒソヒソ
GIGGLE GIGGLE
クスクス
ばたんっ
SHUT
SQUISH
SORRY, SOBA-SSHI!
WELL... I ENDED UP TAKING A COMPLETE DETOUR...
FROM HERE ON OUT, I HAVE TO SOMEHOW GET NANCY ON THE STUDENT COUNCIL'S SIDE!!!
BUT BEFORE THAT...
...THERE'S JUST ONE MORE THING I GOTTA DO!!

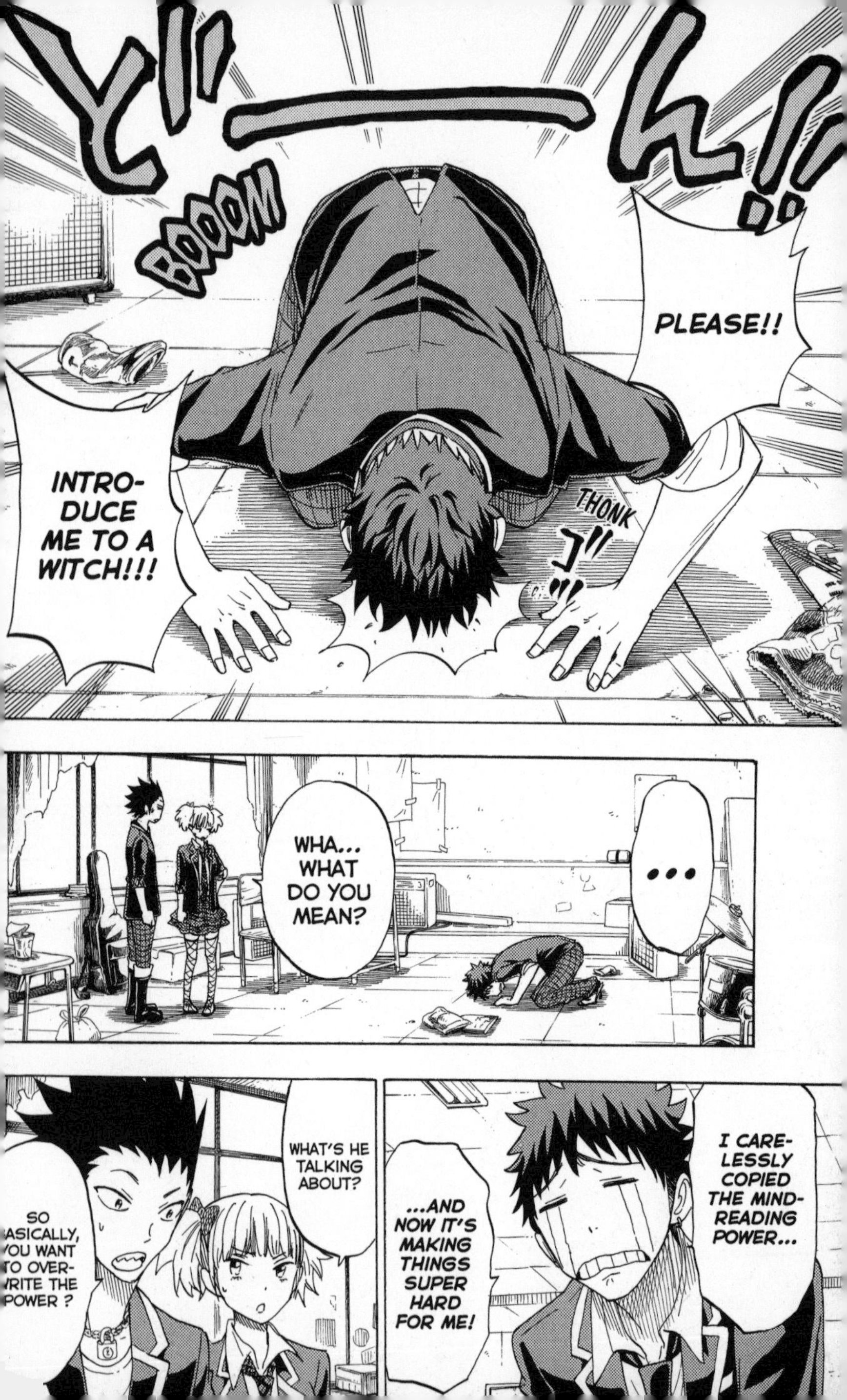
どーーん!!
BOOOM
PLEASE!!
INTRODUCE ME TO A WITCH!!!
THONK
ゴッ
...
WHA... WHAT DO YOU MEAN?
I CARELESSLY COPIED THE MIND-READING POWER...
...AND NOW IT'S MAKING THINGS SUPER HARD FOR ME!
WHAT'S HE TALKING ABOUT?
SO BASICALLY, YOU WANT TO OVERWRITE THE POWER ?

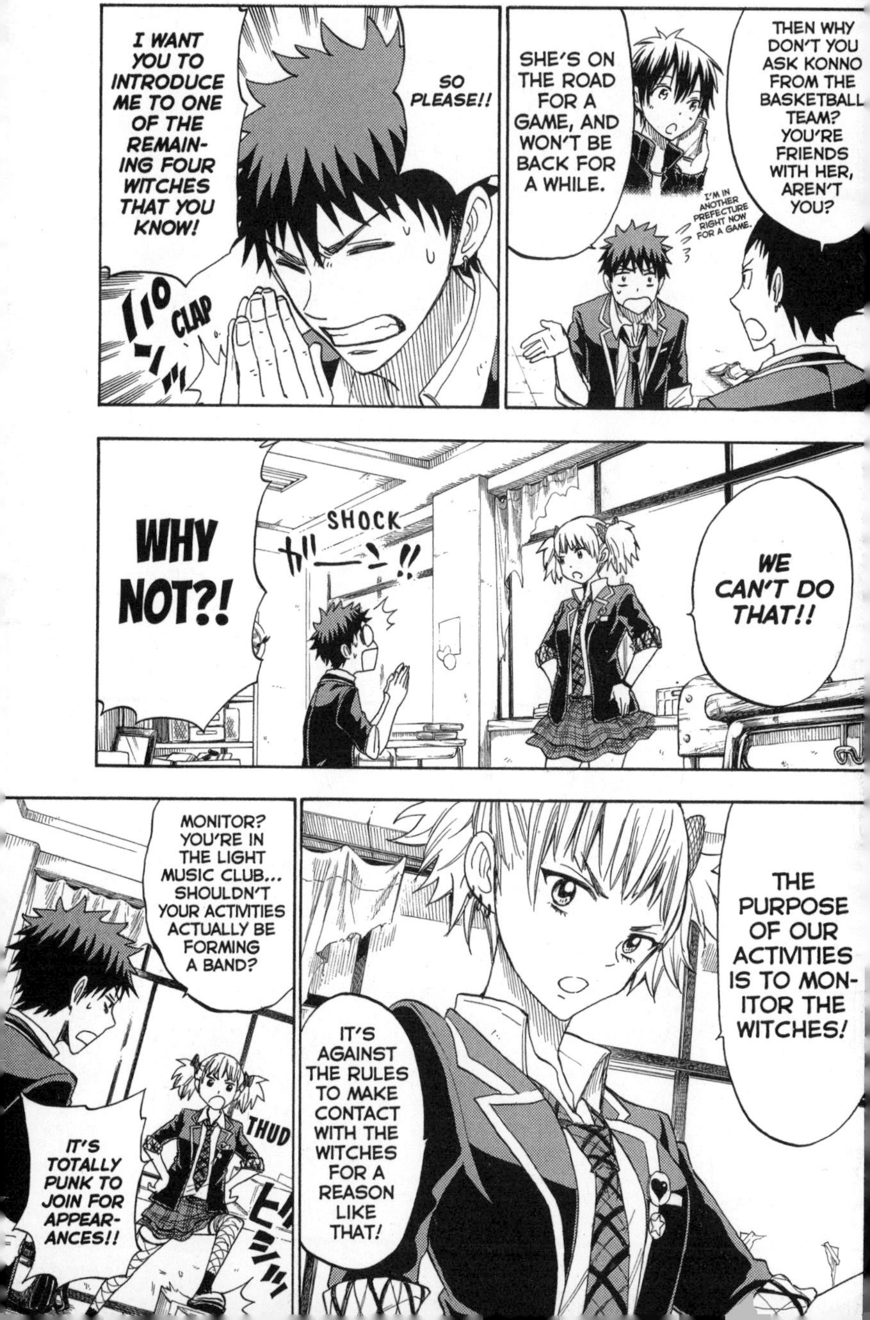
THEN WHY DON'T YOU ASK KONNO FROM THE BASKETBALL TEAM? YOU'RE FRIENDS WITH HER, AREN'T YOU?
SHE'S ON THE ROAD FOR A GAME, AND WON'T BE BACK FOR A WHILE.
I'M IN ANOTHER PREFECTURE RIGHT NOW FOR A GAME.
SO PLEASE!!
I WANT YOU TO INTRODUCE ME TO ONE OF THE REMAIN-ING FOUR WITCHES THAT YOU KNOW!
CLAP
WE CAN'T DO THAT!!
SHOCK
WHY NOT?!
THE PURPOSE OF OUR ACTIVITIES IS TO MON-ITOR THE WITCHES!
IT'S AGAINST THE RULES TO MAKE CONTACT WITH THE WITCHES FOR A REASON LIKE THAT!
MONITOR? YOU'RE IN THE LIGHT MUSIC CLUB... SHOULDN'T YOUR ACTIVITIES ACTUALLY BE FORMING A BAND?
THUD
IT'S TOTALLY PUNK TO JOIN FOR APPEAR-ANCES!!

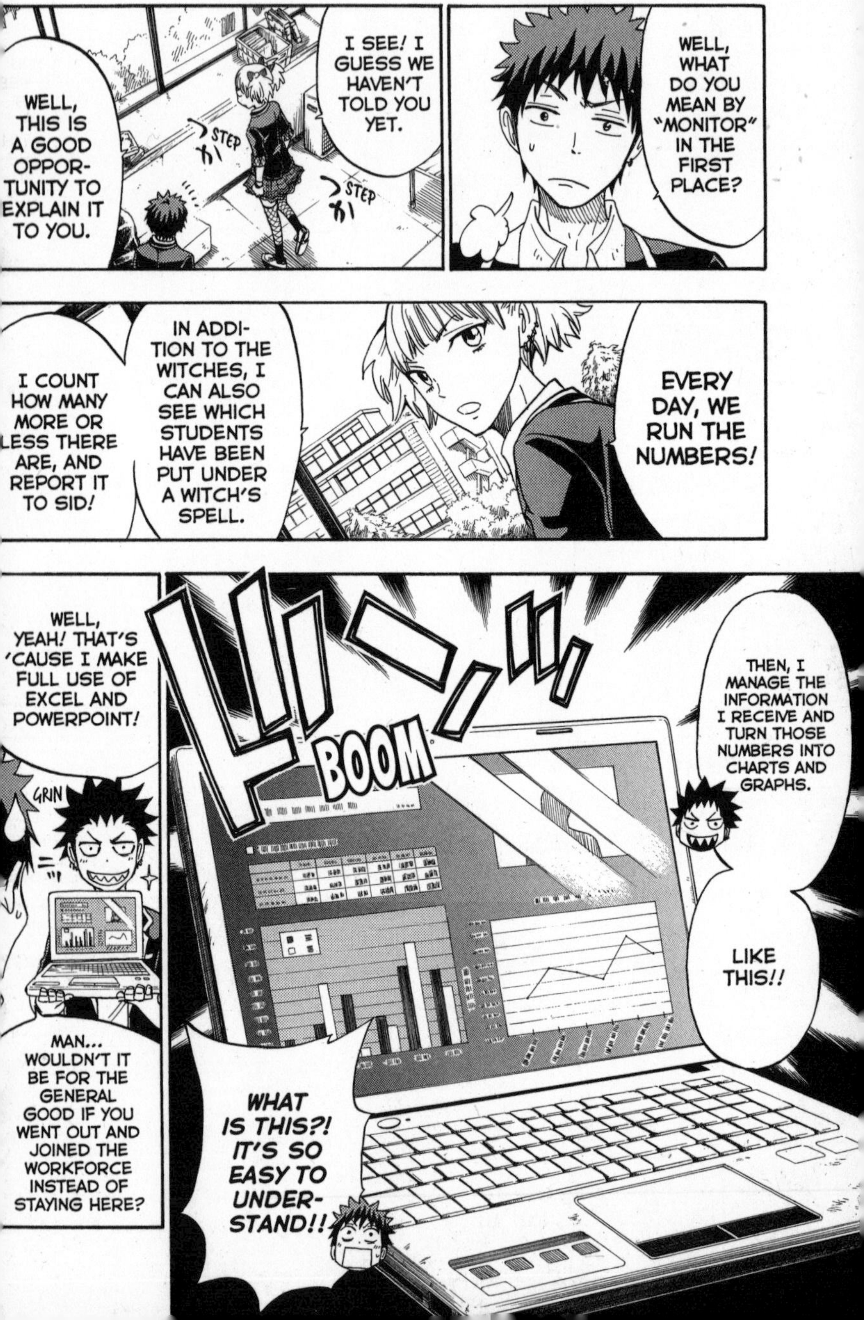
WELL, WHAT DO YOU MEAN BY "MONITOR" IN THE FIRST PLACE?
I SEE! I GUESS WE HAVEN'T TOLD YOU YET.
STEP
STEP
WELL, THIS IS A GOOD OPPORTUNITY TO EXPLAIN IT TO YOU.
EVERY DAY, WE RUN THE NUMBERS!
IN ADDITION TO THE WITCHES, I CAN ALSO SEE WHICH STUDENTS HAVE BEEN PUT UNDER A WITCH'S SPELL.
I COUNT HOW MANY MORE OR LESS THERE ARE, AND REPORT IT TO SID!
THEN, I MANAGE THE INFORMATION I RECEIVE AND TURN THOSE NUMBERS INTO CHARTS AND GRAPHS.
LIKE THIS!!
BOOM
WHAT IS THIS?! IT'S SO EASY TO UNDERSTAND!!
WELL, YEAH! THAT'S 'CAUSE I MAKE FULL USE OF EXCEL AND POWERPOINT!
GRIN
MAN... WOULDN'T IT BE FOR THE GENERAL GOOD IF YOU WENT OUT AND JOINED THE WORKFORCE INSTEAD OF STAYING HERE?

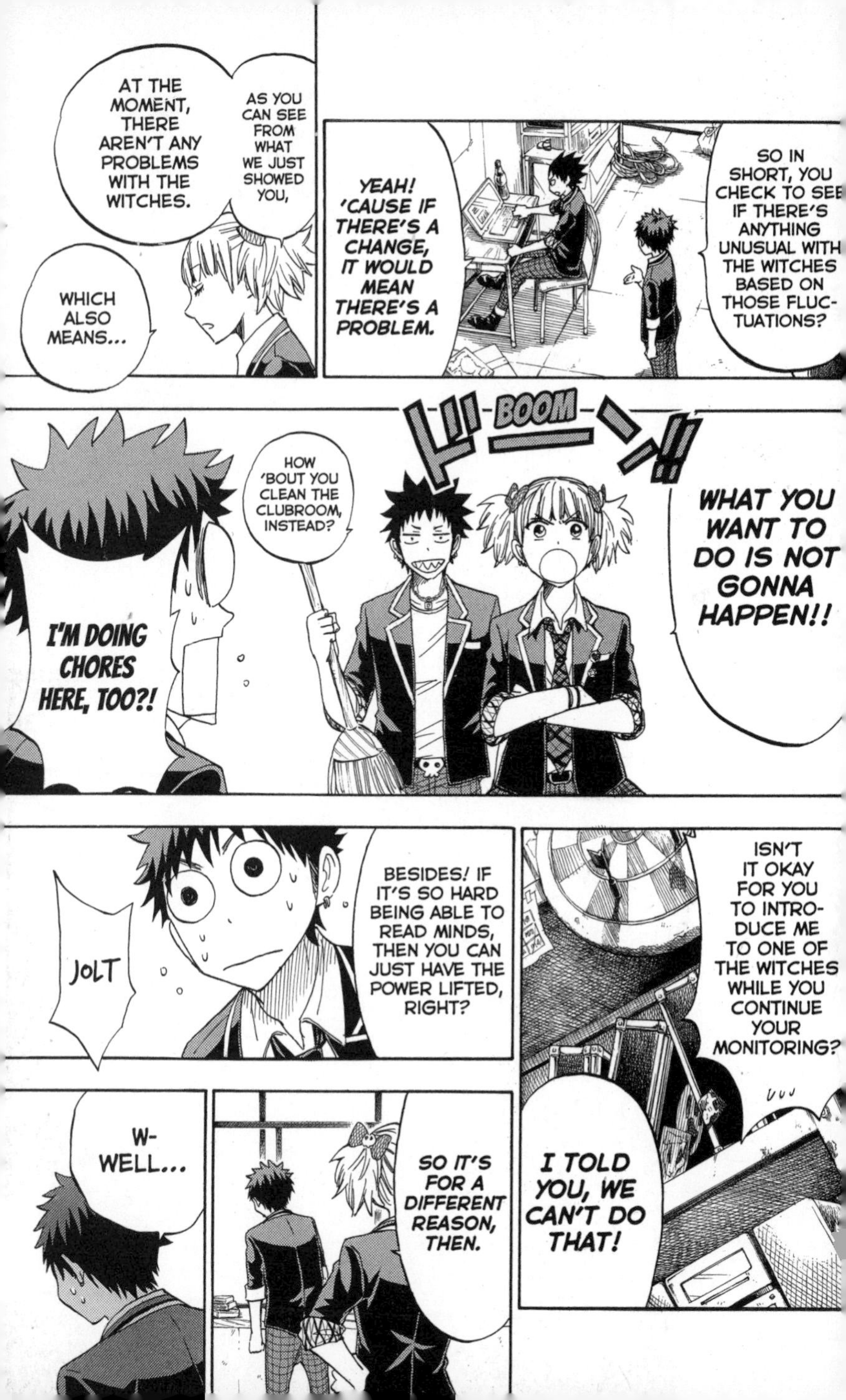

SO IN SHORT, YOU CHECK TO SEE IF THERE'S ANYTHING UNUSUAL WITH THE WITCHES BASED ON THOSE FLUCTUATIONS?
YEAH! 'CAUSE IF THERE'S A CHANGE, IT WOULD MEAN THERE'S A PROBLEM.
AS YOU CAN SEE FROM WHAT WE JUST SHOWED YOU,
AT THE MOMENT, THERE AREN'T ANY PROBLEMS WITH THE WITCHES.
WHICH ALSO MEANS...
WHAT YOU WANT TO DO IS NOT GONNA HAPPEN!!
BOOM
HOW 'BOUT YOU CLEAN THE CLUBROOM, INSTEAD?
I'M DOING CHORES HERE, TOO?!
ISN'T IT OKAY FOR YOU TO INTRODUCE ME TO ONE OF THE WITCHES WHILE YOU CONTINUE YOUR MONITORING?
I TOLD YOU, WE CAN'T DO THAT!
BESIDES! IF IT'S SO HARD BEING ABLE TO READ MINDS, THEN YOU CAN JUST HAVE THE POWER LIFTED, RIGHT?
JOLT
SO IT'S FOR A DIFFERENT REASON, THEN.
W-WELL...

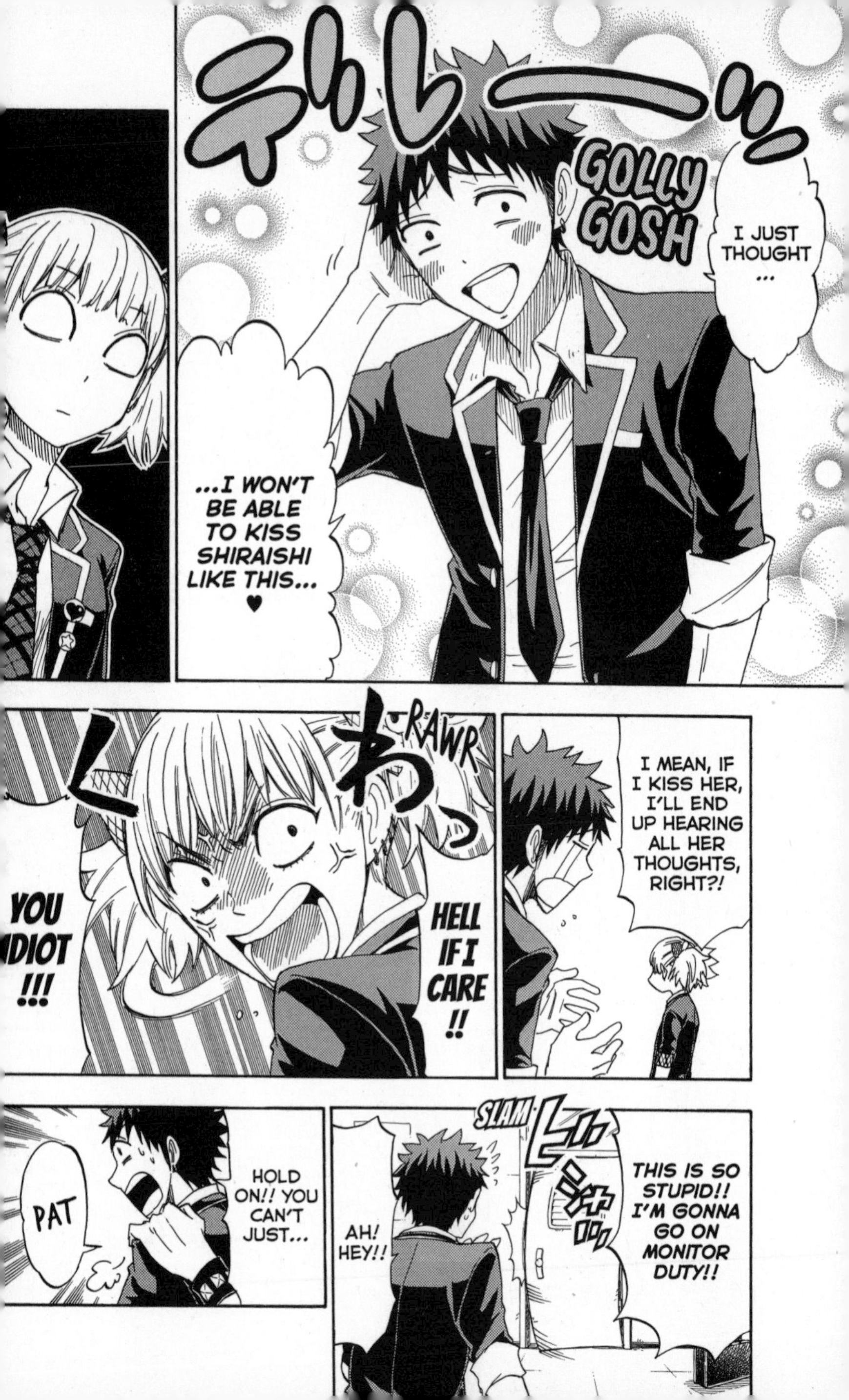
GOLLY GOSH
I JUST THOUGHT ...
...I WON'T BE ABLE TO KISS SHIRAISHI LIKE THIS... ♥
I MEAN, IF I KISS HER, I'LL END UP HEARING ALL HER THOUGHTS, RIGHT?!
RAWR
HELL IF I CARE !!
YOU IDIOT !!!
SLAM
THIS IS SO STUPID!! I'M GONNA GO ON MONITOR DUTY!!
AH! HEY!!
HOLD ON!! YOU CAN'T JUST...
PAT

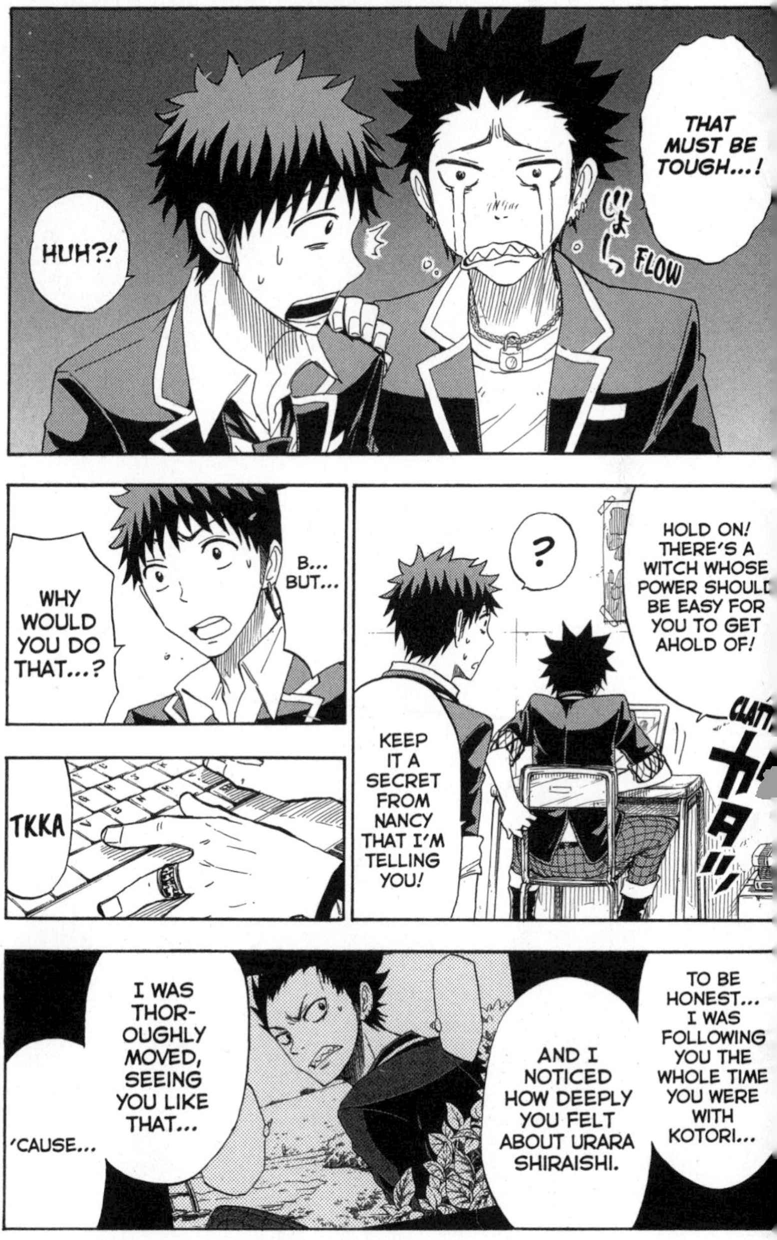
THAT MUST BE TOUGH...!
FLOW
HUH?!
HOLD ON! THERE'S A WITCH WHOSE POWER SHOULD BE EASY FOR YOU TO GET AHOLD OF!
?
CLATT
KEEP IT A SECRET FROM NANCY THAT I'M TELLING YOU!
B... BUT...
WHY WOULD YOU DO THAT...?
TKKA
TO BE HONEST... I WAS FOLLOWING YOU THE WHOLE TIME YOU WERE WITH KOTORI...
AND I NOTICED HOW DEEPLY YOU FELT ABOUT URARA SHIRAISHI.
I WAS THOR-OUGHLY MOVED, SEEING YOU LIKE THAT...
'CAUSE...

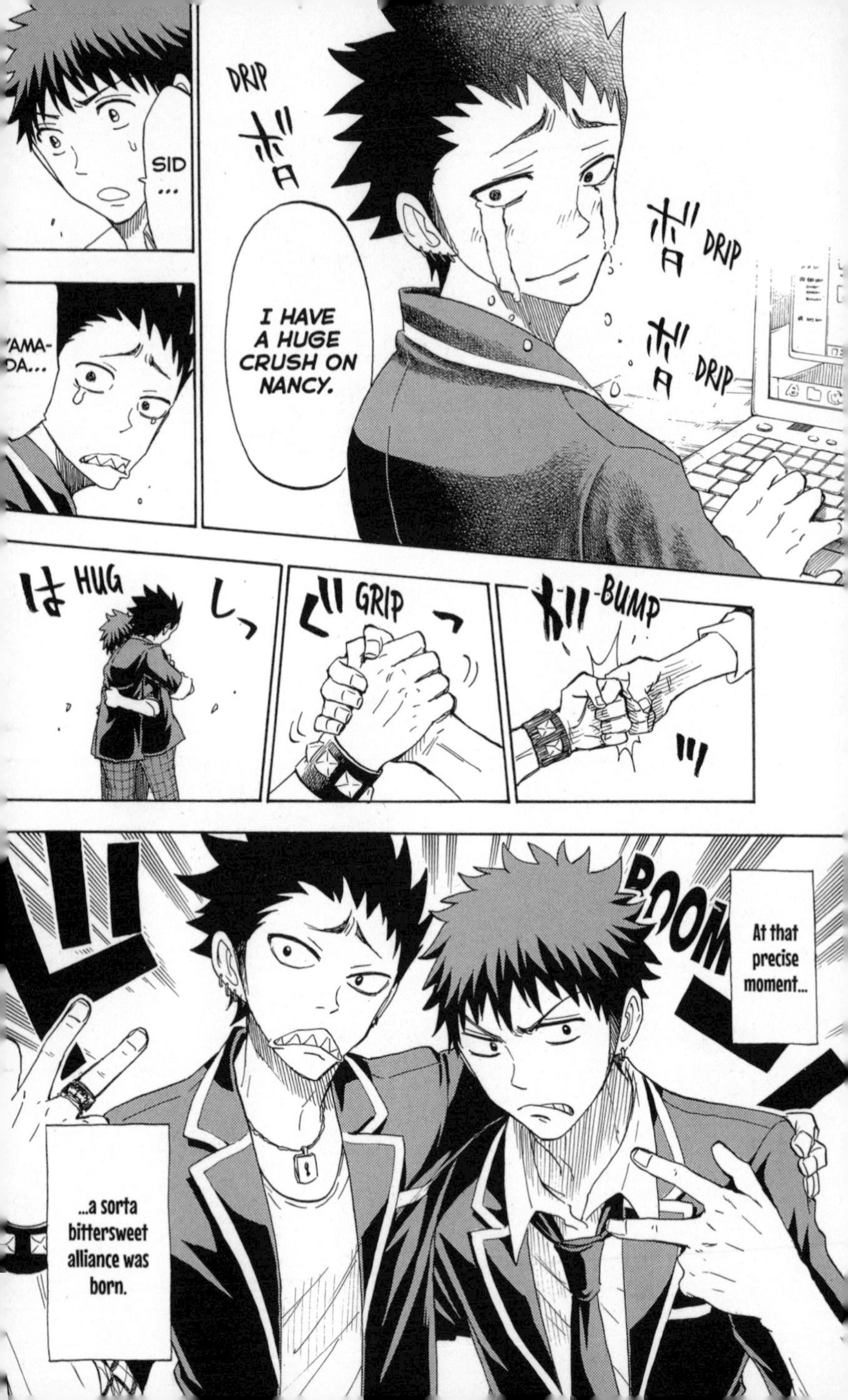

ボタ DRIP
ボタ DRIP
DRIP
ボタ
I HAVE A HUGE CRUSH ON NANCY.
SID ...
YAMA-DA...
ガッ BUMP
ぐっ GRIP
は HUG
しっ
BOOM
At that precise moment...
...a sorta bittersweet alliance was born.

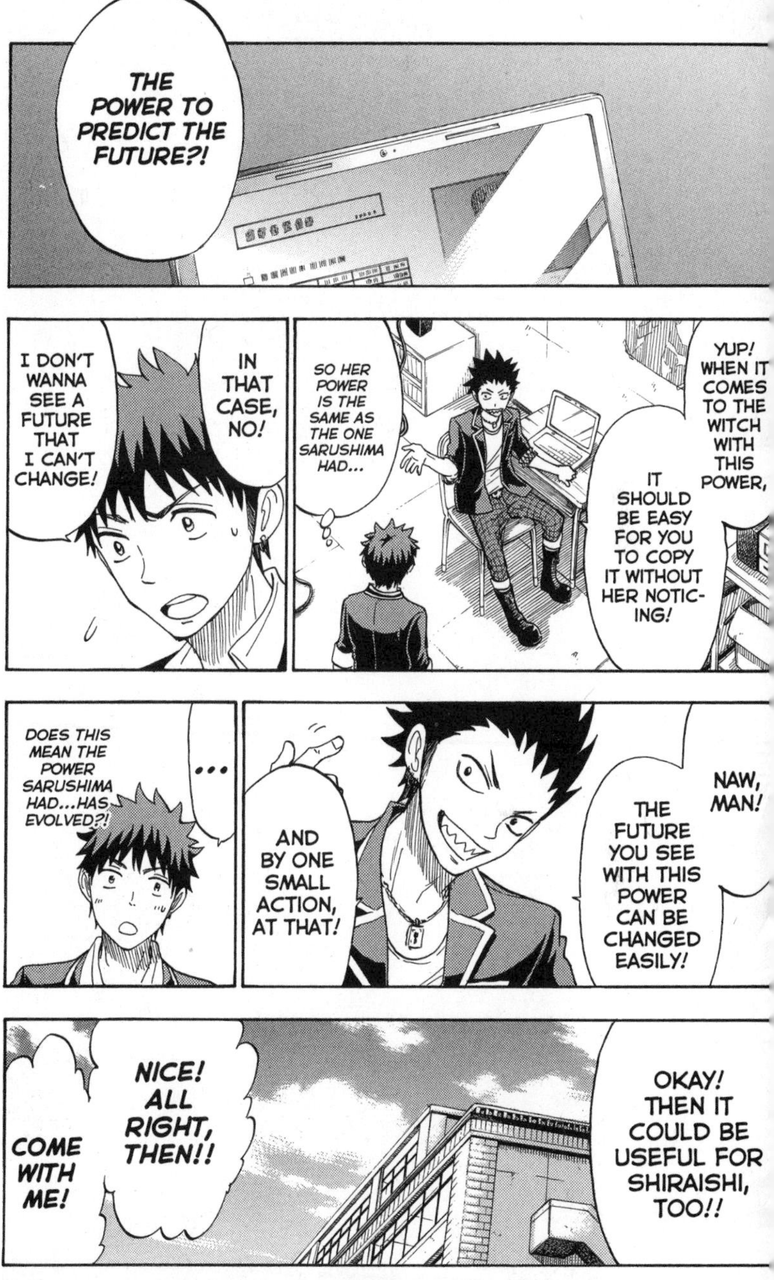
THE POWER TO PREDICT THE FUTURE?!
YUP! WHEN IT COMES TO THE WITCH WITH THIS POWER,
IT SHOULD BE EASY FOR YOU TO COPY IT WITHOUT HER NOTIC-ING!
SO HER POWER IS THE SAME AS THE ONE SARUSHIMA HAD...
IN THAT CASE, NO!
I DON'T WANNA SEE A FUTURE THAT I CAN'T CHANGE!
NAW, MAN!
THE FUTURE YOU SEE WITH THIS POWER CAN BE CHANGED EASILY!
AND BY ONE SMALL ACTION, AT THAT!
...
DOES THIS MEAN THE POWER SARUSHIMA HAD...HAS EVOLVED?!
OKAY! THEN IT COULD BE USEFUL FOR SHIRAISHI, TOO!!
NICE! ALL RIGHT, THEN!!
COME WITH ME!

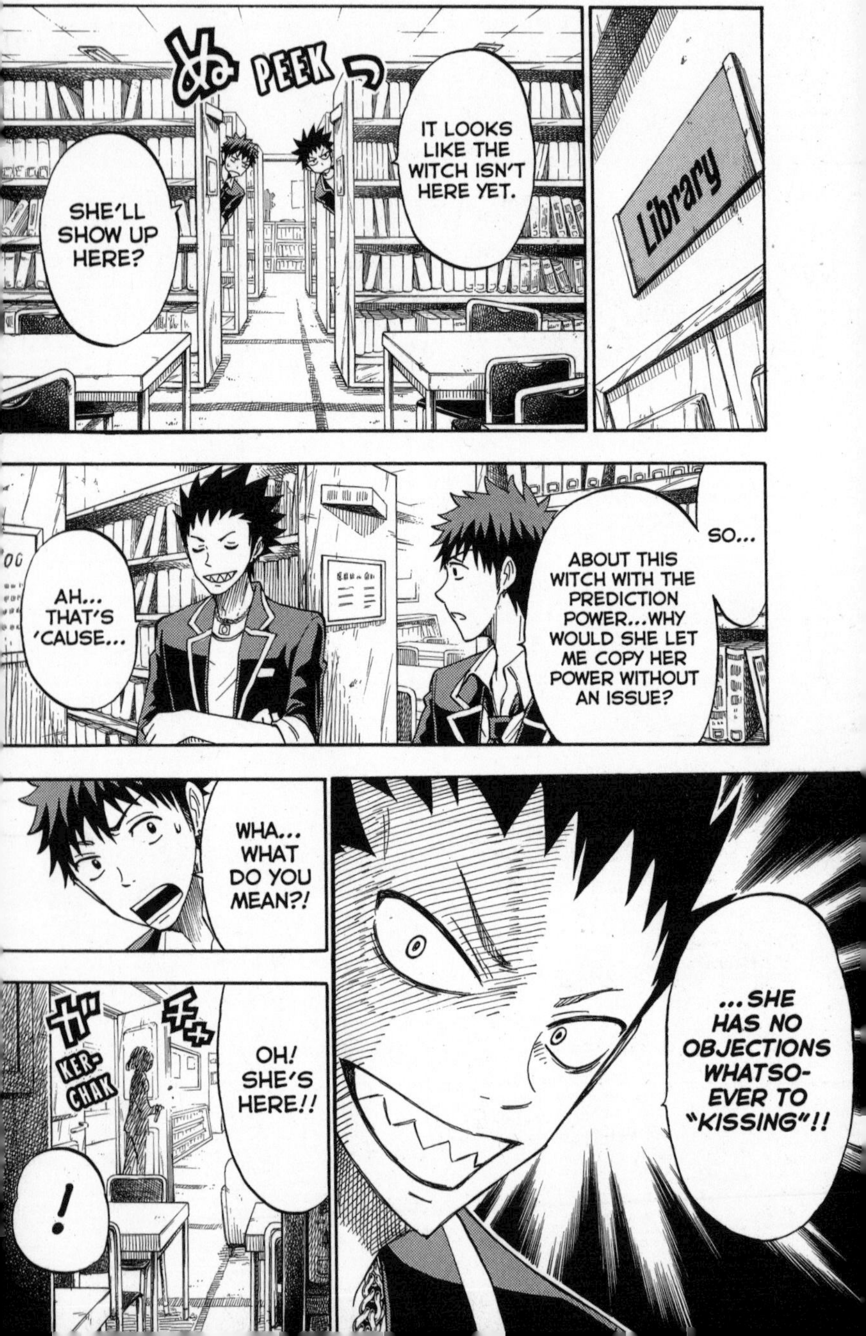
Library
ぬ PEEK っ
IT LOOKS LIKE THE WITCH ISN'T HERE YET.
SHE'LL SHOW UP HERE?
SO...
ABOUT THIS WITCH WITH THE PREDICTION POWER...WHY WOULD SHE LET ME COPY HER POWER WITHOUT AN ISSUE?
AH... THAT'S 'CAUSE...
...SHE HAS NO OBJECTIONS WHATSO-EVER TO "KISSING"!!
WHA... WHAT DO YOU MEAN?!
OH! SHE'S HERE!!
ガ チャ KER-CHAK
!

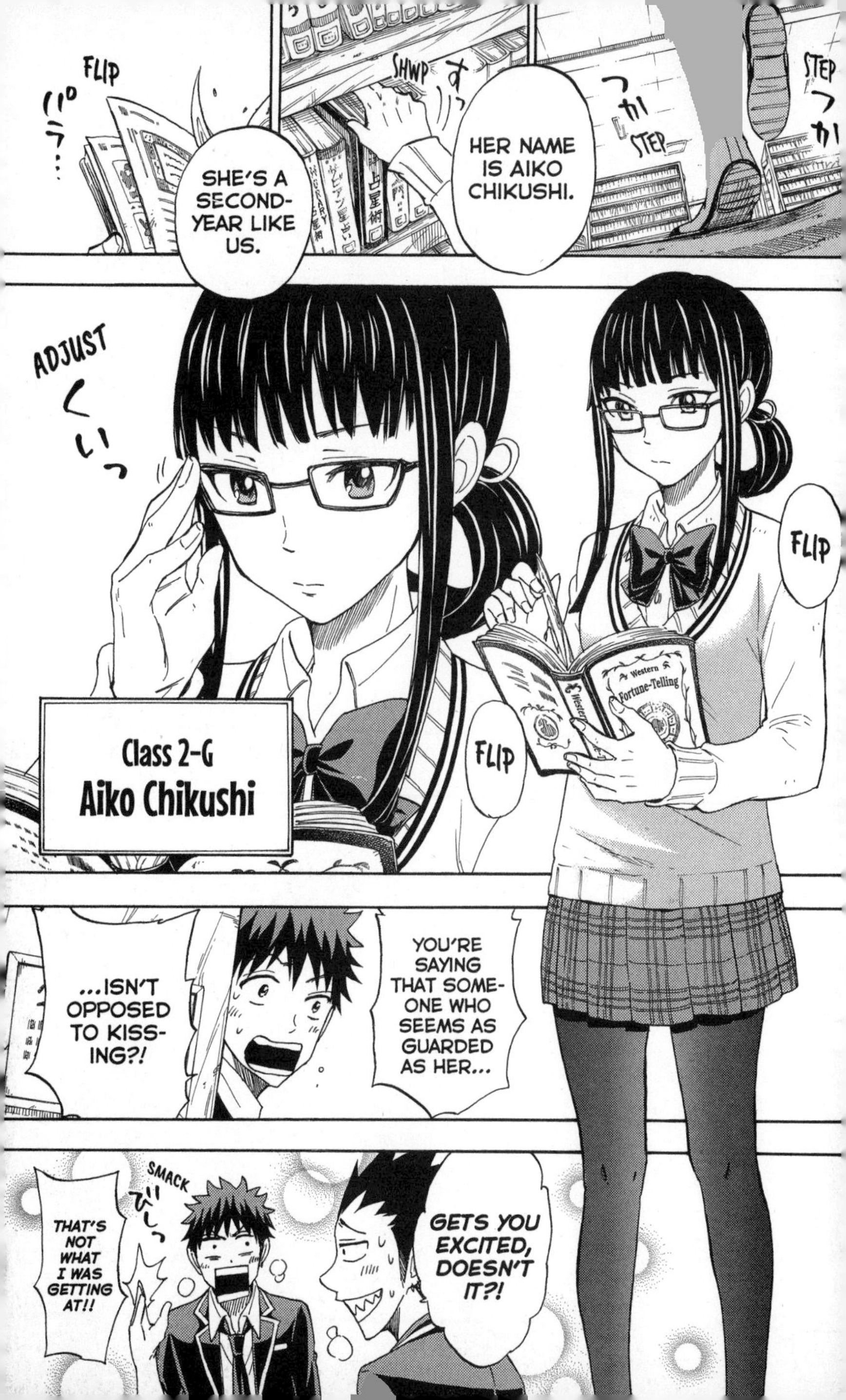
STEP
つかつか
STEP
HER NAME IS AIKO CHIKUSHI.
SHWP
す
SHE'S A SECOND-YEAR LIKE US.
FLIP
パラ…
FLIP
Western Fortune-Telling
Western
FLIP
ADJUST
くいっ
Class 2-G
Aiko Chikushi
YOU'RE SAYING THAT SOME-ONE WHO SEEMS AS GUARDED AS HER...
...ISN'T OPPOSED TO KISS-ING?!
GETS YOU EXCITED, DOESN'T IT?!
SMACK
びしっ
THAT'S NOT WHAT I WAS GETTING AT!!

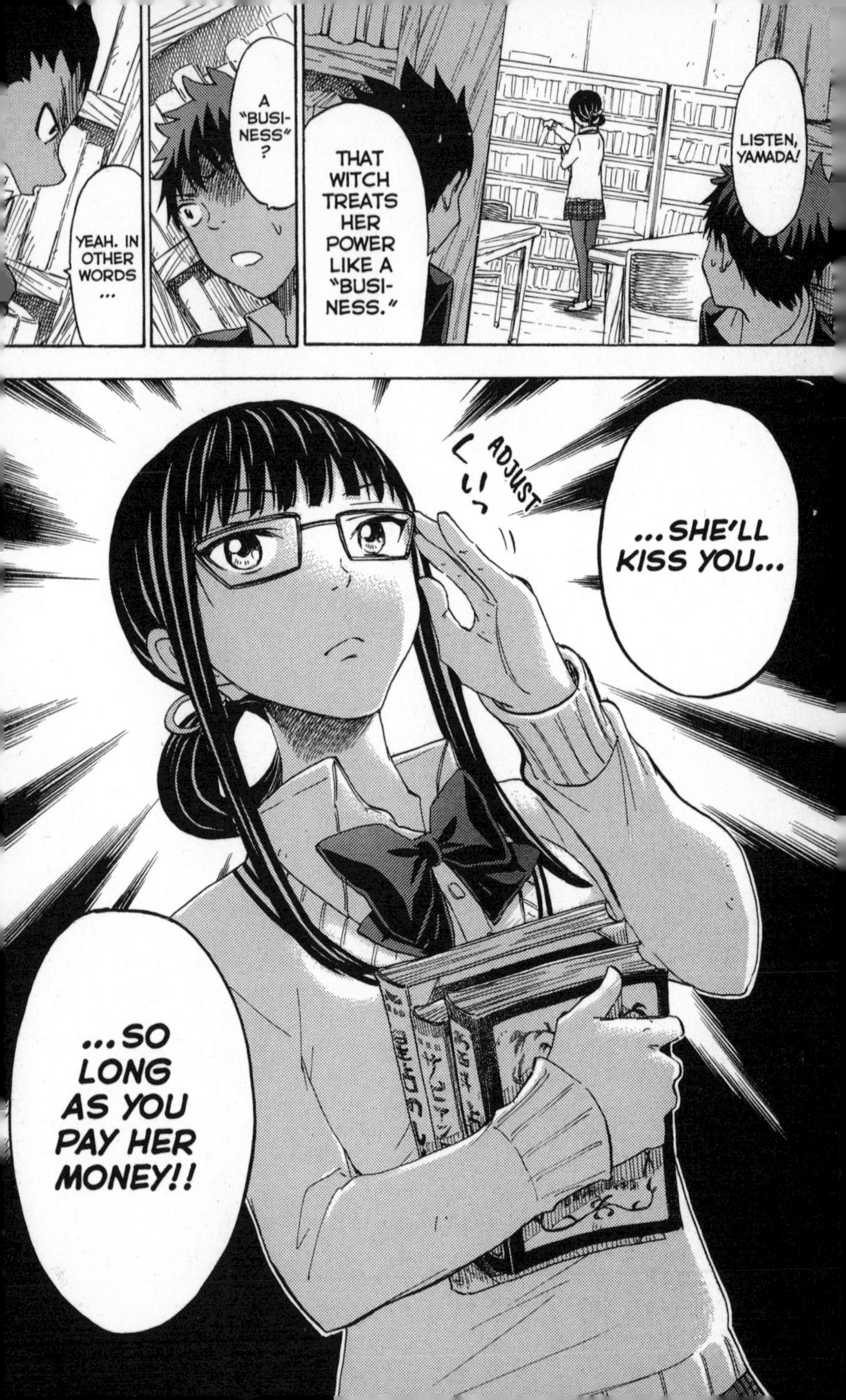
LISTEN, YAMADA!
THAT WITCH TREATS HER POWER LIKE A "BUSINESS."
A "BUSINESS"?
YEAH. IN OTHER WORDS...
...SHE'LL KISS YOU...
ADJUST
...SO LONG AS YOU PAY HER MONEY!!

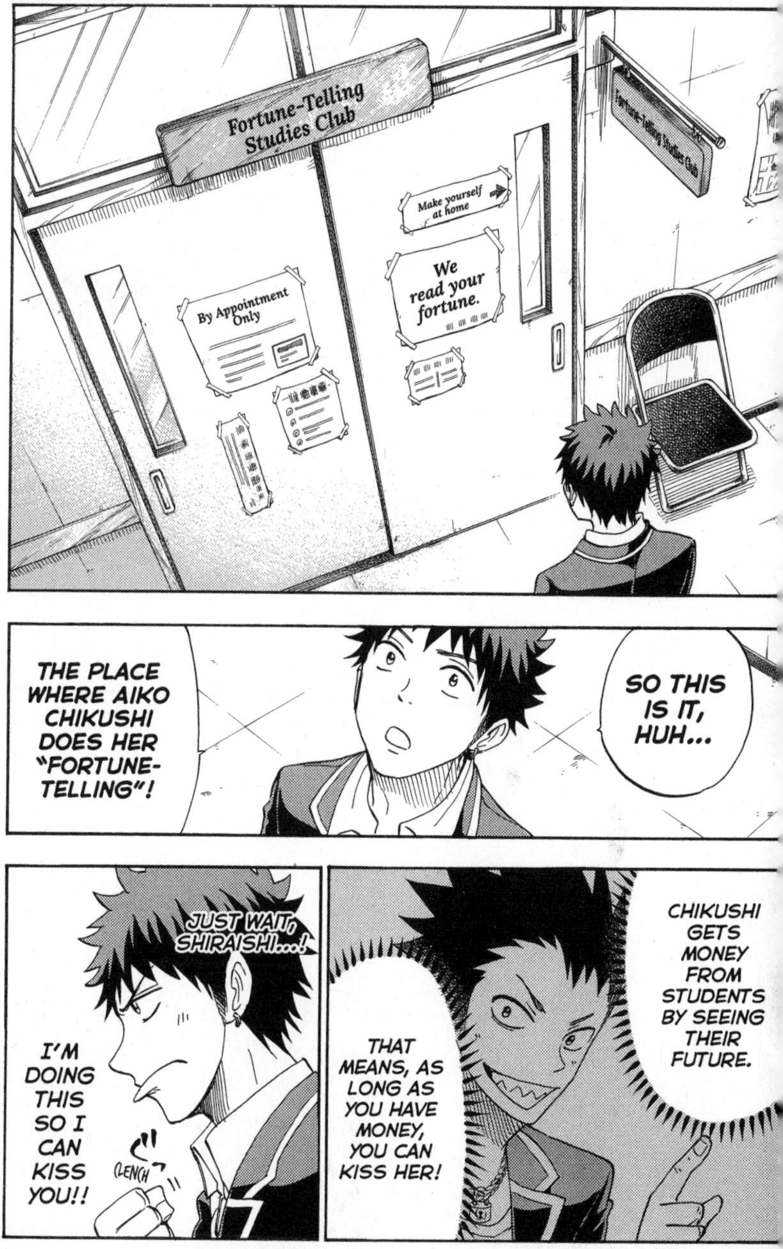
Fortune-Telling Studies Club
Fortune-Telling Studies Club
Make yourself at home
We read your fortune.
By Appointment Only
SO THIS IS IT, HUH...
THE PLACE WHERE AIKO CHIKUSHI DOES HER "FORTUNE-TELLING"!
CHIKUSHI GETS MONEY FROM STUDENTS BY SEEING THEIR FUTURE.
THAT MEANS, AS LONG AS YOU HAVE MONEY, YOU CAN KISS HER!
JUST WAIT, SHIRAISHI...!
I'M DOING THIS SO I CAN KISS YOU!!
CLENCH

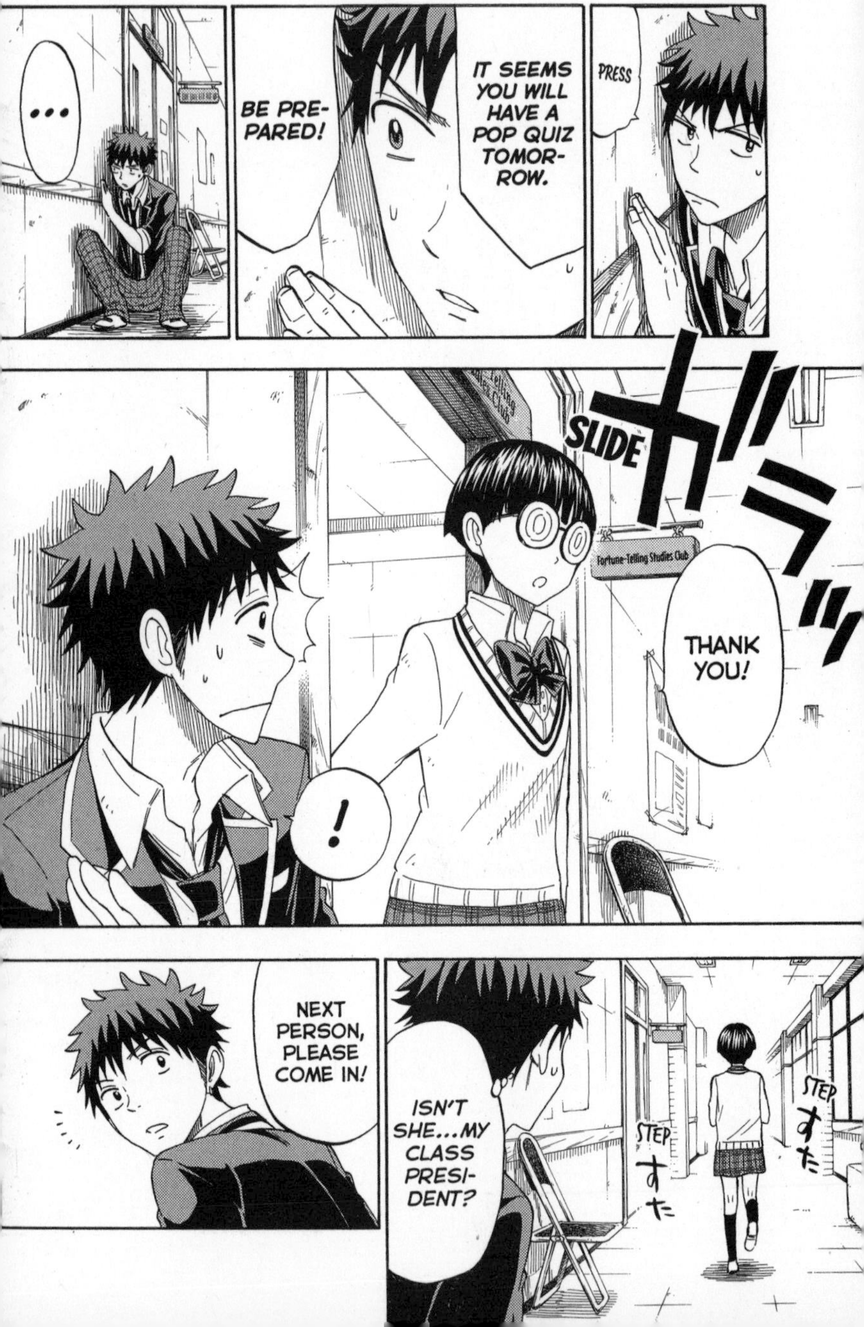
PRESS
IT SEEMS YOU WILL HAVE A POP QUIZ TOMORROW.
BE PREPARED!
...
SLIDE
ガラッ
Fortune-Telling Studies Club
THANK YOU!
!
STEP
すた
STEP
すた
ISN'T SHE...MY CLASS PRESIDENT?
NEXT PERSON, PLEASE COME IN!

CHAPTER 109: The Masked JK

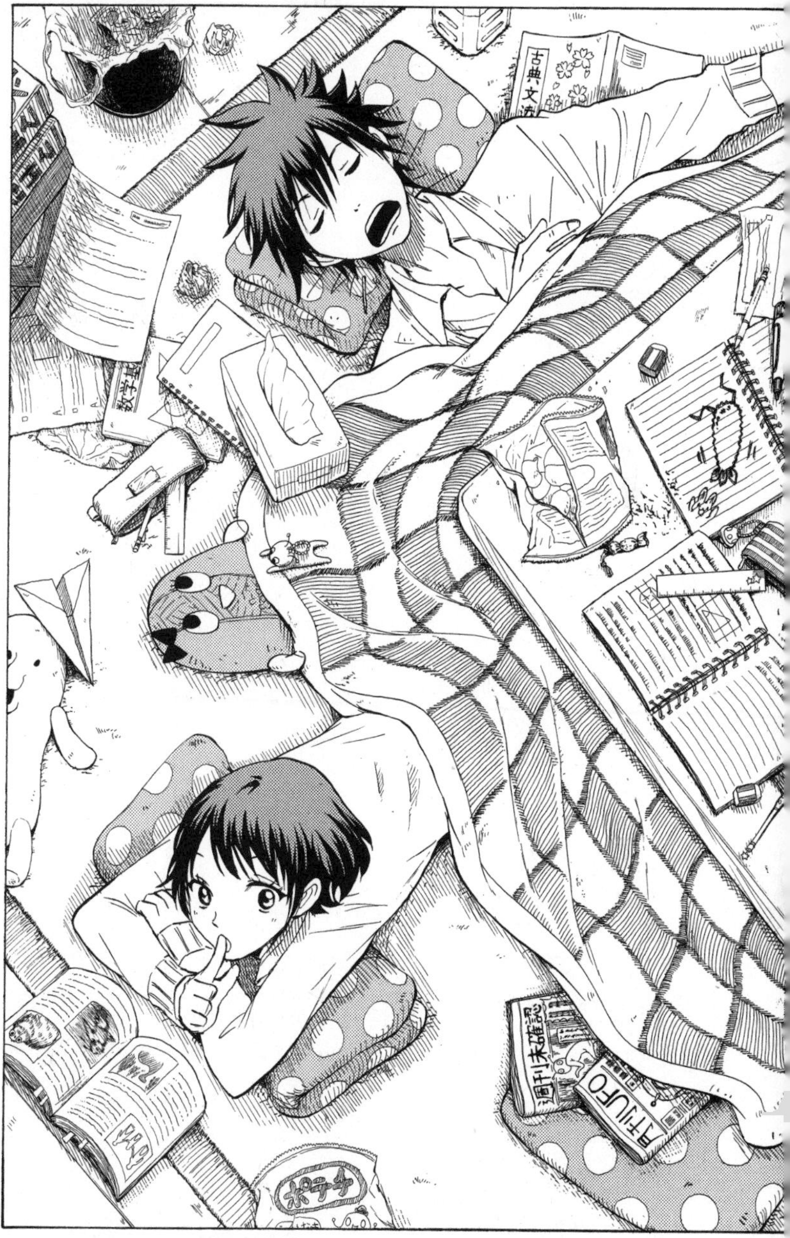

古典文法
数学基
月刊UFO

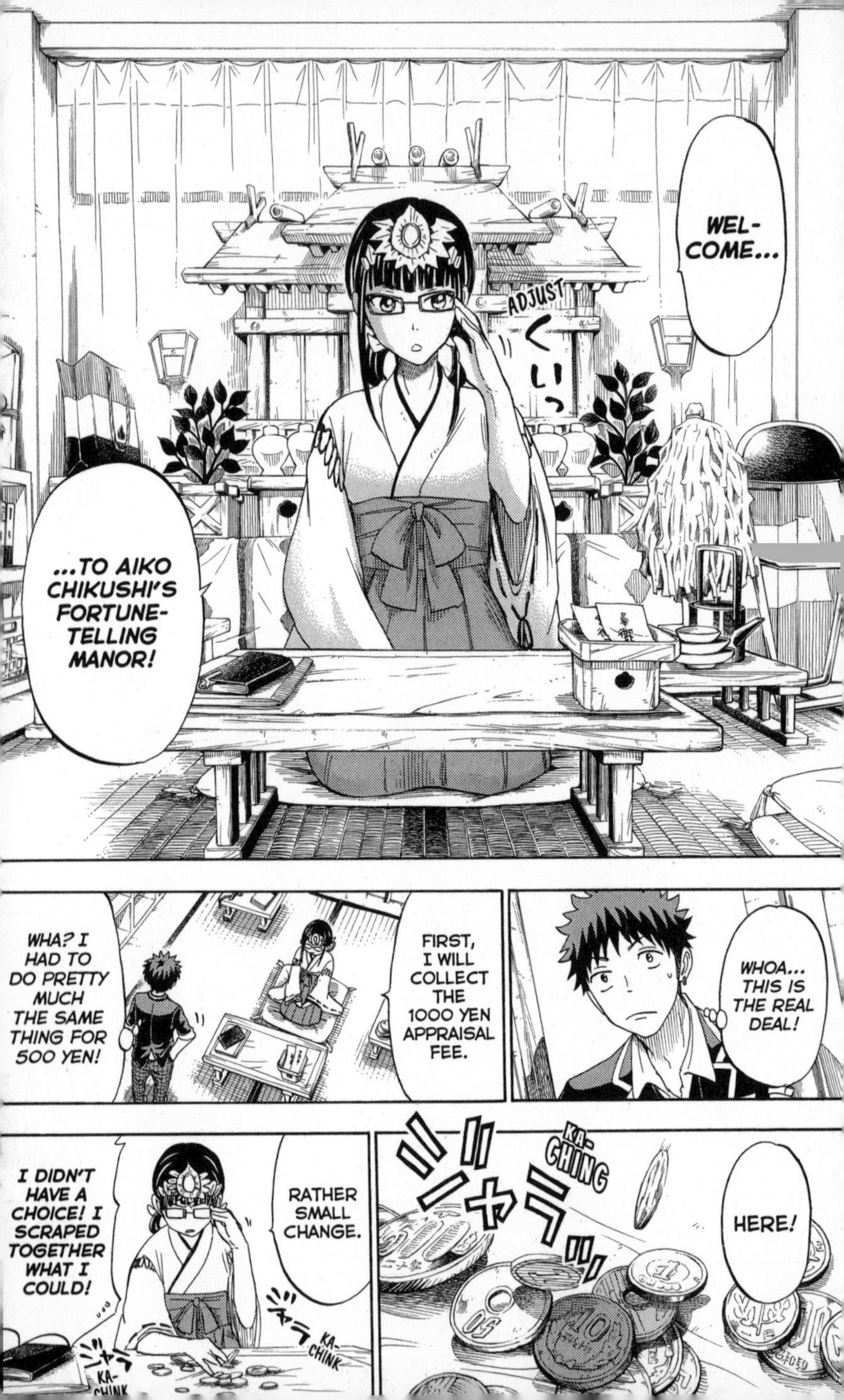
WEL-COME...
ADJUST
くいっ
...TO AIKO CHIKUSHI'S FORTUNE-TELLING MANOR!
WHOA... THIS IS THE REAL DEAL!
FIRST, I WILL COLLECT THE 1000 YEN APPRAISAL FEE.
WHA? I HAD TO DO PRETTY MUCH THE SAME THING FOR 500 YEN!
HERE!
KA-CHING
RATHER SMALL CHANGE.
I DIDN'T HAVE A CHOICE! I SCRAPED TOGETHER WHAT I COULD!
KA-CHINK
KA-CHINK

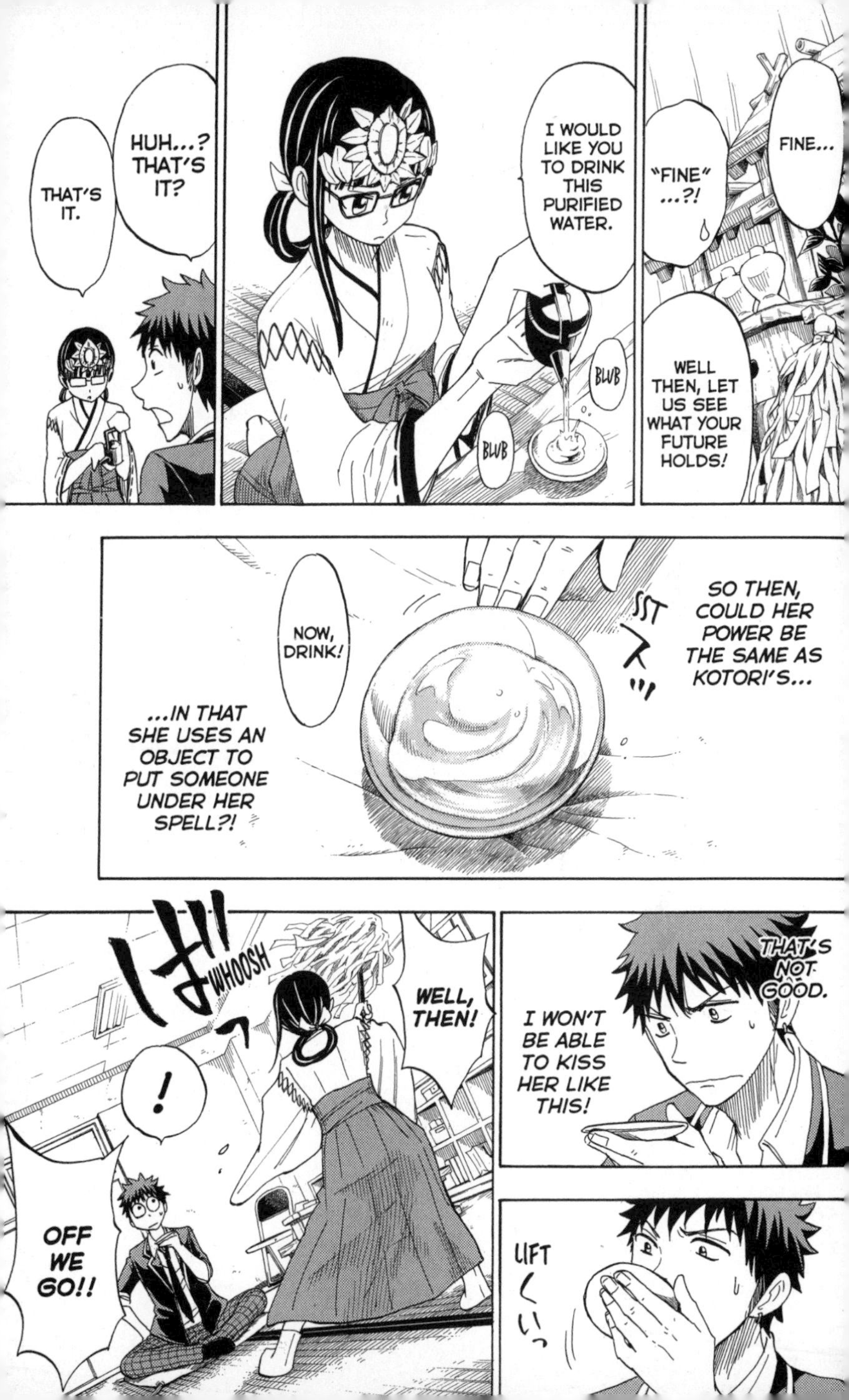
FINE...
"FINE" ...?!
WELL THEN, LET US SEE WHAT YOUR FUTURE HOLDS!
I WOULD LIKE YOU TO DRINK THIS PURIFIED WATER.
BLUB
BLUB
HUH...? THAT'S IT?
THAT'S IT.
SO THEN, COULD HER POWER BE THE SAME AS KOTORI'S...
SST
NOW, DRINK!
...IN THAT SHE USES AN OBJECT TO PUT SOMEONE UNDER HER SPELL?!
THAT'S NOT GOOD.
I WON'T BE ABLE TO KISS HER LIKE THIS!
LIFT
WELL, THEN!
WHOOSH
!
OFF WE GO!!

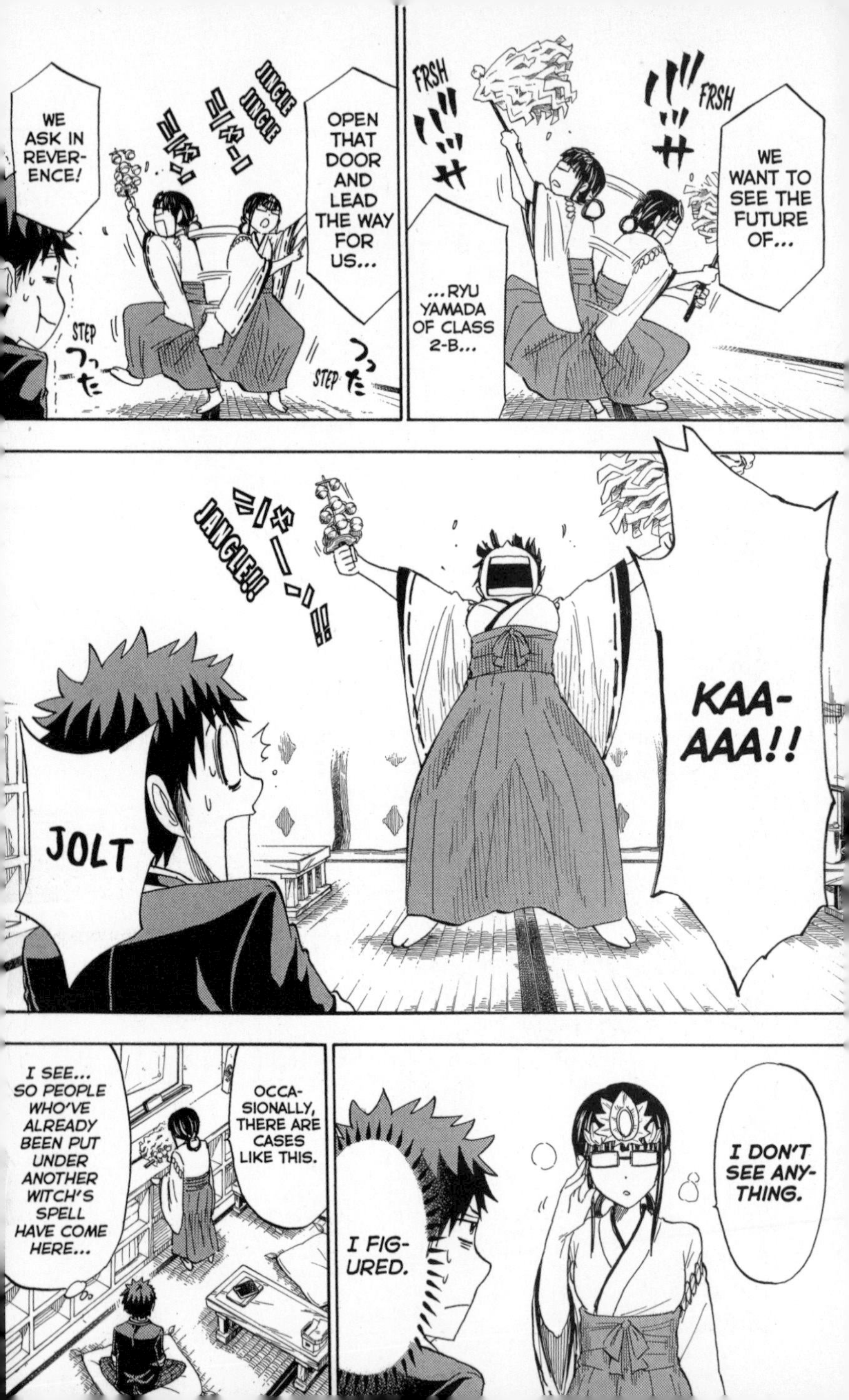

FRSH
FRSH
WE WANT TO SEE THE FUTURE OF...
...RYU YAMADA OF CLASS 2-B...
OPEN THAT DOOR AND LEAD THE WAY FOR US...
JINGLE JINGLE
WE ASK IN REVERENCE!
STEP
STEP
KAA-AAA!!
JANGLE!!!
JOLT
I DON'T SEE ANY-THING.
I FIG-URED.
OCCA-SIONALLY, THERE ARE CASES LIKE THIS.
I SEE... SO PEOPLE WHO'VE ALREADY BEEN PUT UNDER ANOTHER WITCH'S SPELL HAVE COME HERE...

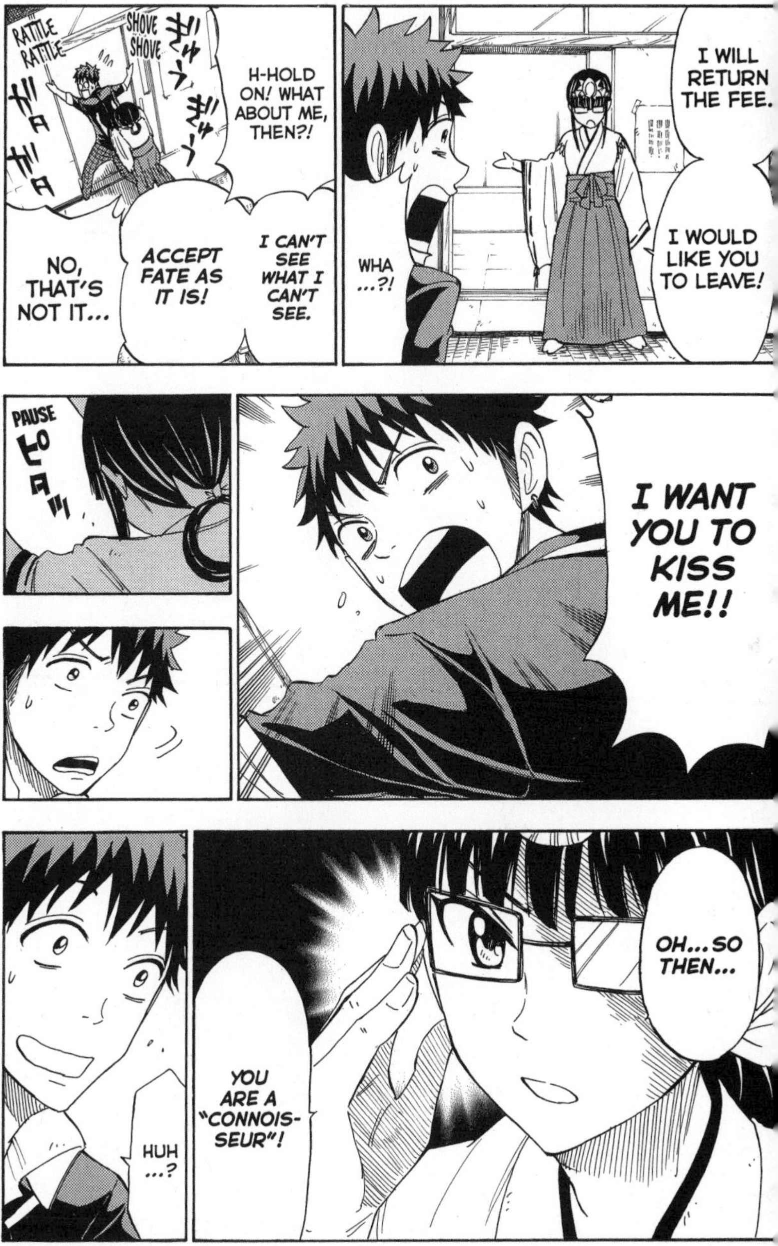
I WILL RETURN THE FEE.
I WOULD LIKE YOU TO LEAVE!
WHA ...?!
SHOVE SHOVE
ぎゅう ぎゅう
RATTLE RATTLE
ガタ ガタ
H-HOLD ON! WHAT ABOUT ME, THEN?!
I CAN'T SEE WHAT I CAN'T SEE.
ACCEPT FATE AS IT IS!
NO, THAT'S NOT IT...
I WANT YOU TO KISS ME!!
PAUSE
ピタッ
OH...SO THEN...
YOU ARE A "CONNOIS-SEUR"!
HUH ...?

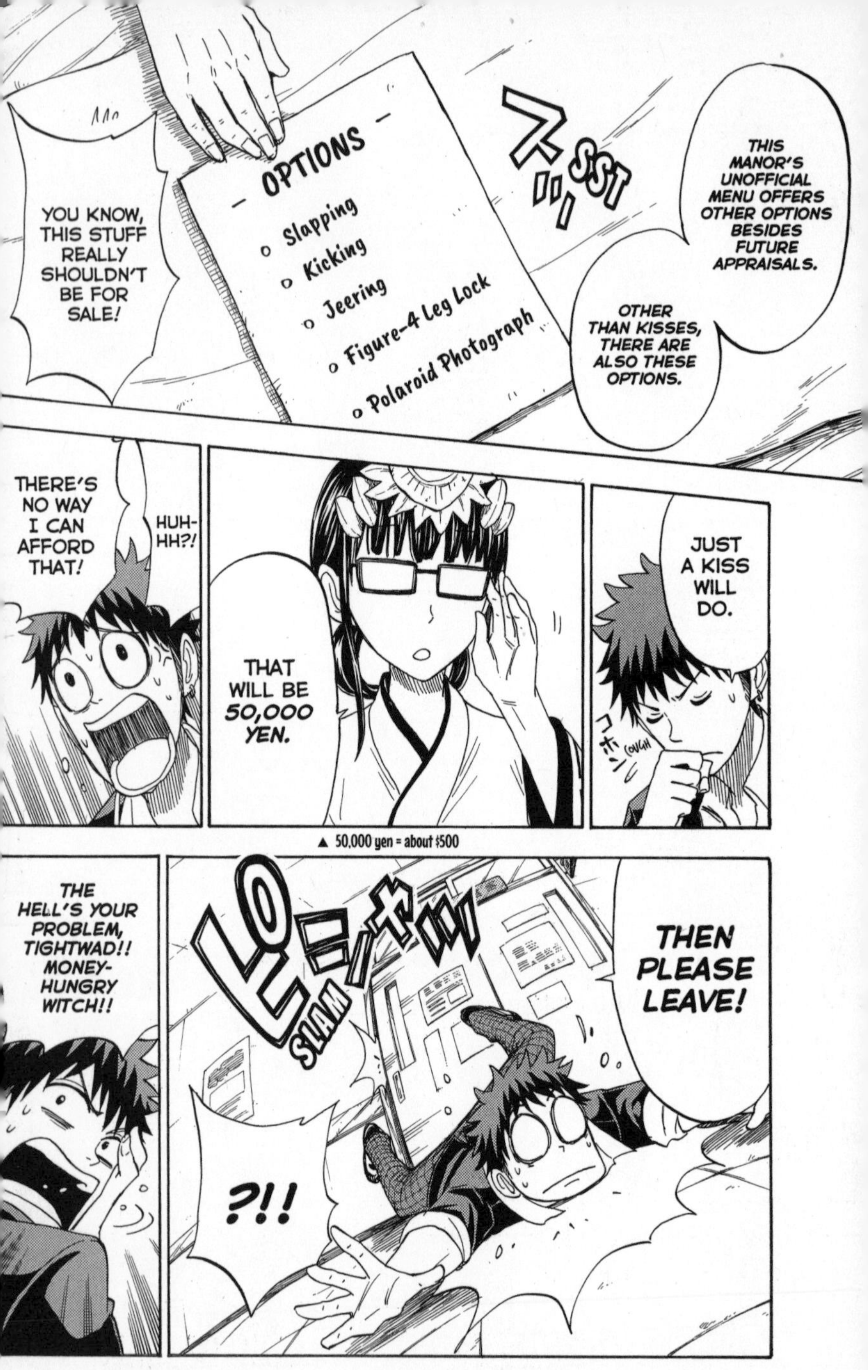
THIS MANOR'S UNOFFICIAL MENU OFFERS OTHER OPTIONS BESIDES FUTURE APPRAISALS.
OTHER THAN KISSES, THERE ARE ALSO THESE OPTIONS.
SST
— OPTIONS —
o Slapping
o Kicking
o Jeering
o Figure-4 Leg Lock
o Polaroid Photograph
YOU KNOW, THIS STUFF REALLY SHOULDN'T BE FOR SALE!
JUST A KISS WILL DO.
COUGH
THAT WILL BE 50,000 YEN.
HUH-HH?!
THERE'S NO WAY I CAN AFFORD THAT!
▲ 50,000 yen = about $500
THEN PLEASE LEAVE!
SLAM
?!!
THE HELL'S YOUR PROBLEM, TIGHTWAD!! MONEY-HUNGRY WITCH!!

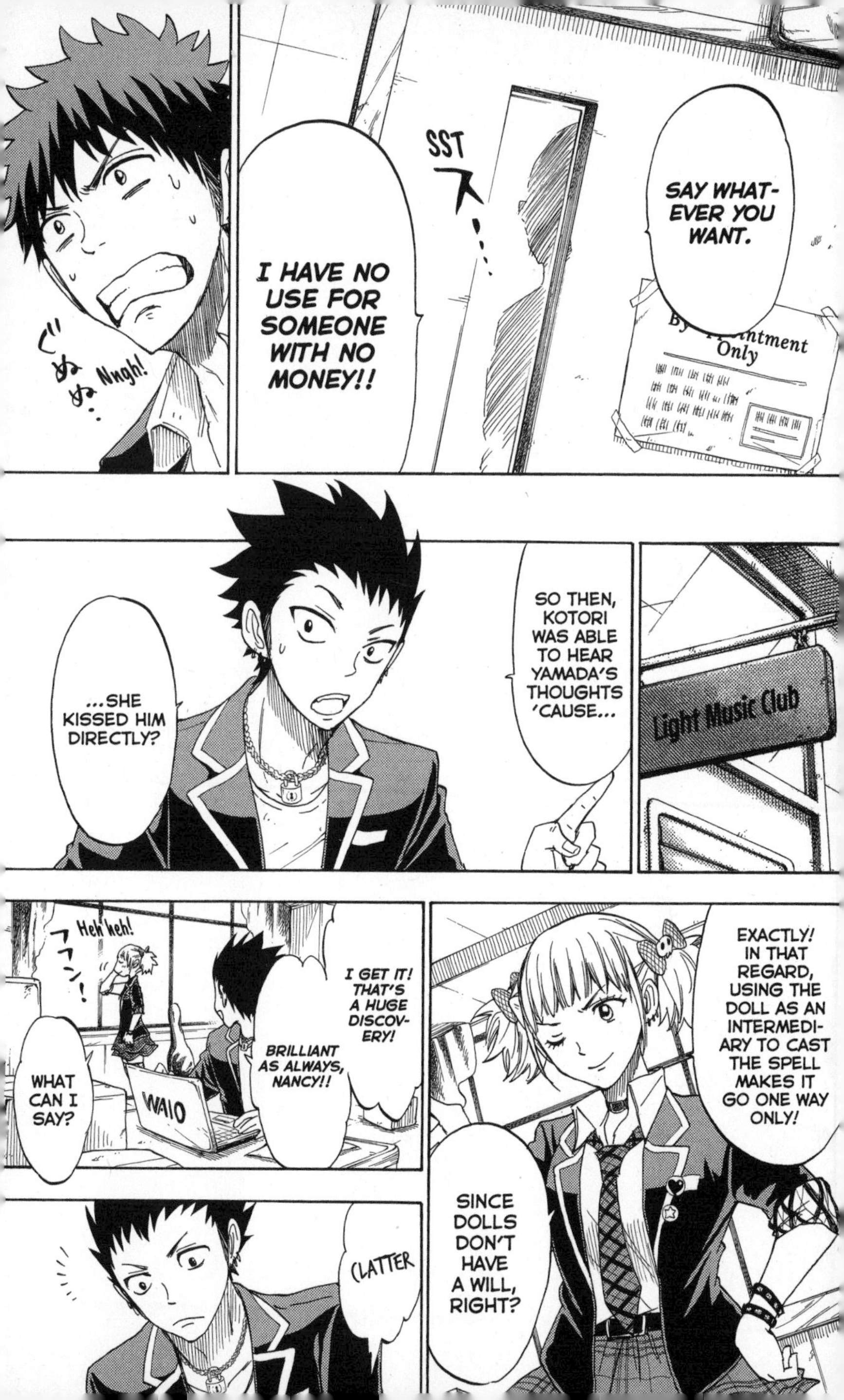
SAY WHAT-EVER YOU WANT.
SST
I HAVE NO USE FOR SOMEONE WITH NO MONEY!!
ぐぬぬ…
Nngh!
Light Music Club
SO THEN, KOTORI WAS ABLE TO HEAR YAMADA'S THOUGHTS 'CAUSE...
...SHE KISSED HIM DIRECTLY?
EXACTLY! IN THAT REGARD, USING THE DOLL AS AN INTERMEDIARY TO CAST THE SPELL MAKES IT GO ONE WAY ONLY!
SINCE DOLLS DON'T HAVE A WILL, RIGHT?
I GET IT! THAT'S A HUGE DISCOVERY!
BRILLIANT AS ALWAYS, NANCY!!
フフン!
Heh heh!
WHAT CAN I SAY?
WAIO
CLATTER

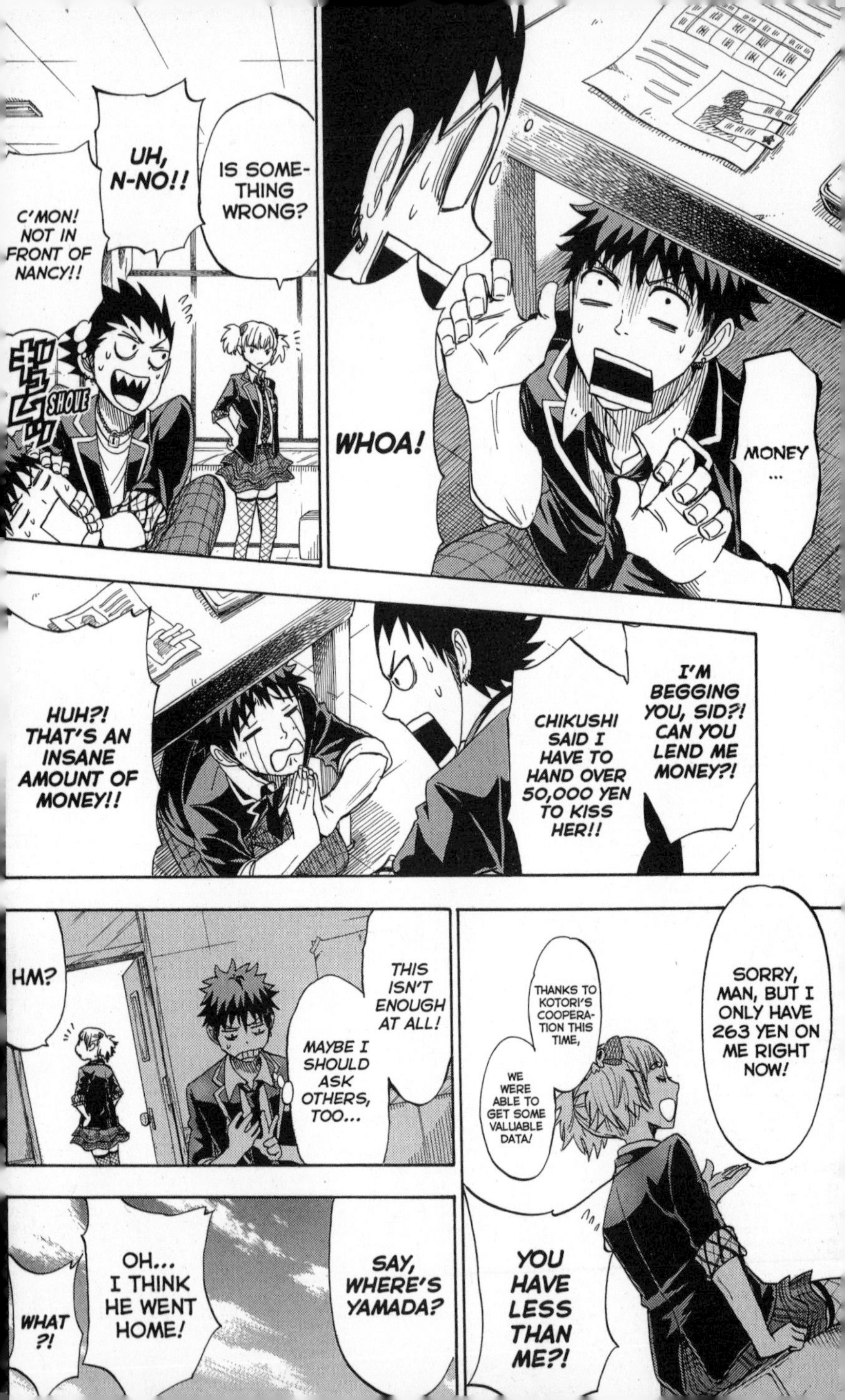

MONEY ...
WHOA!
IS SOME-THING WRONG?
UH, N-NO!!
C'MON! NOT IN FRONT OF NANCY!!
SHOVE
I'M BEGGING YOU, SID?! CAN YOU LEND ME MONEY?!
CHIKUSHI SAID I HAVE TO HAND OVER 50,000 YEN TO KISS HER!!
HUH?! THAT'S AN INSANE AMOUNT OF MONEY!!
SORRY, MAN, BUT I ONLY HAVE 263 YEN ON ME RIGHT NOW!
THANKS TO KOTORI'S COOPERA-TION THIS TIME,
WE WERE ABLE TO GET SOME VALUABLE DATA!
YOU HAVE LESS THAN ME?!
THIS ISN'T ENOUGH AT ALL!
MAYBE I SHOULD ASK OTHERS, TOO...
HM?
SAY, WHERE'S YAMADA?
OH... I THINK HE WENT HOME!
WHAT ?!

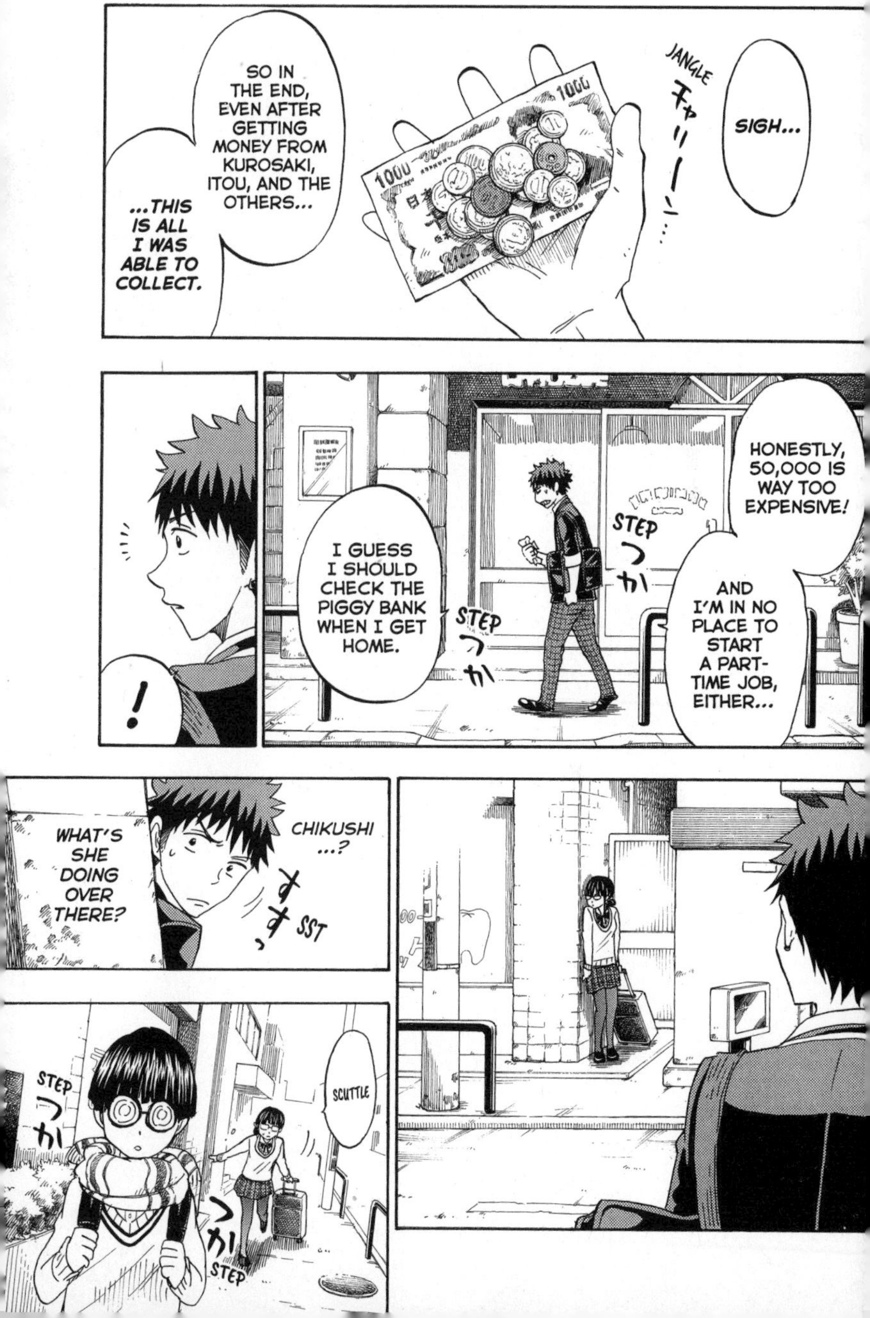
JANGLE
SIGH...
SO IN THE END, EVEN AFTER GETTING MONEY FROM KUROSAKI, ITOU, AND THE OTHERS...
...THIS IS ALL I WAS ABLE TO COLLECT.
HONESTLY, 50,000 IS WAY TOO EXPENSIVE!
AND I'M IN NO PLACE TO START A PART-TIME JOB, EITHER...
STEP
STEP
I GUESS I SHOULD CHECK THE PIGGY BANK WHEN I GET HOME.
!
CHIKUSHI ...?
SST
WHAT'S SHE DOING OVER THERE?
SCUTTLE
STEP
STEP

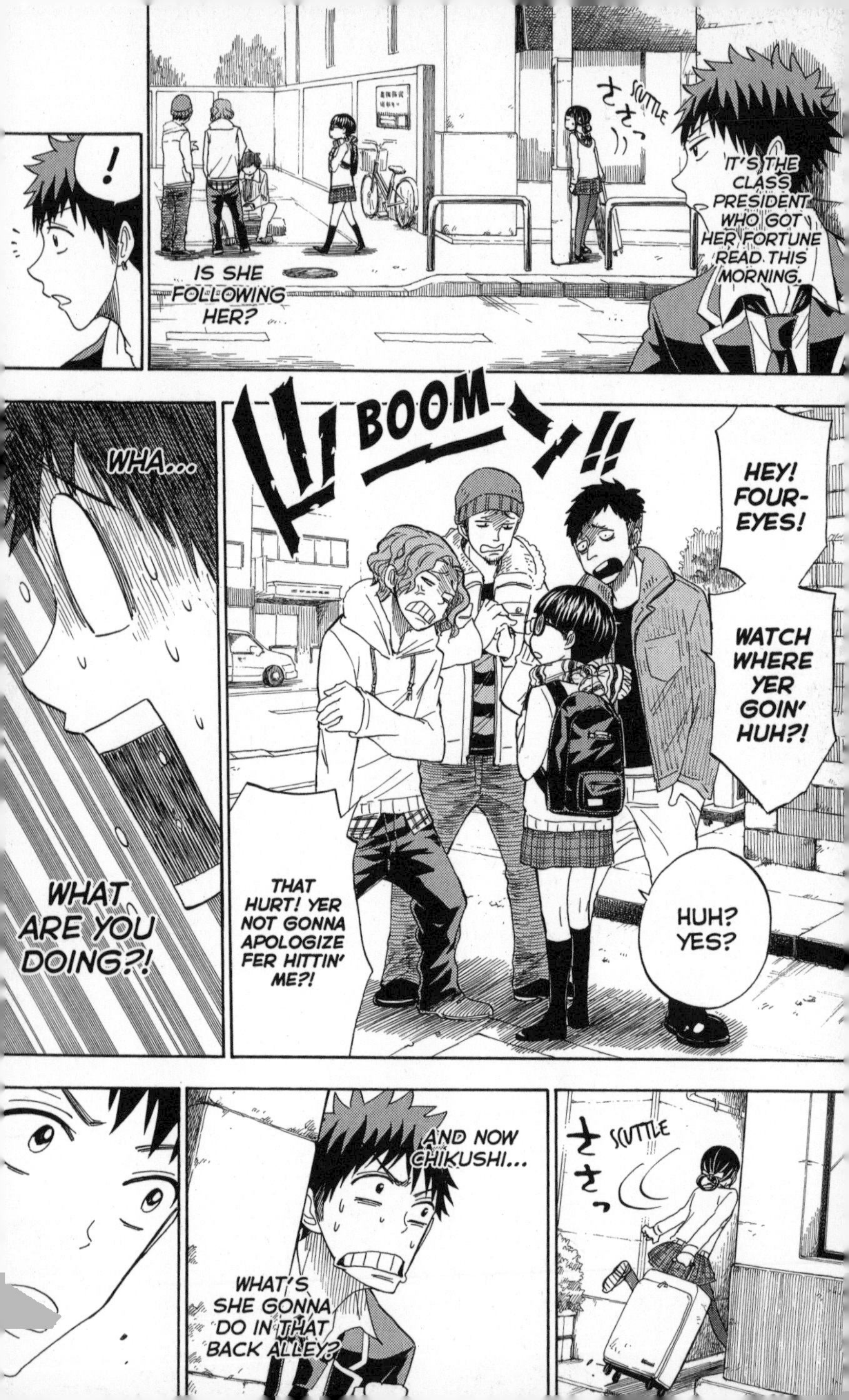
SCUTTLE
IT'S THE CLASS PRESIDENT WHO GOT HER FORTUNE READ THIS MORNING.
IS SHE FOLLOWING HER?
!
BOOM
HEY! FOUR-EYES!
WATCH WHERE YER GOIN' HUH?!
THAT HURT! YER NOT GONNA APOLOGIZE FER HITTIN' ME?!
HUH? YES?
WHA...
WHAT ARE YOU DOING?!
SCUTTLE
AND NOW CHIKUSHI...
WHAT'S SHE GONNA DO IN THAT BACK ALLEY?

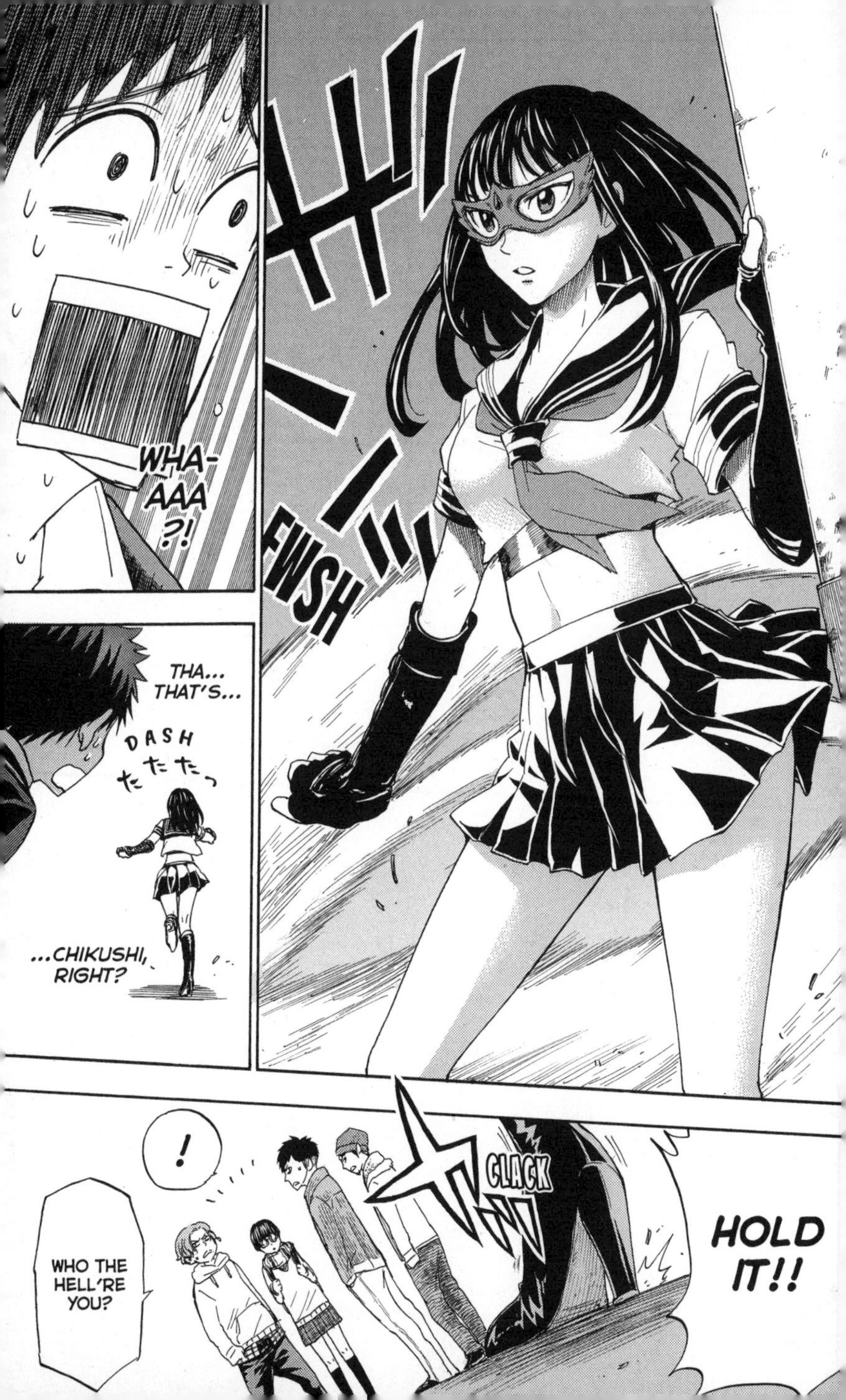
FWSH
WHA-AAA?!
THA... THAT'S...
DASH
たたたっ
...CHIKUSHI, RIGHT?
HOLD IT!!
CLACK
!
WHO THE HELL'RE YOU?

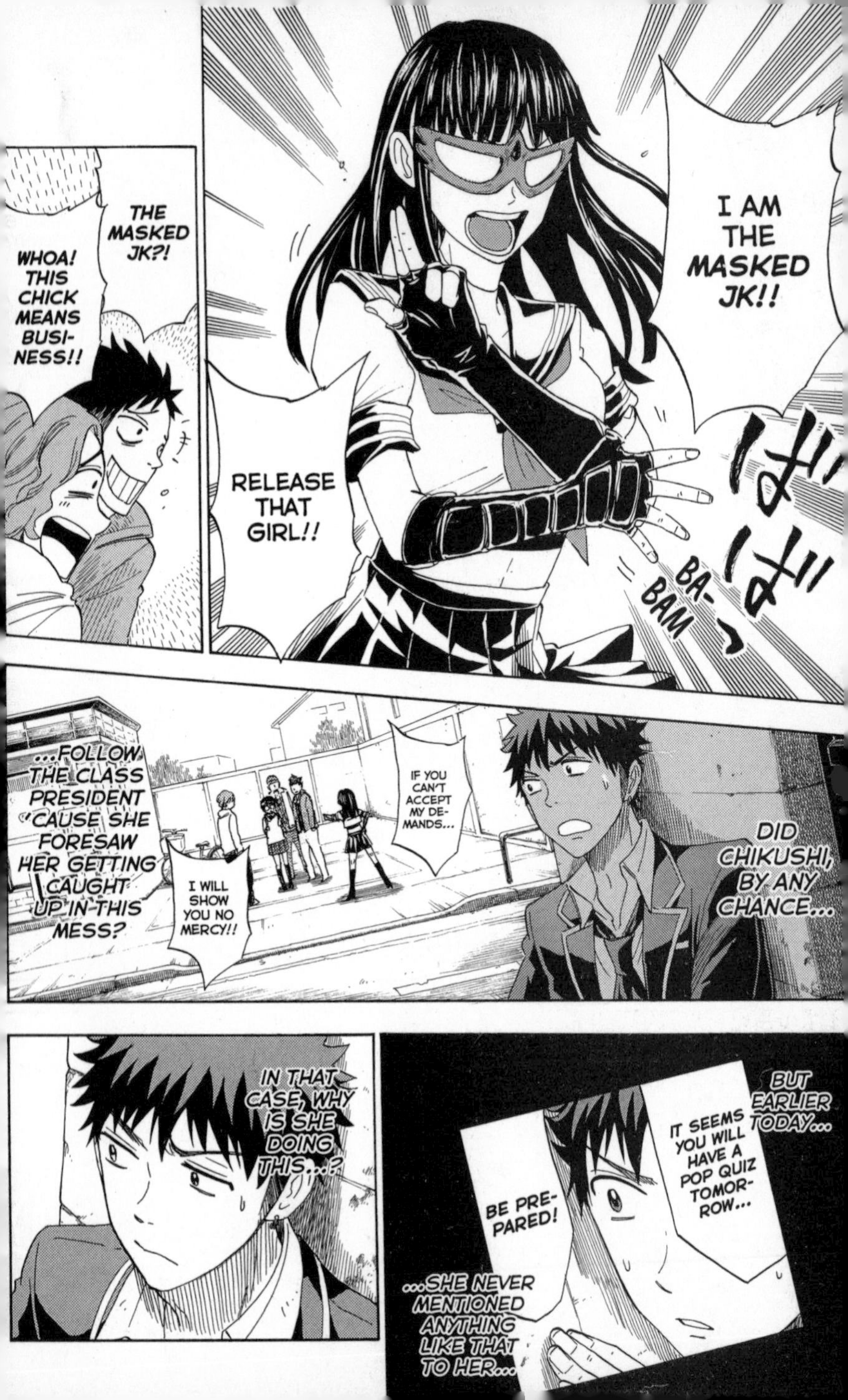
I AM THE MASKED JK!!
BA-BAM
RELEASE THAT GIRL!!
THE MASKED JK?!
WHOA! THIS CHICK MEANS BUSI-NESS!!
DID CHIKUSHI, BY ANY CHANCE...
IF YOU CAN'T ACCEPT MY DE-MANDS...
I WILL SHOW YOU NO MERCY!!
...FOLLOW THE CLASS PRESIDENT 'CAUSE SHE FORESAW HER GETTING CAUGHT UP IN THIS MESS?
BUT EARLIER TODAY...
IT SEEMS YOU WILL HAVE A POP QUIZ TOMOR-ROW...
BE PRE-PARED!
...SHE NEVER MENTIONED ANYTHING LIKE THAT TO HER...
IN THAT CASE, WHY IS SHE DOING THIS...?

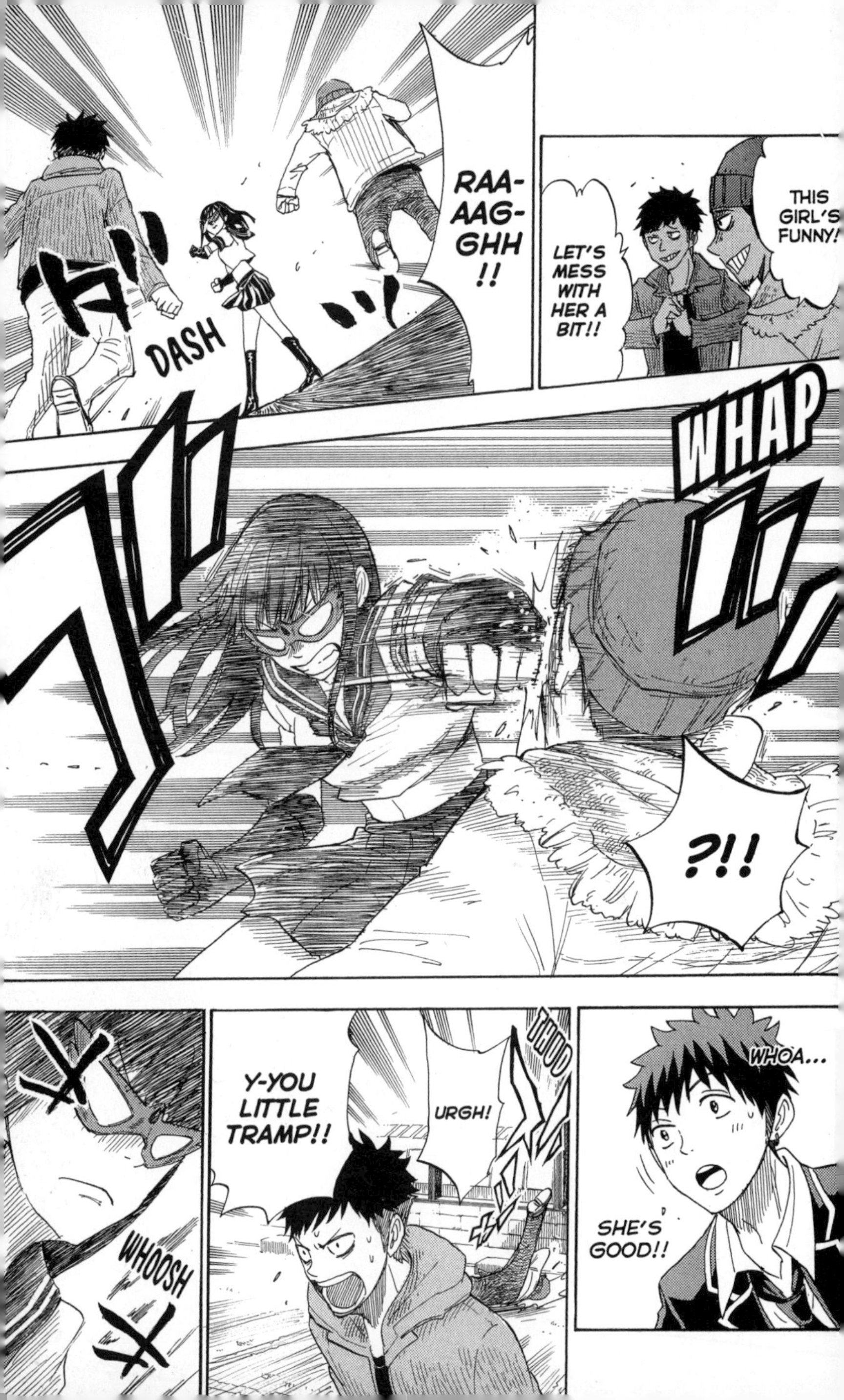
THIS GIRL'S FUNNY!
LET'S MESS WITH HER A BIT!!
RAA-AAG-GHH!!
DASH
WHAP
?!!
WHOA...
SHE'S GOOD!!
THUD
URGH!
Y-YOU LITTLE TRAMP!!
WHOOSH

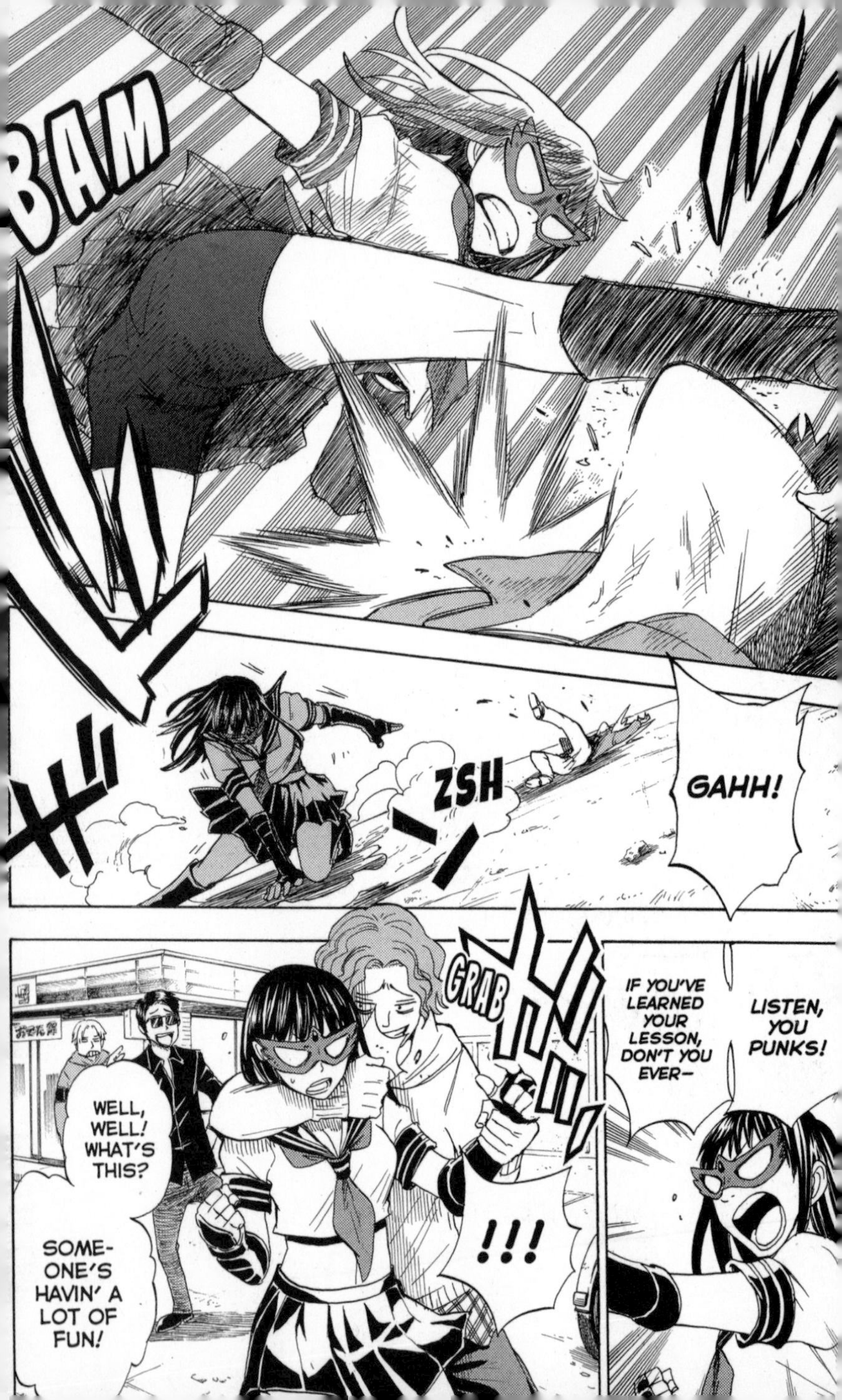
BAM
GAHH!
ZSH
LISTEN, YOU PUNKS!
IF YOU'VE LEARNED YOUR LESSON, DON'T YOU EVER—
GRAB
!!!
WELL, WELL! WHAT'S THIS?
SOME-ONE'S HAVIN' A LOT OF FUN!

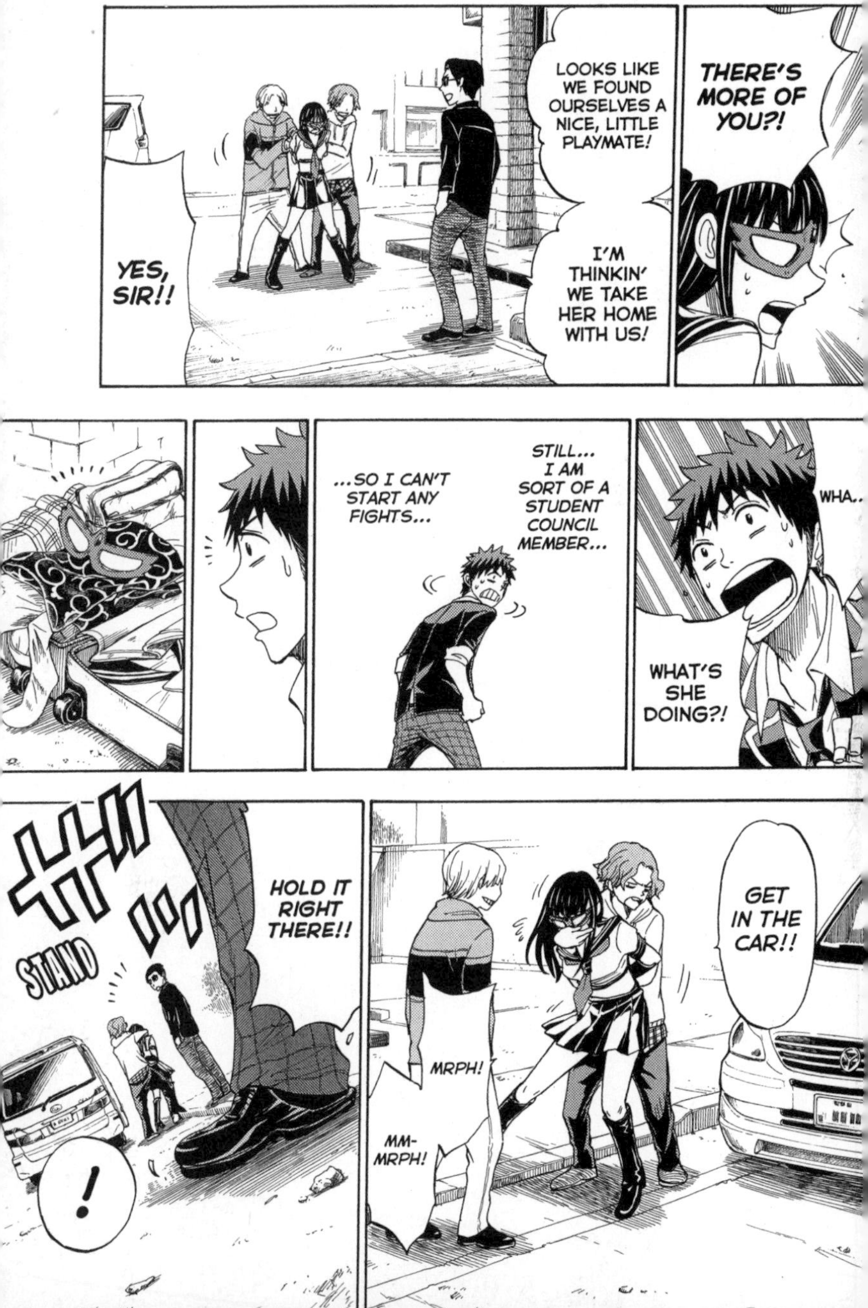
THERE'S MORE OF YOU?!
LOOKS LIKE WE FOUND OURSELVES A NICE, LITTLE PLAYMATE!
I'M THINKIN' WE TAKE HER HOME WITH US!
YES, SIR!!
WHA..
WHAT'S SHE DOING?!
STILL... I AM SORT OF A STUDENT COUNCIL MEMBER...
...SO I CAN'T START ANY FIGHTS...
GET IN THE CAR!!
MRPH!
MM-MRPH!
HOLD IT RIGHT THERE!!
STAND
!

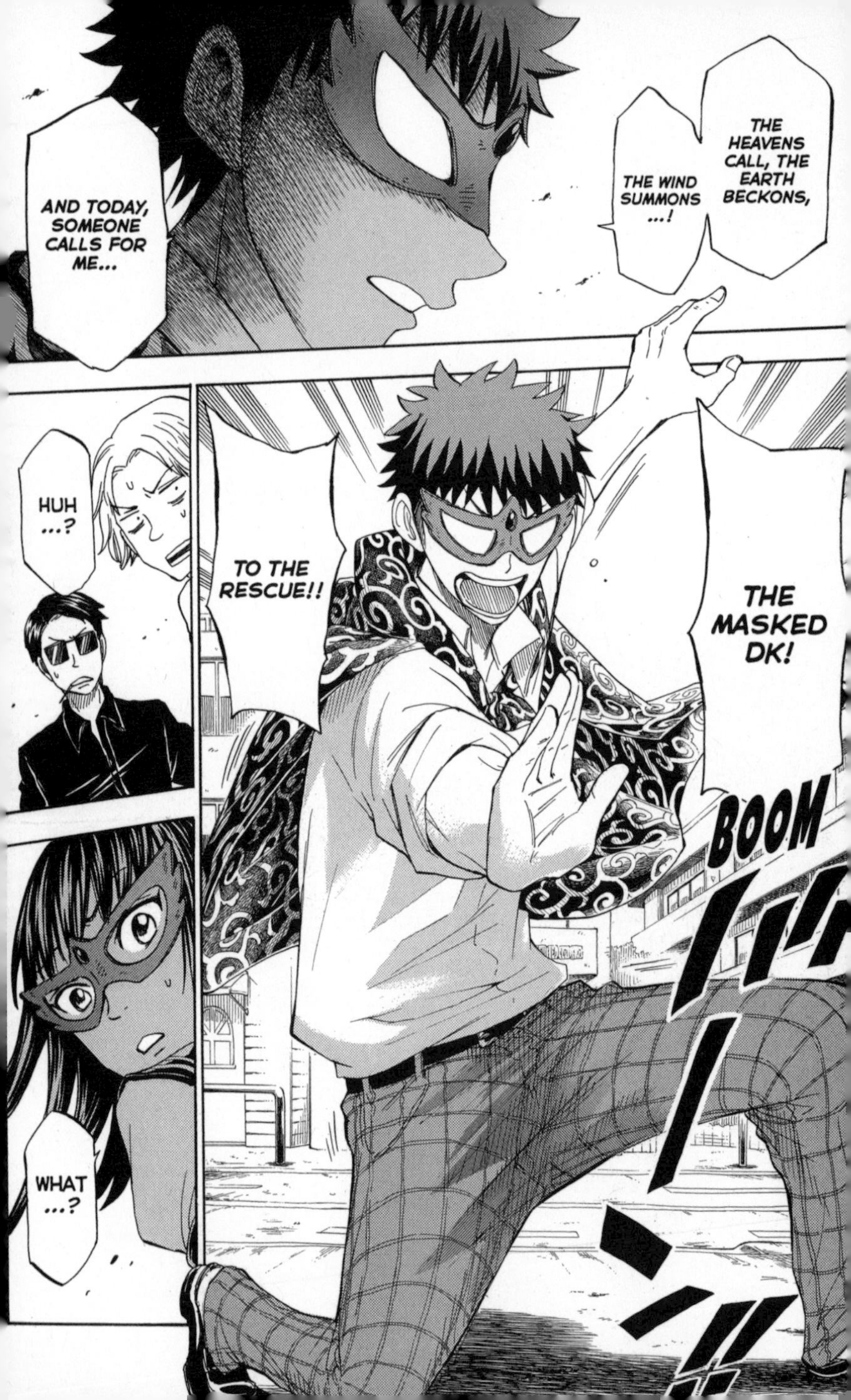
THE HEAVENS CALL, THE EARTH BECKONS,
THE WIND SUMMONS ...!
AND TODAY, SOMEONE CALLS FOR ME...
THE MASKED DK!
TO THE RESCUE!!
BOOM
HUH ...?
WHAT ...?

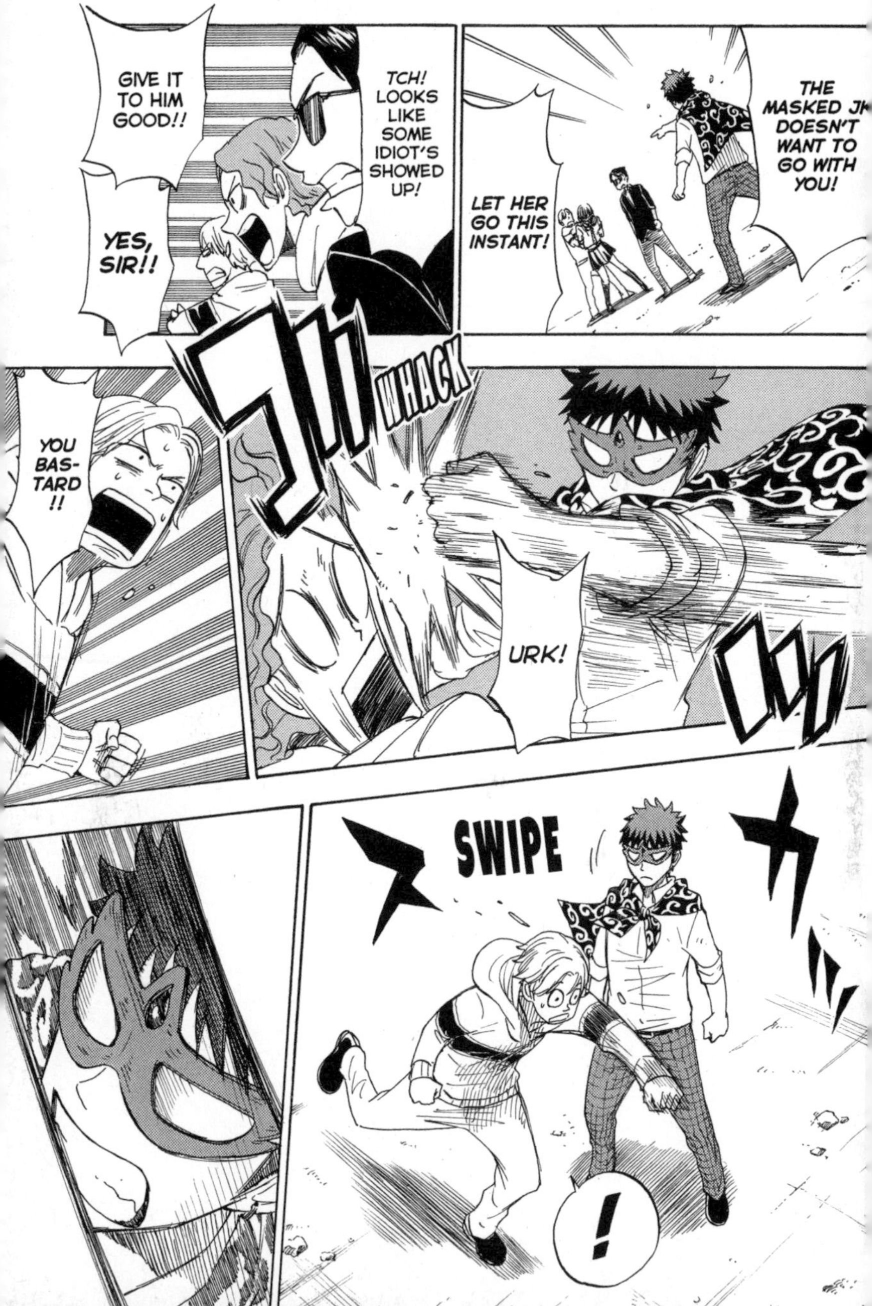
THE MASKED JK DOESN'T WANT TO GO WITH YOU!
LET HER GO THIS INSTANT!
TCH! LOOKS LIKE SOME IDIOT'S SHOWED UP!
GIVE IT TO HIM GOOD!!
YES, SIR!!
WHACK
URK!
YOU BAS-TARD!!
SWIPE
!

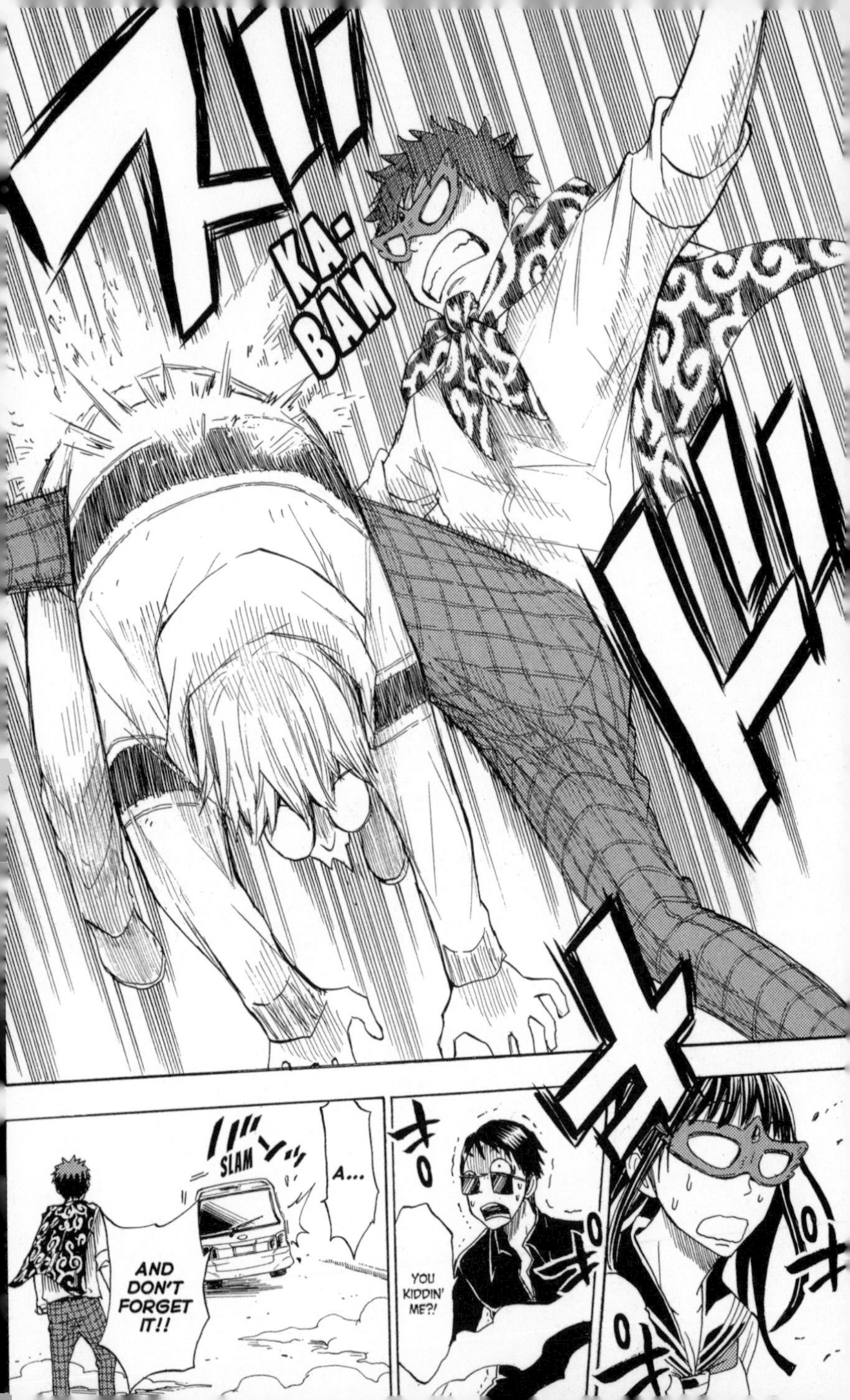
KA-BAM
YOU KIDDIN' ME?!
A...
SLAM
AND DON'T FORGET IT!!

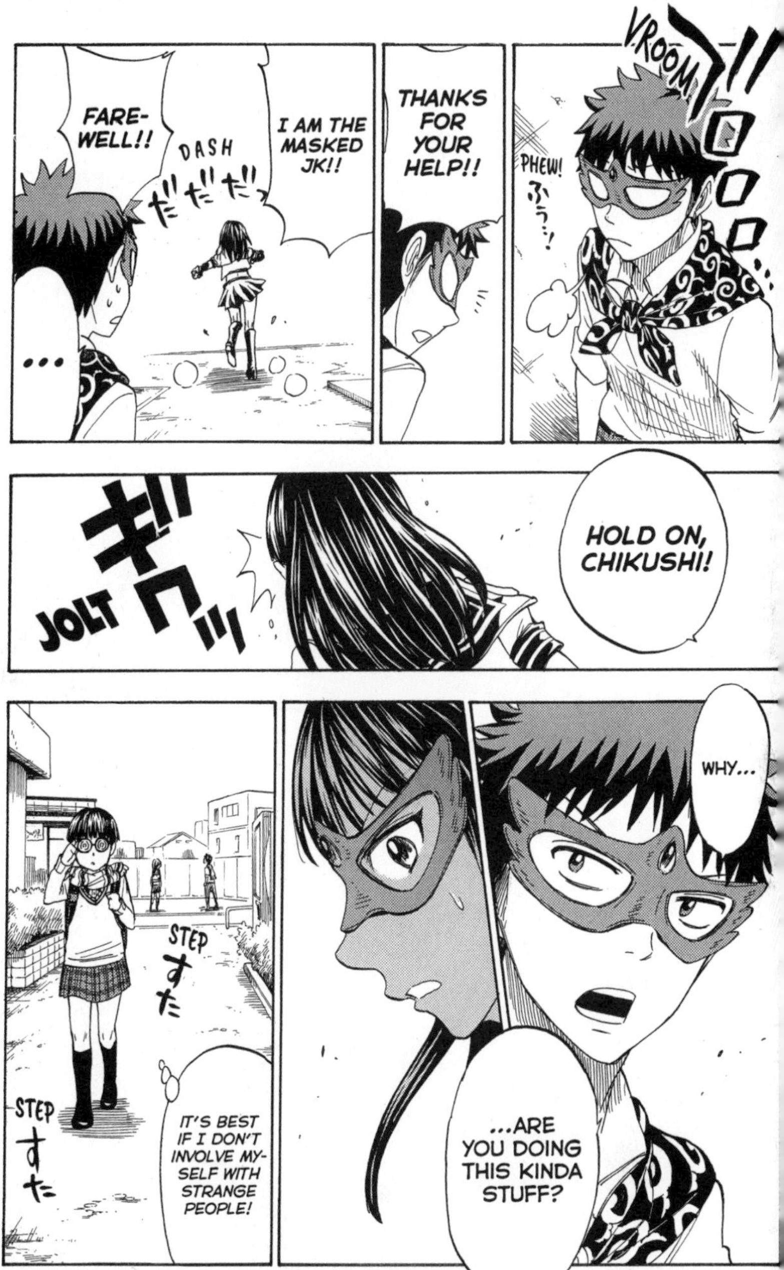
VROOM
PHEW!
ふう…!
THANKS FOR YOUR HELP!!
I AM THE MASKED JK!!
FARE-WELL!!
DASH
だだだっ
...
HOLD ON, CHIKUSHI!
JOLT
ギクッ
WHY...
...ARE YOU DOING THIS KINDA STUFF?
STEP
すた
IT'S BEST IF I DON'T INVOLVE MY-SELF WITH STRANGE PEOPLE!
STEP
すた

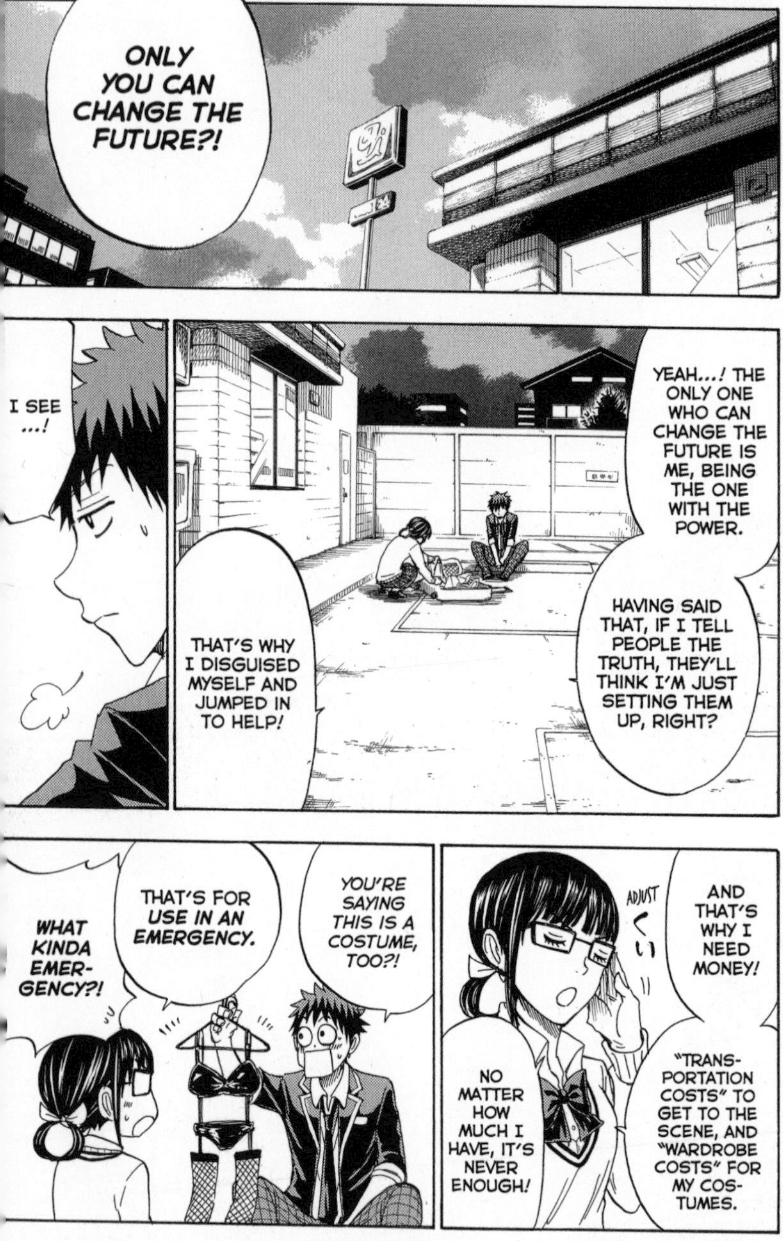
ONLY YOU CAN CHANGE THE FUTURE?!
YEAH...! THE ONLY ONE WHO CAN CHANGE THE FUTURE IS ME, BEING THE ONE WITH THE POWER.
HAVING SAID THAT, IF I TELL PEOPLE THE TRUTH, THEY'LL THINK I'M JUST SETTING THEM UP, RIGHT?
THAT'S WHY I DISGUISED MYSELF AND JUMPED IN TO HELP!
I SEE ...!
AND THAT'S WHY I NEED MONEY!
ADJUST
くい
"TRANSPORTATION COSTS" TO GET TO THE SCENE, AND "WARDROBE COSTS" FOR MY COSTUMES.
NO MATTER HOW MUCH I HAVE, IT'S NEVER ENOUGH!
YOU'RE SAYING THIS IS A COSTUME, TOO?!
THAT'S FOR USE IN AN EMERGENCY.
WHAT KINDA EMERGENCY?!

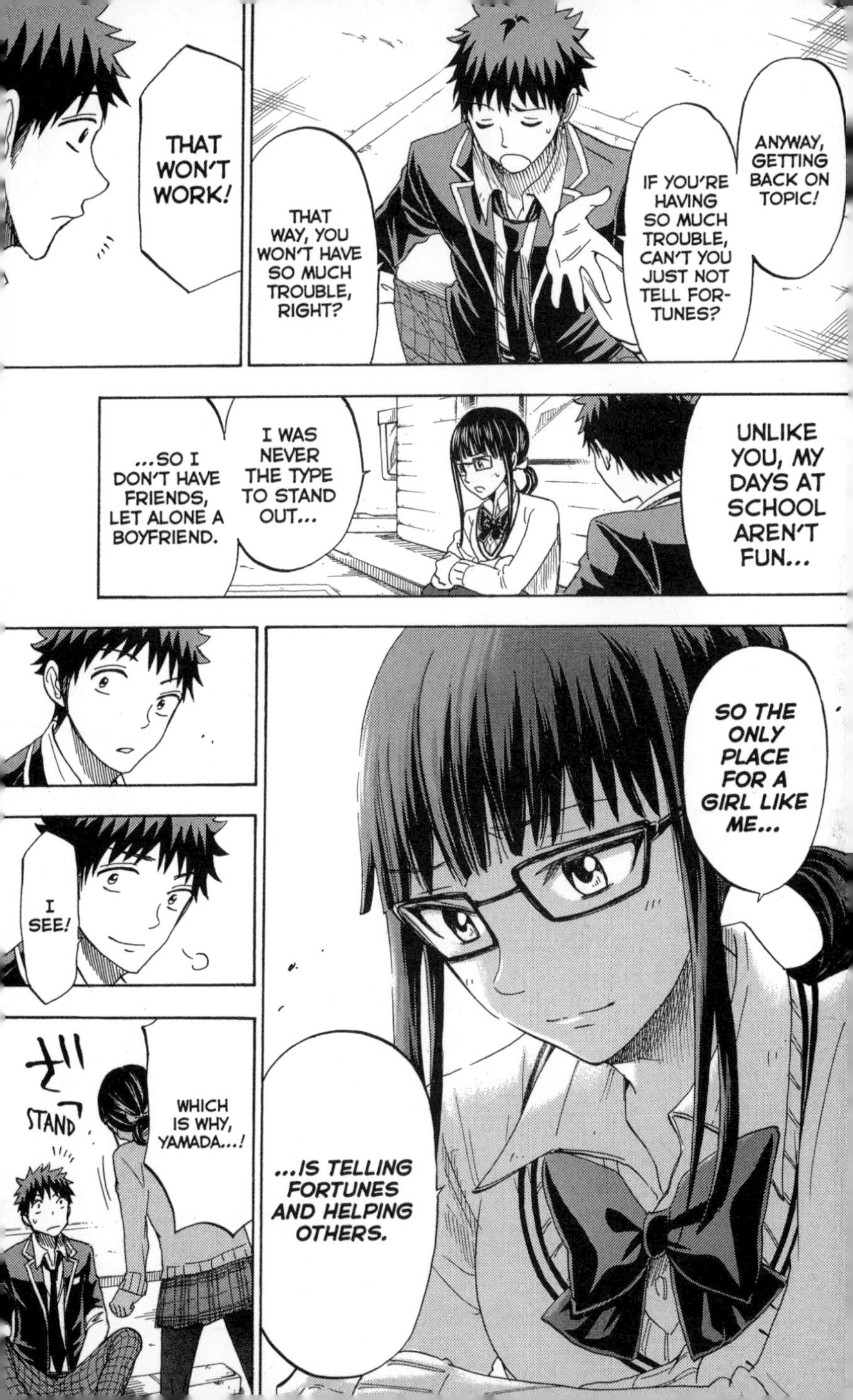
ANYWAY, GETTING BACK ON TOPIC!
IF YOU'RE HAVING SO MUCH TROUBLE, CAN'T YOU JUST NOT TELL FOR-TUNES?
THAT WAY, YOU WON'T HAVE SO MUCH TROUBLE, RIGHT?
THAT WON'T WORK!
UNLIKE YOU, MY DAYS AT SCHOOL AREN'T FUN...
I WAS NEVER THE TYPE TO STAND OUT...
...SO I DON'T HAVE FRIENDS, LET ALONE A BOYFRIEND.
SO THE ONLY PLACE FOR A GIRL LIKE ME...
...IS TELLING FORTUNES AND HELPING OTHERS.
I SEE!
WHICH IS WHY, YAMADA...!
STAND

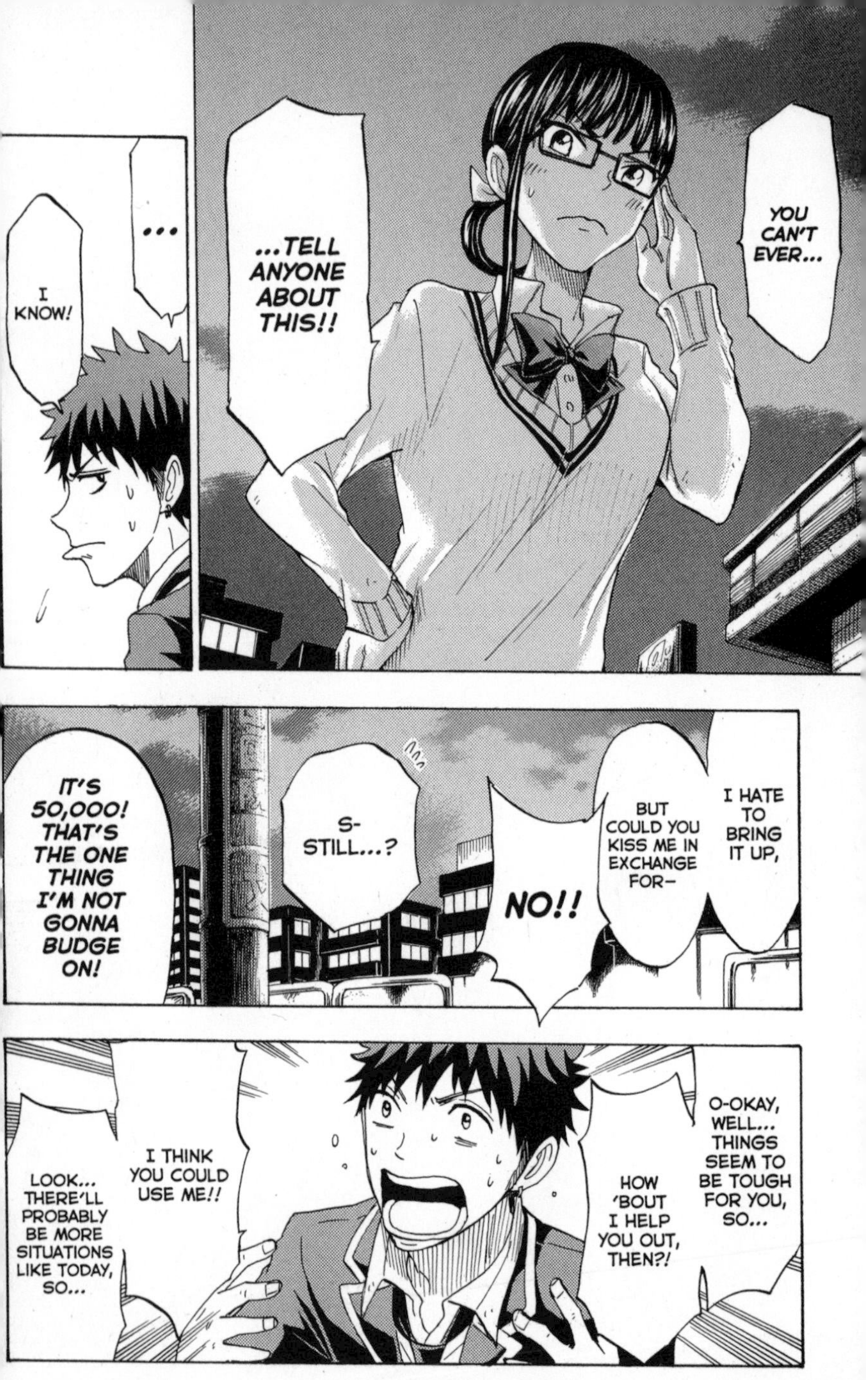
YOU CAN'T EVER...
...TELL ANYONE ABOUT THIS!!
...
I KNOW!
I HATE TO BRING IT UP,
BUT COULD YOU KISS ME IN EXCHANGE FOR–
NO!!
S- STILL...?
IT'S 50,000! THAT'S THE ONE THING I'M NOT GONNA BUDGE ON!
O-OKAY, WELL... THINGS SEEM TO BE TOUGH FOR YOU, SO...
HOW 'BOUT I HELP YOU OUT, THEN?!
I THINK YOU COULD USE ME!!
LOOK... THERE'LL PROBABLY BE MORE SITUATIONS LIKE TODAY, SO...

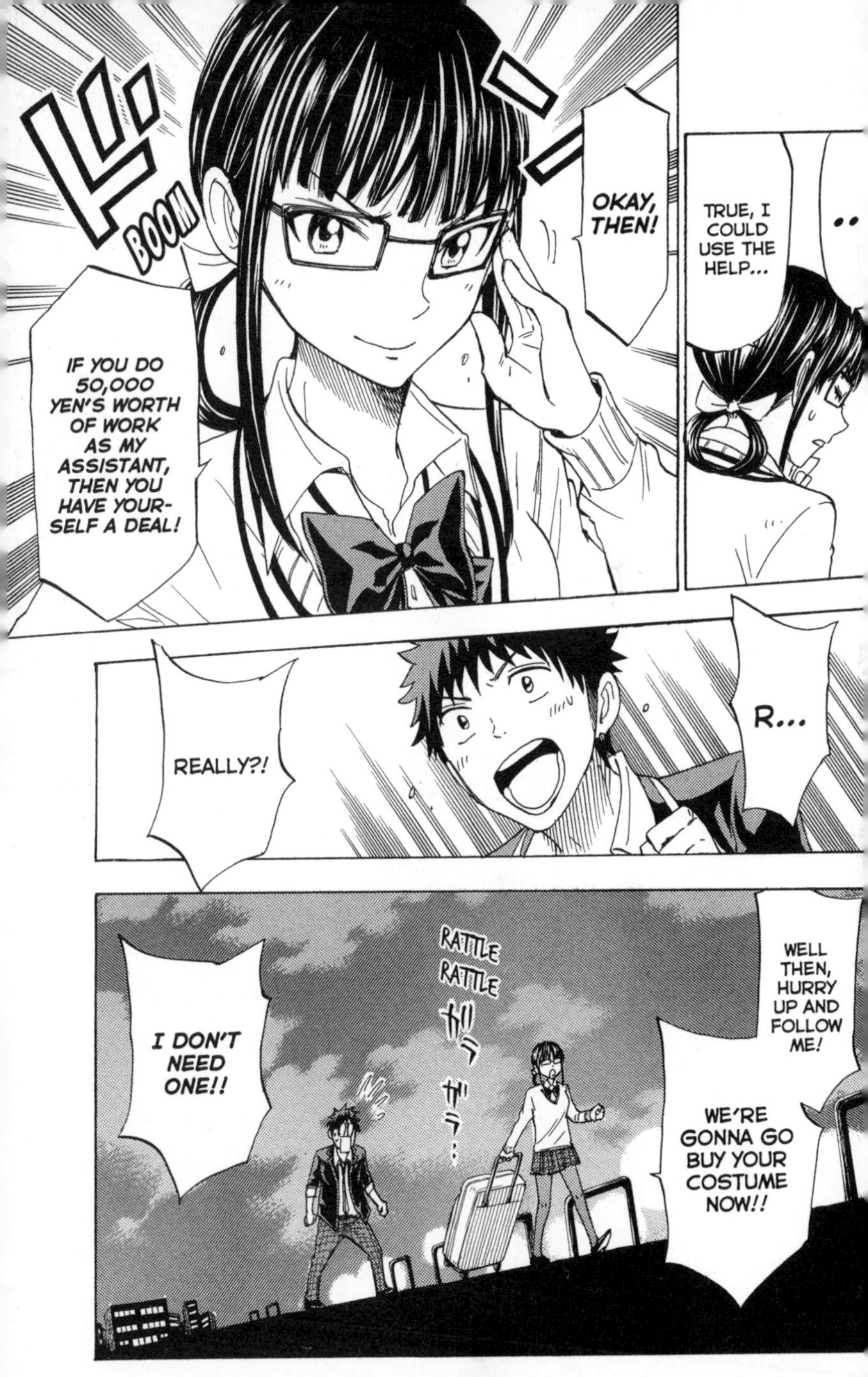
..
TRUE, I COULD USE THE HELP...
OKAY, THEN!
BOOM
IF YOU DO 50,000 YEN'S WORTH OF WORK AS MY ASSISTANT, THEN YOU HAVE YOURSELF A DEAL!
R...
REALLY?!
WELL THEN, HURRY UP AND FOLLOW ME!
WE'RE GONNA GO BUY YOUR COSTUME NOW!!
RATTLE RATTLE
I DON'T NEED ONE!!

Yamada-kun and the Seven Witches

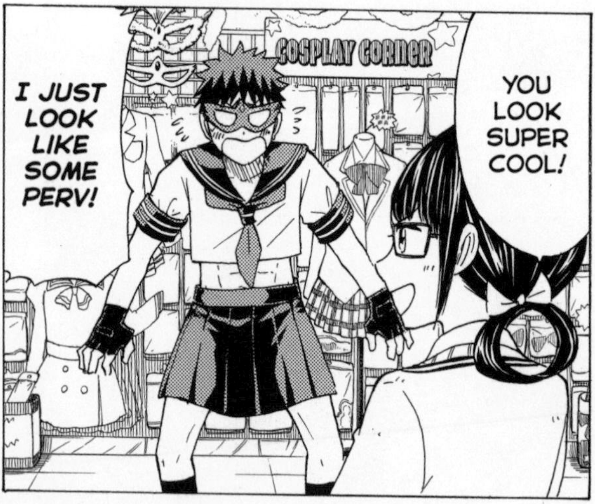
YOU LOOK SUPER COOL!
COSPLAY CORNER
I JUST LOOK LIKE SOME PERV!

CHAPTER 110: So lame...

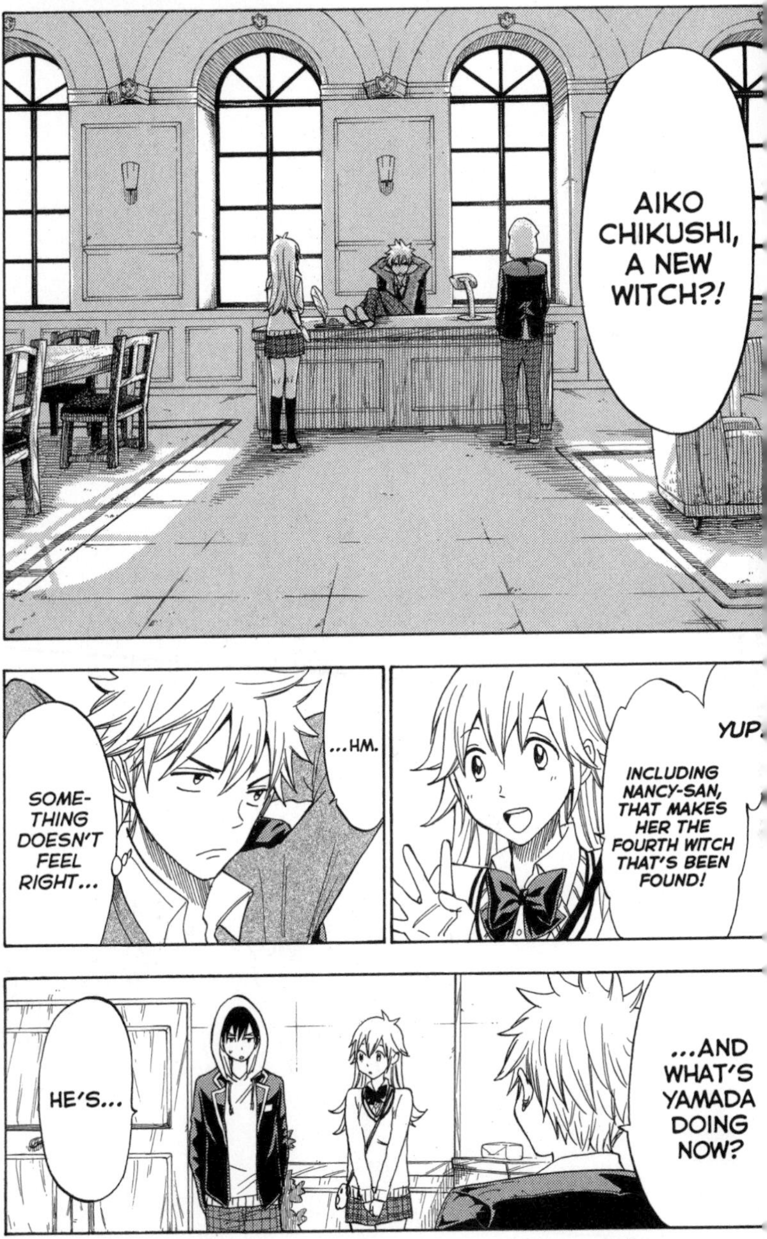
AIKO CHIKUSHI, A NEW WITCH?!
YUP.
INCLUDING NANCY-SAN, THAT MAKES HER THE FOURTH WITCH THAT'S BEEN FOUND!
...HM.
SOME-THING DOESN'T FEEL RIGHT...
...AND WHAT'S YAMADA DOING NOW?
HE'S...

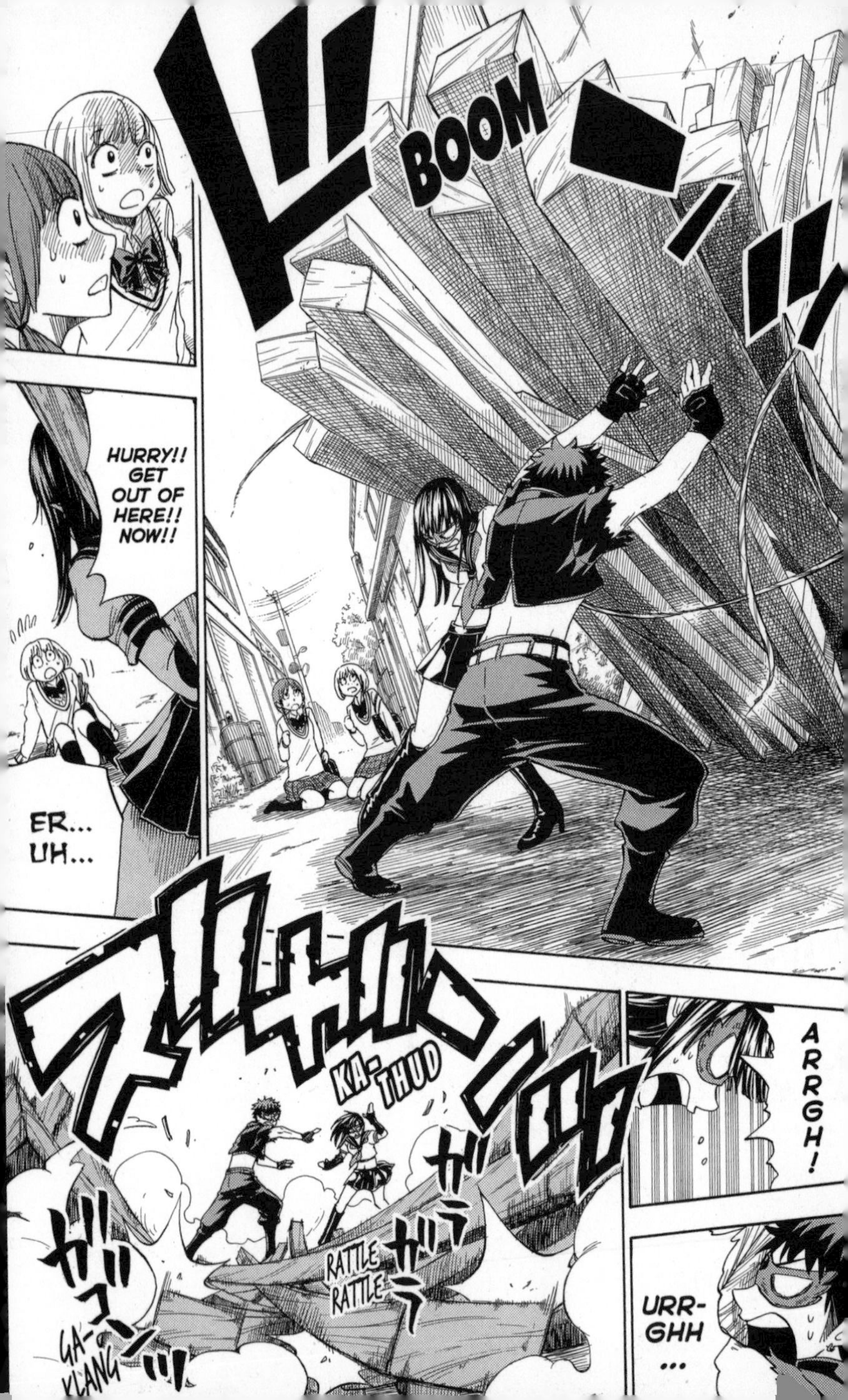
BOOM
HURRY!! GET OUT OF HERE!! NOW!!
ER... UH...
ARRGH!
URR-GHH...
KA-THUD
RATTLE RATTLE
GA-KLANG

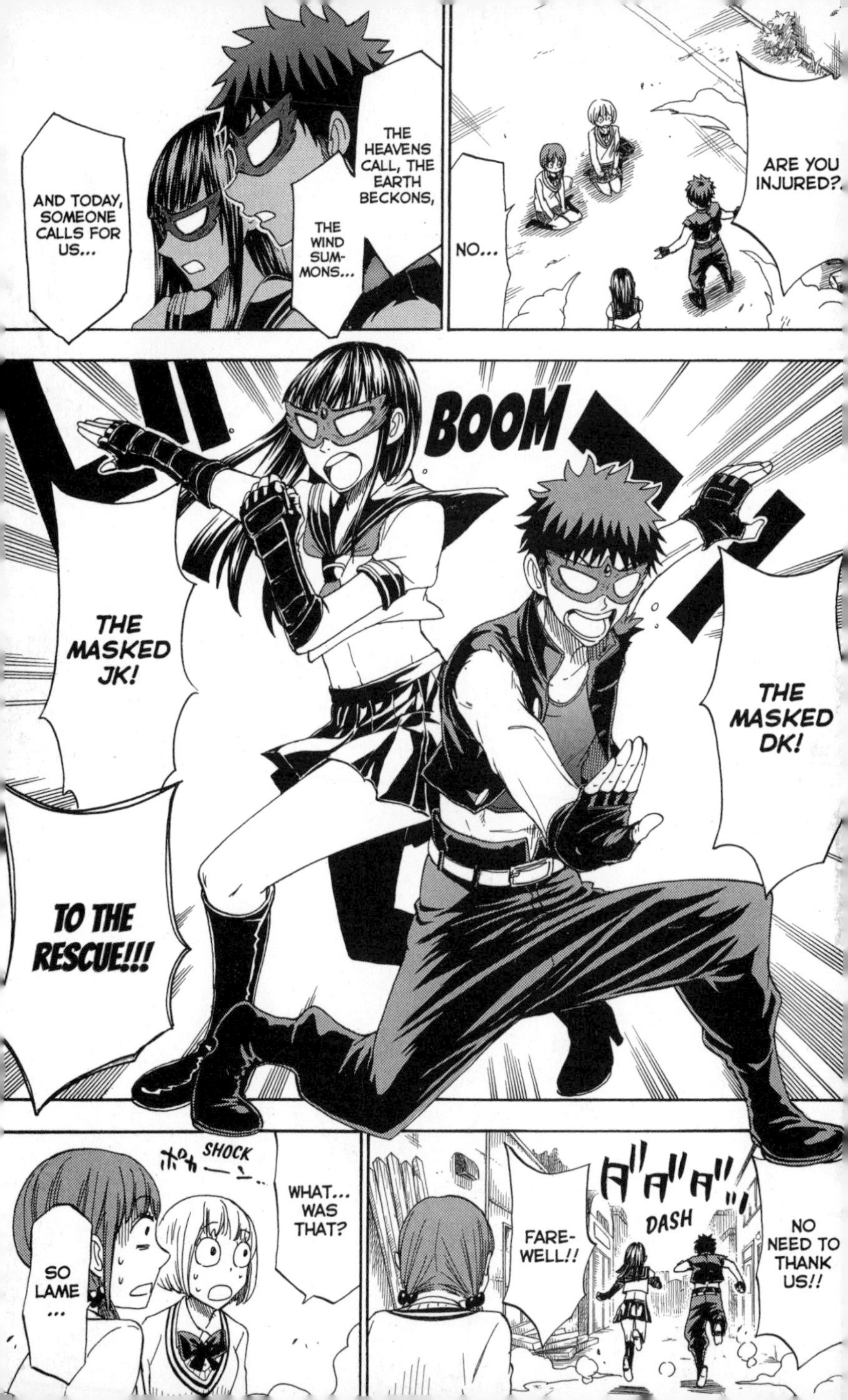
ARE YOU INJURED?.
NO...
THE HEAVENS CALL, THE EARTH BECKONS,
THE WIND SUM-MONS...
AND TODAY, SOMEONE CALLS FOR US...
BOOM
THE MASKED DK!
THE MASKED JK!
TO THE RESCUE!!!
NO NEED TO THANK US!!
DASH
FARE-WELL!!
SHOCK
WHAT... WAS THAT?
SO LAME ...

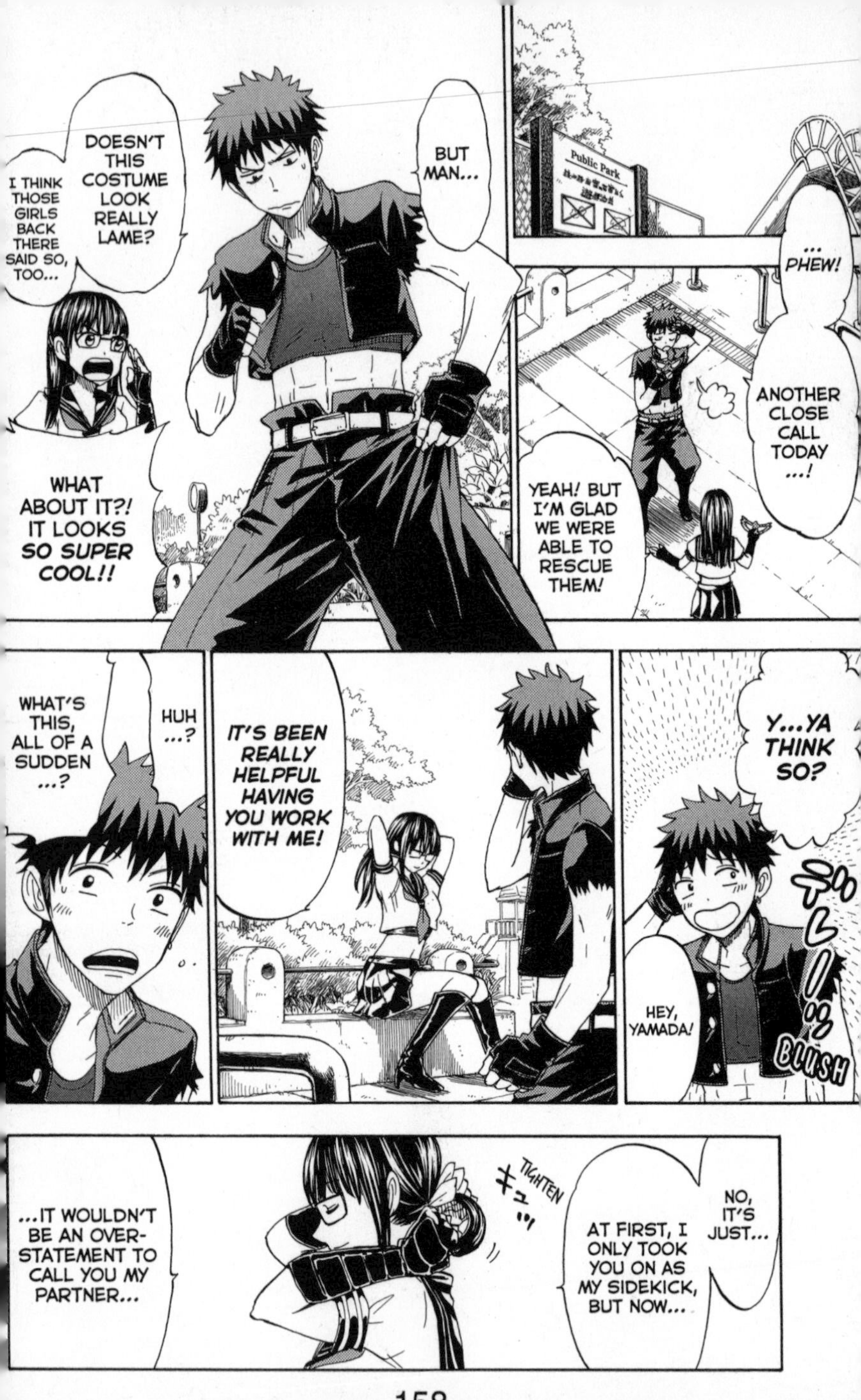
Public Park
...PHEW!
ANOTHER CLOSE CALL TODAY ...!
YEAH! BUT I'M GLAD WE WERE ABLE TO RESCUE THEM!
BUT MAN...
DOESN'T THIS COSTUME LOOK REALLY LAME?
I THINK THOSE GIRLS BACK THERE SAID SO, TOO...
WHAT ABOUT IT?! IT LOOKS SO SUPER COOL!!
Y...YA THINK SO?
BLUSH
HEY, YAMADA!
IT'S BEEN REALLY HELPFUL HAVING YOU WORK WITH ME!
HUH ...?
WHAT'S THIS, ALL OF A SUDDEN ...?
NO, IT'S JUST...
AT FIRST, I ONLY TOOK YOU ON AS MY SIDEKICK, BUT NOW...
TIGHTEN
...IT WOULDN'T BE AN OVER-STATEMENT TO CALL YOU MY PARTNER...

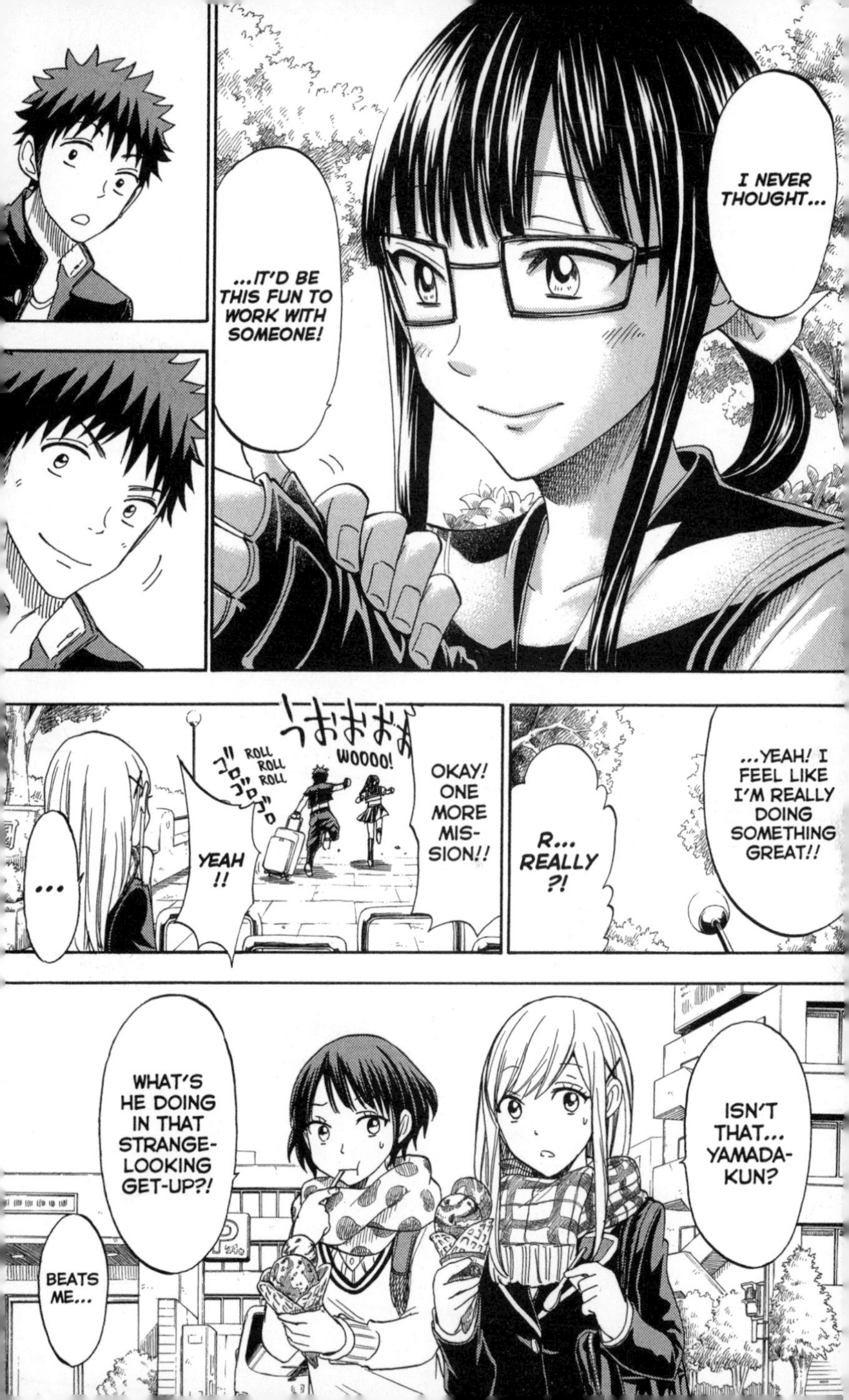
I NEVER THOUGHT...
...IT'D BE THIS FUN TO WORK WITH SOMEONE!
...YEAH! I FEEL LIKE I'M REALLY DOING SOMETHING GREAT!!
R... REALLY?!
OKAY! ONE MORE MISSION!!
うおおおお
WOOOO!
YEAH!!
ゴロゴロゴロ
ROLL ROLL ROLL
...
ISN'T THAT... YAMADA-KUN?
WHAT'S HE DOING IN THAT STRANGE-LOOKING GET-UP?!
BEATS ME...

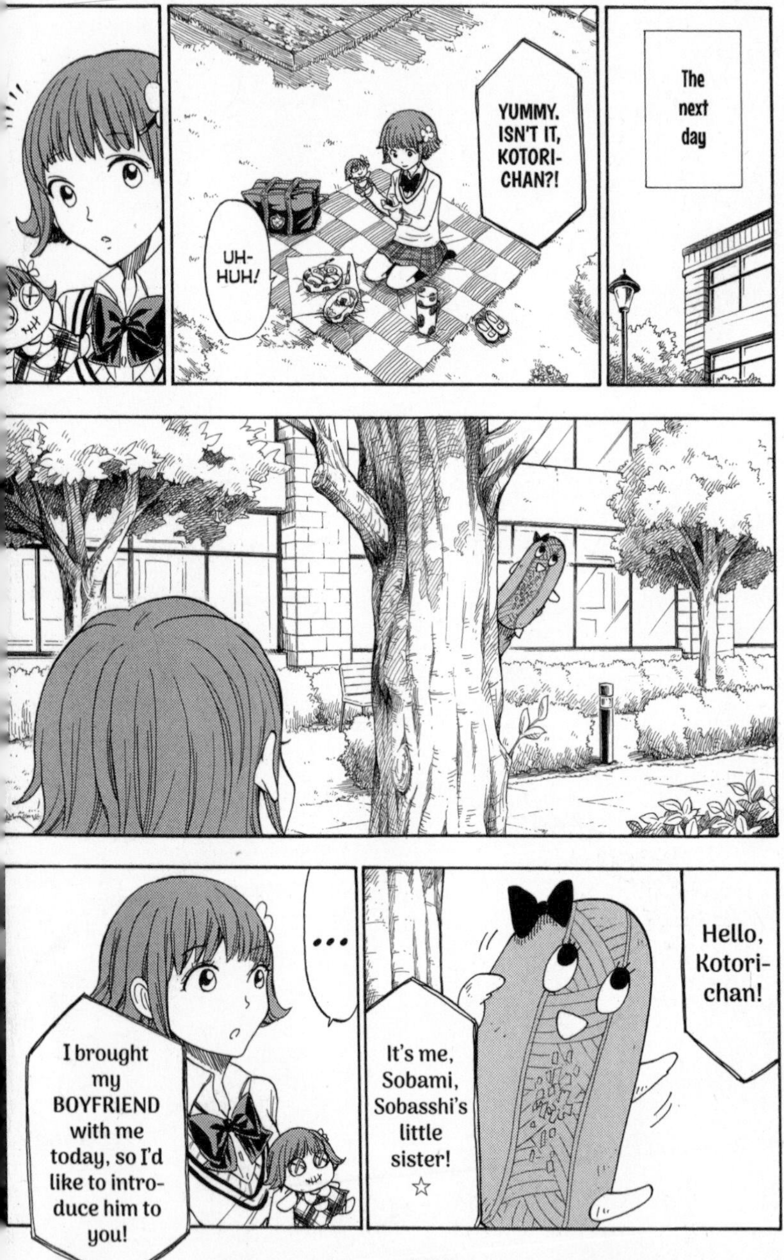
The next day
YUMMY. ISN'T IT, KOTORI-CHAN?!
UH-HUH!
Hello, Kotori-chan!
It's me, Sobami, Sobasshi's little sister! ☆
...
I brought my BOYFRIEND with me today, so I'd like to introduce him to you!

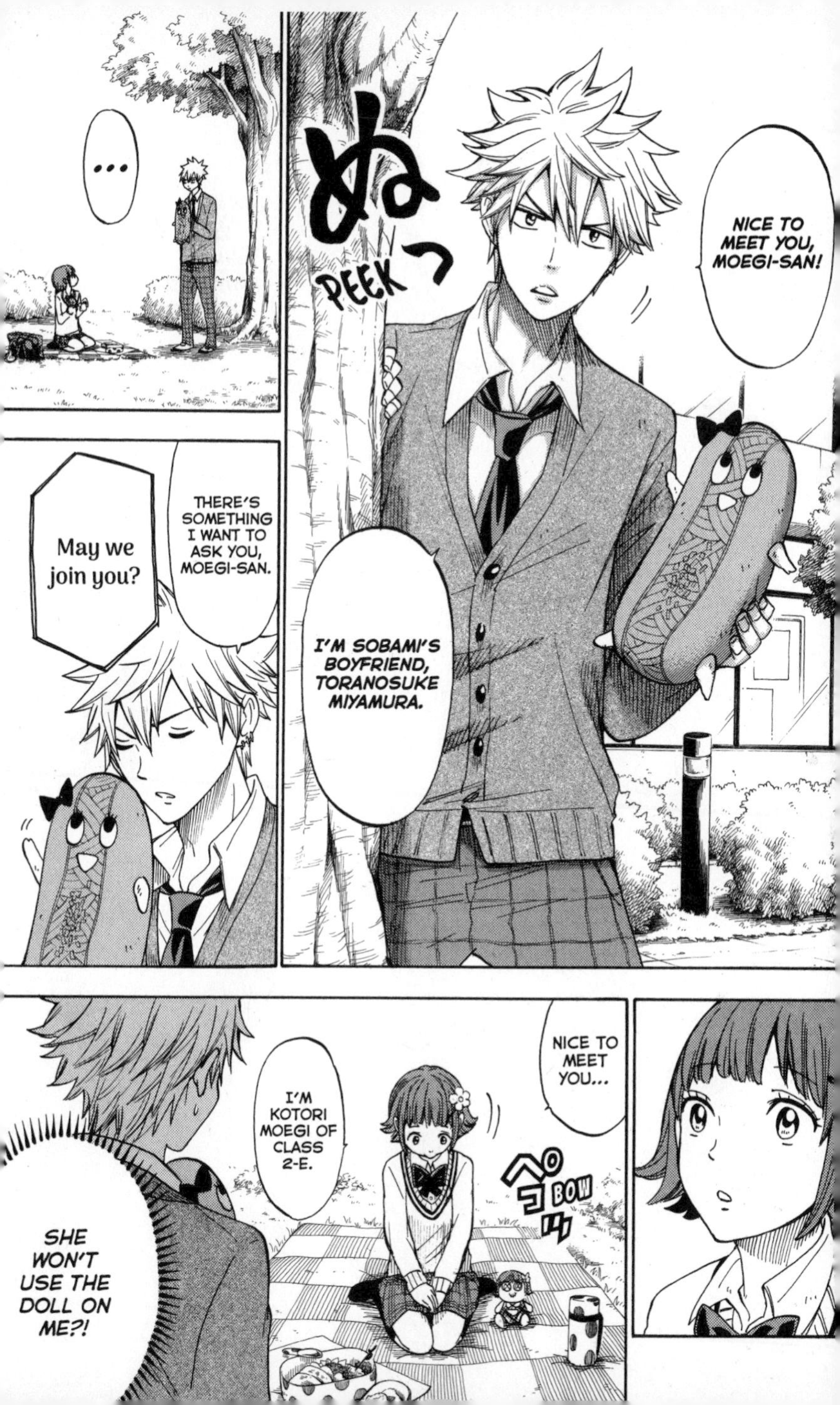
NICE TO MEET YOU, MOEGI-SAN!
ぬっ
PEEK
I'M SOBAMI'S BOYFRIEND, TORANOSUKE MIYAMURA.
...
THERE'S SOMETHING I WANT TO ASK YOU, MOEGI-SAN.
May we join you?
NICE TO MEET YOU...
I'M KOTORI MOEGI OF CLASS 2-E.
ペコッ
BOW
SHE WON'T USE THE DOLL ON ME?!

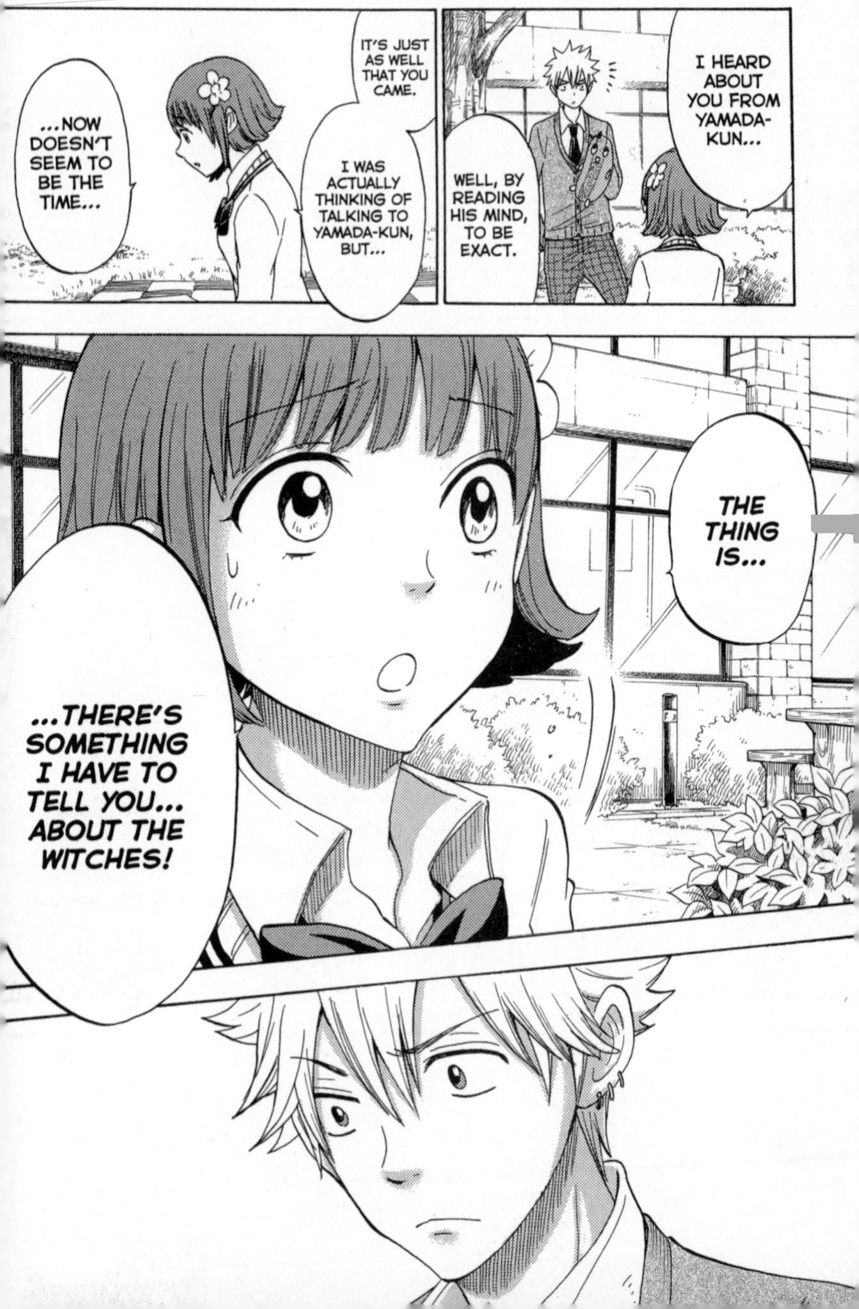
I HEARD ABOUT YOU FROM YAMADA-KUN...
WELL, BY READING HIS MIND, TO BE EXACT.
IT'S JUST AS WELL THAT YOU CAME.
I WAS ACTUALLY THINKING OF TALKING TO YAMADA-KUN, BUT...
...NOW DOESN'T SEEM TO BE THE TIME...
THE THING IS...
...THERE'S SOMETHING I HAVE TO TELL YOU... ABOUT THE WITCHES!

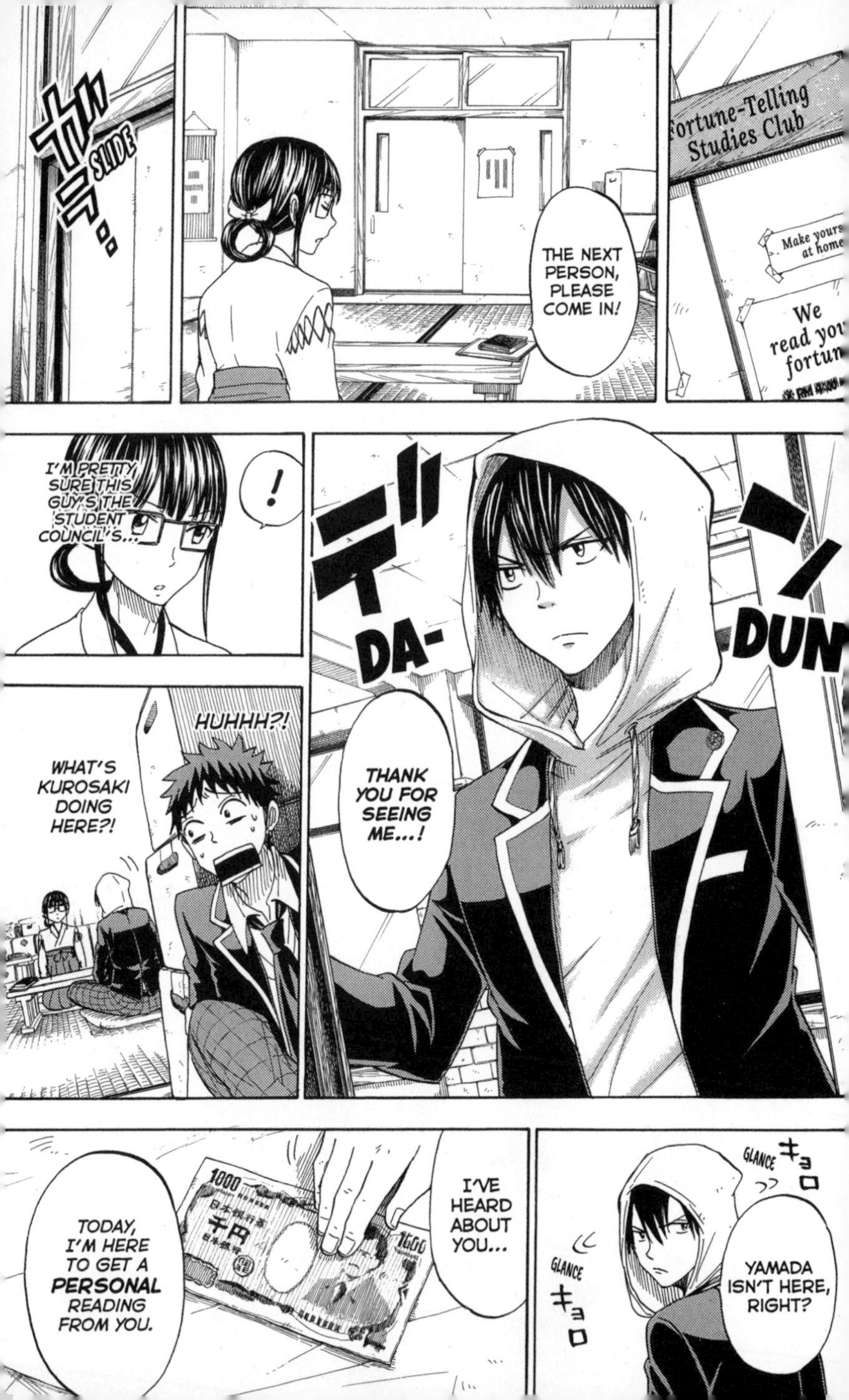
Fortune-Telling Studies Club
We read you fortun
THE NEXT PERSON, PLEASE COME IN!
SLIDE
DA-
DUN
THANK YOU FOR SEEING ME...!
!
I'M PRETTY SURE THIS GUY'S THE STUDENT COUNCIL'S...
HUHHH?!
WHAT'S KUROSAKI DOING HERE?!
GLANCE
キョロ
GLANCE
キョロ
YAMADA ISN'T HERE, RIGHT?
I'VE HEARD ABOUT YOU...
TODAY, I'M HERE TO GET A PERSONAL READING FROM YOU.

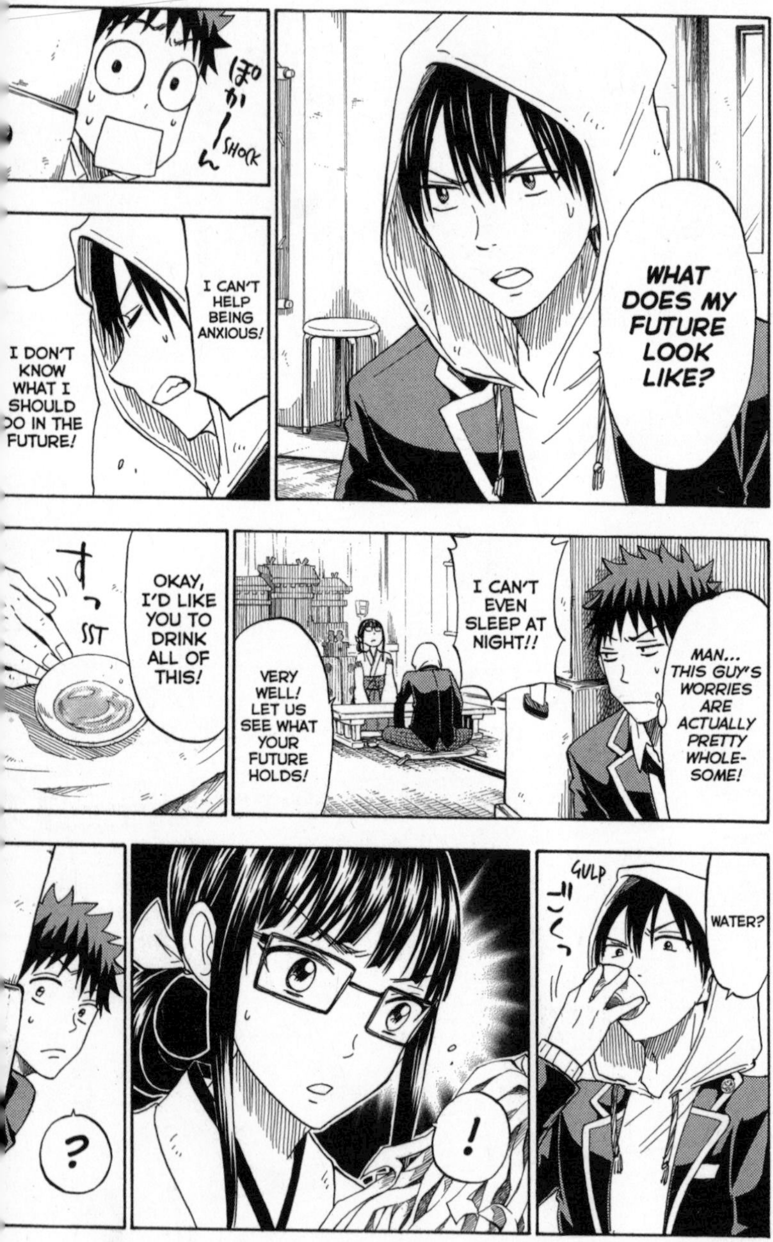
WHAT DOES MY FUTURE LOOK LIKE?
ぽかーん
SHOCK
I CAN'T HELP BEING ANXIOUS!
I DON'T KNOW WHAT I SHOULD DO IN THE FUTURE!
MAN... THIS GUY'S WORRIES ARE ACTUALLY PRETTY WHOLE-SOME!
I CAN'T EVEN SLEEP AT NIGHT!!
VERY WELL! LET US SEE WHAT YOUR FUTURE HOLDS!
OKAY, I'D LIKE YOU TO DRINK ALL OF THIS!
すっ
SST
GULP
ゴクッ
WATER?
!
?

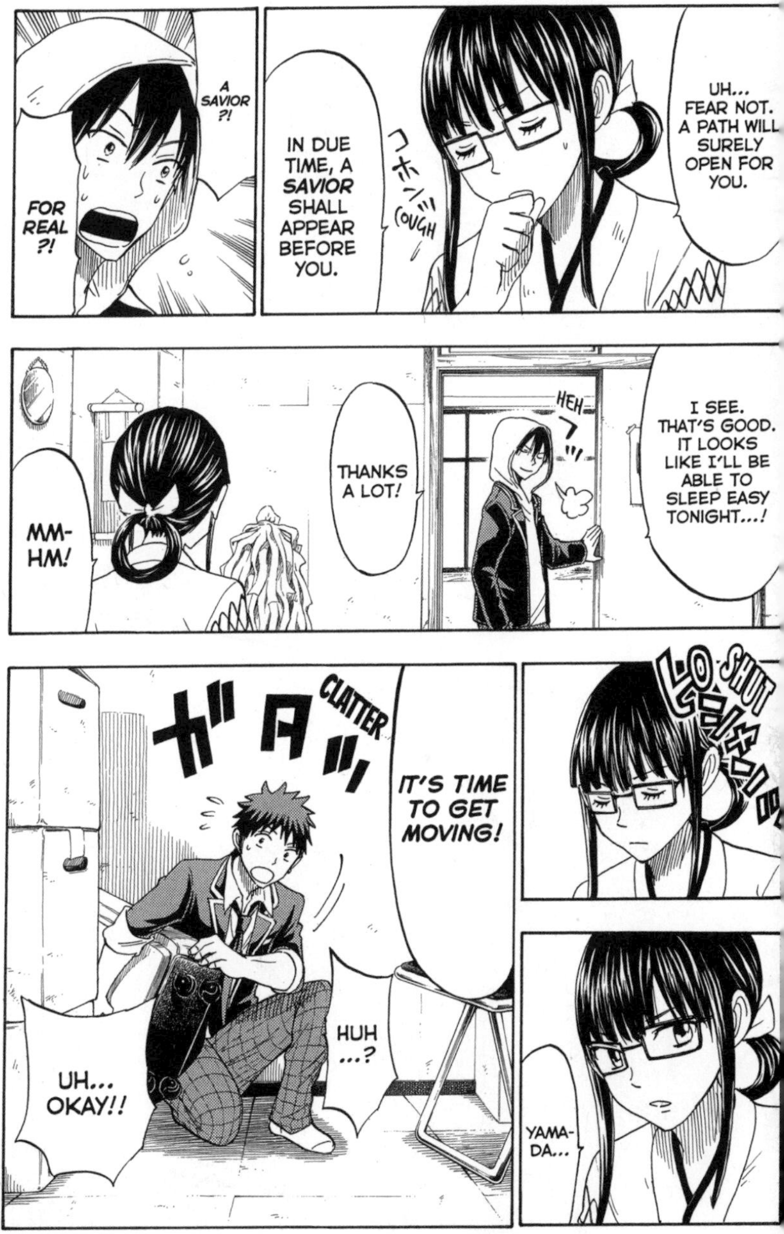
UH... FEAR NOT. A PATH WILL SURELY OPEN FOR YOU.
COUGH
IN DUE TIME, A *SAVIOR* SHALL APPEAR BEFORE YOU.
A SAVIOR ?!
FOR REAL ?!
I SEE. THAT'S GOOD. IT LOOKS LIKE I'LL BE ABLE TO SLEEP EASY TONIGHT...!
HEH
THANKS A LOT!
MM-HM!
SHUT
YAMA-DA...
IT'S TIME TO GET MOVING!
ガタッ
CLATTER
HUH ...?
UH... OKAY!!

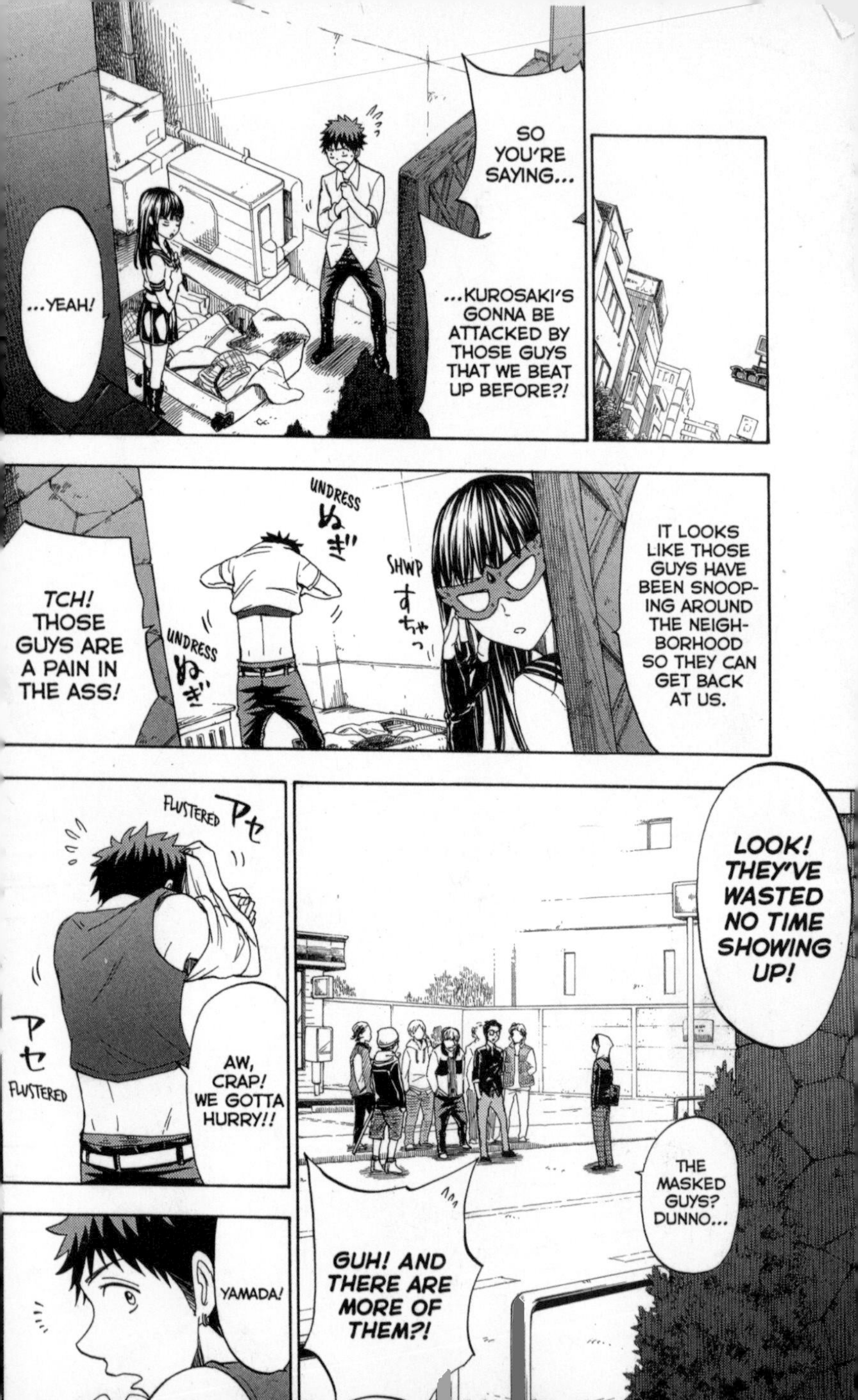
SO YOU'RE SAYING...
...KUROSAKI'S GONNA BE ATTACKED BY THOSE GUYS THAT WE BEAT UP BEFORE?!
...YEAH!
IT LOOKS LIKE THOSE GUYS HAVE BEEN SNOOP-ING AROUND THE NEIGH-BORHOOD SO THEY CAN GET BACK AT US.
SHWP すちゃっ
UNDRESS ぬぎ
UNDRESS ぬぎ
TCH! THOSE GUYS ARE A PAIN IN THE ASS!
LOOK! THEY'VE WASTED NO TIME SHOWING UP!
THE MASKED GUYS? DUNNO...
GUH! AND THERE ARE MORE OF THEM?!
FLUSTERED アセ
AW, CRAP! WE GOTTA HURRY!!
アセ FLUSTERED
YAMADA!

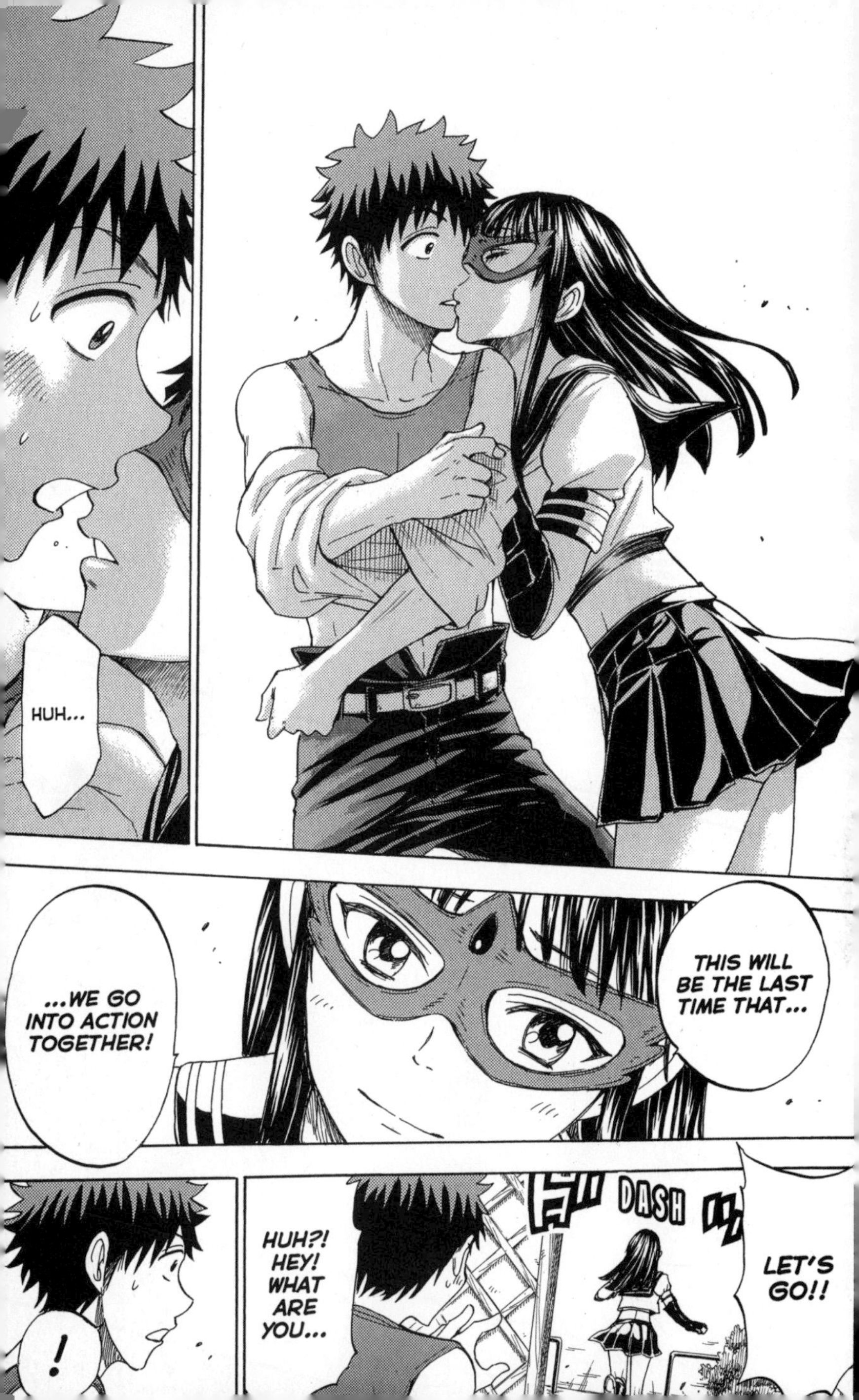
HUH...
THIS WILL BE THE LAST TIME THAT...
...WE GO INTO ACTION TOGETHER!
LET'S GO!!
DASH
HUH?! HEY! WHAT ARE YOU...
!

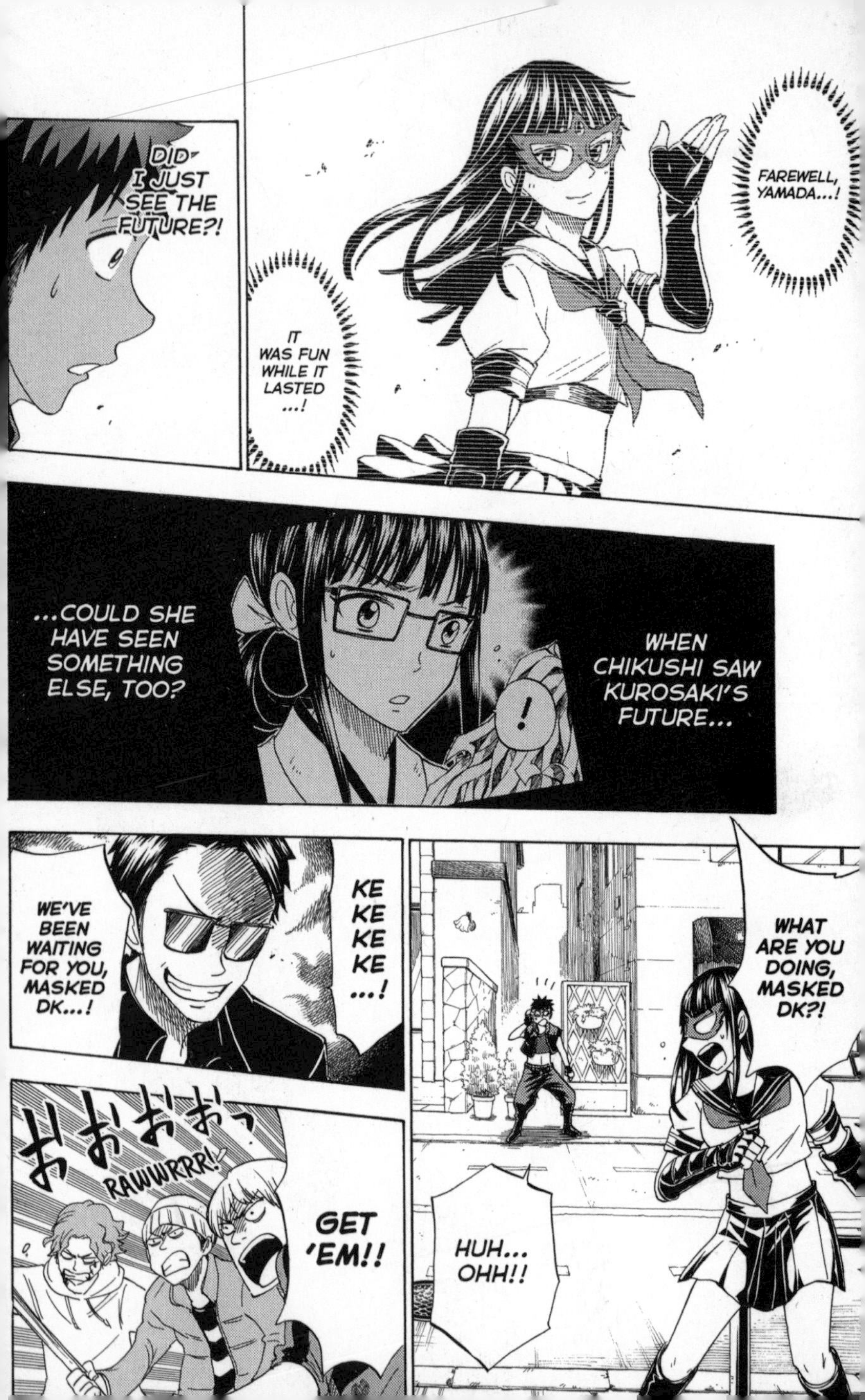
FAREWELL, YAMADA...!
IT WAS FUN WHILE IT LASTED...!
DID I JUST SEE THE FUTURE?!
WHEN CHIKUSHI SAW KUROSAKI'S FUTURE...
!
...COULD SHE HAVE SEEN SOMETHING ELSE, TOO?
WHAT ARE YOU DOING, MASKED DK?!
HUH... OHH!!
KE KE KE KE...!
WE'VE BEEN WAITING FOR YOU, MASKED DK...!
おおおおっ
RAWWRRR!
GET 'EM!!

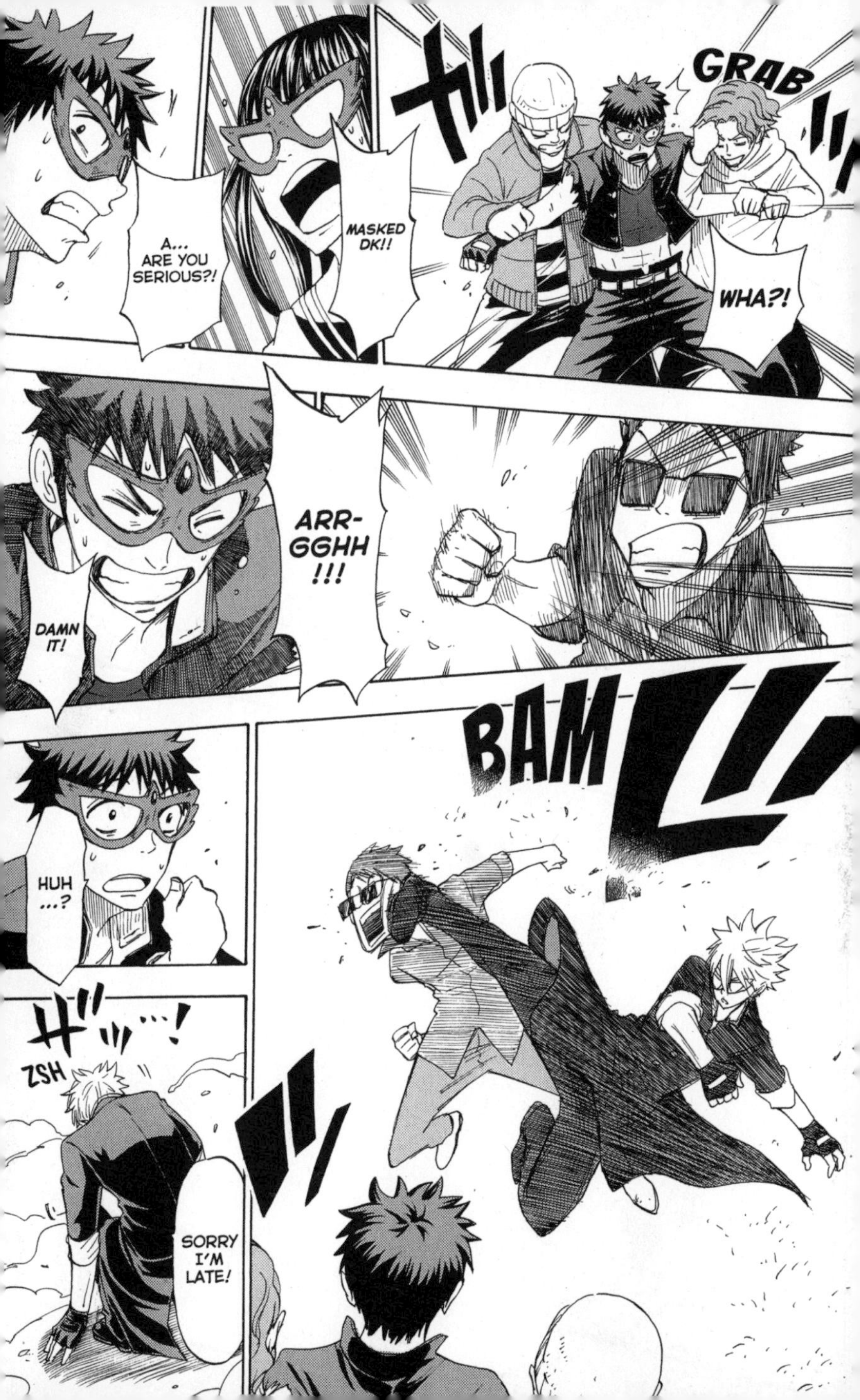
GRAB
WHA?!
MASKED DK!!
A... ARE YOU SERIOUS?!
ARR-GGHH!!!
DAMN IT!
BAM
HUH ...?
ZSH
SORRY I'M LATE!

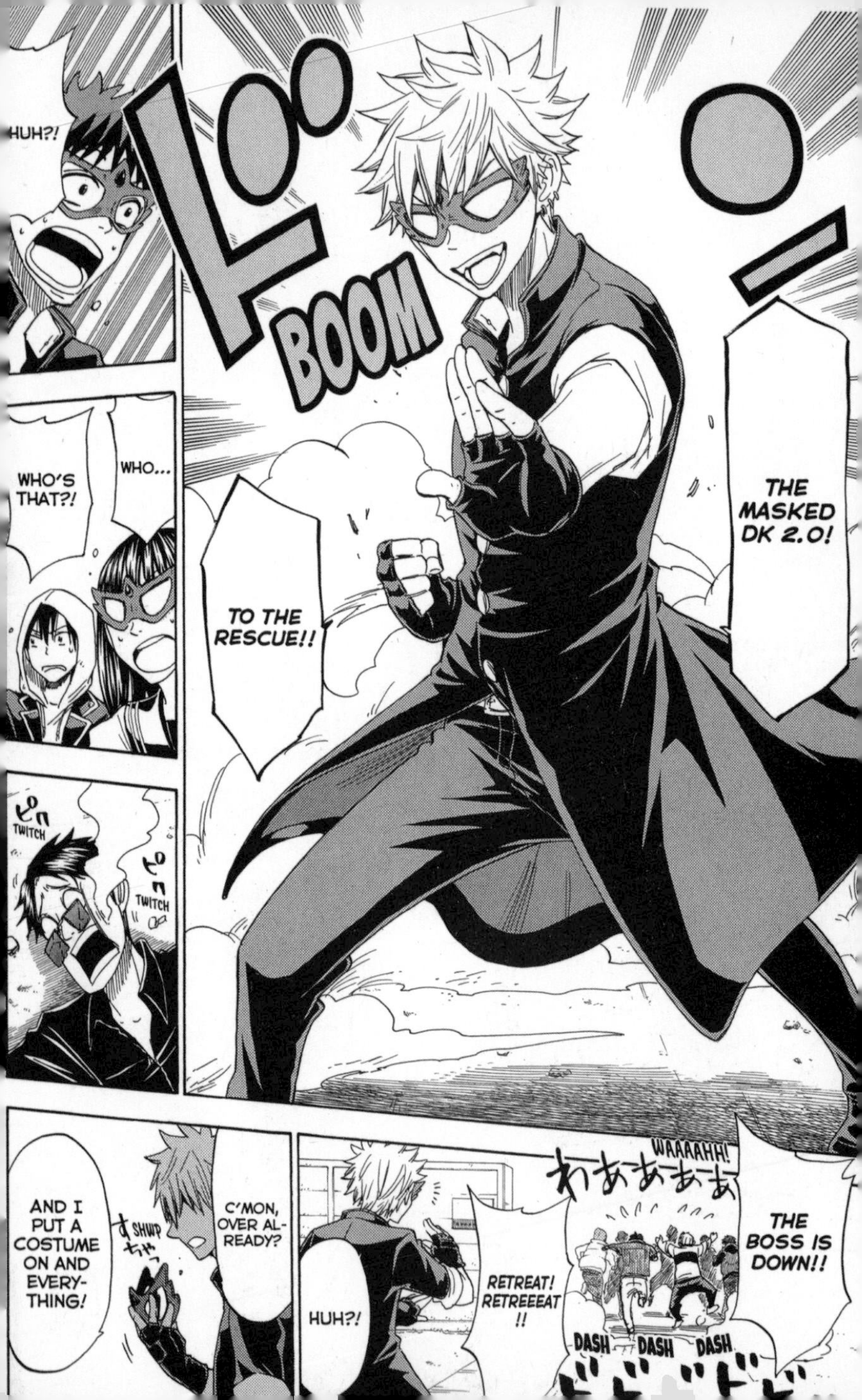

BOOM
THE MASKED DK 2.0!
TO THE RESCUE!!
HUH?!
WHO...
WHO'S THAT?!
ピク TWITCH
ピク TWITCH
わああああ WAAAAHH!
THE BOSS IS DOWN!!
RETREAT! RETREEEAT !!
DASH DASH DASH
C'MON, OVER AL-READY?
HUH?!
すちゃ SHWP
AND I PUT A COSTUME ON AND EVERY-THING!

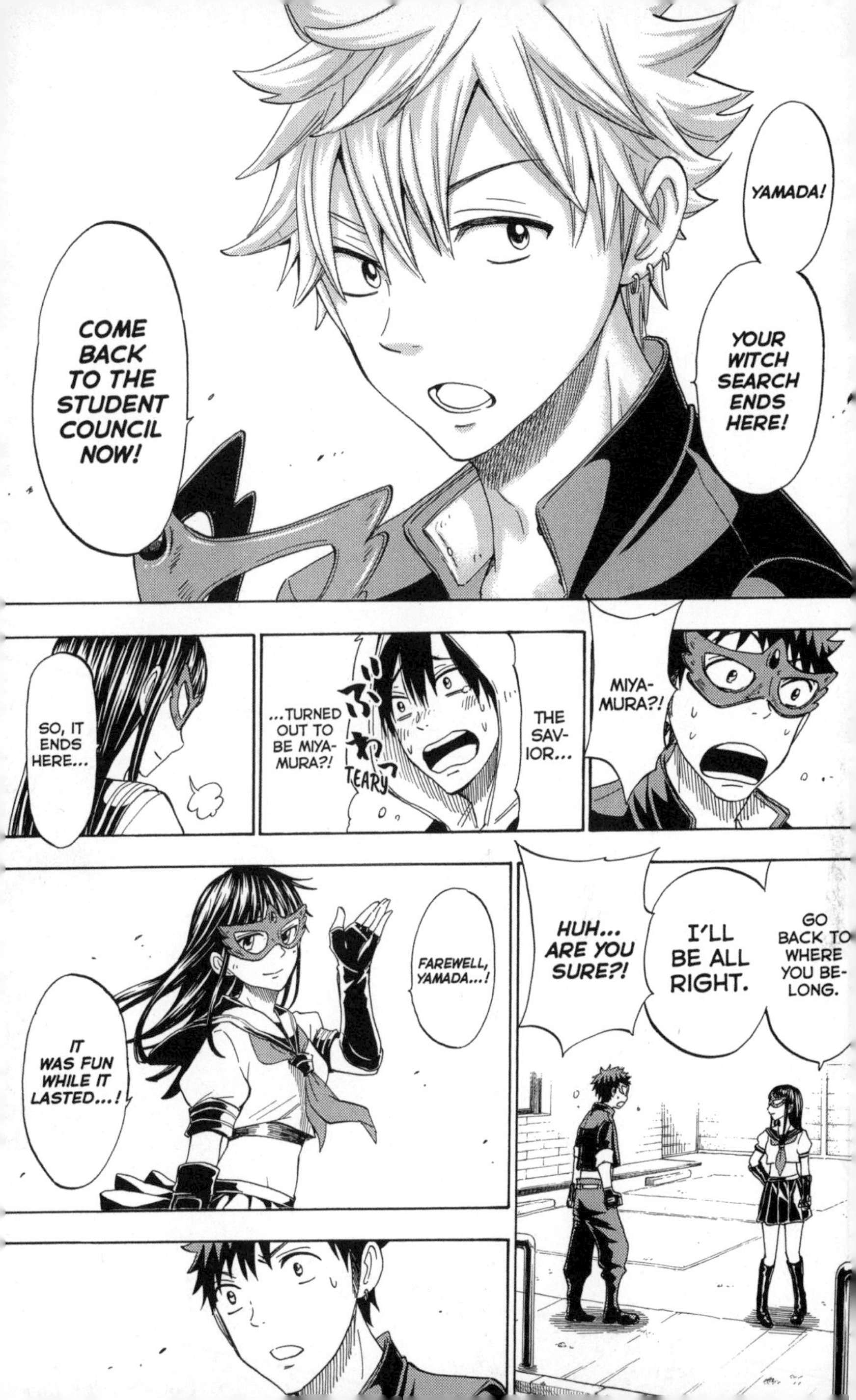
YAMADA!
YOUR WITCH SEARCH ENDS HERE!
COME BACK TO THE STUDENT COUNCIL NOW!
MIYA-MURA?!
THE SAV-IOR...
...TURNED OUT TO BE MIYA-MURA?!
TEARY
SO, IT ENDS HERE...
GO BACK TO WHERE YOU BE-LONG.
I'LL BE ALL RIGHT.
HUH... ARE YOU SURE?!
FAREWELL, YAMADA...!
IT WAS FUN WHILE IT LASTED...!

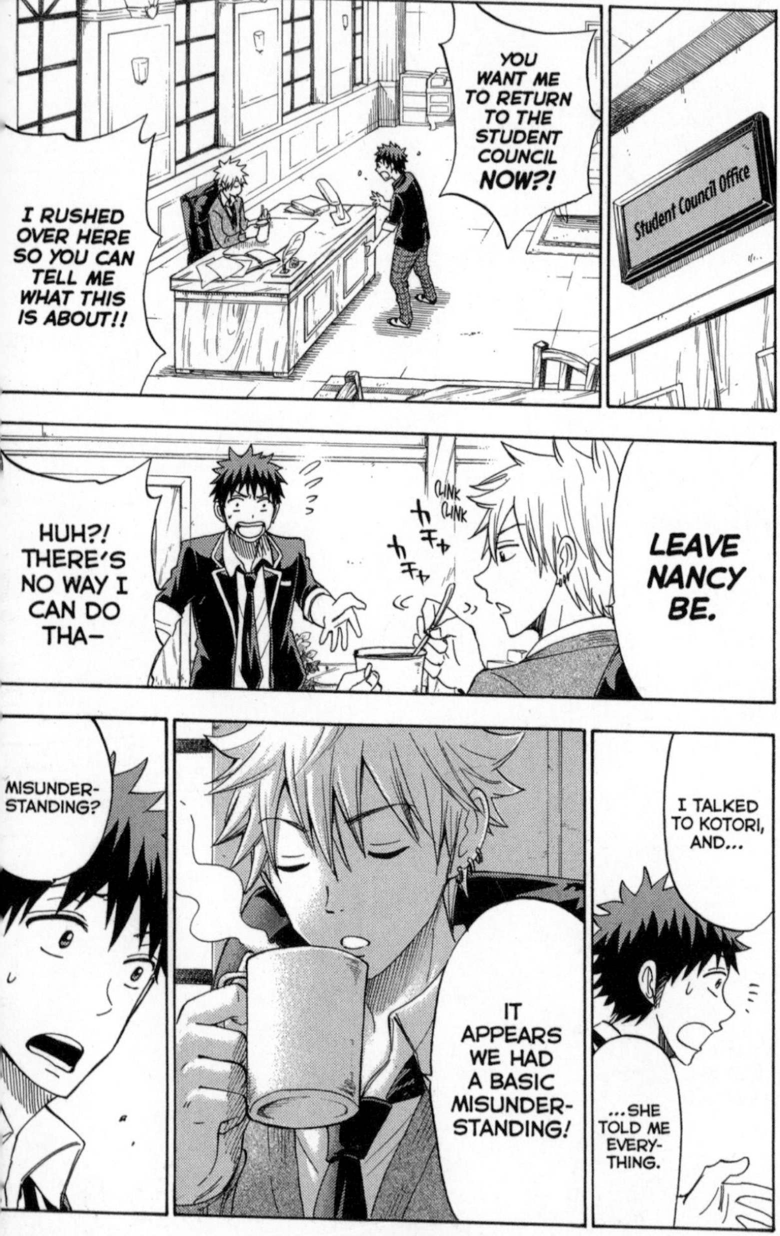
Student Council Office
YOU WANT ME TO RETURN TO THE STUDENT COUNCIL NOW?!
I RUSHED OVER HERE SO YOU CAN TELL ME WHAT THIS IS ABOUT!!
LEAVE NANCY BE.
CLINK CLINK
カチャ カチャ
HUH?! THERE'S NO WAY I CAN DO THA-
I TALKED TO KOTORI, AND...
...SHE TOLD ME EVERYTHING.
IT APPEARS WE HAD A BASIC MISUNDERSTANDING!
MISUNDER-STANDING?

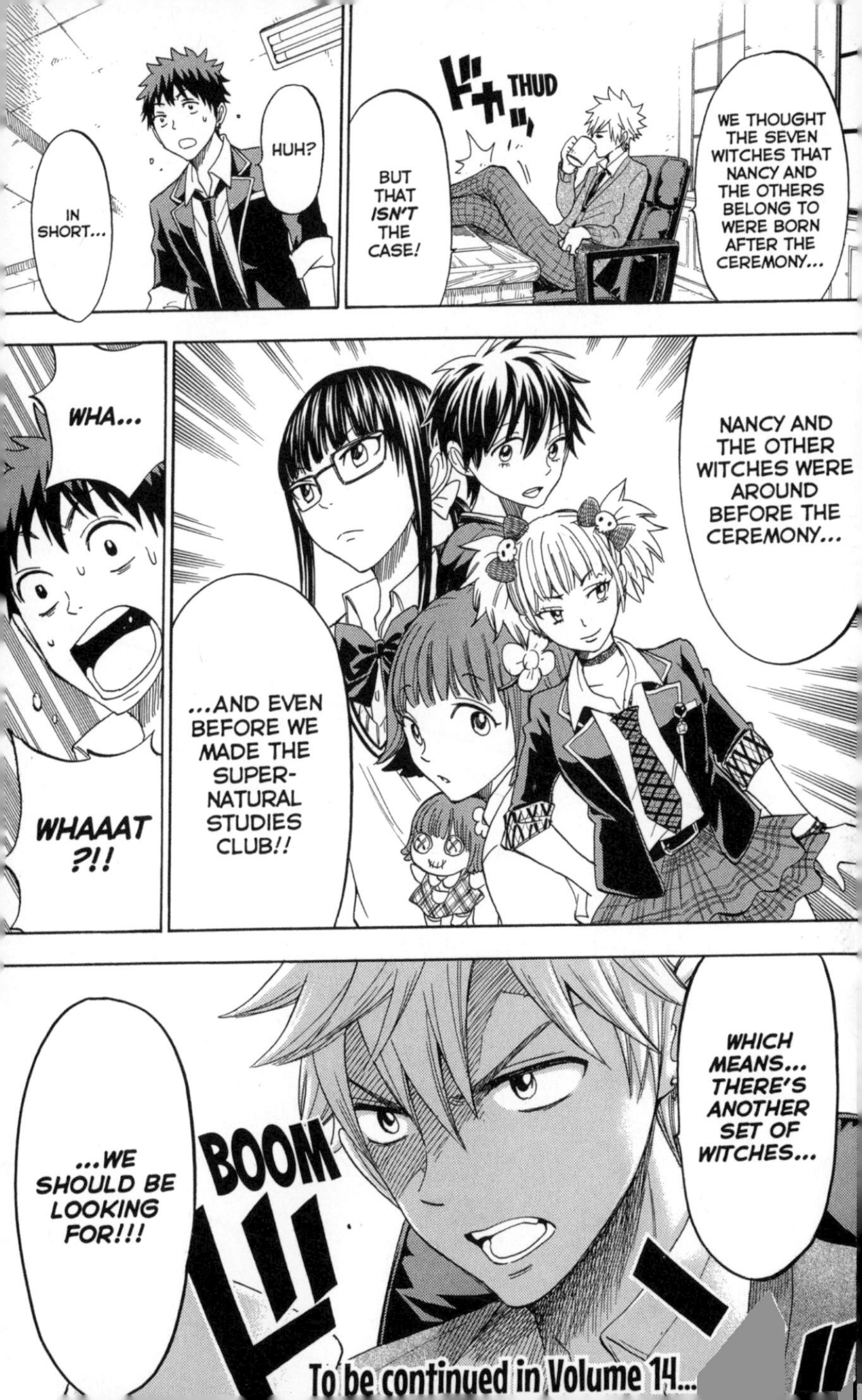
WE THOUGHT THE SEVEN WITCHES THAT NANCY AND THE OTHERS BELONG TO WERE BORN AFTER THE CEREMONY...
ドカッ
THUD
BUT THAT *ISN'T* THE CASE!
HUH?
IN SHORT...
NANCY AND THE OTHER WITCHES WERE AROUND BEFORE THE CEREMONY...
...AND EVEN BEFORE WE MADE THE SUPER-NATURAL STUDIES CLUB!!
WHA...
WHAAAT?!!
WHICH MEANS... THERE'S ANOTHER SET OF WITCHES...
BOOM
...WE SHOULD BE LOOKING FOR!!!
To be continued in Volume 14...

Yamada-kun and the Seven Witches

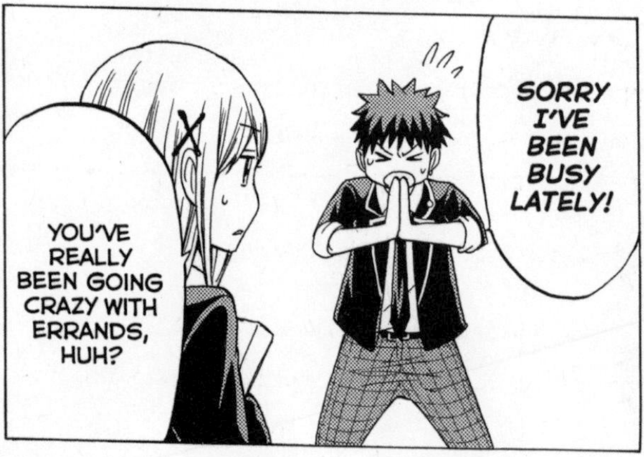
SORRY I'VE BEEN BUSY LATELY!
YOU'VE REALLY BEEN GOING CRAZY WITH ERRANDS, HUH?

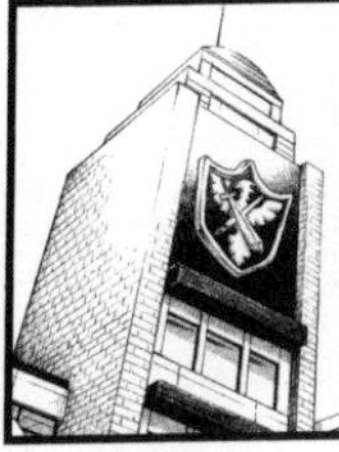

朱雀高等学校 裏ホームページ

SUZAKU HIGH SCHOOL UNDERGROUND WEBSITE

Here it is! The 8th installment of our Q&A session!!

There wasn't enough space for it in the last volume!

Nowadays, the Q&A session is the only chance I can talk to you, Itou-san. I've really missed you.

You're full of it!! How can you say that when you sometimes drop by the clubroom without warning to eat or laze around!

Now, then, shall we get going?!

Hey! You're just gonna ignore the truth?!

Q1. Did Yamada-kun draw the picture of Urara-chan (from LINE?) that's seen on his smartphone?

Kagoshima Prefecture, H.N Inabakun-san

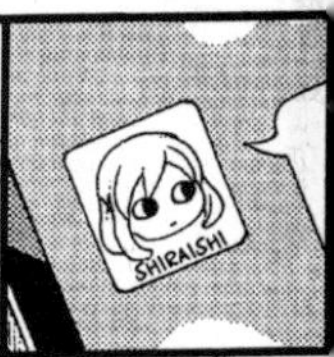
SHIRAISHI

That is indeed Yamada's drawing.

He didn't just draw Urara-chan. He drew all of us and set our icons to those pictures! It'd be nice to show everyone someday.

Yeah! Let's show everyone in the next volume! Stay tuned!

Q2. Where can you buy a smartphone case like the one former president Yamazaki has?

Yamagata Prefecture, H.N S.T.-san

 That was a souvenir I bought when my family and I went to Hawaii. I got it as a joke, but it seems he likes it.

 He has the tastes of a **geezer**, doesn't he?
Not that you're any better, buying something like that...

 Next time, I'll buy a smartphone case for you too.
One with a buff **guy in a swimsuit** on it.

 No, thank you!!!

Q3. Yamada-kun has kissed boys in addition to girls. Which guy was the best?

Kanagawa Prefecture, H.N Shumai-san

 We got Yamada to answer this question directly!!

 **Hmm... Tamaki.**

Why not me, Yamada?!!

Incidentally, Yamada said he's kissed you so often that he's **gotten used to it** now.

Is that so, Yamada? **I'll be right back!** Rattle, rattle, slam!!

Hey, Miyamura! Where are you going?!!

Sigh... anyway, that's all for now!!

We're still accepting questions!
If there's anything you're curious about, or you'd like to ask, send us your questions!

Please send your correspondence here ↓

Yamada-kun and the Seven Witches: Underground Website
c/o Kodansha Comics
451 Park Ave. South, 7th Floor
New York, NY 10016

※ Don't' forget to include your handle name (pen name)!

By the way, what exactly does "best" mean? Hmm???

H-He couldn't be talking about... **Eeeek!!!**

Oh no! In any case, I gotta go after Miyamura!!

Hey, Miyamura?!

Suzaku Gallery

This is where we'll introduce illustrations that we've received from all of you!

Selected artists will receive an original present from Itou-san and yours truly! When you make a submission, please make sure to clearly write your address, name, and phone number! If you don't, we won't be able to send you a prize, even if you're selected! Anyway, looking forward to all your submissions!

Osaka Pref., H.N. Daisy-san

Everyone around Yamada is so lively. That must make it hard to study, right?!

URARA

Saga Pref., H.N. Yuzu-Icecream-san

Shiraishi-san's smile always makes you feel nice. ☆

Tokyo, H.N. Fuunyan-san

Cute couple! I hope that day will come for me someday! ♥

Aichi Pref., H.N. Chiyo Sakakibara

I love you, too! It'd be nice to get more illustrations of me.

山田君と
7人の魔女

Aichi Pref., H.N. Runa Takita-san

Urara-chan and I have always been super close like this! ♥

Yamada-kun to nananin no majo

Hokkaido, H.N. Shion-san

Igarashi-kun starts a new school activity in the Shogi (Japanese chess) club. Is there something to this...?

山田くんと
7人の魔女

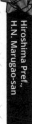

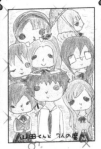

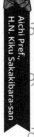

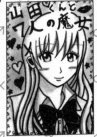

Aichi Pref., H.N. A High School Girl in Aichi-san

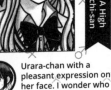

Urara-chan with a pleasant expression on her face. I wonder who those eyes are for?

山田くんと 7人の魔女

Aichi Pref., H.N. Kiku Sakakibara-san

Seven chill-lookin' witches. The arrangement works well.

山田くんと7人の魔女
ベストカップル

Hiroshima Pref., H.N. Marugao-san

This is so nice! I hope that someday someone else and I could also be like this...

山田くんと
7人の魔女

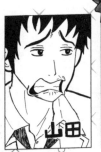

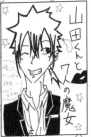

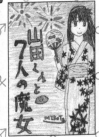

Gifu Pref., H.N. Kaki-koori-san

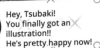

Asuka-senpai enjoying the summer. The fireworks in the night sky further highlight the splendor of a beautiful woman.

山田くんと
7人の魔女

Fukuoka Pref., H.N. Mami-san

Hey, Tsubaki! You finally got an illustration!! He's pretty happy now!

山田

Aichi Pref., H.N. Erina-san

What's wrong, Yamada!! Something must've happened for you to make a face like that, right?!

ウェディングドレス
山田くんと
7人の魔女

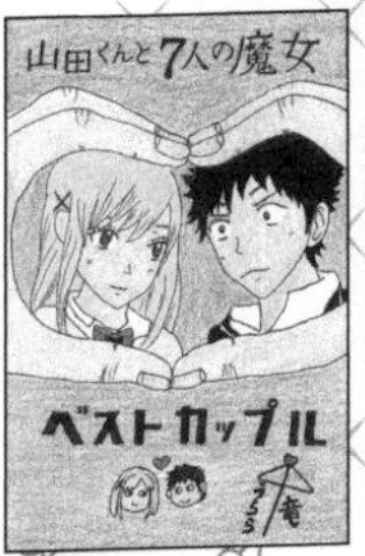

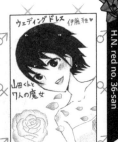

Miyazaki Pref., H.N. red no. 36-san

Oh my! Is this me?! I hope to become a bride like this someday! ♥

Please send your art here ↓

Yamada-kun and the Seven Witches: Suzaku Gallery
c/o Kodansha Comics
451 Park Ave. South, 7th Floor
New York, NY 10016

※ Please clearly write your address, name, and phone number. If your address, name, and phone number aren't included with your submission, we won't be able to send you a prize.

※ And if necessary, don't forget to include your handle name (pen name)!

Please send your letters with the understanding that your zip code, address, name, and other personal information included in your correspondence may be given to the author of this work.

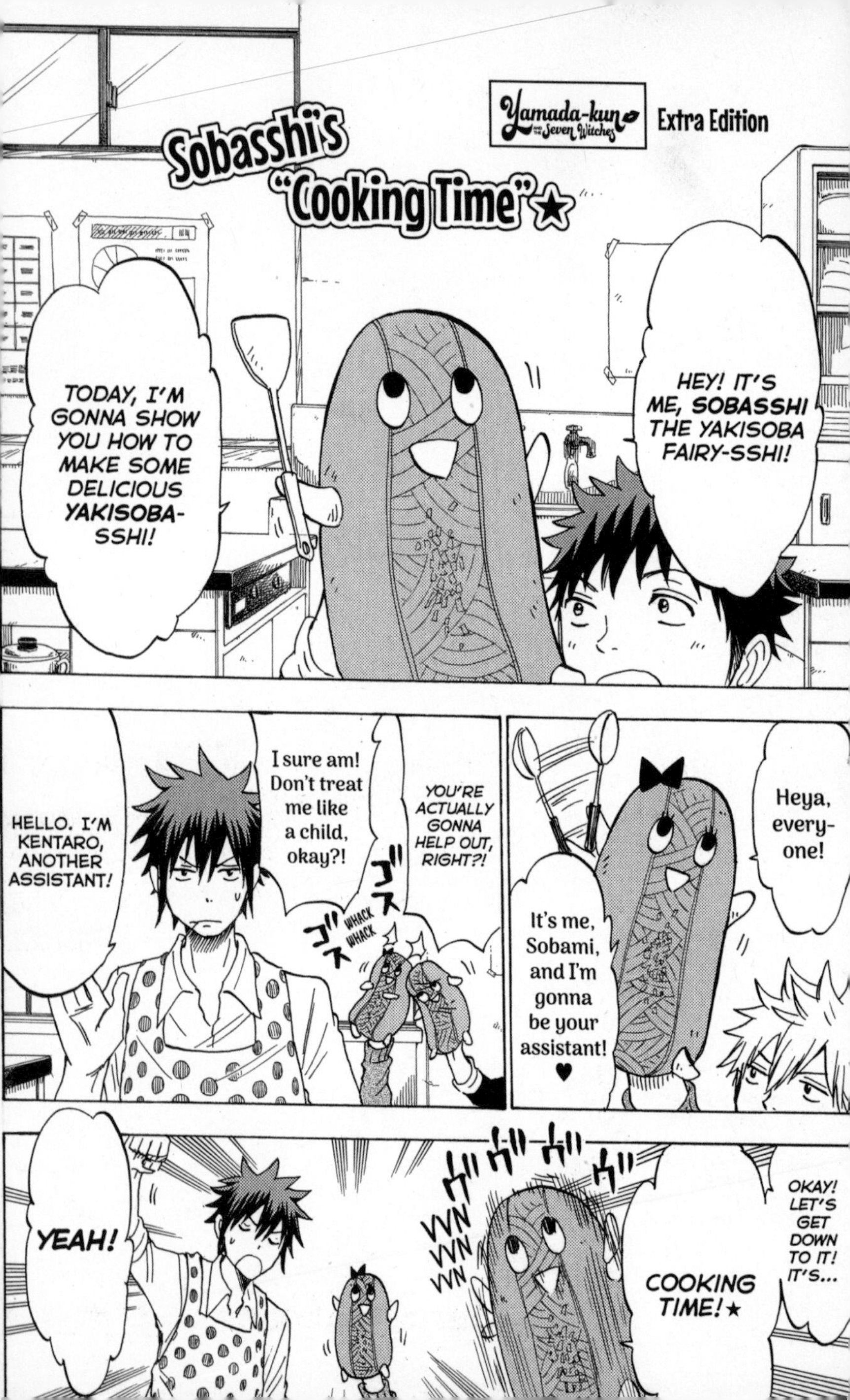
Yamada-kun and the Seven Witches Extra Edition
Sobasshi's "Cooking Time"★
HEY! IT'S ME, SOBASSHI THE YAKISOBA FAIRY-SSHI!
TODAY, I'M GONNA SHOW YOU HOW TO MAKE SOME DELICIOUS YAKISOBA-SSHI!
Heya, every-one!
It's me, Sobami, and I'm gonna be your assistant! ♥
YOU'RE ACTUALLY GONNA HELP OUT, RIGHT?!
I sure am! Don't treat me like a child, okay?!
ゴス ゴス
WHACK WHACK
HELLO. I'M KENTARO, ANOTHER ASSISTANT!
OKAY! LET'S GET DOWN TO IT! IT'S...
COOKING TIME!★
VVN VVN VVN
YEAH!

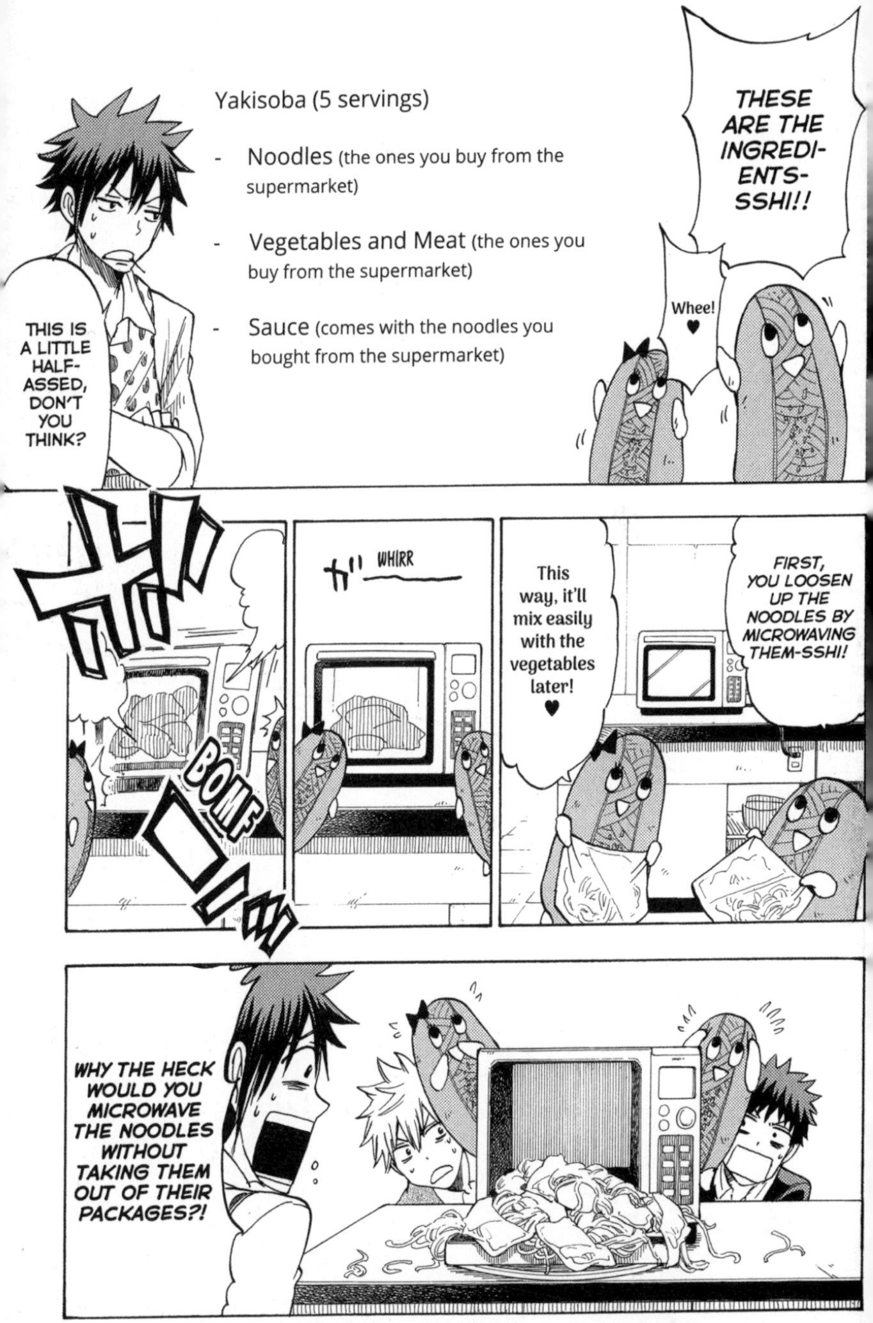

THESE ARE THE INGREDIENTS-SSHI!!
Whee! ♥
Yakisoba (5 servings)
- Noodles (the ones you buy from the supermarket)
- Vegetables and Meat (the ones you buy from the supermarket)
- Sauce (comes with the noodles you bought from the supermarket)
THIS IS A LITTLE HALF-ASSED, DON'T YOU THINK?
FIRST, YOU LOOSEN UP THE NOODLES BY MICROWAVING THEM-SSHI!
This way, it'll mix easily with the vegetables later! ♥
WHIRR
BOMF
WHY THE HECK WOULD YOU MICROWAVE THE NOODLES WITHOUT TAKING THEM OUT OF THEIR PACKAGES?!

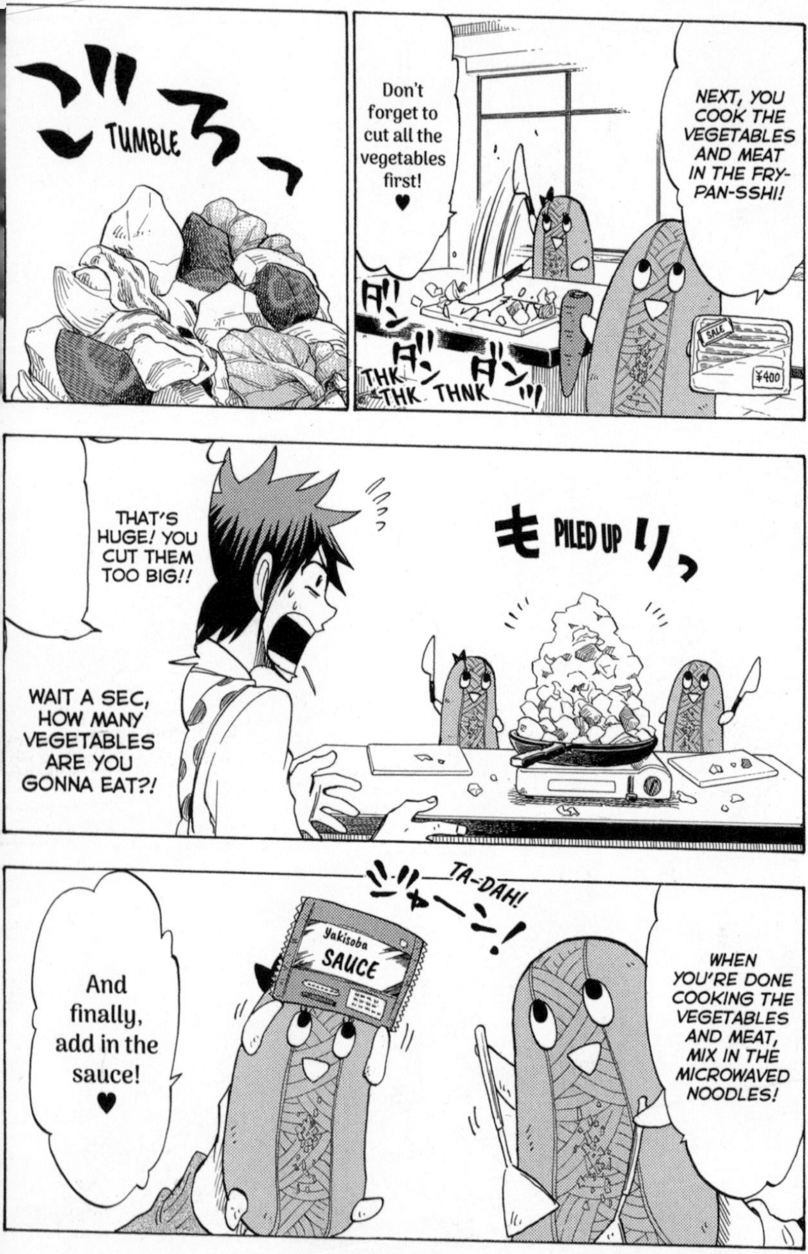
NEXT, YOU COOK THE VEGETABLES AND MEAT IN THE FRY-PAN-SSHI!
SALE
¥400
Don't forget to cut all the vegetables first! ♥
ダン THK
ダン THK
ダンッ THNK
ごろっ TUMBLE
もりっ PILED UP
THAT'S HUGE! YOU CUT THEM TOO BIG!!
WAIT A SEC, HOW MANY VEGETABLES ARE YOU GONNA EAT?!
WHEN YOU'RE DONE COOKING THE VEGETABLES AND MEAT, MIX IN THE MICROWAVED NOODLES!
ジャーン! TA-DAH!
Yakisoba SAUCE
And finally, add in the sauce! ♥

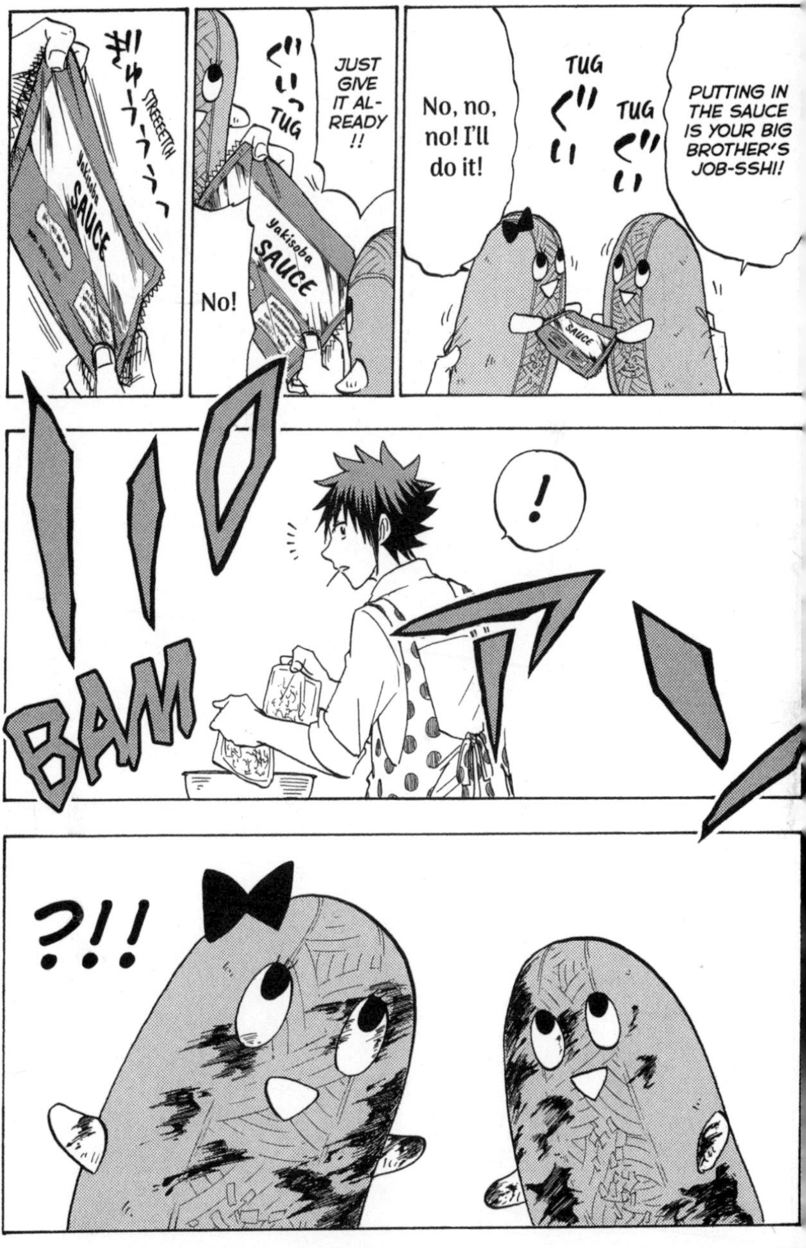
PUTTING IN THE SAUCE IS YOUR BIG BROTHER'S JOB-SSHI!
TUG ぐい
TUG ぐい
No, no, no! I'll do it!
SAUCE
JUST GIVE IT AL-READY!!
ぐいっ TUG
No!
yakisoba SAUCE
STREEETCH
yakisoba SAUCE
!
BAM
?!!

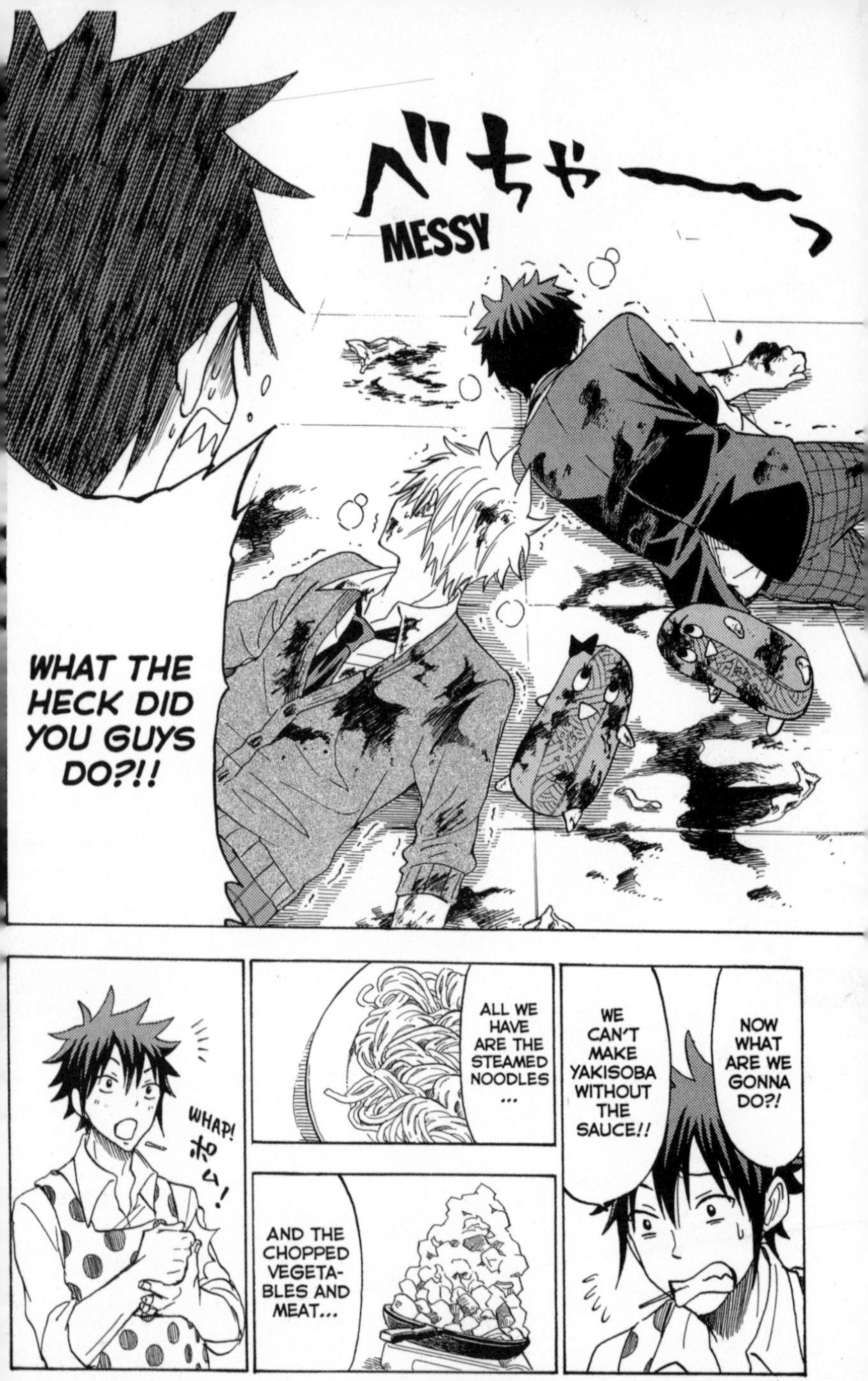
べちゃーーっ
MESSY
WHAT THE HECK DID YOU GUYS DO?!!
NOW WHAT ARE WE GONNA DO?!
WE CAN'T MAKE YAKISOBA WITHOUT THE SAUCE!!
ALL WE HAVE ARE THE STEAMED NOODLES...
AND THE CHOPPED VEGETA-BLES AND MEAT...
WHAP!
ポム!

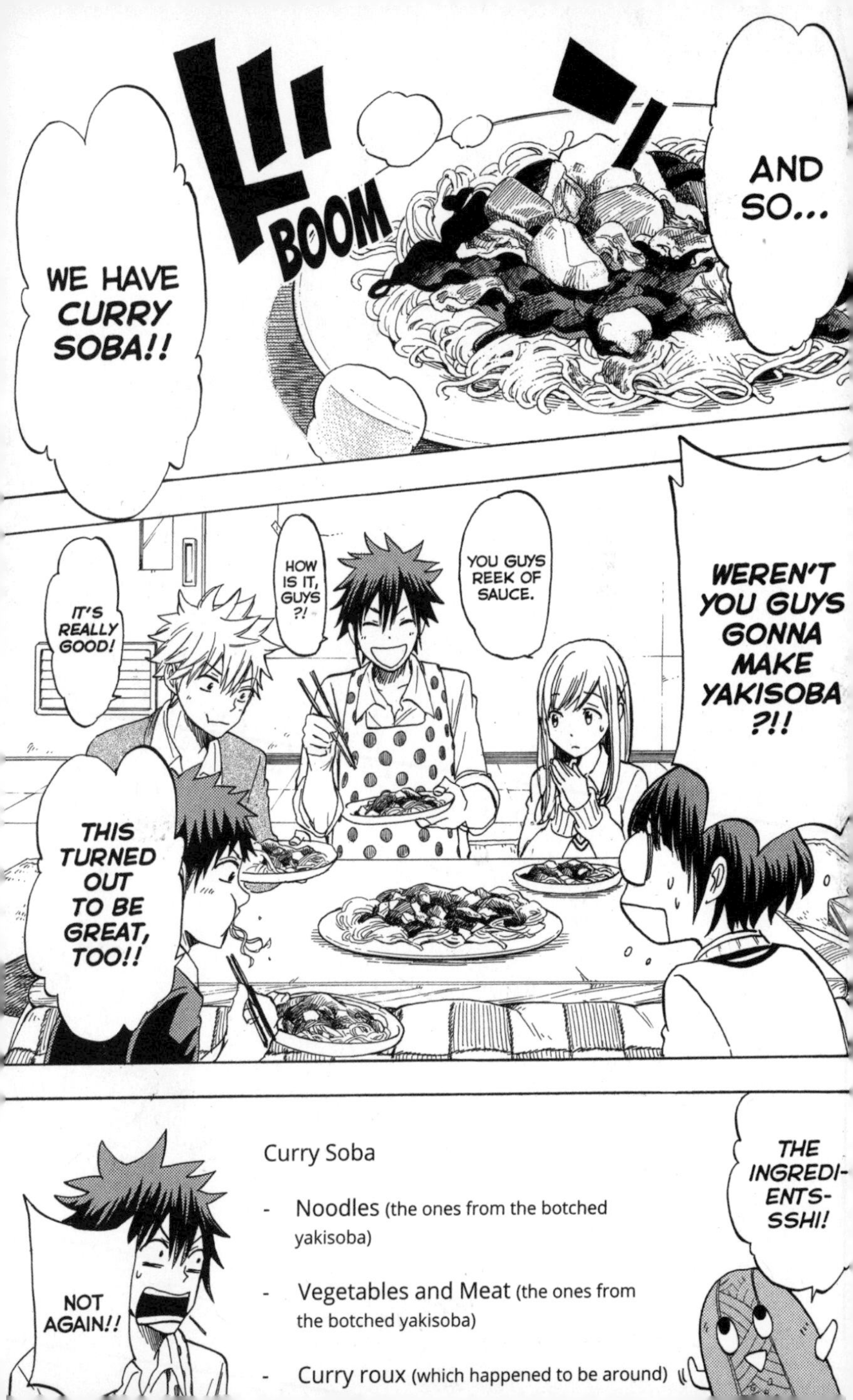

AND SO...
BOOM
WE HAVE CURRY SOBA!!
WEREN'T YOU GUYS GONNA MAKE YAKISOBA?!!
YOU GUYS REEK OF SAUCE.
HOW IS IT, GUYS?!
IT'S REALLY GOOD!
THIS TURNED OUT TO BE GREAT, TOO!!
THE INGREDI-ENTS-SSHI!
Curry Soba
- Noodles (the ones from the botched yakisoba)
- Vegetables and Meat (the ones from the botched yakisoba)
- Curry roux (which happened to be around)
NOT AGAIN!!

Translation Notes

Light Music Club, page 34

This is a direct translation of the Japanese name for this school club, but in some ways, it may be similar to the band club that is more common in American schools. Typically, students in this club form groups to perform "light music," which can be described as popular/band music.

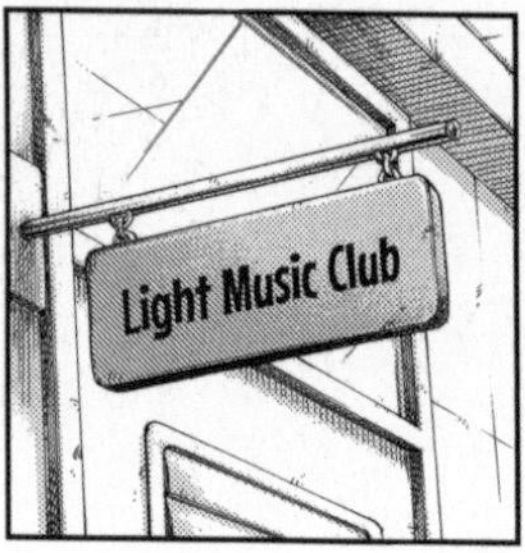
Light Music Club

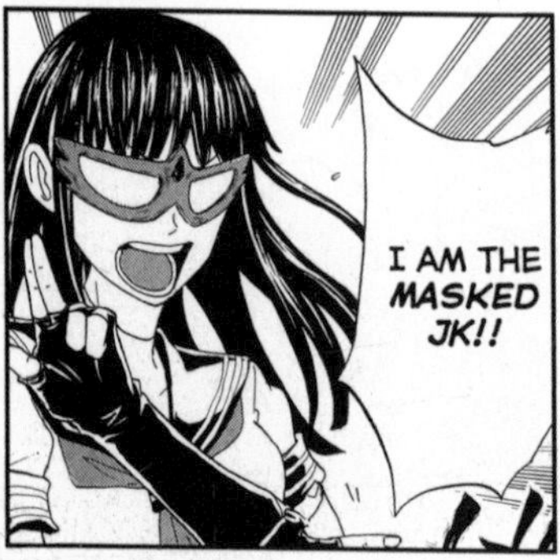
I AM THE MASKED JK!!

JK and DK, page 142

JK and DK are both initialisms to describe high school students. JK stands for *joshi kousei* (EN: high school girl) and DK stands for *danshi kousei* (EN: high school boy).

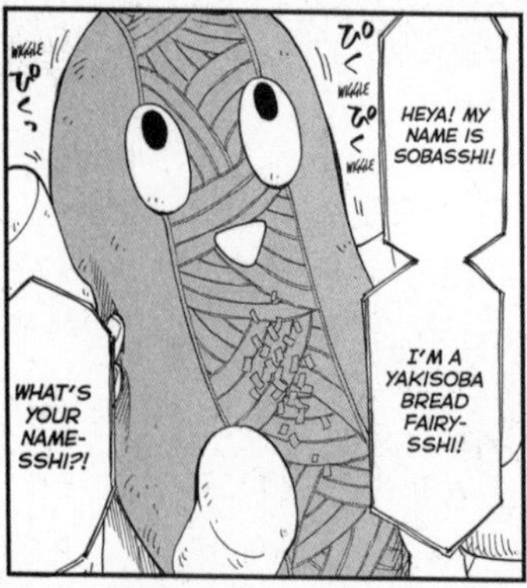
HEYA! MY NAME IS SOBASSHI!
I'M A YAKISOBA BREAD FAIRY-SSHI!
WHAT'S YOUR NAME-SSHI?!

–sshi, page 50

In Japanese media, one way that characters are differentiated is by the addition of a particular ending. For example, to show that a character is feline in nature, that specific character may add *–nyan* (EN: meow) to the end of their sentences, or a talking rock or ball may say *–goro* (EN: roll) at the end of their sentences. In the case of Sobasshi, he ends his sentences in –basshi (which has no real meaning except that it's the end of his name). To makes things work smoothly for the English version, this was shortened to –sshi.

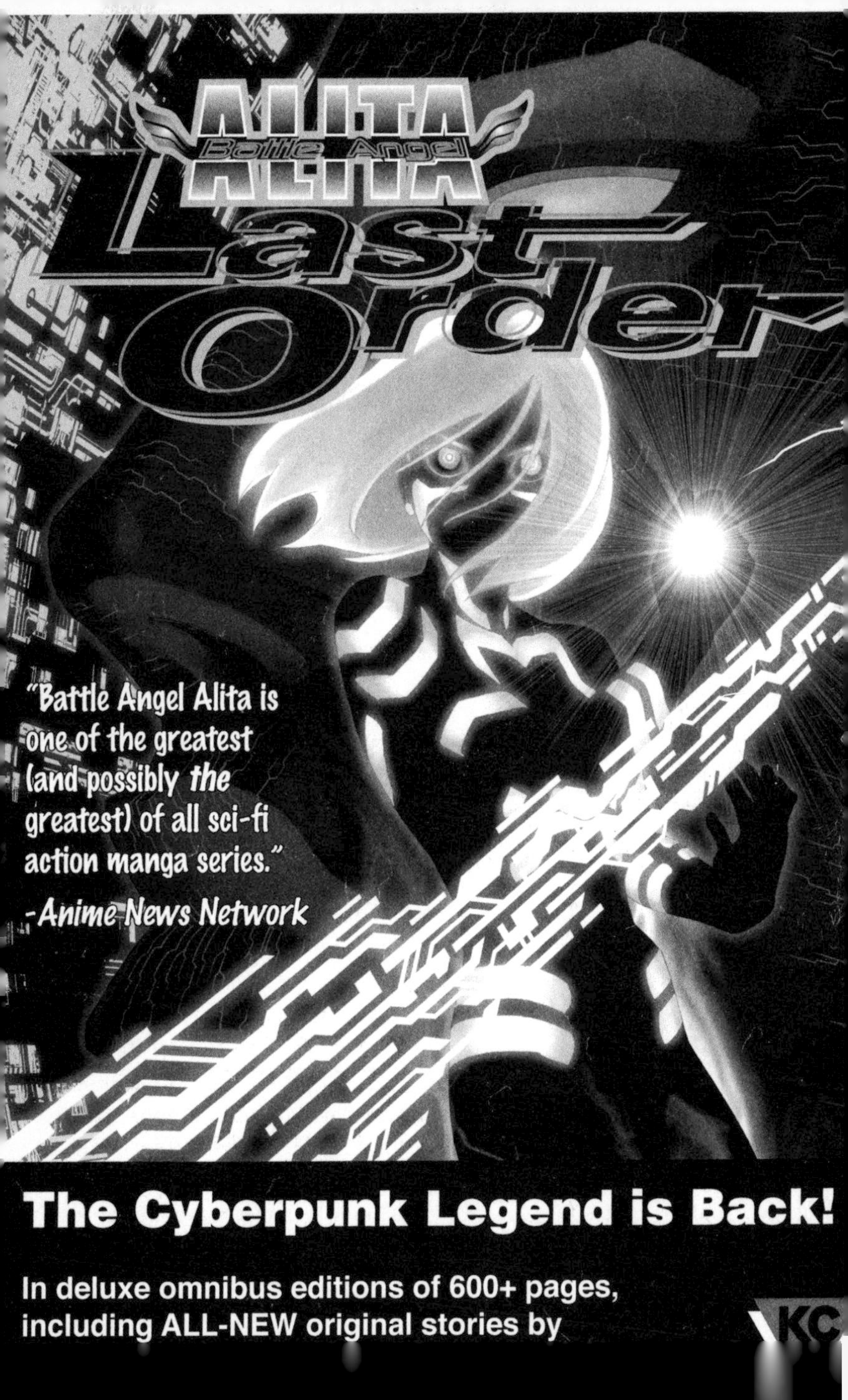
ALITA
Battle Angel
ALITA
Last Order
"Battle Angel Alita is one of the greatest (and possibly *the* greatest) of all sci-fi action manga series."
-Anime News Network
The Cyberpunk Legend is Back!
In deluxe omnibus editions of 600+ pages, including ALL-NEW original stories by
KC

A Silent Voice

KC
KODANSHA COMICS

"The word heartwarming was made for manga like this." –Manga Bookshelf

"A harsh and biting social commentary... delivers in its depth of character and emotional strength." -Comics Bulletin

"A very powerful story about being different and the consequences of childhood bullying... Read it." –Anime News Network

Shoya is a bully. When Shoko, a girl who can't hear, enters his elementary school class, she becomes their favorite target, and Shoya and his friends goad each other into devising new tortures for her. But the children's cruelty goes too far. Shoko is forced to leave the school, and Shoya ends up shouldering all the blame. Six years later, the two meet again. Can Shoya make up for his past mistakes, or is it too late?

Available now in print and digitally!

INUYASHIKI

A superhero like none you've ever seen, from the creator of "Gantz"!

Ichiro Inuyashiki is down on his luck. He looks much older than his 58 years, his children despise him, and his wife thinks he's a useless coward. So when he's diagnosed with stomach cancer and given three months to live, it seems the only one who'll miss him is his dog.

Then a blinding light fills the sky, and the old man is killed... only to wake up later in a body he almost recognizes as his own. Can it be that Ichiro Inuyashiki is no longer human?

COMES IN EXTRA-LARGE EDITIONS WITH COLOR PAGES!

KC
KODANSHA
COMICS

Maria
THE VIRGIN WITCH

"Maria's brand of righteous
justice, passion and plain talking
make for one of the freshest
manga series of 2015. I dare any
other book to top it."
—UK Anime Network

PURITY AND POWER

As a war to determine the rightful ruler of
medieval France ravages the land, the witch
Maria decides she will not stand idly by as
men kill each other in the name of God and
glory. Using her powerful magic, she summons
various beasts and demons —even going as far
as using a succubus to seduce soldiers into submission under the veil of night— all to stop the
needless slaughter. However, after the Arch-
angel Michael puts an end to her meddling, he
curses her to lose her powers if she ever gives
up her virginity. Will she forgo the forbidden
fruit of adulthood in order to bring an end to
the merciless machine of war?

Available now in print and digitally!

KODANSHA COMICS

Yamada-kun and the Seven Witches volume 13 is a work of fiction. Names, characters, places, and incidents are the products of the author's imagination or are used fictitiously. Any resemblance to actual events, locales, or persons, living or dead, is entirely coincidental.

A Kodansha Comics Trade Paperback Original.

Published in the United States by Kodansha Comics,
an imprint of Kodansha USA Publishing, LLC, New York.

Publication rights for this English edition arranged through Kodansha Ltd., Tokyo.

First published in Japan in 2014 by Kodansha Ltd., Tokyo, as *Yamada-kun to Nananin no Majo* volume 13.

ISBN 978-1-63236-142-4

Printed in the United States of America.

www.kodanshacomics.com

9 8 7 6 5 4 3 2 1

Translation: David Rhie
Lettering: Sara Linsley
Editing: Ajani Oloye
Kodansha Comics edition cover design: Phil Balsman